Praise for *Maharanis*

"Imagine Amanda Foreman crossed with Simon Schama and you have Lucy Moore. Brilliant and vivacious, she is that rare thing: a scholar with a popular touch."
—*The New Statesman*

"Moore's fly-on-the-wall approach gives their triumphs and struggles immediacy." —*Publishers Weekly*

"Full of astounding information. Not only does it provide a rare glimpse of the maharanis' struggles, revolutions, lifestyles, but also describes the growing pains of the emerging democratic society in India." —*India Post*

"India's maharanis dazzle the pages."
—*India New England*

"Lucy Moore has captured the richness and tragedy of the Indian princely families in the last days of the Raj and the new world of independence, focusing on the formidable personalities of four princesses as they emerge from purdah to stamp their personalities on their time. Exotic in detail yet clear in its historical treatment, this is a fascinating picture of a vanished world."
—Sarah Bradford, author of *America's Queen*

"You can almost hear the rustle of silk as you leaf through this brilliant and romantic true story of four Indian princesses. As heady as an Indian summer." —*Mail on Sunday*

ABOUT THE AUTHOR

Lucy Moore was born in London, raised in Massachusetts, and educated at Edinburgh University. She writes for a wide variety of British magazines and newspapers as well as *The Washington Times*. She is the author of two previous books of British history.

Maharanis

A Family Saga of Four Queens

LUCY MOORE

PENGUIN BOOKS

PENGUIN BOOKS

Published by the Penguin Group
Penguin Group (USA) Inc., 375 Hudson Street, New York, New York 10014, U.S.A.
Penguin Group (Canada), 90 Eglinton Avenue East, Suite 700, Toronto,
Ontario, Canada M4P 2Y3 (a division of Pearson Penguin Canada Inc.)
Penguin Books Ltd, 80 Strand, London WC2R 0RL, England
Penguin Ireland, 25 St Stephen's Green, Dublin 2, Ireland (a division of Penguin Books Ltd)
Penguin Group (Australia), 250 Camberwell Road, Camberwell,
Victoria 3124, Australia (a division of Pearson Australia Group Pty Ltd)
Penguin Books India Pvt Ltd, 11 Community Centre,
Panchsheel Park, New Delhi – 110 017, India
Penguin Group (NZ), cnr Airborne and Rosedale Roads, Albany,
Auckland 1310, New Zealand (a division of Pearson New Zealand Ltd)
Penguin Books (South Africa) (Pty) Ltd, 24 Sturdee Avenue,
Rosebank, Johannesburg 2196, South Africa

Penguin Books Ltd, Registered Offices:
80 Strand, London WC2R 0RL, England

First published in Great Britain by Penguin Books Ltd 2004
First published in the United States of America by Viking Penguin,
a member of Penguin Group (USA) Inc. 2005
Published in Penguin Books (UK) 2005
Published in Penguin Books (USA) 2006

10 9 8 7 6 5 4 3 2 1

ISBN 0 14 30.3704 8
CIP data available

Printed in the United States of America
Set in Monotype Bembo

Contents

List of Illustrations

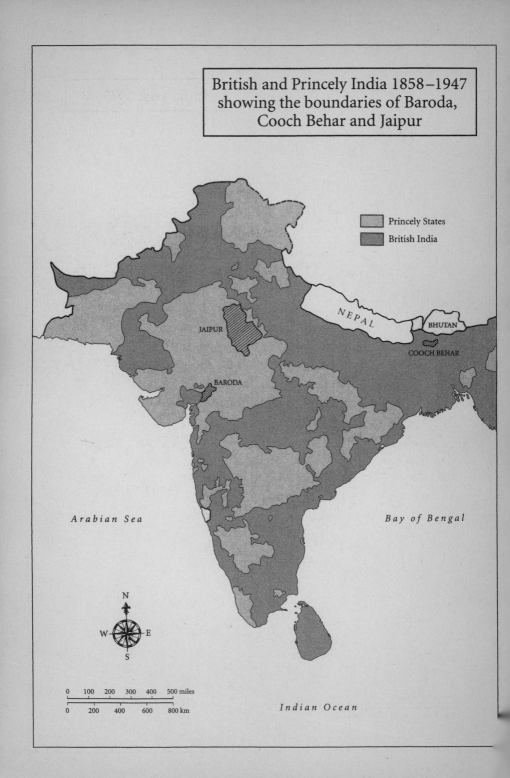

British and Princely India 1858–1947 showing the boundaries of Baroda, Cooch Behar and Jaipur

Princely States
British India

NEPAL

BHUTAN

COOCH BEHAR

JAIPUR

BARODA

Arabian Sea

Bay of Bengal

N
W   E
S

0   100   200   300   400   500 miles
0   200   400   600   800 km

Indian Ocean

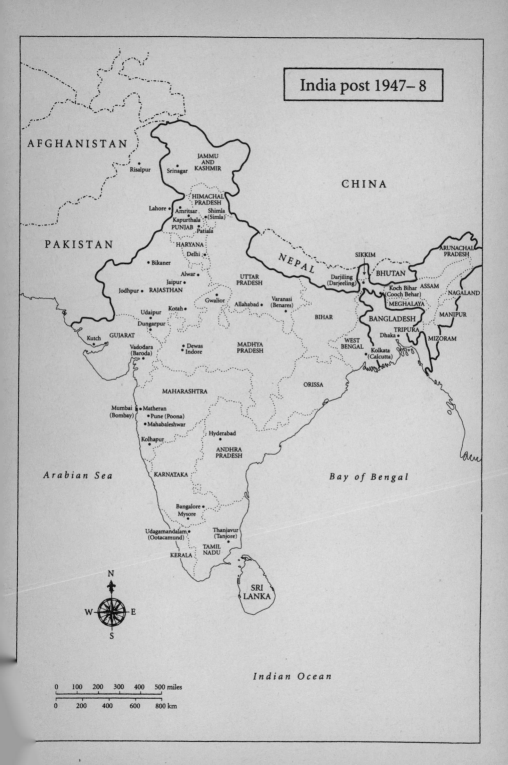

India post 1947– 8

AFGHANISTAN

CHINA

Risalpur

JAMMU
AND
KASHMIR

Srinagar

HIMACHAL
PRADESH

Lahore   Amritsar   Shimla
         Kapurthala   (Simla)
         PUNJAB   Patiala

PAKISTAN

HARYANA

Delhi

NEPAL

SIKKIM

ARUNACHAL
PRADESH

Bikaner

Alwar
Jaipur
Jodhpur   RAJASTHAN

UTTAR
PRADESH

Darjiling
(Darjeeling)

BHUTAN

Koch Bihar   ASSAM
(Cooch Behar)

NAGALAND

Gwalior   Allahabad

Varanasi
(Benares)

MEGHALAYA

MANIPUR

Udaipur   Kotah

Dungarpur

BIHAR

BANGLADESH

Kutch   GUJARAT

Vadodara
(Baroda)

Dewas
Indore

MADHYA
PRADESH

WEST
BENGAL

Dhaka

Kolkata
(Calcutta)

TRIPURA

MIZORAM

MAHARASHTRA

ORISSA

Mumbai
(Bombay)

Matheran
Pune (Poona)
Mahabaleshwar

Kolhapur

Hyderabad

ANDHRA
PRADESH

Arabian Sea

KARNATAKA

Bay of Bengal

Bangalore
Mysore

Udagamandalam
(Ootacamund)

Thanjavur
(Tanjore)

TAMIL
NADU

KERALA

SRI
LANKA

N

W   E

S

Indian Ocean

0   100   200   300   400   500 miles

0   200   400   600   800 km

The Gaekwad Family

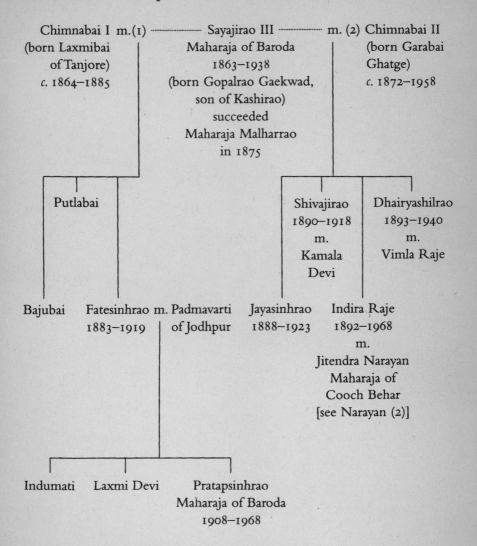

Chimnabai I m.(1) ········· Sayajirao III ········· m. (2) Chimnabai II
(born Laxmibai   Maharaja of Baroda   (born Garabai
of Tanjore)   1863–1938   Ghatge)
c. 1864–1885   (born Gopalrao Gaekwad,   c. 1872–1958
                           son of Kashirao)
                            succeeded
                        Maharaja Malharrao
                             in 1875

Putlabai   Shivajirao   Dhairyashilrao
                                  1890–1918   1893–1940
                                      m.   m.
                                   Kamala   Vimla Raje
                                    Devi

Bajubai   Fatesinhrao m. Padmavarti   Jayasinhrao   Indira Raje
          1883–1919   of Jodhpur   1888–1923   1892–1968
                                                        m.
                                                Jitendra Narayan
                                                 Maharaja of
                                                 Cooch Behar
                                                [see Narayan (2)]

Indumati   Laxmi Devi   Pratapsinhrao
                        Maharaja of Baroda
                           1908–1968

Every effort has been made to ensure these names and dates are correct but in some cases they have been difficult to verify.

The Narayan Family (1)

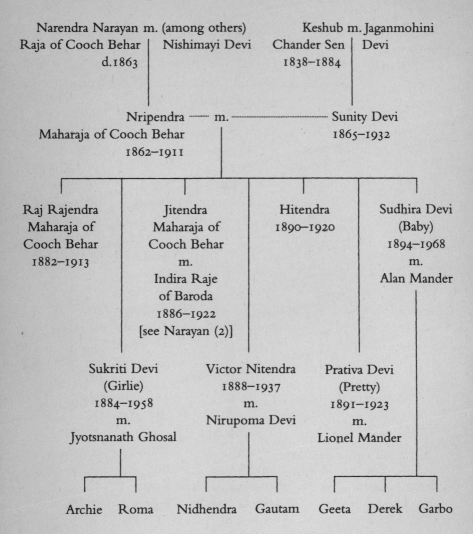

Narendra Narayan m. (among others)
Raja of Cooch Behar | Nishimayi Devi
d.1863

Keshub m. Jaganmohini
Chander Sen | Devi
1838–1884

Nripendra ⋯⋯ m. ⋯⋯ Sunity Devi
Maharaja of Cooch Behar   1865–1932
1862–1911

Raj Rajendra
Maharaja of
Cooch Behar
1882–1913

Jitendra
Maharaja of
Cooch Behar
m.
Indira Raje
of Baroda
1886–1922
[see Narayan (2)]

Hitendra
1890–1920

Sudhira Devi
(Baby)
1894–1968
m.
Alan Mander

Sukriti Devi
(Girlie)
1884–1958
m.
Jyotsnanath Ghosal

Victor Nitendra
1888–1937
m.
Nirupoma Devi

Prativa Devi
(Pretty)
1891–1923
m.
Lionel Mander

Archie   Roma   Nidhendra   Gautam   Geeta   Derek   Garbo

The Narayan Family (2)

Jitendra Narayan m. Indira Raje
Maharaja of Cooch Behar · of Baroda
1886–1922 · 1892–1968

Jagaddipendra (Bhaiya)
Maharaja of Cooch Behar
1915–1970
m.
Gina Egan

Gayatri Devi (Ayesha)
b. 1919
m.
Man Singh (Jai)
Maharaja of Jaipur
[see Jaipur]

Kamala Devi (Baby)
b. c. 1925
m.
Rao Raja
Bijai Singh of
Jodhpur

Ila Devi
1914–1945
m.
Romendra
Kishore Deb
Burman of Tripura

Indrajit
1918–1951
m.
Kamala Devi
of Pittapuram

Menaka Devi
b. 1920
m.
Yeshwantrao Singh
Maharaja of
Dewas Jr

Devika Devi
b. 1938
m.
Prithvi Raj
(Pat)
of Jaipur
[see Jaipur]

Uttara Devi (Honey)
b. 1942
m.
Brijraj Singh
Maharao of
Kotah

Udaya (Pixie)
b. 1950
m.
Rudendra
Pratap Singh
Rani of Pyagpuy

Harsh Kumari
b. 1953
m.
Raja Chandra
Vijay Singh

**Manabender
Kishore
(Bhim)**
1937–2002
m.
Reeta Roy

**Bharat
(Habi)**
b. 1941
m.
Srimati (Moon
Moon) Sen

Virajendra
Maharaja of
Cooch Behar
1944–1992
m.
(1) Reena
(2) Anna
(3) Surekha Guring

**Lakshman
Singh
(Bunny)**
b. 1951
m.
Lata Kumari

The Jaipur Family

Man Singh II (Jai) Maharaja of Jaipur 1911 –1970

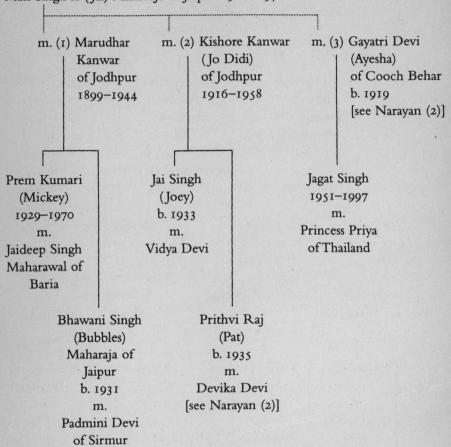

m. (1) Marudhar
Kanwar
of Jodhpur
1899–1944

m. (2) Kishore Kanwar
(Jo Didi)
of Jodhpur
1916–1958

m. (3) Gayatri Devi
(Ayesha)
of Cooch Behar
b. 1919
[see Narayan (2)]

Prem Kumari
(Mickey)
1929–1970
m.
Jaideep Singh
Maharawal of
Baria

Jai Singh
(Joey)
b. 1933
m.
Vidya Devi

Jagat Singh
1951–1997
m.
Princess Priya
of Thailand

Bhawani Singh
(Bubbles)
Maharaja of
Jaipur
b. 1931
m.
Padmini Devi
of Sirmur

Prithvi Raj
(Pat)
b. 1935
m.
Devika Devi
[see Narayan (2)]

I

In November 1911, it might have seemed as if every one of India's
nearly 300 million inhabitants was heading for Delhi. The vast subcontinent's dusty highways were crowded with a caravan of carts
drawn by bullocks and camels, pony-traps, gilded palanquins,
humble bicycles and elephants with painted faces, all piled high
with people and trunks and packages, travelling towards the crumbling red sandstone majesty of the old Mogul capital on India's
northern plains. Every now and again a motorcar – modern and
exotic – sped past, horn blaring. The scents of gasoline and drying
dung hung in the air. Silky reddish dust settled thickly on everything, dulling the rainbow hues of the women's saris. Jewel-adorned
maharajas with their veiled maharanis and sprawling retinues,
bearded soldiers in kilts and turbans, white-swathed brahmins and
arrogant British administrators with their lipsticked wives were all
on their way to the great Coronation Durbar, intended to celebrate
the accession to the throne of Britain's new king, and India's new
emperor, George V, and to demonstrate to all the world that the
British ruled the greatest empire in history.

The word durbar was traditionally used in India to describe a
ruler or raja's court, his government, or his levees, but its most
common use was for his great receptions, held in a durbar hall or a
tented camp as he moved around his lands. It was a way for his
people to see their king, to pay their respects and receive his
government first-hand. The magnificence of the raja's clothes,
his servants, his elephants and nautch, or dancing, girls, all attested
to his wealth and power. He sat cross-legged on his gaddi, a
cushioned stool-throne that symbolized his dominion, receiving
his retainers' homage. He had the sole right to wear in his turban a
jewelled, plumed aigrette, called a kalgi. Behind him stood liveried
retainers in uniforms of dark velvets and cloth of gold. Some held

over his head a fringed chatri, or large parasol; others fanned him with huge peacock-feather fans; still others bore the royal chamars, or fly-whisks, made of yaks' tails set in ornate silver handles. Here, surrounded by evidence of his majesty, the raja ritually received the tribute of his subjects.

In the autumn of 1911, India was gathering to pay homage to its foreign overlords in the person of the viceroy, Lord Hardinge, the King-Emperor's representative in India and the supreme governor of Britain's possessions there. He had ordered the erection of a vast tented city, Coronation Park, on the plains just north of Delhi, a quiet provincial town. Far from being a random choice, this was a site layered with imperial significance. During the rebellion (known by the Victorians as the Indian Mutiny) in the summer of 1857, Delhi, as the seat of the last surviving Mogul emperor, had been the symbolic centre of the rising. The British had camped on the site of the future Coronation Park before re-capturing Delhi and asserting their complete control over northern India. Both the first British durbar in 1877, during which Queen Victoria was declared Empress of India, and Lord Curzon's durbar in 1903, celebrating the accession of her son, Edward VII, had been held there.

What the previous year had been fields of 'waving corn' was at the start of December 1911 a canvas city, the white peaks of its tent roofs like thousands of sails on a dusty sea. Coronation Park covered 28 square miles and contained 233 separate campsites. A light railway snaked through the site between sixteen mini-stations, though this was the first durbar at which automobiles were the preferred mode of transport. Every important state had its own motor-fleet; the official cars of India's richest state, Hyderabad, were all chrome yellow. Inside the camp, 40 miles of dirt road had been covered with a thick layer of black oil to stop dust blanketing everything. The newfangled electricity lighting the camp could have illuminated the British cities of Portsmouth and Brighton combined. Bakeries, dairies, butchers and fruit and vegetable markets supplied the camp's population of 250,000 with fresh food. Water was piped into each campsite. Thirty temporary post offices had been erected and 116 post-boxes dealt with letters addressed in India's twenty major languages; telegraph wires stretched, crackling, overhead.

The King's camp alone spread over 83 acres. A broad red gravel drive approached the central reception tent between manicured lawns edged with potted ferns, palms and flowerbeds. The rose-bushes had been imported from England. The main shamiana, or marquee, was held up by slim white and gold columns; its walls were pale blue. Crystal chandeliers, powered by electricity, shed a glow over the proceedings. Persian carpets covered the boarded floors. The nearby state dining tent, similarly decorated, held 145 British and thirty Indian diners on the night of the state banquet.

The King's 120 predominantly English guests stayed in his camp. Their tents were warmed during the cool winter nights either by fires burning in marble fireplaces or, only in the King's camp, by electricity. The guests ate in three dining tents, smaller and less formal than the banqueting tent, hung with rich red drapes, and spent what spare time they had in pale blue and old-rose tented drawing rooms, or (if they were male) in the smoking and billiards tents. Kitchens, garages and servants' quarters clustered behind the main living tents. In the stable tents, every horse had its own syce, or groom, who slept alongside his charge.

Each of the important Native States – as the British insisted on referring to the hundreds of princely states whose domestic administration was controlled by a maharaja rather than the British Government of India – was required to attend the Durbar, and each had its own campsite. These were grouped together by region in a vast semicircle, some distance away from the main encampments of the King, the Viceroy and the British governors of the eleven provinces of British-run India. The campsites were laid out strictly in order of status and precedence; it would not have done for a mighty Rajput maharaja to find himself next to a mere raja from the eastern hills near Assam. The Maharaja of Baroda's camp even had a wooden pavilion, befitting his status as the third ranking (after Hyderabad and Mysore) prince in India. The emerald lawn was edged with palm trees and red gravel paths led to the canvas sleeping, dining, drawing, billiards and bath tents. Sunflowers, the

Baroda state emblem, grew along the site's railings. Overhead, saffron bunting snapped in the wind.

It had rained for two days before 12 December, the day on which the main ceremony was to take place. 'This transcended a joke,' observed a journalist, apparently worried that God was teasing the King by withholding fine weather from his Durbar. But on the morning of the 12th, the sun soon burned through the fine dawn mist. Before noon, the King-Emperor, George V, and his Queen-Empress, Mary, emerged from their dressing tents robed in ermine and purple satin, their sparkling crowns heavy on their heads. Escorted by scarlet-coated bodyguards and the Imperial Cadet Corps astride black chargers with snow leopard skins as saddle cloths, the royal couple drove in an open landau drawn by four horses to the durbar arena in which they would receive the homage of their Indian subjects.

Fifty thousand spectators were standing in the sunshine to watch the ceremony. Many had been transported to the durbar site from the Punjab, north of Delhi, to bolster the crowd. The Royal Pavilion stood at the heart of a semicircular amphitheatre almost 500 yards across. As the King and Queen arrived at the red and gold cupola and mounted the dais on to their gilt and marble thrones beneath it, a salute of 101 shots sounded, the Royal Standard was hoisted up the flagpole, the guards saluted, and 'God Save the King' rang out across the regimented plain. With a roll of drums the Durbar was declared open.

Using the ancient ritual of the durbar was just one example of how the British manipulated India's indigenous iconography to reinforce their position of dominance – or, as they termed it, their paramountcy. Like the Moguls before them, they embraced the durbar as a means of displaying their power to the Indian people and the Indian princes. Another demonstration of the way in which the British imposed their command through ceremony was the strict hierarchy into which they ordered the princely states, publicly displayed by gun salutes. The states were divided into 118 'salute states' ruled by maharajas, 117 non-salute states whose rajas (meaning king, as opposed to maharaja which means great king) were more like clan leaders and 327 minor states under thakurs, or lords, with no jurisdictional powers. Some thakurs ruled 'kingdoms' of less than a square mile. Salutes for the top 118 states ranged from a 9-gun salute to a 21-gun salute for the five premier princes. The viceroy, the head of the Government of India, was awarded a 31-gun salute.

Originally, gun salutes were a way of allotting rank to regional rajas and nawabs, or Muslim princes, whose lands and wealth varied enormously. However, because gun salutes were not strictly apportioned, they were used by the British administration to solicit support and reward obedience. They soon became hotly contested marks of imperial favour.

'If you were a prince with no gun salute, then every two penny-halfpenny Political Agent [the Government of India official detailed to every state; also known, in larger states, as the Resident] could come and visit you every three months and ask to see the accounts,' remembered one member of a former princely family. 'Whereas if you had a high enough gun salute, then the Political Agent could only come to you like a chaprassi [messenger], and if you had a 19-gun salute then you were left alone, because only the Viceroy could come and bother you. So the higher the gun salute, the less trouble you had – and this was the attraction.'

This was a common misconception among the smaller states about the bigger ones. The truth was that the British liked inter-fering in all the princely states, regardless of their wealth or status, though their interference was seldom appreciated. The British ruled a land they never really understood, for all their individual, specialized knowledge of Bengali waterways or Sanskrit poetry, and the princely states were the most elusive areas of all.

Imperial rituals like the Coronation Durbar illustrated the gulf between what the British thought about princely India and what the Indian princes thought about the British in India. Viceroys adored the extravagance and exoticism of durbars. Less than a decade earlier, Queen Victoria was barely in her grave before Lord Curzon begged to be allowed to represent her heir, Edward VII, at a magnificent reception to be held in honour of his coronation.

Many maharajas, on the other hand, endured them, acutely conscious of being forced publicly to demonstrate their submission to an alien power. Their homage was never as uncomplicated, or as unqualified, as the British liked to believe.

Before the 1911 Durbar, four of the five senior princes of India (Hyderabad, Mysore, Baroda and Gwalior; the fifth was Kashmir), each entitled to a 21-gun salute, requested exemption from paying homage to George. They did not want to bow down to him as vassals but to meet him as his allies and equals. Their appeals were rebuffed. One of the four, the Maharaja of Baroda, had suggested 'some alteration in the manner in which the poor native princes were to be received by the king'. By this, he meant some less deliberately humiliating reception. His request was ignored.

Sayajirao* Gaekwad, Maharaja of Baroda, was a reserved, gentle man of forty-eight. Of medium height, tending to portliness, he had a neat head of black hair streaked with grey, a clipped moustache, and intelligent, kindly brown eyes. He governed one of the richest and best-run states in India, situated in modern Gujarat, midway up the western coast of the subcontinent. Under his guidance, Baroda boasted compulsory education (not yet instituted in British India), modern hospitals, colleges, museums, libraries and railways. The Maharaja's politics were conspicuously liberal and progressive, and he was the only 'native ruler' who dared declare openly his longing for the day when India would throw off the British yoke.

In the years before 1911, resentment and frustration had built up on both sides as the Gaekwar (as he was known by the British, who generally misspelt Gaekwad, both a family name and an honorific) fought to retain his autonomy in the face of British officiousness and interference. In 1904 Baroda had been forced to request permission from Lord Curzon, whom he loathed, to travel to Europe for his health; having received this permission, he deliberately refused to return in time to welcome the Prince and Princess of Wales to

* '-rao' is a masculine Marathi honorific suffix; the female version is '-raje' (or '-devi' in Bengali).

Baroda when they toured India in 1905. Capping this snub, in the face of intense British disapproval Baroda continued to hire brilliant young Indian officials openly in favour of India's independence; his wife and children were outspokenly anti-British. Though Sayajirao had already been called into the India Office to discuss the 'disloyalty' of his attitude, like a truant child, until 1911 any incident had been avoided which might crystallize the hostility building up between the British and Baroda.

The Maharaja arrived at the amphitheatre on the morning of 12 December wearing Baroda court dress, a long double-breasted coat of fine, patterned muslin, tied at the side, over a pink and gold brocade tunic and plain white trousers, tight round the calves and loose from the knee up. A large plume of diamonds blazed in his neat, brick-red pugree (type of turban; see Glossary) and he wore a pearl and diamond collar. Quite deliberately, on this occasion, he had left off the ceremonial jewelled sword, carrying a gold-topped cane instead. He also neglected to wear the pale-blue satin sash and diamond Star of India, the highest imperial order. When he sat down in the front row of the maharajas' enclosure, he handed his necklace to his unadorned youngest son, Dhairyashil, sitting behind him. It was an inauspicious start.

The British liked their maharajas dazzling. The court outfit of the Maharaja of Patiala's son was a silk turban draped with strings of pearls and set with a diadem. Around his neck hung a collar of diamonds and four or five other diamond and emerald necklaces. His coat was fastened by diamond buttons, his wrists encircled by diamond bracelets, his waist bound by a diamond belt and a gold lamé scarf held together with a single fist-sized emerald. To appear without this brilliant display on the day of the durbar, just as when he wore European instead of Indian dress to official functions, was an assertion of Baroda's personal taste: unlike most maharajas, he seldom wore jewels, and resented being expected to do so to please the British. It was also intended to be, and was seen as, a calculated affront.

During the ceremony, each prince was to pay individual obeisance to the King-Emperor, approaching the marble dais, bowing three times, and reversing back to his seat. No one was ever permitted to turn their back on the King-Emperor. Baroda was third in order of precedence after Hyderabad and Mysore. When his turn came, he approached the dais jauntily, his walking-stick swinging, and bowed only once, perfunctorily, before turning around and returning to his seat. A newsreel cinematograph shows him looking confused as he retreated, perhaps because he had not bothered to attend the rehearsal. Some accounts reported he waved his stick at the King and Queen, but this was not true. His approach was not dramatically dissimilar from those of the men who preceded and followed him. But there had been definite intent in his defiance of the ceremony's conventions, and this had not passed unnoticed.

Later that evening, as he strolled through the gaily twinkling campsites of Coronation Park, the Maharaja stopped at the castellated camp gates of his friend, the Governor of Bombay, Sir George Clarke. Pointedly, he was told Clarke was not 'at home' to him. The next morning, an Indian friend, Gopal Krishna Gokhale – one of the founders of the Indian National Congress (later the political party Congress) and an early mentor of Mohandas Gandhi – rushed into the Baroda camp, beneath the wind-blown orange bunting, and told the Maharaja that his bow, or lack thereof, had been taken as an insult to their Majesties. Baroda, aware the damage had been done, took advice from his Resident and wrote immediately to apologize to the Viceroy. Hardinge, a stickler for etiquette (especially where it concerned him; in this case, he saw an insult to the King as an insult to his own person) and already furious because the Maharaja had not stood up when he (Hardinge) entered the room on a previous occasion, refused at first to accept it. There were calls for Baroda's deposition, even his deportation; at the very least, said many, his gun salute should be reduced.

While the Maharaja pondered the price of disloyalty, not everyone in the Baroda camp was worried about political niceties. Baroda's beautiful, wilful daughter, Indira, was unconcerned by the furore her father's demonstration had caused. In a month she was due to become the second wife of an immensely rich maharaja. The arranged match, uniting two powerful kingdoms, was a source of great satisfaction to her parents. Her trousseau lay ready in silken piles in her rooms in the rambling palace at Baroda. But Indira spent her time at the Durbar not with her family and fiancé, but in the camp of her school friends, Princesses Prativa and Sudhira of Cooch Behar, nicknamed Pretty and Baby.

Cooch Behar, far off in the north-east of India, was a lush, remote state whose glamorous ruling family was immensely popular with the British. As a family, they 'had the gifts of good looks and high style'. Elegant Maharaja Nripendra Narayan, who had died two months earlier, had served as ADC (aide-de-camp) to King Edward VII; his third son, Victor, was named for his godmother, Queen Victoria.

The degree of the Cooch Behars' integration into British society and manners was unique among Indian princely dynasties. Though several maharajas had, by the early twentieth century, decided that European polish was essential if they were to be well treated by the British (and several more decided that they liked the freedom, flowing alcohol and loose women available abroad) most retained their familiar habits at home and never lost their reserve with the British ruling classes. The Cooch Behars, though their state was geographically remote, traditional in custom and relatively un-important politically, were in England well-known members of Edwardian high society in England.

The Cooch Behars were as unorthodox in religious matters as they were well connected in Britain. Despite her prominence on the social scenes of Calcutta, Darjeeling and London, the Maharani of Cooch Behar, Sunity Devi, was a devoted member of the Brahmo Samaj, a Hindu reform movement that sought to fuse eastern and western cultures and membership of which made her and her family literally outcasts in the eyes of traditional Hindus like the Barodas.

Pretty and Baby had been to boarding school in Eastbourne, on England's south coast, with Indira of Baroda. It was only natural that on seeing her in Delhi the Cooch Behar princesses should ask

Indira to visit their camp. There she met their tall, handsome second brother, Prince Jitendra, 'like some kind of fairy-tale prince, splendid-looking and full of charm, impulsive, generous, and amusing company'.

Twenty-five-year-old Jit (as he was known) was the most engaging of the seven Cooch Behar children, with a slangy Etonian manner, a ready smile and 'astonishing grace in everything he did'. A member of the elite Imperial Cadet Corps which had escorted the King and Queen to their thrones on durbar day, he wore its gold-embroidered, knee-length ivory coat and sky-blue sash and turban with panache.

As they danced together – itself a scandal, since only very sophisticated Indians danced in the European style; it was considered immodest – Jit asked Indira why she looked so sad. If she was about to be married, he said, she 'should be over the moon'. 'I'm miserable *because* I'm getting married,' she replied.

'Well, why don't you marry me?' came Jit's response. What started as a throwaway comment developed quickly into a whirlwind romance that would scandalize the community into which they had been born and mark the beginning of social changes that would transform it entirely. During the bustle and furore of the Durbar, in the freshness of the desert mornings or in the evenings, when electric lights gradually turned the campsite into an illuminated fairyland, Indira and Jit took advantage of their nearness to steal away for snatched hours together, defying her parents' wishes and convention. Again and again Indira ignored her parents' warnings to have nothing to do with 'certain people', and returned in secret to the Cooch Behar camp to meet her lover and plan their future.

Five days after Baroda's 'inadequate obeisance' had caused such a scandal, Madhavrao Scindia, the Maharaja of Gwalior, stout and self-important, came to visit his prospective father-in-law at the Baroda campsite. Unaware that his fiancée had fallen in love with another man, he called informally to offer his support and to say goodbye to the family; he would see them all in a few weeks when he came to Baroda to marry Indira. Later that day, the Barodas and their attendants boarded their private train south. Some hours into the journey, Sayajirao received an express telegram from the Maharaja of Gwalior, still in Delhi, that read, 'WHAT DOES THE PRINCESS MEAN BY HER LETTER?'

Indira had left a letter for her intended husband before leaving Coronation Park. Without consulting her parents, she had informed Gwalior that she could not marry him, and that their wedding, years in the planning and scheduled to take place in just over a month, was off. When questioned, Indira calmly answered that she had indeed written to Scindia cancelling the wedding, and explained it was because she was in love with, and engaged to, Jit Cooch Behar.

Her parents were aghast. Jit's elder brother had just ascended the Cooch Behar gaddi, so Jit was unlikely ever to become maharaja himself and their beautiful, intelligent daughter would never be a maharani in her own right. Even worse than this disappointment, for the proud Barodas, was the dishonour of a connection with the Cooch Behars. Though the family were kshatriyas, the warrior caste to which all Indian rulers belonged, Cooch Behar was only a small 13-gun salute state. Their bloodline, admittedly far more ancient than the Gaekwads', was deemed (by India's purer princely families) tainted over centuries of intermarriage with princesses from the tribal kingdoms that bordered them in the foothills of the Himalayas. Finally, and most importantly, Sayajirao and Chimnabai considered the Cooch Behars overly Anglicized – as Brahmos, they weren't even proper Hindus – and, what was worse, fast.

Marriages in princely India were not affairs of the heart but affairs of state, arranged on behalf of the bride and groom by their parents and governments. Two years earlier, after meeting the seventeen-year-old Indira in London, Maharaja Madhavrao Scindia of Gwalior had asked the Maharaja of Baroda for Indira's hand in marriage. Extensive negotiations, consultations and comparisons of horoscopes complete, Sayajirao, hugely gratified, accepted Scindia's proposal on his daughter's behalf.

The match would be a union between two of India's most

important princely states. Baroda and Gwalior were two of the five states accorded the highest ceremonial honours of the British Empire in recognition of their pre-eminent wealth and political influence. The states were relatively close to each other geographically, Baroda in Gujarat on the western side of India and Gwalior in the northern centre. Both families were descended from eighteenth-century generals who had helped the Marathas conquer central India. That these two powerful states should be joined by marriage was a source of pleasure and pride to both maharajas. Madhavrao Scindia doted on his spirited, beautiful bride-to-be; Sayajirao of Baroda was delighted to ensure that his only daughter and favourite child would be married to one of India's premier princes, her future security and position assured.

Thirty-four-year-old Gwalior was much respected by the British. An earlier viceroy, Lord Curzon, had told Queen Victoria in 1900 that he was the most intelligent and promising of the younger princes. In contrast E. M. Forster, for a time secretary to the Maharaja of Dewas Senior, thought Scindia 'in private life an insolent and surly buffoon and in public a militarist and an obscurantist', and noted his well-known penchant for tiresome practical jokes. One April Fool's Day, recalled another British visitor approvingly, 'Our poached eggs were made of stone, our matches were duds, our cigarettes exploded, our ham sandwiches were lined with pink flannel, our chairs were uncertain, and when we came to play bridge in the evening our pencils boasted rubber points!'

Lieutenant-Colonel Dunlop Smith was more positive. He considered Scindia 'able, ambitious, and most energetic, thoroughly loyal, but resentful of any interference by either Government or the Gwalior Resident'. When the 'interference' took the form of an official reprimand for removing his pugree after the Viceroy had left a reception, it is small wonder that the Maharaja occasionally allowed his frustration to show. Gwalior initially made every effort to cooperate with the British, trying hard to win their approval and friendship. But the British, with 'their arrogance and prejudice, managed to alienate them [the princes]. Even the most broad-minded of them tended to be excessively sensitive, and the line between subservience and an acceptable level of familiarity was very thin.'

Scindia later named his two children George and Mary after George V and Queen Mary, but his daughter-in-law said this was only outwardly a token of his esteem for the King-Emperor. 'No one ever dared to call them by these names in his hearing'; they were always called by their Indian names. George – or Jivajirao – 'never set foot in England so long as the English were ruling India'. Scindia's policy towards the British was, as his family's always had been, one of intense distrust masked by extravagant courtesy. Only the British seemed to think his *politesse* was sincere. Certainly the nationalist Sayajirao wouldn't have wanted his daughter to marry a prince in the pocket of the Government of India.

Another point in his favour was that Scindia was immensely rich – almost as rich as Baroda himself. His vast palace in Gwalior, Jai Vilas, or Home of Victory, was built for the Prince of Wales's visit to India in 1876. The two crystal chandeliers in the hall, the larger boasting 248 candles, were so heavy that twelve elephants had been led up on to the roof of the hall while it was being built to ensure it was strong enough to bear their weight. They illuminated a mirror-filled durbar hall 50 feet wide by 90 feet long, and 40 feet high. A small silver electric train ran round the huge dining table, stopping in front of diners to dispense port, chocolates and cigarettes. At either end of the room stood marble busts of King George and Queen Mary, garlanded, on feast days, with golden marigolds.

Despite the lip-service paid to the Empire, Gwalior was run on decidedly traditional lines. 'There seems to be a great deal more servility here than in any state I have been in,' commented one of the Maharaja's British guests in 1918. 'Everybody spends all his time in our presence bent to the ground.' Deference approaching worship was the normal attitude to the prince and his family in every Indian state; the greeting for a member of an Indian royal family was the deeply respectful mujira, bowing low to the ground and touching the royal feet. Gwalior was not unusual in receiving this homage from his people.

In the summer of 1911, after her engagement to Gwalior had been announced, Indira visited London with her parents. Her exotic beauty and background made her the darling of the gossip columns. Scindia threw a lavish party to celebrate their betrothal at Ranelagh Gardens. Indira spent her days in the city's shops, putting together her trousseau, part of which included furniture and heavy Irish linen sheets embroidered with the initials I S, for Indira Scindia, beneath a coronet.★ But her mood was too restless, too brooding, for an excited young bride-to-be. She returned home that autumn distracted and thoughtful.

Though she had consented to the match, Indira did not see the desirable suitor her father presented to her, but a blustering, stout man twice her age. She was unusually well educated for a woman, Indian or British, born in the late-Victorian period, and had inherited the intellectual curiosity that marked both her parents; but Scindia made no secret of his disdain for the life of the mind. Finally, and decisively, he failed to win her emotionally.

The fact that Gwalior already had a wife might not have put Indira off if the situation had been handled sensitively. Although her father was opposed to polygamy in principle and committedly monogamous in practice, most Indian princes at the turn of the twentieth century had several wives as well as a harem of concubines living in their palace's zenana, or women's quarters. Although often attributed to Muslim influence, polygamy had been a part of princely life in India for many centuries, ensuring an ample supply of male heirs and acting as binding alliances between states. Out of deference to local custom, the British had never made an effort to legislate against it. Indira might have hoped to be the most senior maharani in a zenana, but she would not have expected to be the only maharani there, whichever prince she married.

Scindia's first wife, Chinku Raje, had not produced a son, and so he looked for another bride. Indira fitted the bill perfectly: she was young (thus fertile) and not only of the right caste and clan but

★ See page 80. This was a political as well as a decorative statement: Indian princes were forbidden by the British government from wearing or using crowns.

from the only Maratha family the Scindias considered their equals. She was also a future queen to her fingertips, beautiful, charming and assured. From her father's point of view, the fact that Scindia's existing wife had not borne him an heir meant that if Indira did, she would take precedence over his first wife. Sons were far more important than wives' feelings or husbands' affections. For his part, Gwalior believed he was in love with Indira, swearing he could not marry her if she did not love him, declaring he already had one marriage of convenience and did not want another; but he never promised her the moon.

From Gwalior's point of view, their marriage had to be a business arrangement as well as a romance. Regardless of whether or not he loved Indira there were conventions to be obeyed and obligations to be met. Indira's primary duty as maharani would be to produce an heir, and to that end Gwalior would visit her apartments regularly. But he could not neglect his first wife – her family, to whom he was now bound as her husband, and who had paid him a large dowry on the marriage, would object – and he would not want to neglect his mistresses, one of the accepted pleasures of his rank. During the negotiations for the marriage, Scindia sent his aide-de-camp to discuss with Indira's family the day-to-day regime under which she would be living as his wife, when she would be known as Second Her Highness. They would ride together at dawn on Mondays, Indira was informed, and he would spend the night with her on Thursdays. The other evenings were reserved for his first wife and mistresses.

Living in purdah, Indira would not see her husband – or any other man, including her beloved brothers – at other times. She would have her own apartments on the women's side of the palace and a generous allowance, but no freedom. In Urdu, the word purdah means curtain, behind which a woman must always be hidden. The seclusion of women of high status had been a feature of Indian society before the first Muslim invasions in the twelfth century, but under Mogul rule from the fifteenth to the eighteenth centuries it had grown more rigid.

By the late nineteenth century, purdah meant the domestic

segregation of men and women and the prohibition of women being seen in public or, sometimes, even leaving their homes. After marriage, a bride would move into her husband's family home, where she was often discouraged from retaining contact with her own family, and was not allowed to meet anyone except the other women and children of the zenana. The only man she would see was her husband, and then only when he chose. For his part, he lived freely. Fidelity was not part of his marriage contract. But a woman's chastity was intimately connected to her family's honour, and it was protected like treasure. Men were thought incapable of controlling themselves in the presence of females; the purdah was a woman's defence against sexual predators and their own base instincts.

For a princess brought up in purdah, marrying a prince and moving into his zenana was simply the next stage in her life, the start of her cloistered adulthood. For Indira it would have been incarceration. She was as independent as she was wilful, and had no desire to be buried alive in the harem of a man she did not love or respect. Her first response to the betrothal was to try to establish her power within the relationship, and a measure of control over her future life. She 'refuses to keep purdah, insists on six months [each year] in Europe, and even, so report says, demands the key of the Treasury, besides a written guarantee that any boy of hers shall succeed to the throne,' noted an observer.

As long as her emotions were not engaged elsewhere, however, Indira was willing to go ahead with the match regardless of her feelings for Gwalior. It was her duty, and her parents, despite their liberalism, had always instilled in her the importance of doing one's duty. But duty would take second place when love entered the equation.

Indira and Gwalior's wedding was due to take place six weeks after the Durbar, on 25 January 1912. Royal astrologers had been consulted to find the most auspicious date; ceremonial routes for the procession through Baroda had been mapped, houses along the way had been whitewashed, and leafy arches to welcome the bridegroom already hung over the streets. Hundreds of guests had been invited. Invitations were often works of art in themselves: when a princess from Jaipur married in 1910, the invitation, illustrated like a manuscript illumination, arrived 'enclosed in a long bag of red silk embroidered with gold and closed at the mouth with a heavy seal of wax'. Colourful street decorations and traditional festivities, like elephant fights, displays of gymnastics, cheetah hunts and fireworks were also planned.

But 25 January dawned, and passed without event. Word went out that the marriage had been postponed 'entirely for personal reasons', a sign that Indira's parents still hoped they could avert the scandal of a broken betrothal and, still worse, an elopement. Not guessing the truth, newspapers speculated that, shocked by Sayajirao's behaviour at the Durbar, Scindia had drawn back from the alliance. Behind closed doors the Barodas did all they could to persuade Indira to change her mind but to no avail. Her heart was set on Jit, and his on her. Cupid, Jit later wrote, 'must have constructed a special arrow, dipped in a special love-potion, and given his bow an extra severe twang, when he pierced that part of me which lies on the north-western side of my body'.

Behind closed doors, Indira sulked and raged by turns, declaring 'that she would give up Jit, marry someone in her own caste, leave him the day she was married and go off to London or Paris and live as a divorcee'. Her mother, Maharani Chimnabai, 'in stern and appalled lectures' made her feel 'so small, so despicable, so disloyal for having disgraced her own family and, so to speak, let the whole side down that only the support and affection of her brothers gave her a sense of proportion about the affair and lent her the courage to stick to her guns'.

In August 1912 the Princess returned Scindia's engagement ring and other presents to him, expressing her sorrow at the outcome of events and emphasizing her culpability. Gwalior's letter back to her father was dignified and kind. He thanked Sayajirao and Chimnabai for all their kindness and consideration for him, and wished Indira happiness and prosperity with his 'friend Cooch Behar, Jit'. He signed himself, 'Your child'.

'Had such a thing happened in earlier times Gwalior would have invaded Baroda with an army!' fumed Chimnabai when she read the letter, adding that her daughter would never marry Jit Cooch Behar. 'Outwardly the Maharaja of Gwalior took his disappointment bravely, but inwardly he was greatly distressed,' observed Sayaji's friend, the Aga Khan. Still in need of a second wife (and a son), Scindia married nine months later.

Throughout that autumn and winter, on the surface, life at the vast Baroda palace of Laxmi Vilas continued as usual. Chimnabai paid her annual homage to the Cobra, Great Protector of Women, in the Nag Panchmi festival. Though the Maharani lived in purdah, she was an important element of Baroda's social and religious fabric. Traditionally, women performed many essential Hindu ceremonies, ranging from daily puja (prayers) for the family's wellbeing, to initiation ceremonies for children as they grew up and prayers and fasting for their husbands' long lives, to annual events like this, in which Chimnabai as the representative of Baroda's women made an offering to the snake-god . Additionally, in many states maharanis (and maharajas) performed Islamic as well as Hindu ceremonies as a demonstration of inclusivity to their Muslim subjects.

With the entire armed forces of Baroda leading the procession, all the palace ladies were carried out to the marquee on elephants, concealed behind curtains in their purdah howdahs, or elephant saddles. They dismounted down elaborately curtained ladders and entered the marquee through a curtained tunnel. There, surrounded by priests, the cast-off skin of a cobra was stretched out on a laurel branch. Chimnabai bowed before the altar as the pandits chanted mantra after mantra and offered the god flowers, sweets and ghee. Then Chimnabai retreated, joined hands with Indira, who was wearing a large pearl nose ring, and the other ladies, and they all circled, singing, round the dais.

As the weather grew warmer, a highly jewelled Chimnabai fulfilled another of her official roles, presiding over a ladies' durbar during which the women of Baroda presented their petitions to her just as their menfolk did to her husband. The Maharani reclined on a pile of red velvet and gold cushions at one end of the vast golden hall. She wore a glowing rose-coloured sari of Benares silk; diamond anklets and toe-rings glittered on her bare feet. The supple silver figure of a dancer kept time to the sitar, veena and tabla played by a group of women as Chimnabai's visitors approached her and salaamed down to the ground with their hands to their foreheads. Each woman offered Chimnabai a handful of tilgul, a sweet made from cinnamon and molasses which was customarily given in springtime; in return paan, rice and sugar cane, symbolic of good wishes, were distributed. At other times a servant poured sesame seeds into the open hands of Chimnabai's petitioners.

Indira attended the durbar too, but her mind was thousands of miles away. She was refusing to countenance other proposals of marriage, turning down a South Indian raja, 'most devoted, twice her age and smiled upon by authority' who she knew 'would give her a good time, as he liked Europe better than India' but whom she could not accept because she loved Jit. Her persistent disobedience shocked even British observers, but Indira stood firm.

Jit's allure was as compelling as it was heady. For Indira, brought up in an environment where duty always took first place, Jit, 'the most spoiled of them all because he had such winning ways', represented a glamorous new world, a thrilling mixture of exoticism and western modernity, with its strong cocktails and uninhibited new dances. A whiff of pleasurable scandal clung to the reputation of the Cooch Behar family, like the daring music-hall songs they sang by the piano in the palace's white and gold drawing room. Jit's love letters to Indira from this period were 'full of descriptions of the enticing life in Cooch Behar and of the festivities of the winter in Calcutta, the spring in Darjeeling [the nearest hill-station to Cooch Behar], the gaiety, the balls, the fancy-dress parties, the visits of polo teams, the cricket matches, and the big-game shoots'.

By February 1913, after over a year of clandestine correspondence with Jit, and unchanging opposition to him from her parents, Indira could stand the stalemate no longer. From her bedroom in Laxmi Vilas, she wrote formally to her father saying that she wished to be married in Calcutta on 18 March, and planned to leave Baroda three days earlier. She still hoped for her parents' consent, but it was clear that she had decided she could wait no longer.

Permission was not granted, and Indira began searching for an alternative route to freedom. Her main problem was that, although she belonged to one of the richest families in the world, she had no access to any money of her own. Her valuable jewellery was state property, and had to be signed out by the state treasurer every time she wore it; her allowance was generous but meticulously itemized, and anything she did not spend had to be returned. She knew her father would cut her off if she ran away. Jit could not help: as a second son, he had no money either. 'How money or its need spoils happiness,' she lamented. They would have to find another way.

Meanwhile, Indira's brother Jayasinh was married that February, his happiness a sharp contrast to her own predicament. His wedding was celebrated with all the customary flourish and fanfare, including a performance by Baroda's celebrated troupe of trained emerald-green parrots. They rode bicycles, turned somersaults, fired minia-ture silver cannons, loaded cameras and took photographs, drove each other in tiny carriages and pairs, swung through hoops and shot arrows with little bows; one even played a piano while another danced. The festivities culminated with a riotous mêlée inside the guarded palace gates – everyone involved in the wedding from Maharani Chimnabai down to the Barodas' youngest son, 'that young villain, Dhairyashil', wildly throwing red powder over everyone else as fireworks exploded overhead. The madness lasted, recorded an unamused (and crimson-stained) Miss Tottenham, Chimnabai's English companion and lady-in-waiting, until four in the morning, when the bridegroom's party finally claimed victory.

Colonel Impey, as Resident the official representative of the Government of India in Baroda, reported back to Calcutta soon after Jayasinh's wedding. 'The Gaekwad has been largely occupied with the affairs of his family,' he observed. Sayajirao was, he said, in poor health, failing to attend more than one of the numerous ceremonies at the wedding and a few minutes at the banquet, where the dewan (chief minister) read his speech for him. This speech, however, was satisfactorily laced with declarations of attachment to George V and the British Empire. 'I mention this fact as in my previous report [in October 1912] I alluded to another speech in which the Gaekwad had let slip an opportunity of expressing in public his loyalty and the necessity of loyalty.' The British were keeping a close eye on Sayajirao after his disappointing behaviour at the Durbar.

Indira's chance came in April, when the Barodas received reluctant permission to sail to Europe for Sayajirao's health; they planned to take her with them in the hopes of distracting her. She and Jit plotted that he would meet her in Bombay, where she and her parents were due to embark. He would then take her to Calcutta where they would be married. In her apartments in the rambling palace at Baroda, amid the piles of trunks and packing cases overflowing with gilt-edged saris and peignoirs trimmed with coffee-coloured Brussels lace, the princess smoked cigarette after cigarette, planning her escape.

A telegram ordering Jit not to come to Bombay was dispatched to Cooch Behar from Baroda before the family left for Bombay on 13 April, but it arrived too late. When they reached Bombay Sayajirao summoned Jit to the marble durbar hall in his palace, Jaya Mahal. In a gallery above, the Maharani watched from behind a thin bamboo screen. Jit entered, walked the great empty length of the room towards Sayajirao, and bowed. 'I wish you to know that it is quite impossible for me to allow you to marry my daughter. It can never be, and my attitude will never change,' said the Maharaja. 'It is very hard,' replied Jit slowly. The interview was over. Afterwards Chimnabai spoke to Jit briefly, and he asked to see Indira for a last time. They were granted five minutes together.

Later in the afternoon, a surprisingly cheerful Indira went to her dressmaker's, accompanied by her mother's English companion, Miss Tottenham, who had been instructed not to let her out of her sight. Coming out of the fitting room, the princess kissed the modiste overly fondly. 'Should I have been warder there also?' wondered Miss Tottenham. When they reached Jaya Mahal, she realized her mistake. Indira had given the seamstress a letter for Jit, which had been brought to Chimnabai and Sayajirao by a servant loyal to them. In it, she outlined her plan – hatched during their brief meeting that morning – to escape the palace with Jit's help and make her way to his hotel.

That night, the palace was guarded only by the Maharaja's most trusted servants. Indira could be seen in her room pacing restlessly to and fro in front of the window, as if she were waiting for someone. An hour before midnight, Jit did try to enter the palace grounds, but was apprehended and turned away. Miss Tottenham escorted Indira to the boat at nine o'clock the next morning, and kept a close watch on her before the gangplank was drawn up lest she tried to escape.

On board the ship, a despondent Indira read in the newspapers the reports of her forthcoming nuptials, already announced by the Cooch Behars to the Calcutta press.

Great preparations are in progress at 'Woodlands', Calcutta, the residence of the Maharajah of Cooch Behar, for the wedding of Maharaj Kumar Jitendra Narayun, the brother of the Maharajah, and Princess Indira, the only daughter of His Highness the Gaekwar. The marriage will take place on Monday next. The bridegroom is very popular in sporting circles in Calcutta.

Sayajirao and Chimnabai were furious about the misleading publicity. If the Maharani met her daughter as they took their evening walks on deck, she would hiss biting words to her in Marathi, or cut her altogether. Indira, with a note of hysteria in her forced laughter, tried to ignore her parents in the confined space of the liner. The newspaper reports had made her a celebrity on board, and she was protected by admirers advocating her romantic cause who objected to obedient Miss Tottenham checking all Indira's shore-bound telegrams and trying to enforce a bedtime of 10 p.m. 'It's Father's own fault,' Indira told Miss Tottenham desperately. 'I could have married at sixteen, but Father said I was too young and should wait longer so that I might have a voice in the matter myself.' Picking up her gold tongue-scraper, she went on, 'Now I taste all the bitterness of life. I make my own choice, and yet here I am a prisoner.'

The Barodas, relieved to have given Jitendra the slip and hoping their stay on the Continent would distract their recalcitrant daughter, disembarked in France and after a short stay in Paris went to Evian-les-Bains. As usual when the Maharaja was away from India, a man from Scotland Yard was trailing Sayajirao, who, it was feared, was in contact with Indian nationalists living in Europe. These revolutionaries-in-waiting found it easier to agitate for independence at a safe distance from the vigilance of the Government of India. With his reputation of sympathy for 'insurrectionists', the Maharaja was considered too powerful a symbol for the nationalists, who saw him as a potential leader of an independent India, to leave unwatched while he toured Europe. The detective noticed a suspiciously bearded man hanging around the Barodas' hotel and assiduously reported it back to the India Office. But it was no rebel or enemy of the Empire, just a clandestine lover, newly landed in Europe, making contact with his princess in her high tower. If Chimnabai and Sayajirao had thought that taking Indira away from India would loosen the bond between her and Jit Cooch Behar, they were wrong.

Thirty years earlier, it would have been inconceivable that a princess should defy her parents and society's accepted order as Indira had done, but – for all their disapproval of their daughter's rebellion – the Princess of Baroda was every inch the product of her parents' marriage. In its own way, and for its times, the union of Chimnabai and Sayajirao Gaekwad was as unconventional as Indira intended hers should be.

Indira's mother, Chimnabai, had married the Maharaja of Baroda in an arranged marriage in 1885 when she was fourteen. An Indian prince or princess in the nineteenth century did not expect to marry for love; Indira's determination to do so was astonishing even three decades later. In this culture, where wives might be discarded for not bearing sons and dying on their husbands' funeral pyre was seen as a privilege, love and affection counted for less than duty, honour and tradition. Marriage was seen as a dynastic arrangement, forged between families or states – not individuals. Love followed the wedding ceremony, rather than developing before it; the feelings of the bride and groom were irrelevant.

'There is no other god on earth for a woman than her husband,' states the *Padmapurana*, a Hindu text dating to AD 750. 'The most excellent of all the good works that she can do is to seek to please him by manifesting perfect obedience to him. Therein should lie her sole rule of life.' The highest religious dharma, or observance, was pativrata, a wife's complete devotion to her husband, whatever his sins or faults. 'Let his defects be what they may, let his wickedness be what it may, a wife should always look upon him as her god, she should lavish on him all her attention and care, paying no heed whatsoever to his character and giving him no cause whatsoever for displeasure.'

Contemporary westerners either deplored or idealized the Indian attitude to women and marriage. Feminists such as the investigative journalist Katherine Mayo, in her incendiary *Mother India*, published in 1929, railed against what they saw as the injustice and nigh-bestial depravity of Indian society. 'We husbands often make our wives so unhappy that we might well fear that they would poison us,' Mayo cites a typical Indian husband as saying. 'Therefore did our wise ancestors make the penalty of widowhood so frightful – in order that the woman may not be tempted.'

Traditional moralists in the Victorian mould, on the other hand, saw much to admire in the Indian woman, who served her man with such strength and dignity. One of the numerous books on India written by former British civil servants and soldiers there quotes a letter from a Hindu wife to her husband:

I could not forget you, for you are to me what the broad deep sea is to the fish . . . Why do you praise me so much? I am not worthy of praise. Nor could I become estranged from you. You alone are my lord and master, you alone can fathom the depths of my heart and understand its desires. For me there is not your equal in the world.

As this devoted letter shows, love did exist in Indian society; but it was expected to come only after marriage. The idea of romance now paramount in western society had no Indian equivalent except in extramarital affairs between, for example, a prince and a court-esan, or a neglected young wife and a humble but adoring gardener who dared not approach her. Tales of passion unrequited, thwarted and doomed are still the mainstay of Indian cinema, but love was what grew between a husband and wife over the years, rooted in the shared life they built together.

In arranged marriages between royal houses, cultural, political and financial issues were even more important than for ordinary citizens, and traditional customs were followed with still greater rigidity. Matchmakers and astrologers checked that clan lineages were pure and horoscopes compatible. Dowries, 'burdens of pride', were pitilessly negotiated in inverse proportion to the bride's status and beauty.

A suitable future maharani was young, sometimes as young as four or five and never more than a year or two into her teens, fertile and preferably pale-skinned. Her family would be of the ruling warrior caste, kshatriya, to which all princely and aristocratic families belonged. Hindu society is divided into four castes: brahmins, traditionally priests; kshatriya, warriors or rulers; vaisya, merchants; and shudra, farmers. Beneath these were the untouchables (today known as dalits) who performed the menial tasks the upper castes scorned, like sweeping, leather tanning and latrine cleaning. There were also thousands of subdivisions of each caste, called jatis. Losing caste – through intermarriage, travelling across the 'black water', or ocean, carrying the corpse of someone from another caste, or even eating food prepared by someone from the wrong caste – was the gravest dishonour not just for an individual, but for his or her entire family. These rigid proscriptions were part of the reason it was so hard for the British to assimilate into Hindu society; they maintained a social status quo that had existed for thousands of years. The British, themselves no strangers to hierarchical social systems, saw caste distinctions as a valuable method of social control and made no effort to weaken them.

A future maharani must also belong to the right clan, which denotes tribal affiliation rather than social station. The Gaekwads of Baroda were Marathas, a fierce people who occupied the high plateau country inland from what is now Mumbai. Marathas held themselves to be superior to the effete Rajputs of northern India and the jungly tribal kingdoms of the north-east. For their part, the ancient Rajput clans, many of whom claimed descent from the gods and who had dominated northern India since before the Mogul conquest, considered the Marathas peasant upstarts.

The first and greatest Maratha leader, Shivaji, defied Mogul authority in the seventeenth century and as Mogul power declined in the eighteenth century, the Marathas united to form a confederacy under a handful of warlords, the Gaekwads of Baroda, the Scindias of Gwalior, the Holkars of Indore, the Peshwas of Poona and the Bhonsles of Nagpur. Growing increasingly powerful, the warlike Maratha dynasties began to dominate central India until their land, much of it seized from the old Rajput dynasties, stretched down from the south-western edge of the Himalayas across the Deccan to the great southern kingdoms of Mysore and Hyderabad. This put them on a collision course with the British East India Company, also intent on controlling north India. A series of Maratha wars ended in 1818 with British acceptance of the Maratha dynasties, but at the price of their recognition of British suzerainty. The Marathas relinquished their ambition of succeeding the Moguls as overlords of India reluctantly, if at all.

Chimnabai, as a young and beautiful Maratha kshatriya, was eminently suitable to become Maharaja Sayajirao's maharani. Their wedding was marked by all the customary celebrations. There were demonstrations of equitation and swordsmanship, wrestling matches, horse races, performances by schoolchildren, animal displays, traditional dances, fireworks and a ploughing competition. There was a huge feast, and a procession through Baroda's streets in which horses and elephants were caparisoned with richly embroidered velvets and cloth-of-gold, and wore headdresses made from plumes of ostrich feathers. Strings of gold coins were tied into the horses' manes, and gold and silver bells tinkled from gold-draped, silver-wheeled carts drawn by pairs of white bullocks. The Maharaja's elephant, presented to him by Queen Victoria, carried a howdah of solid gold, encrusted with blazing jewels which required twenty-four men to hoist it up on to the animal's back. At the end of the day, the elephant was rewarded for its efforts with a pint of sherry.

But the nervous fourteen-year-old bride did not watch any of the public displays in her honour and her face was not glimpsed by the crowds cheering her name. Chimnabai would have seen her new home for the first time from behind a heavy veil as she was led out of her closed train compartment and into a little carriage like a 'biscuit-tin on wheels' drawn by two snow-white bullocks. As she was driven to the rambling zenana of the crumbling white palace, Nazar Bagh, in which the ruling family of Baroda lived, she was hidden behind tightly drawn curtains. She would not have expected ever to look openly at the outside of the palace in which she would spend the rest of her life.

Forbidden to all men and most foreigners, zenanas were places of mystery and enchantment. The correct elevation of a zenana's garden walls was high enough 'that no man standing on an elephant can overlook them'. An intrepid English traveller, Fanny Parks, visited a zenana in Calcutta in the 1830s and was unsurprised that no men were permitted inside it, because the ladies' apparel 'consisted of one long strip of Benares gauze [expensive silk gauze from Varanasi, with an almost iridescent sheen to its brilliant colours] of thin texture, with a gold border, passing twice round the limbs, with the end thrown over the shoulder. The dress was rather transparent, almost useless as a veil: their necks and arms were covered with jewels.' Parks also noted how curious the cloistered women were about the outside world. They observed all comings and goings through screens, and knew everyone's name and business. 'They were very inquisitive; requested me to point out my husband, inquired how many children I had, and asked a thousand questions.'

Zenanas rang with the sounds of music and song, children playing, whispers, chatter and the tinkling of anklets; there was scarcely a moment of solitude. In the mid nineteenth century, the women of the royal zenana at Oudh (the area around Lucknow) whiled away their days with archery, reading and reciting poetry, or riding ponies in their lush walled garden. They had a large silver swing, which was especially pleasant in the humidity of the monsoon; they resembled dazzling parakeets in a cage as they swung, silk-swathed, behind their high walls. Languid by night, they smoked hookahs, or indulged, heavy-lidded, in opium, taken daily as a syrup from the poppies in their garden and rolled by hand into edible black pellets.

The uninterrupted monotony of life behind zenana walls often bred deception and quarrels in royal households, especially where a prince had more than one wife. Rival ranis and courtesans plotted against each other, encouraged by their servants and guardian eunuchs. 'A common complaint is, "Such a one has been practising witchcraft against me." If the husband make a present to one wife, even if it be only a basket of mangoes, he must make the same exactly to all the other wives to keep the peace.' The very architecture of zenanas – cramped, unlit rooms, a maze of narrow passages and staircases, 'the ever present screens of marble tracery that may hide or reveal so much' – fed this impression: 'all these things breathe of plot and counter-plot, league and intrigue'.

But for all the scheming that could develop in this enclosed world, old women looking back on zenana life after its demise remembered zenanas as places of companionship and warmth, of mutual support rather than repression. 'Zenana life, for all its limitations, had profound and solid compensations, too.' There were strict rules about behaviour – a junior wife could never look a more senior zenana woman in the face, for example – but these were customs with which every bride would have been acquainted from childhood in her own home.

Chimnabai was lucky that Sayajirao had no other wife waiting to welcome her to Baroda. As a legacy of his British education, Sayajirao believed passionately in monogamy in a world where polygamy was universally accepted. She still had to face the ladies of the zenana, but being the Maharaja's only wife granted her automatic status. Her proud Maratha blood gave her strength. Many years later, her niece said that being a Maratha woman, she hated 'to beg or say Yes, Yes, to everything which does not agree to my view, I don't say that I am always right but I will not give in to please anybody or to gain anything': it might have been Chimnabai herself talking.

Chimnabai's bridegroom, waiting for her on the other side of the purdah, was a man whose defining characteristic was his determination to govern Baroda well, and to show the British that Indians were fit to rule themselves. As his friend the Aga Khan said, he 'possessed a sturdy independence of character, and the awareness that the honour and dignity which he had inherited were not only his own personal right but were attributes indissociable from the race and nation to which he belonged. For him, India always came first. Neither family nor class nor creed mattered more than this simple, spontaneous, and all-embracing loyalty.'

Though his warm-hearted modesty of manner was enormously

charming, all through his life Sayajirao held himself aloof even from
the people closest to him. This was the legacy of his unusual
upbringing.

In 1870, Khanderao Gaekwad, the jovial and popular Maharaja
of Baroda, died. Flamboyant Khanderao had been unenthusiastic
about administration but passionate about jewels. In 1867 he bought
one of the largest diamonds in the world, the 125-carat, rose-tinted
Star of the South; his armoury boasted a pair of solid silver cannon.
Though the British government might have preferred Khanderao
to take a little more of an interest in the ruling of his state, and a
little less in his pleasures, for them he was, in many ways, an ideal
maharaja. He was popular with his people, and therefore his state
was internally secure. He was also loyal to the Government of India
and compliant with their policies.

His younger brother, Malharrao, was a different story. Because
Khanderao was childless, Malharrao was expected to succeed him.
In 1863 Malharrao had been found guilty of scheming to kill
his brother and take his place on the throne. He had paid a
British sergeant to shoot Khanderao; when his plot was discovered,
Malharrao was imprisoned alone in a dark, narrow cell in a village
outside Baroda city. When Khanderao died seven years later, the
British Resident, Colonel Barr, rode out to Malharrao's prison and
invited him to the capital – but only as Regent. Khanderao's young
bride, Jamnabai, was pregnant. No decision about the succession
could be made until Khanderao's baby was born. If it was a boy, it
would be king. If a girl, the Regent would become maharaja.

Malharrao had not sat in prison for all those years to be thwarted
on his release by a slip of a seventeen-year-old girl who might or
might not have been carrying Baroda's legitimate heir in her belly.
He hired sorcerers to kill Jamnabai, and had her food poisoned.
But the steely Jamnabai refused to eat anything she had not cooked
herself, and slept with a dagger under her pillow and a snarling dog
tethered to the bedpost.

Her baby, born in July 1871, was a girl. Triumphant, Malharrao
showered the streets of Baroda with gold coins. Jamnabai beat a

tactical retreat to Poona, but continued to barrage Colonel Phayre, the self-righteous British Resident who had replaced Barr, with reports of Malharrao's misrule, of rampant extortion, torture and murder. Like Khanderao, Malharrao spent money liberally, casting a pair of cannons in solid gold (trumping his brother's silver pair) that weighed 280 lbs each, and commissioning a large carpet woven entirely of pearls for a local temple, but which he then kept for himself. On a trip to Bombay in 1874, Malharrao admired a British Highland regiment so much that he decided to dress one of his own battalions in the same way. Their kilts did not look quite right at first, though, until the soldiers were given pink calico tights to cover up their incongruously brown legs.

Phayre was easily convinced of Malharrao's unsuitability to rule, and keen to see him dethroned. According to Phayre, Malharrao responded with characteristically underhand methods, apparently spiking the Resident's sherbet with a compound of arsenic and ground-up diamonds. Phayre was dismissed in December 1874, but Malharrao was nevertheless deposed on 10 April 1875 for misrule. The new Resident, Sir Richard Meade, agreed that Jamnabai, now Queen Regent, could adopt a suitable boy to bring up as her dead husband's heir. The news that the Gaekwad throne waited for a young man to claim it spread through the kingdom.

The Gaekwad realm was the third richest in India. Baroda, flat and fertile, covering 8,000 square miles, was known as the garden of Gujarat. Cotton, millet, maize, opium poppies and fruit trees flourished in its fields and orchards. In 1877, its population numbered more than 2 million people, mostly prosperous smallholders, with almost 90,000 in Baroda city. Baroda's army comprised 11,000 soldiers, larger than any other Maratha kingdom's. Its annual tax revenue was £2,000,000, of which the maharaja received one in every thirteen, an astonishingly large annual income by any contemporary standards, though other accounts say the Gaekwad took only one-tenth of Baroda's revenue. Because the states were governed absolutely, there was no constitutional limit on the maharajas' privy purses; some princes took as much as a third or a half of their states' revenues for their private use.

During the years of Mogul rule, the first Gaekwad had seen a Muslim butcher drive a herd of cattle past his fort. Horrified at the prospect of their slaughter (cows are sacred to Hindus), he opened a small side door, or kavad, into the fort, into which the cows ran, escaping their persecutor. The words for cow (gai) and door (kavad) were joined to create a name, Gaekwad, as a testament to his piety in saving the cows, and courage in defying his country's invaders. The Gaekwads, far from trying to cover up their humble rural origins, were proud of their name and background.

Baroda's association with the British forces in India began after the Maratha wars and the final destruction of the Maratha armies in 1818. In 1857, Khanderao backed the British in the Indian Mutiny, now recognized as the first step on the path to Indian independence. Horrified by the violence and bloodshed of the rebellion – and determined to ensure that their rule would never be challenged again – when peace was restored in 1858 the British government claimed India for the first time as a subject land governed by a viceroy in the name of the crown and a secretary of state answerable to Parliament in London. Three-fifths of the subcontinent that had formerly been dominated by the East India Company now became British India, ruled autocratically in eleven provinces by a multitude of British administrators and soldiers as a colony of the British crown.

The remaining two-fifths, covering a third of India's land mass and constituting perhaps a quarter of its population, were princely or 'native' states ruled by maharajas or nawabs in alliance with the British government. The states that had remained loyal to Britain during the rebellion were seen as invaluable 'breakwaters in the storm' and a deliberate policy was followed by the British thereafter of 'increasing the consequence of, and placing trust in, the native chiefs'. As long as they paid taxes to the Government of India, the maharajas were permitted to rule according to their traditional local customs along broadly feudal lines, with the maharaja as absolute despot in his own lands. They were subject to the British in two important areas. The British demanded control over the princes' foreign policies and forbad them from waging war independently;

they also insisted on certain administrative standards being met across the subcontinent.

Good government, as Viceroy Lord Mayo told the princes in 1858, with typically Victorian high-mindedness and optimism, was key.

If we support you in your power we expect in return good government. We demand that everywhere through the length and breadth of Rajputana [roughly modern Rajasthan], justice and order shall prevail; that every man's property shall be secure; that the traveller shall come and go in safety; that the cultivator shall enjoy the fruits of his labour and the trader the fruits of his commerce; that you shall make roads and undertake the construction of those works of irrigation which will improve the condition of the people and swell the revenues of the states; that you shall encourage education and provide for the relief of the sick.

But though the declared intentions of the British were often admirable – and individual soldiers and civil servants were frequently principled, sympathetic and knowledgeable – at bottom every aspect of India's government was dominated by the need to maintain Britain's moral, ideological and economic superiority over what they considered to be a subject race.

Arthur Balfour, discussing Britain's troubled presence in Egypt in 1910, articulated the fundamental argument for ruling over subject peoples without their consent: that empire was justified by the advantages it conferred. 'If it is our business to govern, with or without gratitude, with or without the real and genuine memory of all the loss of which we have relieved the population and no vivid imagination of all the benefits which we have given to them,' he demanded, 'if that is our duty, how is it to be performed?' In the same speech, he referred to the British as the 'dominant race'. This sentiment was a prerequisite for empire building. 'We happen to be the best people in the world,' declared that arch-imperialist Cecil Rhodes, 'with the highest ideals of decency and justice and liberty and peace, and the more of the world we inhabit, the better it is for humanity.'

Though racism ran right through Indian society under the British, the princes were secure with their boundaries, riches and privileges guaranteed by the paramount power. They had only to toe the British line to retain their authority. But British restraints on the princes' foreign policies and the complete ban on warfare were hard for proud, martial rulers to take. Psychologically, too, the British presence was a double-edged sword for the princes. 'We started feeling that they [the British] were essential to our survival,' said one former prince, 'whereas originally it was we who had been essential for British survival.'

This almost unwitting Indian complicity in British rule is one of the most complex and controversial aspects of Indian colonial history. The British governed India through a strange alchemy of conviction, on their side, and an irresistible suspicion, on the Indians', that western civilization was intrinsically superior to Indian culture – more modern and therefore more desirable. The British and many of the Indians they ruled were in thrall to this illusion, and this is why, with a proportionately tiny governing class (the Indian Civil Service numbered about 1,000; as late as 1921 there were only 156,000 white people in India), the British managed to maintain their control. It was a conjuring trick, the emperor's new clothes; and in the 1870s, only a few Indians in princely India or British India had begun to consider the possibility that the emperor might be naked.

In the early summer of 1875, when the heat was becoming unbearable and the monsoon was still months away, Maharani Jamnabai followed her Resident's advice, and summoned the men of the extended Gaekwad family to Baroda city with their sons, so that one of them might be chosen to succeed her deposed brother-in-law.

Kashirao, the headman of a hamlet several days' travel from Baroda city, took two of his sons and one of his nephews to the state's capital. Although he and his family were farmers, they were kshatriyas, of the warrior caste, and distantly related to the ruling Gaekwad family. The four walked 300 miles from their village to the palace, along interminable dusty tracks, past oxen drawing trickles of water up from deep wells and brightly clad women working in the parched fields. Though there was a new train line in Gujarat, they could not afford tickets.

The three boys were asked individually why they thought they had come to Baroda. The eldest replied, 'To see the sights'; the youngest wasn't sure. The middle boy, Gopalrao, unhesitatingly declared, 'I have come here to rule.' Another story describes the three unsophisticated boys sitting at dinner with the Maharani and Sir Richard, unsure of how to eat in such grand surroundings. The eldest and youngest were too bewildered and nervous to move; from beneath his eyelashes, Gopalrao watched Jamnabai, and copied her. The astrologers confirmed Jamnabai and Meade's choice. They saw in Gopalrao's stars 'a powerful sovereignty, extension of territories, ever-increasing riches, and the enjoyment of a rule unhampered by foes'.

On 25 May 1875, Gopalrao was declared Maharaja of Baroda. Two days later, he was formally adopted by Jamnabai, and given a new name, Sayajirao. Resident Sir Richard Meade lifted him on to the gaddi – intended to underline, should such a reminder be needed later, how directly Sayajirao was indebted to the British for the 'sudden flick of destiny' that had catapulted him in the space of a few weeks from a future as the middle son of a provincial farmer to ruler of one of India's grandest and richest states. All the traditional festivities of installation were observed: gifts were exchanged, gun salutes fired, sugar distributed among the people, prisoners freed and the poor fed.

Part of the reason Sayajirao had been chosen was his obvious intelligence and good health (the Prince of Wales was told that Jamnabai had chosen at random 'a beautiful boy she had seen playing, half-naked, in the alleyways'). 'He is a small, delicately framed lad for his twelve years . . . with a bright pleasant face.' He looked adequate to the challenges ahead of him. These challenges would be great, especially mentally, for, at twelve, Baroda's new maharaja spoke only his native Marathi, and could not read, write or count. The entire education of an ideal prince would have to be packed into six years, including learning to speak fluent Gujarati and Hindi as well as English, and the classical education the British deemed necessary.

Sayajirao was installed in the enormous old palace of Nazar Bagh. With him came his family – his two brothers, who were to join his lessons and be company for him, and his parents, whom he seldom saw. One of the saddest stories about Sayajirao's youth is his memory of seeing his father from the window of his balcony, from which he used to wave at him. He did not dare call out for fear of making Jamnabai, his adopted mother, jealous. 'I have never had any family life, no kissing – to mention a small point – no familiarity, all salaams!' he recalled years later. 'This was so when I was a boy.' This perhaps accounts for the 'sad, subdued look' observed in his mild eyes by one of the Prince of Wales's companions later in the year.

It was lucky then that Sayajirao's English tutor, Mr Elliot, was such a success. Honest, wise and gentle, utterly straightforward, he earned Sayajirao's love as well as his respect. His classes consisted of philosophy, history, political science, geography, chemistry and mathematics, as well as sport and etiquette. Sayaji learned to speak, read and write in English, Marathi, Gujarati and Urdu, and devoured the works of Bentham and Mill, Shakespeare and Lewis Carroll.

Later Sayajirao had his favourite book, *Alice's Adventures in Wonderland*, translated into Marathi, his mother-tongue. At first glance, it seems an odd choice for a statesman – until one remembers how Sayajirao came to power. All of a sudden, his world had been turned upside-down; nothing was as it seemed, and impossible things were now possible – even after breakfast. Like Alice, he was an innocent in a strange world for which he knew none of the rules. This insight offers us a rare glimpse of Sayajirao's vulnerability. He learned his lessons so well that he rarely let his mask slip.

Sayajirao's first public appearance as maharaja outside Baroda was in November 1875 during the state visit to India of Edward, Prince of Wales (later Edward VII). The young Maharaja travelled to Bombay for the official reception. 'This boy, aged twelve years, who a few months ago was only a village lad in comparative poverty, bears himself with perfect composure and dignity, and appears to his inferiors every inch a king, as though he had sat on the Gadi for half a century,' observed one onlooker. 'He fell naturally and with genuine grace into a tone of perfect equality and frank boyish cordiality, well blended with dignity, in his intercourse with the Prince of Wales.' The Prince advised him to carry on with his English, and urged him to take up riding. Edward also commented on how well Sayajirao was adapting to his new circumstances. 'The Little Gaekwar of Baroda, who is as old as our oldest boy [Prince Albert, or Eddy], seems really a very intelligent youth, though only six months ago he was running about the streets adorned with the most limited wardrobe.'

Now he was a maharaja, Sayajirao's new wardrobe was far from limited; the Prince of Wales himself might have envied it. Sayajirao appeared at the reception as dazzling as a 'crystallised rainbow' in the Baroda jewels. 'He was weighted – head, neck, chest and arms, fingers and ankles – with such a wonder of vast diamonds, emeralds, rubies and pearls, as would be worth the loot of many a rich town.' They included a seven-stringed necklace of magnificent pearls the size of marbles; the 128-carat Star of the South, bought by Khanderao, as the centrepiece of a necklace made up of five rows of 500 diamonds and two further rows of emeralds; its matching plume of diamonds, worn in the turban; and the 70-carat Akbar Shah diamond, thought to have been one of the eyes of a peacock on the Moguls' solid-gold Peacock Throne, taken from the Diwan-i-Khas (Hall of Public Audience) in Delhi when the Persians sacked the city in 1739. The one type of jewel Sayajirao was not wearing was sapphires, because, allied to the turbulent planet Saturn, they were thought to bring bad luck. There were no blue stones in the Baroda treasury.

In hesitant English, Sayajirao presented Prince Edward with a silver tea service engraved with scenes from Hindu mythology, and an accompanying crib entitled, 'Hindoo Mythology Popularly Treated: Being an Epitomized Description of the Various Heathen Deities Illustrated on the Silver Swami Tea Service'. At the time,

Sayajirao's British advisers clearly thought this was an appropriate present for Edward, illuminating in digestible form the spiritual life of the millions of Indians who would, one day, be his subjects. Did they not suspect how galling it would be for Sayajirao, graciously permitted by them to retain his religion, then to see his deities dismissed as heathen idols decorating a teapot?

The fun-loving Prince of Wales invited himself to Baroda. He was keen to see the traditional elephant fights for which the city was famous. When the royal train pulled into Baroda station, the Prince was met by Sayajirao's own elephant, with its face saffron-painted, ears of pale yellowish-green, and false tusks and anklets of gold. Edward climbed a silver ladder to the golden howdah, a magnificent seat atop the beast's back, and sat beneath a cloth-of-gold canopy. The second elephant was almost as gorgeous, painted French grey and red, with a silver howdah, ankle and tusk rings. As the procession of elephants carrying the royal party left the station, another row of elephants salaamed them. The route to the Residency was 'hung with lamps and festooned with bright green leaves and flowers' as the elephants, followed by bands and the 3rd Hussars and Baroda Horse regiments, passed along it. 'The people seemed very comfortable,' observed a member of the cortège, 'no sign of the wretchedness we are so fond of attributing to Native Rule.'

The Agga, Baroda's arena, measured a massive 180 yards by 60, with 20-foot walls punctuated by huge archways. At one end was a three-storey grandstand for spectators. The Prince's party, moustached and dignified in white flannel suits and sola topis, watched a series of contests: pairs of human 'wrestlers', bare-knuckle fighting; rams, buffalo and rhino; an elephant versus a man on horseback; and, finally, the disappointing pièce de résistance, two elephants in combat. 'I rather suspect that these elephants were sly old fellows, who, like the gladiators in olden times, did not hurt each other a bit more than necessary and often "made believe" in a sadly deceptive fashion,' commented one of the Prince's companions. The reluctant opponents had to be provoked into battle with an inventive array of devices, ranging from shouts, flag-waving and cold water to fireworks and lance-pricks. Disapproving English newspapers reported Prince Edward 'highly delighted' by the spectacle.

Sir Bartle Frere wrote to Queen Victoria★ from Baroda that her son's visit 'had the most marked and powerful effect in reconciling all classes to a complete change of rulers, and to a transition from a regime of frightful tyranny and corruption to an orderly and well-regulated native administration'. Indeed: his few days there, most of which were spent in pursuit of game, must have made all the difference.

In fact the real reason Baroda was settling down was its satisfaction with the young maharaja and its new dewan, Sir Tanjore Madhavrao, who was sorting out the mess in which the two previous maharajas, Khanderao and Malharrao, had left Baroda. In 1875 Baroda was on the verge of bankruptcy, what with their precious artillery, huge diamonds and astonishing generosity to shrines. Sayajirao ordered one each of the gold and silver cannons melted down into currency, and retained the remaining two for ceremonial use.

The year 1881 was an important one for Sayajirao. He began the year by marrying. According to custom, his advisers had chosen a suitable girl whom he would not see until their wedding day. She was Maharani Jamnabai's niece, a princess from Tanjore (Dewan Sir Tanjore's home state) called Laxmibai, and in January 1881 the couple endured a month of nuptial ceremonies and celebrations. The famous tight-rope walker, Charles Blondin, was brought over from England to perform at the festivities. According to tradition, to underline her new identity as a bride and her allegiance to her new family, her name was changed from Laxmibai to Chimnabai. Six days after their wedding, Sayajirao laid the foundation stone for Baroda's new palace, just outside the old city walls. It was to be called Laxmi Vilas, meaning home of the goddess of wealth (Laxmi),

★ Though she soon tired of reports of his 'progresses', as she wrote to her daughter Vicky. 'There is such a constant repetition of elephants – trappings – jewels – illuminations and fireworks' (quoted in S. Weintraub, *The Importance of Being Edward*, p. 234).

and a reference to his bride's childhood name. Their first son was born that summer.

At the end of the year, three months before his nineteenth birthday, Sayajirao was formally invested with his powers as maharaja in a pandal, or marquee, in the grounds of Nazar Bagh, where he and his household still lived in the heart of old Baroda. The Viceroy, Lord Ripon, gave a speech that was, according to an Indian onlooker, 'dignified . . . but perilously close to the pompous'. Although Sayajirao had performed the 'social and public functions' of the role since his installation, he was now handed the reins of government. All power in Baroda now rested in him.

'May you always be zealous in performing your duties,' went the ancient prayer for an Indian king. 'May you always give in just measure. May you always be humble in the presence of the wise. May you always be in control of your emotions. May your zeal always be tempered by humanity. May you always be learned. May your presence always be regal. May you always possess the virtues of the divine King Rama.'

One of his first actions was to sack his capable, but obsequiously pro-British, dewan. Madhavrao had quarrelled with Sayajirao's beloved tutor, Elliot, who had remained in Baroda and was still a powerful influence there. Though no longer his tutor, Elliot was a mentor to the lonely young man and Sayajirao relied on him enough to get rid of the man who had brought peace, prosperity and order to Baroda. Elliot would be Sayajirao's most trusted adviser for the next fourteen years.

Emblematic of the importance Elliot and Sayajirao attached to education was the foundation of Baroda College in 1882. Twenty years later, Sayajirao lamented 'the uneducated losing so much pleasure in their lives through lack of the power to appreciate what is beautiful'. Education would, he believed, 'bridge the gulf between the East and the West and make all who possessed it able to meet on an equal footing'. In 1876–7, the percentage of Baroda's revenue spent on education was just 1 per cent; by 1933–4, it had jumped to 17 per cent.

No sooner had the intrigue of ousting Madhavrao been resolved than Sayajirao was struck by a devastating blow. His bride of three years, with whom he'd fallen deeply in love, died of tuberculosis, leaving behind two tiny daughters, a son – and a devastated widower. Sayajirao, barely out of his teens, was heartbroken for 'the mild, charitable, amiable woman, the devoted mother and loving wife'.

He lost his appetite and developed the chronic insomnia that would plague him for the rest of his life. Lacking anything else to hold on to, the young maharaja was inconsolable. Ever since his adoption and the move to Baroda city, Sayajirao had felt isolated by his new responsibilities despite the opulence all around him. He had hoped his wife would be his life's companion but she had died and left him alone again.

Despite the hundreds of retainers and servants whose only wish was to serve their king, and the complete lack of privacy, palace life could be intensely lonely for a maharaja. Because all power rested in the prince's person, palaces ran on intrigue, competition and jealousy. The maharaja was either on his guard against syco-phants or revelling in their flattery. Access to the maharaja and his favour meant everything: how then could he trust anyone? Everything centred around him, but he could open his heart to no one. This was especially hard for Sayajirao, who had been born to a simpler life.

After some months, with no sign of Sayajirao's heart mending, his advisers counselled him to remarry. He knew it was the right thing to do, no matter how hard it might be, but he had one, highly unconventional, condition: he must see the girl before he made up his mind. Sayajirao's demand was staggeringly modern, and would have been granted only because he was a maharaja, and the privilege of marrying a daughter to him outweighed the indignity of having to allow him to inspect her first.

Two suitable candidates were hurriedly found for the mourning prince. One was another girl from Tanjore, his first wife's home state, and the other was Garabai, the daughter of a noble, Baji Rao Ghatge, from nearby Dewas. After many days' deliberation,

Sayajirao chose Garabai. They married on 25 December 1885. Garabai was given Chimnabai as her new name, becoming the second Chimnabai of Baroda.

Immediately after his remarriage, Sayajirao demonstrated his continuing intentions to move away from the accepted ideal of marriage by drawing up a plan for his bride's studies and engaging two women to teach her to read and write English and Marathi. Folk tradition was deeply suspicious of women being educated, though there was a parallel tradition, especially at Mogul courts, of literate and creative purdah princesses. The Mogul empress Nur Jahan was not only an excellent shot who rode into battle on an elephant, but also made perfume, wrote poetry and designed gardens, buildings and clothes; the fifteenth-century Rajput princess Mirabai is called the Sappho of India.

In some regions courtesans were the only type of women who were educated as a matter of course. From mother to daughter, they kept alive the traditional dance forms, wrote and recited poetry, and played musical instruments. The association of learning with sexual licence discouraged ordinary women from seeking education, even if they could afford it. There was also a commonly held belief that if a married woman touched a book, her husband would die – the worst fate that could befall a wife.

But Sayajirao, playing Pygmalion, wanted his consort to be a companion, not just his brood-mare. Later, he said he and his wife agreed 'an educated lady in the house is more able to shed the light of enlightenment and true happiness than one who is ignorant and open to the cruel and interested intrigues of her surroundings, which have been a great bane of Hindoo wealthy families'.

The young couple took another dramatic step away from the traditional Indian way of life eighteen months later when they set sail for Europe. Devout Hindus automatically lost caste by travelling over the 'black water' and coming into contact with so many non-Hindus. The world outside India was still a mystery to most Indians, and in the main they considered it a mystery not worth

unravelling, if not downright dangerous, but Sayajirao was fascinated by what he had heard of Europe from his beloved tutor. His
health had not recovered from the debilitation that followed his
first wife's death, and it was decided another sweltering summer in
Baroda would only make him worse. Western doctors were to be
consulted, and mountain air taken.

Their entourage numbered fifty-five, including a pandit, or
priest, a barber, a tailor and a doctor. Two brahmin cooks
would prepare their meals in kitchens separate from the rest of
the ship, as eating food prepared by a non-brahmin was forbidden
to high-caste Hindus. They took with them all their groceries for
the journey, two cows for their milk, and a supply of ayurvedic
medicines.

Chimnabai was accompanied by two Englishwomen, Mrs
Elliot, the wife of Sayajirao's tutor, and her own companion,
Mrs Taylor, several Indian maids and her sister. When they reached
Bombay, Mrs Elliot and Mrs Taylor went off on a secret mission,
buying a supply of 'socks, shoes, petty coats and other garments'
for the Indian women. These purchases had to be kept secret so
the people of Baroda would not 'discuss what these ladies wore in
Europe'.

They travelled by steamer, the journey taking just under
three weeks. During the day, passengers strolled around the
decks – the Maharaja was an 'indefatigable promenader' – and
at night, in white tie, dined in palm-filled dining rooms. The British
saw these liners as playgrounds, entertaining themselves on board
with amateur theatricals and impassioned flirtations; the Barodas
kept themselves to themselves, particularly on this first, unfamiliar
passage.

For Chimnabai and Sayajirao, this was the start of a lifelong
love-affair with Europe. They travelled for five months through
the Continent, renting a house in Paris and touring Switzerland,
enraptured by the serenity of the mountains and green pastures,
so unlike Baroda's dusty plains. They visited palaces, museums,
churches – and barracks, dockyards, prisons, factories and sewage
plants. Everywhere they went Sayajirao took notes, meticulously

examining everything to see how it could be used to improve Baroda. He observed methods of road-laying, railway planning, museum curating and calico-printing; he visited poultry farms to see if Indian chickens could be persuaded to lay more eggs. Electricity, in particular, sparked his imagination: he wanted electric lifts and lights and bells installed in his new palace, still un-finished, and gas and electricity brought to the people of Baroda city.

They finally reached England at the end of November 1887, and on 2 December went to Windsor to pay their respects to Queen Victoria. The Barodas and their party travelled by special train from Paddington to Windsor. The platform had been cleared of men when they arrived so the ladies could disembark and get into their closed carriage unseen.

An ardent Indophile, the Queen had just taken an Indian man-servant, Abdul Kareem, known as the Munshi, into her service, and was learning Hindi. As promised by the Viceroy, Lord Dufferin, on this visit Victoria invested Sayajirao with the GCSI (Knight Grand Commander of the Order of the Star of India), the highest order of the Indian Empire, entitling the holder to wear at cere-monies a purple robe and a gold chain decorated with elephants, lotus flowers and peacocks.

Victoria's diary entry for their visit is the first glimpse we have of Chimnabai's character independent of her husband – although she seems to have been confused about what the Maharani was wearing. Chimnabai customarily wore a Maratha sari, which ties between the legs; this may have given the impression that she was wearing trousers. 'The Maharani bent low and shook hands. She is a pretty little thing and wore a close-fitting jacket and trousers, no petticoat, of pale blue satin, over the whole a long crimson and gold gauze veil, which passed over her head and covered her completely, excepting her face which she uncovered as she came into the room.

'She had splendid jewels on,' Victoria continued, in a description that chimes better with what we know of Chimnabai later. 'She looks very gentle but is said to be very wilful and to wish to see everything without being seen. She regretted not having seen Bertie. Both Princesses had a red spot painted in the centre of their foreheads [a bindi; see Glossary]. The maharani understands a little English, and says a few words, but her sister does not.'

The foreignness of Britain could be as intimidating as it was unfamiliar but the eighteen-year-old Chimnabai, as Victoria's description attests, carried herself with characteristic presence, dignity and self-composure. Her petite frame and fair skin belied her inner strength. A British woman once asked her whether she ever felt awkward not knowing British customs and manners. 'If I do not know what to do, I do nothing,' she replied with proud simplicity.

Of the next five years, Chimnabai and Sayajirao spent almost four outside Baroda, to the vexation of a succession of local Residents, who toed an uneasy line between their dual roles as representatives of the British government in the Indian states and political advisers to them. Formal complaints were made of the Maharaja's 'absenteeism'. But having discovered he could sleep well in a cool climate, Sayajirao was determined not to become ill again by remaining in Baroda during the hot weather. Even if he was in good health, spending too long in Baroda could be a strain. 'The atmosphere . . . was such that unless he could escape to England or abroad for three months in the year he felt he would go insane,' said a grandson of the Nawab of Bhopal of his grandfather, many years later, 'because as a ruler you were always on show, and with everybody saying "Yes, Sir" and "No, Sir" and "Whatever you want, Sir," it does tend to drive even the sanest man a little bit bonkers.'

In 1888, Sayaji visited Europe again, this time accompanied only by Mr Elliot as Chimnabai had just given birth to their first son, Jayasinhrao. The party numbered only fifteen. Though some maharajas travelled in flamboyant state, after his initial visit Sayajirao preferred to travel modestly, if not exactly in discomfort. For him, this was one of the great pleasures of foreign travel. 'I can hardly compare my life in England, where I am a private gentleman, with my life in India, where I am a ruling Prince,' he said in 1901, 'but the high level of intelligence usual in England and my coming into contact with men of different cultures, pursuits and interests, makes life, and especially a holiday, more enjoyable and more instructive.'

Chimnabai and their two small sons accompanied Sayajirao to Europe three years later. This time, they spent three months in Switzerland, returning to 'the tried and true friend St Moritz'. Both Chimnabai and Sayajirao were recuperating from illnesses; Sayajirao had suffered from pneumonia the previous winter. He consulted the celebrated Dr Charcot in Paris. His ailments – a non-specific combination of sleeplessness and stomach aches, later diagnosed as neurasthenia (a general medical term for fatigue and anxiety, no longer in use) – improved.

While Sayajirao was away, Baroda's administration was overseen by a specially appointed council headed by the dewan. It was in constant contact with the Maharaja, who insisted on being intimately involved in the minutiae of government. Serially numbered dispatch boxes from Baroda, containing the papers of state, arrived each week; telegraphs and letters came daily. Death sentences, for example, were pronounced first by the district judge, then confirmed by the High Court, then sent to the Maharaja for appeal. Sayajirao listened to his dewan's opinion, the opinion of his deputy, generally a judicial officer, and then, if desired, he asked for more information. Before deciding, he heard the report of a Judicial Committee. This process might take up to three weeks, and could easily be done if he were at one of the Indian hill-stations (it was usual during the hottest months of the year for all government to be conducted from a hill-station) or even in Europe.

Matters were also referred to the Resident, who was intended to represent the British government in the state and the state to the British government. Baroda was blighted in the late 1880s and 1890s by a series of petty, incompetent Residents, from the 'grasping Reynolds' to the 'actively malign Colonel Biddulph', who, in 1888, tried to remove Sayajirao from his throne. 'The effects of my absence are determined very much by the personal characteristics of this officer,' Sayajirao wrote in 1901. 'The result of my being away is to make his intervention in the administration more frequent and more felt.' This was not, he added, necessarily a good thing: 'The result of this external and, I might almost say, needless intervention, is that it multiplies and accentuates the slight inconveniences of my absence into serious difficulties, and creates new ones. Uncertainty and want of confidence in the indigenous Government is promoted.'

While the British were displaying the patronizing officiousness that blighted so many of the Empire's achievements, Sayajirao and Chimnabai were coming into contact for the first time with Indian nationalist intellectuals such as G. K. Gokhale, mentor to the young Mohandas Gandhi, and Mohammad Ali Jinnah. These men and women were passionate idealists and intellectuals whom the British regarded as dangerous seditionists. Many among them were involved in the foundation of the Indian National Congress, a pressure group which saw itself as the voice of India, in 1885. The Indian National Congress later became simply Congress, and still later, after Independence, the political party Congress.

Sayajirao was not present at their inaugural meeting in Bombay, but he was aware of the Indian National Congress's progressive aims of social reform and greater Indian representation in India's government, and donated money to their cause. In 1892, Sayajirao also contributed £1,000 to a leading Congress member, Dadabhai Naoroji, previously Dewan of Baroda under Malharrao, who was running for Parliament in England. When Naoroji won the seat of Finsbury Central by five votes later that year, he became the first Indian member of the British Parliament.

The following year, Sayajirao hired the brilliant young Aurobindo Ghose, also a prominent member of Congress, who had topped the Indian Civil Service candidates' lists but failed the final exams because, on principle, he refused to sit the riding test that was a mandatory grading element, but which he saw as a test of acquired English superiority irrelevant to administrative skills. The Indian Civil Service, generally known as the ICS, was a 'vast club' that controlled almost all the senior administrative positions in the Raj. Discrimination against Indian applicants was inherent in the system; the highly competitive examination favoured an Oxbridge education and had to be sat in England, thus putting it out of reach of the vast majority of potential Indian candidates. The first Indian to pass into the ICS was Satyendranath Tagore in 1863, but it was still highly unusual for Indians to do so in the 1890s when Ghose was an applicant. Ghose stayed in Sayajirao's service for over a decade, and as his views became more defiantly and violently nationalistic, Sayajirao promoted him to the position of his personal secretary and made him tutor to his children. The Maharaja of Baroda's Anglophilia was rapidly dissolving.

Chimnabai and Sayaji were in Baroda in February 1890 when the royal household moved into the glorious new palace of Laxmi Vilas. Though, modestly, Sayajirao said it had neither all the advantages of an Indian palace nor all the conveniences of a European house, he declared he thought it left nothing to be desired. Set in 700 acres of parkland on the outskirts of Baroda city, Laxmi Vilas 'had an almost fairy-tale aspect . . . [with the sun] gilding its domes and towers, [and] the pools of purple shadow, under its many arches'. Monkeys swung from a profusion of Mogul domes, drooping Bengali canopies, Rajput carvings and Gujarati towers, and ran through the palace's great halls and courtyards.

In the woods surrounding Laxmi Vilas flew parrots, woodpeckers, orioles, minars and quail; peacocks strutted across the lawns in front of the palace. Mr Goldring from Kew Gardens in London had designed the gardens. The park was crisscrossed by walks and encircled by a riding track, on which Sayajirao rode every day before breakfast. It was a sportsman's dream, with an immaculate cricket-ground, a two-mile racecourse, racquets and fives courts, a boat house on the Vishnamitri river which flowed through the grounds, a croquet lawn, a rifle range, a golf course and stables filled with horses. Sayajirao's soldiers exercised on the parade ground. A little temple stood in a clearing. Painted statues of Hindu gods and goddesses rose on pedestals out of a marble swimming pool.

The palace was designed by Major Charles Mant, the principal architect of the late nineteenth-century Indo-Saracenic style, whose aim was to 'unite the usefulness of the scientific European designs together with the beauty, taste, grandeur and sublimity of the native style', and which can best be seen in the public buildings of Kholapur in Maharashtra. But Mant died suddenly with three major palaces barely begun. 'He lost control of his senses, became convinced that his palatial designs would fall down because he had done the sums wrong, and died tragically while still in his forties.'

Laxmi Vilas was completed by Robert Fellowes Chisholm at a cost, in the end, of £180,000. Its layout was traditional, divided into three parts: public rooms, centred round the enormous durbar hall, where twelve workmen from the Murano glass company in Venice spent eighteen months laying the gold mosaic, a design of Hindu gods and goddesses, on the walls; the Maharaja's apartments; and the women's quarters in which Chimnabai and the children lived. Its frontage was over 500 feet; Sayajirao is said to have scootered down the marble corridors from his apartments to the dining room. There were no external doors, partly because with 200 servants and a permanent military presence the palace was never unguarded, partly because the mystical awe in which India's princes were held meant there was no fear of attack or robbery. The ceiling of the covered porch that led to the durbar hall was high enough that visitors could ride their elephants right up to the doorway before dismounting.

Elements of the palace's planning and decoration were appropriated from both Indian and European fashions. Externally, the domes and turrets celebrated India's indigenous architectural styles; there was a billiard room (Sayajirao and his sons loved billiards, and always played after dinner – and sometimes after breakfast); western visitors were catered for with generous guest apartments. They were entertained in drawing rooms furnished with French antiques and heavy with the rich scent of incense burning in braziers to repel the thick clouds of mosquitoes that plague Baroda. There were five courtyards inside the palace, where plants were reflected in cool pools of water and classical marble statues stood like ghosts among the greenery. Each night, visitors were given embossed cards to fill in specifying what mode of transportation they required for the following day: horse, elephant or Rolls-Royce.

The family ate, European-style, in a dining room on Chimnabai's side of the palace. The food might be Indian or European, though Chimnabai preferred Indian. When they ate Indian food, the royal family were served on gold thalis, or plates, with silver used for guests. Chimnabai explained to one visitor that these were more economical than china as they did not break. Every evening before dinner, an old woman waited in the hall to present Sayajirao with a tiny bouquet, for which responsibility she was given a pension.

After dinner, a jug and basin were wheeled round the table so everyone could wash their hands and mouths, Indian-style. Then Chimnabai prepared paan, a traditional digestive, from an emerald- and diamond-studded gold paan box, its segments opening out from the centre like petals of a lotus. Paan is made by wrapping a slice of areca nut with slaked lime and spices in a betel leaf; it might also contain more exotic ingredients, such as gold leaf or ground-up pearls. The little green package, smelling freshly of soap and euca- lyptus, is then chewed. As the men headed off to the billiard room, they helped themselves from a tray of betel nut, cardamom, almonds and cloves, other digestives.

The staff was a similarly exotic *mélange*. An English major-domo – the imposing Mr Pluck, who wore a dark-blue coat with gold buttons and a velvet collar – presided over the household, which included a French chef, an Irish Sergeant-Major in charge of the stables, Sayajirao's English valet, and Chimnabai's English com- panion and Swiss lady's maid. The Indian bodyguards wore 'white buskins and gauntlets, scarlet tunics slashed with gold, shining Wellingtons and dolmans of pale heliotrope edged with fur'. In future years, the garages were manned by Italian chauffeurs, because the Baroda cars were Italian-made; cars belonging to members of the Baroda family had red number-plates, and were the only vehicles allowed to drive through the narrow streets of the old city. Three white-uniformed ADCs took it in turn to be on duty for a twenty-four-hour stint. They had to be polite, amusing and good at tennis, riding and bridge; and they were required to carry a notebook and pencil at all times, in case workaholic Sayajirao needed to make a note of something. Servants were everywhere, all the time: privacy was a luxury maharajas and their families never enjoyed.

Chimnabai's apartments were decorated with silver furniture, delicately embroidered curtains and hangings, and rich carpets. Her toilet set was made of ivory and gold, and her jewels tumbled out of gold boxes. There were piles of dazzling saris in sandalwood chests, drawers of European lace ('she confessed to being rather extravagant in the matter of lace'), and feather-light cashmere shawls of fuchsia and emerald and luminous mouse-coloured natural wool.

Her daily bath – still a rarity among the British – was taken sitting on a stool. Cool water was scooped out of a large silver ewer on a stand with a smaller silver vessel, and poured over the body. Fine-ground gram (chick pea) flour was a natural, exfoliating soap. Sindur, the vermilion powder used for the bindi on the forehead, was kept in a tiny round pot.

Chimnabai would lie on a pile of silken cushions in the cool light of the trellised marble porch, working on an embroidery frame, with musicians playing softly or someone reading to her, as her ladies took turns fanning her with two enormous ostrich-feather fans.* She was a skilled sitar and veena player herself and had a pleasant singing voice. Dampened blinds of khus grass sent vetiver-scented breezes through her chambers. When she strolled through the palace grounds in the afternoon, whistles were sounded to shoo all the gardeners out of her path lest they catch sight of their queen.

'Here,' as one visitor to Baroda said, 'there is nothing to mar the effect of living in fairyland.'

---

* When her granddaughter Ayesha read this in draft she snorted (elegantly) at the thought of the upright, energetic Chimnabai behaving in so languid a manner, but this description does come from an eye-witness, the Reverend Weeden, who spent a year in Baroda in about 1910 and knew the family well.

Like Sayajirao of Baroda, Nripendra Narayan, Maharaja of Cooch Behar, came to the throne young and under the watchful gaze of the British government. Cooch Behar was a small, jungle-bound state in the far north-east of India, much less wealthy and influential than Baroda, but important to the British because of its strategic situation on ages-old trade routes that connected Calcutta, the centre of British government in India, with Nepal, Tibet, Assam and Burma. The Cooch Behar crest shows a blade of grass with which a legendary ancestor sliced off an enemy's head before presenting it to Kali, the terrible goddess of destruction and regeneration especially venerated in Bengal. The first raja, Visvasimha, established the Narayan dynasty at the start of the sixteenth century, though 'according to popular tradition his race had been founded by the love of a god and a maiden . . . [the Cooch Behar rajas were] always great rulers, great lovers, and great fighters'.

Nripendra ascended the Cooch Behar gaddi in 1863 as a ten-month-old baby. Concerned about Bhutanese incursions and wary of a long regency, the government of India wasted no time offering their help to the Cooch Beharis. Though, like Maharani Jamnabai of Baroda, the powerful women of the court – particularly Nripendra's grandmother, Rani Kameshwari, and his stepmother, Dangar Aii Debati – were determined to dominate policy from the zenana, refusing the British was not an option.

Nripendra's father, Narendra, who died when he was barely out of his teens, had steadfastly refused to allow the British to interfere with his rule or modernize his habits. Raja Narendra had several wives and dozens of concubines, all of whom plotted and intrigued against each other for Narendra's favour and to promote their children by him. He seems to have viewed his women as sport: he was notorious for getting drunk and attacking them, trying to chop off their heads. On one occasion, he swung at one of his wives – Nripendra's mother, Nishimayi, a beautiful local girl from a nearby village – with his sabre. His sword just glanced her, nicking the tip of her little finger.

When Nripendra succeeded Narendra, the British (as in Baroda) were resolved to give the young prince a western education and transform the primitive state through its ruler. They were determined not to repeat the mistake they had made in allowing the unruly Narendra, Nripendra's dead father, to remain in his state as a child-king. 'He had, before he left Cooch Behar, learnt to indulge in all his fancies,' the British Resident, Colonel Haughton, reminded the ranis after his death. 'He was flattered and humoured till it became the habit to indulge without restraint in every fancy.'

When he was five years old, the new raja – a 'frank, open-hearted boy' – was taken to the Wards' Institution at Benares (now Varanasi), a school set up by the British for the sons of Indian nobles. Though the British believed 'he would be better educated if he was kept away from the disturbances of the state and of the family', the ladies of Cooch Behar – Narendra's wives, mistresses, sisters, mother, aunts and all their servants – deeply suspicious of the British way of doing things, came too, and lived there in what became known as Cooch Behar Palace.

Six years later, Nripendra was sent to Patna, where he studied at Government College. Like Sayajirao, he had an English tutor and guardian, St John Kneller, who joined his household in 1872. To the horror of his Indian family, closely observing the foreign influences on him, Nripendra was told to erase the sandalwood paste on his forehead after prayers, was encouraged to wear British clothes and to eat and drink (admittedly only tea or gingerade) sitting at a table with his tutors – all of which was forbidden by the Hindu religion. 'When I am under somebody's control what strength have I of my own?' asked the helpless boy.

When Victoria was proclaimed Empress of India at the Delhi

Durbar in 1877, Nripendra was elevated to the rank of maharaja, hailed, for the first time, with a 13-gun salute. Because so few rajas in Bengal had been recognized as maharajas by the British (others included Tripura and Manipur), this was a signal honour.

The following year, the Government of Bengal decided that Nripendra ought to be sent to school in England. The palace ladies were outraged: how would he remain Indian if he was sent away? They were convinced that he would never return, or, if he did, he would be unrecognizably westernized. They insisted that, if he were to go, he must marry an Indian girl first so he had something to come home for; any other wives could come later.

Proposals for the young Maharaja flooded in: one man from Madras offered a dowry of Rs 3,00,000 over and above the jewellery with which he would endow his daughter. But the British were adamant that if Nripendra were to marry so young, it must be to an educated girl who could share the new life they had mapped out for him. The bride they were seeking had to meet with the approval of Nripendra's mother and grandmother as well as that of his English advisers. It was a nigh impossible combination: a girl traditional enough to please the orthodox ranis of Cooch Behar, and yet progressive enough for the modernizing British.

They settled on Sunity Devi, the pretty eldest daughter of the Bengali religious reformer Keshub Chunder Sen. She was well educated, but also modest and feminine. As a holy man's daughter, her virtue was unimpeachable; her family were also, necessarily, kshatriya, the warrior caste.

At first, Sunity's father refused the Cooch Behar offer. Disingenuously, he said his daughter was neither very pretty nor very well educated, 'not a suitable bride for a young Maharaja'. The truth behind his hesitation was that he knew how unpopular his agreement to the match would be among his followers. Sunity Devi was thirteen years old, a decent age for an Indian bride, but Keshub Chunder Sen had agitated to have the minimum marriage age for girls raised to fourteen, and could not be seen to condone child-marriage. On the other hand, as Maharani of Cooch Behar, she would be in a position to effect enormous reform herself. Eventually he was persuaded that the marriage would enhance Cooch Behar's spiritual good. He began to see the match as God's will, and made up his mind to approve it.

Keshub Chunder Sen was a charismatic priest who has been described as the Martin Luther of Hinduism. His mantra was 'One God, One Life, One Wife'. The faith he preached was the Brahmo Samaj, founded in 1828 by the octolingual (Bengali, Sanskrit, Persian, Arabic, English, Greek, Latin and Hebrew) scholar Raja Rammohun Roy. It was a reformist, monotheistic wing of Hinduism. Like Unitarianism, theosophy and spiritualism, Brahmoism was part of the broader search for truth that characterized populist nineteenth-century intellectual life. Rationalist and egalitarian, it held that mankind could achieve its full potential – its full perfection – through the union of social reform and superstition-free spirituality. All religions were seen as equally valid: 'nothing sacred to others [is] to be reviled or treated with contempt'. It 'aimed at purifying Hindu society by a return to the philosophical basis of the ancient Hindu scriptures, rejecting the idolatry and superstition of later generations, and with them social evils like caste prejudice and the suppression of women'. The first Brahmo temple opened in Calcutta in 1830 dedicated to 'the Eternal, Unsearchable, and Immutable Being who is the Author and Preserver of the Universe'.

The Tagore family, the great Bengali intellectual dynasty, put their influential weight behind the new religion and by mid-century Brahmoism was seen in Calcutta as an essential mark of modernity and progression. Dwarkanath Tagore was a successful businessman and philanthropist seen by the British as 'living proof of how British enlightenment could transform India for the better'. But inherent to his Anglophilia (Bengal born and bred, Tagore retired to Surrey where he died in 1846) was a core of national pride. Dwarkanath, like Rammohun Roy, believed and proclaimed that Indians could benefit enormously from interaction with Europeans; the subtext was that, once these necessary political, artistic, spiritual and social lessons had been absorbed, Indians would be capable of ruling themselves. The very process of acquiring western ideas contained within it the desire to throw off foreign rule. In the early 1840s the Governor-General, Lord Ellenborough, observed to Dwarkanath that if 'the natives of India' were properly educated, 'we [the British] should not remain in the country for three months'. 'Not three weeks,' replied Tagore. Dwarkanath's son, Debendranath, was Keshub Chunder Sen's early spiritual mentor. Debendranath's children included Satyendranath, the first Indian to pass into the Indian Civil Service in 1863; the poet, mystic, novelist and nationalist Rabindranath, winner of the 1913 Nobel Prize for Literature; and his sister, the novelist Swarnakumari.

Keshub Chunder Sen was a tall, broad-shouldered man, habitually swathed in a black cloak, possessing hypnotic charm. He was remarkably good-looking, with wavy dark hair, a warm smile and serene brown eyes. The Viceroy, Lord Dufferin, said he had never seen a handsomer man. 'Mr Keshub is no ordinary man,' said another friend, 'as you can tell by the perfect shape of his feet and the pink sole.'

In 1862, when Sen declared his allegiance to the Brahmo Samaj, he broke with his family, who refused to accept his renunciation of caste. (As Sunity Devi later pointed out, 'If one believes in caste, one can never believe in universal brotherhood.') Sen's wife asked if she could go with him when he left the extended Sen family home to live at the Tagores'. 'I want you to realise your position fully,' he told her. 'If you come with me, you give up caste, rank, money and jewels. The relations who love you will become estranged from you. The bread of bitterness will be your portion. You will lose all except me. Am I worth the sacrifice?' Putting her devotion to her husband above her responsibility to his family and her religion, she followed him.

In 1870, Sen was brought to England by a Unitarian association, and spent six months giving lectures all over the country. Echoing the ideas of Roy and Tagore, Sen declared he had come to London to extend his countrymen's heartfelt thanks to the British – not for railways or riches, but for 'revolutionary reform'.

When India lay sunk in the mire of idolatry and superstition, when Mahometan oppression and misrule had almost extinguished the spark of hope in the native Indian mind, when Hinduism, once a pure system of Monotheism, had degenerated into a most horrid and abominable system of idolatry and polytheism, when the priests were exceedingly powerful, and were revelling in their triumphs over down-trodden humanity, the Lord in His mercy sent out the British nation to rescue India.

It is no wonder his audience cheered their hearts out: this was exactly how the British liked to regard their imperial role.

It is no wonder, either, that even Queen Victoria demanded an audience with the celebrated reformer. On 13 August Sen went to Osborne House, the Queen's residence on the Isle of Wight, where he was served a vegetarian luncheon (he was vegetarian and teetotal), and then taken in to see the Queen and Princess Louise. He gave Victoria a pair of portraits of his wife, with which he reported her 'much pleased' – so pleased in fact that she requested a portrait of him as well and presented him with inscribed copies of her two books, *Early Years of the Prince Consort* and *Highland Journal*.

Sen's views on the British conquest of India were not limited to gratitude. He stressed that the British had a responsibility to their colony. 'If you desire to hold India, you can only do so for the good and welfare of India,' he exhorted his listeners, advising them first to promote education in India, then to develop a single vernacular language to unite the country, and next to allow Indians to hold office in India. Foreign control was a good thing only up to a certain point: 'the growth of society must be indigenous, native, natural'.

For women, too, Sen recommended home-grown development. 'There are some not only in India but in England, who think that if native women don't wear crinoline, speak French and play on the piano they are past redemption ... I for one protest against these ideas and projects of denationalising the Indian nation,' he told one audience. 'At least spare us the crinoline.'

Contrary to popular western opinion,* he said, Indian women were full of vigour and strength; but early marriage and perpetual widowhood were heavy burdens for them to bear. Education would free them to become 'good wives, mothers, sisters and daughters'. Bengal, the most progressive region of India, was seeing at this time an explosion of academic opportunities for women. In 1863, there were only 2,500 female students at ninety-five girls' schools in the area; less than thirty years later, there were more than 80,000 students at over 2,000 schools.

But for all his spiritual zeal and proud patriotism, Keshub Chunder Sen was a paternalist at heart and saw the role of women always in relation to men. 'In those things wherein man excels woman, let man's voice be heard; where woman excels man, let her voice be heard. The true prosperity of society depends on the harmony of the sexes.' Harmony, for him, did not mean equality. Educating girls, he believed, served no other purpose than to produce good wives and mothers. Female students at the ashram's school were taught subjects 'likely to be useful to them', which did not include geometry, logic, science or history.

Though Sen did not advocate female emancipation, he did oppose child-marriage. In 1872, at Sen's urging, the British government passed a Marriage Act (known as the Brahmo Marriage Act) setting the minimum age for marriage at fourteen for girls and eighteen for boys. Arguments in favour of child marriage pervaded mainstream Hindu and Muslim culture in India. Fathers dared not expose their pubescent daughters to the pressure of adult desires, especially in extended family households; giving a 'damaged' daughter in marriage was a slur on a father's honour. The younger she was, the more likely the child-bride was thought to be to accept

---

* 'Hindoo women are degraded, they are totally devoid of all delicacy, their ideas and language are coarse and vulgar, their terms of reproach and abuses are gross and disgusting in the extreme,' wrote Flora MacDonald in 1883, revealing the prejudice and ignorance that underpinned so many western observations of Indian life at this time. 'Although they manifest much shyness and outward modesty there is little real virtue of the higher order among them' (*Western Women*, p. 100).

the customs and disciplines of her new family, and venerate and respect her husband unconditionally.

Concerns about young brides being physically immature for the sexual and reproductive duties of marriage were dismissed by the insistence that child-marriage was usually just a very binding proposal. By custom, consummation generally did not take place until puberty, even if the young bride went to live with her husband's family before its onset, but what today would be regarded as sexual abuse of child-brides was a major source of concern to British and Indian reformers from the mid nineteenth century.

Once Sen was reconciled with his parents, he and his wife and ten children lived in a sprawling compound, Coolootola, built by Sen's grandfather and filled with nearly fifty aunts, uncles, cousins and grandparents. It was 'an enchanted place', with its six courtyards, cool dark interior rooms and deep, mossy wells. This was a traditionally run household, acceptable – just – to the ranis of Cooch Behar. The nineteenth-century activist Pandita Ramabai described a similar home, in which

men spend their evenings and other leisure hours with friends of their own sex, either in the outer courtyard or away from home. Children enjoy the company of father and mother alternately, by going in and out [of the purdah and non-purdah areas] when they choose . . . The women of the family usually take their meals after the men have had theirs, and the wife as a rule, eats what her lord may please to leave on his plate.

Here, as all over India, women held the family together, performing the rituals and observances that maintained the family's structure and coherence. There was a strict purdah area, in which the elder ladies of the house gambled at cards and the young wives surreptitiously embroidered slippers for their husbands, not wishing to show their devotion too publicly. The children had the run of the complex for their games of hide-and-seek and scared each other with ghost stories in neglected stairways.

Dominating proceedings from Coolootola's zenana was Sunity's handsome grandmother, Sharadasundari Devi, who 'exacted and received the utmost deference from her daughters-in-law'. The whole family called her Thakoorma, which means 'father's mother' in Bengali. In Indian families everyone is defined by their relationship to one another. Instead of using their given names, Sunity Devi would have called her aunts and uncles by different, specific nouns according to whether they were her father's or mother's siblings and whether they were older or younger. The very language used reinforced the fundamental cultural assumption that individual identity was subordinate to family solidarity and preservation.

In the afternoons, after school, Sunity and her female cousins would bathe and dress their hair, and put on fine muslin saris before going up on to the roof of the old house to enjoy the evening breeze. Sometimes they caught sight of a distant splash of colour on another roof, and knew other girls were also taking advantage of the cool of sunset. As they sat up above the city, singing and telling stories, the chime of bells, the trumpeting of conch shells and the faint scent of incense and flowers drifted up to them while the older women of the house prostrated themselves before their gods at arati, or evening prayers.

Sunity Devi's mother was 'the best type of Hindu woman. Gentle, loving, and self-denying, her whole life was beautiful in its goodness and simplicity.' She was a small woman with tiny hands and feet, a beautiful singing voice and a gift for story-telling – all traits her daughter would inherit. She lived for her husband, and encouraged her children to do so too. 'We led our lives secure in the belief that the religion practised by my father was the highest. His life and his teachings were so beautiful that it was impossible not to try to live up to his ideals, and his yoke was so light that we never felt it.'

On the morning Sunity was to meet Nripendra's advisers her parents told her that the Englishmen coming to see the school were coming to see her, 'and if we all agree, perhaps some day you will marry a handsome young maharaja'. Shy and feverish, dressed in a mauve and gold sari and adorned for the occasion with her mother's jewels, the petite Sunity was taken into a reception room. She played a simple minuet on the piano and answered a few questions put to her in English. A Mr Dalton observed every move she made, and described it all in a letter to Nripendra. He was impressed, as he told Sen: 'I thought your daughter a very charming young lady, and in every way a suitable bride for the Maharajah.'

Though the British were confident that Sunity Devi was the right girl for Nripendra, there were still some final negotiations to be made. Nripendra himself had been unwilling to marry and then immediately leave his bride, but he had been persuaded by the argument that another suitable girl would not easily be found, and was 'charmed at the beauty and virtue of Srimati Sunity'.

Sen, who wished to delay the wedding at least until his daughter was fourteen, was promised that since Sunity would not live with her husband until he returned from England a year or two hence, the ceremony – which the British were trying to rush through before Nripendra could happily leave his mother and India – would be more of a binding betrothal than an actual wedding. At his request, Nripendra wrote directly to Sen assuring him of his sincere attachment to the principles of monogamy and monotheism. Nripendra's mother won the concession that the Brahmo infidel (in her eyes), Sen, who had lost caste by travelling across the ocean, should not give his daughter away at the wedding ceremony. But at least the young couple were happy: from the moment Sunity, blushing, looked up into Nripendra's eyes for the first time, and saw them fixed adoringly on her, she loved him, and knew he loved her.

On 28 February 1878, the Sen family and assorted friends and followers left Calcutta for the long journey to Cooch Behar, nestled in the foothills of the Himalayas. Before the direct train line was laid in 1894, the way north from Calcutta was arduous, beginning with four hours on a broad-gauge train line from Howrah station. The party then steamed across the Ganges, which was so broad it took an hour to cross. There followed ten hours on a narrow-gauge train, three hours being poled down the Brahmaputra River in a houseboat, then six hours over a swamp, perched on a swaying elephant, and 30 miles on the Cooch Behar's private miniature railway before the final leg, a 25-mile drive in a carriage. Nripendra was one of the first Indian princes to purchase motorcars in the 1890s; these, together with the direct rail line from Calcutta to northern Bengal, made reaching Cooch Behar far easier.

They arrived in a lush and verdant land. Legend has it that the god Shiva chose Cooch Behar as his earthly home because it was so beautiful. Flying over Cooch Behar – with the white crags of the Himalayas apparently floating beside you above the hazy blue of the horizon, and the foothills below like a herd of ghostly elephants – it looks more water than land, silver webs and ribbons of water gleaming in the sun. When the rivers are in spate Cooch Behar is like a tropical Venice, and the easiest means of transportation, until the advent of railways, was by boat. For centuries, the land-locked state even had its own navy.

The wedding was due to take place on 6 March, and Sunity, though she had met Nripendra several times in Calcutta (chaperoned, of course), would not see him in Cooch Behar until the marriage ceremony. On their arrival, there was some final confusion about exactly what form the wedding would take. Sen insisted it was to be a Brahmo ceremony, free from what he scathingly called idolatry. This was unacceptable to the traditionalists of Cooch Behar, who had been persuaded to accept Sunity Devi but saw no reason to embrace her father's ideas, and hoped she would relinquish them when she became maharani. They were also upset that neighbouring rajas from Bijni, Dorong, Parbatjoar and Lakhipur refused to attend the wedding of a Cooch Behar prince to the daughter of an outcaste Brahmo.

The day of the wedding dawned, and the palace priests came to the house the Sens were staying in to discuss the service. Sen refused to allow any Hindu rites to be performed, and for a while it looked as though the wedding would have to be postponed, or even cancelled. Much later, after hours of debate, Sunity was told to get ready. Weeping, she touched her parents' feet and bid them farewell. She and her sister Bino rode in a palki through the narrow, teeming streets of Cooch Behar, brightly illuminated in celebration of their maharaja's wedding, to the palace zenana.

There she was met by Nripendra's mother who performed varan, the traditional welcome to the bride. Sunity, tired and confused, stood at the centre of a great crowd of women, all examining her and commenting on her looks. Suddenly, she heard a soft whistle outside and knew – for she had often heard his whistle in Calcutta – that it was Nripendra, letting her know he was there, waiting for her.

The next morning, Sunity was bathed and dressed by the palace women, and did not break her fast. According to her grandmother, she was petrified with fear, and begged her to stay with her, saying, 'I don't know what these people will do to me.' Nripendra's grandmother, the dowager rani, approached with the priest, and asked Sunity to hand him a gold coin, some water and tulsi (basil leaf, used in religious ceremonies) – part of the traditional Hindu marriage rites which Sen had specified must not be part of his daughter's wedding. 'I immediately took these things away from her [Sunity] and threw them down,' reported Sharadasundari Devi indignantly. 'I said "What are all these customs of yours? One should not indulge in such bad omens or else these will bring bad luck to you as well as us."'

Darkness fell. The auspicious hour chosen by the pandits came and went. The music stopped. One by one, the lights over the palace were extinguished. Nripendra, his eager face set, spoke at last in the words of a fairy-tale. 'Now give good heed to my words. I am going to bed. If I am to marry this girl, wake me up. Otherwise have my horse in readiness, for I shall ride away from Cooch Behar for good and all tomorrow morning. If I cannot marry this girl, I will marry no one.'

At midnight Sen's door burst open and the British officer who had negotiated the wedding rushed in, waving a telegram from the Lieutenant-Governor of Bengal ordering the wedding to take place as planned – simply, according to Brahmo custom, but in the presence of the palace's Hindu priests. Both sides could claim to have won the dispute. There was another auspicious hour at 3 a.m.; if they hurried, Nripendra and Sunity could still be married.

Fireworks fizzed and exploded above as the mournful song of conch shells, the traditional Bengali welcome for a bride, sounded in the streets of Cooch Behar. Sunity Devi, wearing a pale-blue sari heavily embroidered with gold and a glittering gold and red veil, was carried on a wooden plank, according to tradition, around Nripendra. 'He was like a wonderful picture, one mass of gold from head to foot, and the shimmering fabric seemed moulded to his fine figure.' She was brought closer and closer to him until a scarf was thrown over the couple and their eyes met for the first time as man and wife.

A few days after the ceremony, Nripendra escorted his bride back to her father's home and left India for two years in Europe. There he visited Italy, Austria and Germany, as well as Britain, where he spent several happy weeks shooting in Scotland and Ireland. As a Brahmo, no religious or caste observances restricted his association with non-Hindus, so, unlike most Indian princes (except Muslims), he could immerse himself completely in European culture and society. 'I am, for good or bad,' Nripendra used to say, 'what the British made me.'

His faithful retainer, who in about 1915 wrote an account of his life serving Nripendra, described the Maharaja's heart like 'that of a boy's full of joy, love and boyish pranks', and praised his 'English virtues': courage, tenacity and patience. 'Although he was the proudest of men,' observed Sunity Devi later, 'his simplicity was such that he believed his joie de vivre would pass unnoticed, and that he might be allowed to live as a man and not a maharaja.' These attributes made Nripendra enormously popular in British society, where he was seen as the ultimate example of an Indian prince with all the advantages of a British upbringing, education and manners. He preferred European food, and lived, according to his wife, 'like an Englishman', though, she insisted, 'he was entirely Indian at heart'.

Sunity Devi, now Maharani of Cooch Behar, remained intensely conscious of the controversy her marriage had caused and the damage it did to her adored father's reputation. 'It was left for me to prove the success or failure of the first Indian marriage which had defied traditional custom,' she declared, exaggerating only a little, and she never forgot her self-appointed role as her father's, and Brahmoism's, champion. This was difficult, given that her evangelizing Brahmoism was highly unpopular in Cooch Behar and the palace ladies there were determined to convert her to Hinduism. They would 'threaten and scold' her by turns to reject her father's faith and return to the old ways. But, secure in her husband's admiration for the British, and passionately convinced of her father's rectitude, Sunity was unswayed.

Their 'real' marriage took place in 1881 at Sunity's family home, Lily Cottage, when she was sixteen and Nripendra eighteen, in her father's Church of the New Dispensation, unhampered by the presence of the Cooch Behar palace pandits and according to the rites in which she believed. 'In quiet ways, we had gathered the fragrant flowers of friendship's garden,' she wrote of the day in her autobiography, in the sentimental imagery so beloved of the Victorians, 'and there we had seen the roses of love which were blooming for us.'

To celebrate, Nripendra gave his bride a little ring of turquoise and diamonds which she never took off, treasuring it more than any of the other magnificent jewels he later gave her. They set off on their honeymoon, alone together for the first time. Sunity's face was damp with tears but radiantly happy as Nripendra sang her a Bengali love song, 'He who has not undergone suffering cannot know love'. They travelled by train to Burdwan, where, when they disembarked, Sunity was escorted by 'a bevy of maidens' through a tented tunnel from the car to the carriage. Only when she was safely on her way to the palace, unseen, were the draperies withdrawn and Nripendra introduced to the officials gathered on the platform to welcome and congratulate him.

This strict purdah would remain the pattern of Sunity Devi's early years as maharani. Nripendra, despite his English gloss, preferred his wife to remain cloistered. At first, not even his own cousins were allowed to meet his bride. Nripendra felt strongly that Sunity should not meet men whose own wives were still in purdah. Since very few women at this time had come out from behind the veil, there were very few men she could meet. He had firm ideas: Sunity must not wear pearls next to her skin, must not speak or laugh loudly, nor ride, dance or play tennis. When questioned about his disapproval of these things (not by Sunity), he replied, 'I prefer *my* wife to do what I like. I don't care a bit what other women do.' There was pressure from his family, too. 'I have often been asked by my husband's relations to remember who I am,' Sunity Devi wrote much later, 'and not speak to any and everybody, and lower my position.'

They lived a freer life in their palatial Calcutta townhouse, Woodlands, than in Cooch Behar. Nripendra, still a minor and not yet installed as ruler, studied law at the elite Presidency College. In her pale-blue and pink sitting room, like any accomplished Victorian girl, Sunity read, painted and sketched, and planned her first forays into entertaining.

Her first child, named Raj Rajendra, or King of Kings, was born at home in Calcutta on 11 April 1882. Sunity Devi was allowed to nurse little Rajey herself, something royal mothers rarely did. The birth of her son, the first born to a Cooch Behar maharaja's principal wife for generations, made Sunity Devi popular for the first time both among the people and in the palace of Cooch Behar. The weeks after Rajey's birth were a whirl of congratulations: even Keshub Chunder Sen, weakened by ill-health, and an aged brahmin servant of Nripendra's frolicked happily in the spring sunshine, sprinkling water coloured with magenta dye on each other in celebration, a custom usually reserved for the festival Holi.

Though Sunity Devi and Nripendra insisted that Rajey's upbringing be as simple as possible, that resolution was hard to keep when even the cow who produced his milk was guarded by sentries. More children followed at almost two-year intervals: Sukriti, meaning good deeds, known as Girlie, in January 1884; Jitendra in December 1886; Victor in 1888; Hitendra, or Hitty, in 1890; Prativa, or Pretty, in 1891; and the youngest, Sudhira, nicknamed Baby, in 1894. The birth of a second son secured the succession, dispelling the old ranis' secretly hatched plans for Nripendra to take another wife.

As the mother of four healthy boys, Sunity was increasingly confident in her position to spend more time in Cooch Behar. Though she admitted to 'advanced Western ideas' when she was away from the state, in Cooch Behar Sunity Devi made a point of being 'the zenana lady who enters into the lives of the people. Many who at first looked upon my marriage with disfavour took me to their hearts when they found that I was just like all their Maharanis, and that I loved them.' Like her mother and grandmother – good Indian housewives – before her, at Cooch Behar she chopped vegetables for the family's meals, prepared betel nut and made sweets that her husband and children loved.

At first, the young family lived in the old palace, but soon Sunity and Nripendra built a new palace, a long colonnaded Italianate villa with a central silver dome modelled on St Peter's in Rome, with a swimming pool, tennis courts, nine-hole golf course and polo ground in the surrounding park. Despite their modern, European palace, Sunity Devi insisted on remaining in purdah while living in the Cooch Behar zenana 'where none of the other women had even seen the front of the palace'.

By the time they moved into their new home, Nripendra had reached his majority and been installed as maharaja. Considerate and measured, he was respected both by his own people and by the British government in Calcutta. While Baroda lay at the southern edge of a large area ruled by proud princes almost independent of direct British influence, there were only a few small princely states in Bengal; most of the region was administered by the British from Calcutta. Maintaining good relationships with the Government of Bengal and the Government of India (separate entities; Bengal was one of British India's administrative regions) made Nripendra's own government that much easier.

Cooch Behar was a small state of 1,300 square miles (just smaller than the area of modern urbanized London) and a population of about 600,000 people, though it had been so well managed during Nripendra's minority that he found himself a rich man when he formally ascended the gaddi in 1883. Nripendra did not share Sayajirao of Baroda's commitment to proving the British wrong by governing better than they could have done, but in accordance with the standards set during his British education he established and funded colleges, laid railway lines and broad red gravel roads edged with palm trees and built whitewashed hospitals and public buildings. Cooch Behar's neat, well-shaded main square, laid out around a huge water tank, was 'a microcosmic model of Benthamite principles', complete with two schools, a court-house, jail, record office and printers. To this day it is the only fully planned town in eastern India.

Despite Nripendra's westernized aspirations and lifestyle and close ties to the British government, Cooch Behar was still a deeply traditional state. Early in his reign, Nripendra was surprised during the rainy season to see people passing his palace with their umbrellas furled. He speculated to a friend that perhaps they were afraid the rain would spoil their umbrellas. 'Maharaja, it has nothing to do with their foolishness,' replied the friend. 'Your subjects are a bit scared to open their umbrellas in front of you. That's why they are passing by the palace road with their umbrellas closed.' Nripendra, appalled, ordered his secretary to make it known he wanted people to use their umbrellas; but it would take more than that to shake his people's awe of his majesty.

In parallel with his administrative duties in Cooch Behar, Nripendra was an active supporter of the British military presence in India. In 1883, he was made an Honorary Major in the Indian Army (the Indian regiments of the British Army under the separate command of a British commander-in-chief). Four years later, he was given the rank of Honorary Lieutenant-Colonel. The reason these titles were only honorary was that Indians were barred from joining the British Army at all or from being commissioned officers in the Indian Army. It was not thought right that British soldiers should have to take orders from an Indian, even if he were an Indian prince. There was also the ominous shadow of the Indian Mutiny of 1857, regarded by many Indians today as a war fought for independence; the British were terrified that if they allowed Indians access to military power it might one day be used against them. But though Nripendra loved Cooch Behar, for him that love was not incompatible with steady loyalty to the British Empire to which he owed so much.

Nripendra and Sunity's growing family was joined in their new palace by an English nurse, Mrs Eldridge, who greatly amused Sunity Devi when she first arrived by her open fascination with her. When asked why she was so interested in Sunity, she replied, 'Well, your Highness, when I came to take up my duties with you, I expected to find a stout, dark, uneducated lady. I must say, now that I've seen you, I'm so taken aback I can hardly believe my eyes.' The Maharani, in her early twenties, was a petite woman with a gentle face and manner. She had 'very delicate features, and most lovely eyes, with exquisitely moulded hands and arms'.

Photographs show Sunity wearing richly embroidered, heavy dresses that were a combination of full nineteenth-century ball-gown (always made by the best Paris couturiers) and sari. Designed to display rank and decorum but reveal nothing of the person within, they lacked both Oriental fluidity and Occidental chic. To modern eyes they look desperately uncomfortable, but they were much admired by her contemporaries, and she was considered both a fashion plate and a model for cosmopolitan Indian women of the late nineteenth century.

Sunity and her friends, two sisters-in-law from the Tagore family with whom she had been brought up, were among the first Indian women to venture into British society in India. While in Baroda Chimnabai Gaekwad refused to alter her traditional costume a jot for her British overlords, these progressive Bengali ladies wanted clothes that took into account both European fashions and Indian proprieties. They began wearing tailored blouses, a cross between an English bodice and an Indian choli, and petticoats beneath their saris: it was the birth of the modern way of wearing a sari. Although it was traditional in Bengal to throw the long end of the sari over the right shoulder, Sunity and her companions were the first to put it over their left shoulders, which in years to come became the most common method of tying a sari.

As with Nripendra, Sunity's British accomplishments made her a popular figure on the Calcutta social scene during the cold weather season between December and March. Their names feature more regularly than any other princely family's on the viceregal guest lists. Sunity Devi embraced Victorian high-mindedness, *politesse* and morality. Her aesthetics and accomplishments were Victorian: she painted and sketched, got up tableaux in the palace at Cooch Behar, and prepared curries and pickles herself in the royal kitchens. Even her piety was Victorian in tone. She described her daughter Pretty as looking 'as if a fairy had dropped her from heaven'.

The Marchioness of Dufferin, whose husband was viceroy in the late 1880s, grew very fond of Sunity Devi during her tenure of Calcutta's lemon-yellow Government House. Hariot Lady Dufferin's diary charts the course of their friendship, from January 1885 when Sunity brought Rajey to lunch and they all went to the Zoological Gardens together ('She is very nice, and seems so pleased to come here, and keeps telling me she feels so at home') to March 1887 when Sunity Devi took her to meet the Sen family ('two grandmothers, an aunt, some cousins and several sisters') at Lily Cottage.

On their visit to Lily Cottage, Lady Dufferin and her companion were hung with garlands, necklaces and bangles made of flowers and tinsel, 'which gave all the effect of large rubies and emeralds on pearl chains. A crown of the same kind was prepared for me, which, however, I could not attempt to place on the top of my fashionable bonnet.' They saw Sunity Devi's mother's hard wooden bed – a common widow's penance; Keshub Chunder Sen had died in 1884 – and Sen's flower-draped marble pulpit. 'Some of the sweets were sent to us after,' Lady Dufferin recorded with gentle amusement, 'and a white sugar statue of a scantily clothed lady was placed before Dufferin at dessert.'

Lady Dufferin was impressed by how quickly Sunity had learned foreign ways, and how fluent her English was. Both Woodlands in Calcutta and the palace at Cooch Behar were decorated in the European style; little Rajey, not yet three, already rode a pony like an English boy. The Maharani, observed Lady Dufferin, wore 'native dress, but has very smart shoes and stockings, while her sisters and sisters-in-law had bare feet'. She 'never seems the least awkward or put out'.

Soon after arriving in India in 1885 Lady Dufferin conceived a scheme to 'promote female medical tuition, medical relief and the establishment of hospitals for women all over the country'. Her husband gave it his blessing and within five years Lady Dufferin's Fund had set up scores of 'female hospitals', medical centres for women and schools, largely paid for by the generosity of the Indian princes. In order to please Lord Dufferin, the princes competed with each other to see who could contribute the most.

'To begin with,' commented Sunity Devi,

women of high caste could not do work of this kind [in hospitals] as they thought it lowered their position; secondly, zenana ladies, however poor, did not wish to be trained or study with men, therefore in the beginning only very common women took up the medical profession, but now many advanced women have taken it up and have studied hard and taken degrees, thus serving their country, for which we owe much gratitude to Lady Dufferin.

Friendships between British and Indian women, like that between Sunity Devi and Lady Dufferin, were restricted only to the more sophisticated upper classes from both nations, but they did help to break down India's caste and purdah barriers. Lady Dufferin went to one of Sunity Devi's sari dinners, wearing a sari herself, and sat on the floor eating with her fingers in true Indian fashion. Her successor, Lady Lansdowne, said Sunity, 'never made any distinction between English and Indians at her parties, and her tactful consideration made her very popular'. These tentative steps towards greater mutual understanding helped build an important trust between Indian and British women independent of their husbands and fathers.

In Baroda, the Gaekwad family was settling into its huge new palace, Laxmi Vilas. Chimnabai had four children in quick succession: Jayasinhrao in 1888, Shivajirao in 1890, Indira Raje, the only girl, in 1892, and Dhairyashilrao in 1893. Sayajirao also had three children by his first wife, so in 1895 there were seven children ranging from two to thirteen years old in the Baroda nursery.

Theoretically, the Indian custom of having several wives, mothers-in-law and their respective children all living communally in the zenana made for one big happy family. The present Maharaja of Kapurthala remembers of his childhood

four of my grandmothers living together in the same house and there was no jealousy or friction between them, despite the fact that there was a senior Maharani who was really the person who had pride of place. The others didn't resent it at all . . . When we used to be taken down to see them . . . They treated all the children just as their own children . . . For us they were all our grandmothers.

It is hard to know how the elder Gaekwad children were affected by their stepmother's arrival in Baroda. According to one source, they loved Chimnabai as their own mother. Fatesinh, Sayajirao's eldest son, was found in tears as a small boy having been told she was not his real mother. But there were also rumours later that Chimnabai had tried to persuade Sayajirao to change the succession in her son's favour.

From the moment they were born, when their mother's chamber walls were washed and repainted after the defilement of childbirth, Indian princes' and princesses' lives were dominated by ritual and ceremony. 'Fondled, indulged, and scrupulously guarded, he is kept like a jewel within its velvet case'. Each day, the royal baby was anointed with a black spot that would mar his perfection, and thus ward off bad luck. Every whim was anticipated. 'Put your foot forward and your shoes were put on. Lift a finger and your hair was combed! We never raised our voices. We just had to look and by our gesture the work was done.' Cosseted and fawned on, they were sheltered to the point of claustrophobia and were never crossed or disciplined.

If this was true for all Indian princelings, then it was especially so for heirs-apparent. The 'yuvraj would always be given the most attention and the second son got less. Or if they [the palace servants] noticed the ruler had a favourite child then that child would get more attention and I don't think these attitudes had a beneficial effect on the little children because they naturally grew up being jealous of each other,' remembers one member of a princely family. 'This estrangement really started right from child-hood, which led to quarrels and strained relationships between family members in adulthood, and it certainly affected the children's minds psychologically.'

Girls were not welcomed with quite the same enthusiasm as boys. A nineteenth-century Rajput father would order songs and music to be played, and sweets to be distributed among his friends, when a son was born; for a daughter, he would announce 'that "nothing" has been born into his family, by which expression it is understood that the child is a girl and that she is very likely to be *nothing* in this world, and the friends go home grave and quiet'.

While a boy would remain with the family, helping to work the land or following his father's business, and carrying on the family name, a girl would be married by her early teens, packed off with a large dowry – often crippling her family but a crucial badge of status and thus never shirked – to live with her husband's family by whom, if she did not bear sons, she would be despised. As Surat Kumari, a female Bengali writer, asked in her short story 'Beloved, or Unbeloved?', 'A bride's of value only to keep the lineage alive: for what else does one take on the burden of bringing in an unwanted girl from another family?'

This led to high rates of female infanticide, especially among the

Rajput families of Rajasthan and central India for whom concepts of tradition and duty were especially precious and rigid. Opium was a favoured method, since it was commonly given to children anyway to make them sleep; or 'a skilful pressure on the neck, which is known as "putting the nail to the throat"'. In 1870, a report revealed that in one state 300 children had been stolen by wolves; all 300 were female. The population census of 1880–81 showed there were 5 million fewer Indian women than men, the result of poor hygiene and medical standards as well as infanticide, but still a dramatic statistic.

These habits were beginning to change towards the end of the nineteenth century. The Maharaja of Bharatpur's sister was to be married in a year of 'severe scarcity and distress'. According to custom, the family wanted the wedding to be an extravagant demonstration of their wealth and power. The Resident there, Michael O'Dwyer, protested to a council member that there was no need to spend so much since there had been no royal wedding in Bharatpur for over 200 years; there were no precedents to be lived up to because there had been no brides in Bharatpur for eleven generations. 'Sahib, you know our customs, surely you know the reason,' replied the old man. 'There were daughters born, but till this generation they were not allowed to grow up.'

Unlike the rulers of Bharatpur and most other Indian princely families, the Gaekwads were a very modern family for their times. All the children, even Indira, their only daughter, were given an English education. They wore both Indian and western clothes and ate both European and Indian food. Chimnabai's quarters were officially a zenana, but were not cut off from the rest of the palace. Though she deplored the 'absurd' custom of purdah, Chimnabai realized that, as Sayajirao observed, 'no one in India, not even myself, her husband, can at the present time [1901] lift up the veil. In fact, though women generally, as Her Highness thinks, require more freedom, the men, of whom the greater part are uneducated, do not favour female freedom or female education.'

The Maharani's daily routine in Baroda was therefore more restricted than it was when they were abroad. Chimnabai rose early and read, usually in English, with a female companion, until breakfast. Keenly interested in current affairs, she always read the Indian and British newspapers, and loved English novels. In the late 1890s, she often read with Cornelia Sorabji, the first Indian woman to qualify as a lawyer – even though, in both British and Indian courts, she was prohibited from practising until 1919. Sorabji's family, Christianized Parsis from Bombay, were family friends of the Gaekwads.

On her return to India from Oxford in 1894, Sayajirao invited Miss Sorabji to Baroda to assess the system of compulsory education he had just instituted there. She was disappointed: though shiny new schools had been built in the rural cotton-growing areas, the farmers didn't send their children to them because they wanted them to work in the fields. 'What puzzled me was his [the Director of Education's] glowing printed report on the success of the scheme . . . "Oh, that is for the Maharajah Bahadur [Victorious King],"' he told Miss Sorabji. '"It would not be respectful to tell His Highness that a scheme, in which the Durbar [Maharaja] is so greatly interested, was a mistake!"' Compulsory education was subsequently dropped, and revived again a decade later with more success.

One of her unofficial duties was teaching the Maharaja to row: his staff were afraid he would injure himself, and they would be blamed; but doughty Miss Sorabji, Thames-trained, had no such scruples. 'The boat was best Oxford, and the oars and rowlocks familiar friends.'

Chimnabai and Sayajirao dined, European-style, with their family and any guests. Their servants who waited on them did not speak English or Marathi, 'so that we can talk amongst ourselves *sans gêne*'. None the less, some rituals survived: on entering the room she and her daughter knelt and touched their foreheads to the ground before the Maharaja in obeisance. Customs like this gave British visitors to India the impression that despite the veneer of modernity, nothing really had changed. It was still, as one old India hand observed, 'the middle ages in sepia'. But times *were* changing, especially in Baroda.

When Sayajirao returned to Baroda in January 1895 from another European tour, he found 'agitation and intrigue rampant' and wrote to complain to the Governor of Bombay, Lord Reay, in what one modern historian has described as the first articulate critique of British paramountcy made by an Indian ruler, that British rule was systematically undermining India's monarchies, its indigenous power structures, seeking to make the states dependent on the Raj by gradually eating away at their power. Every time Sayajirao left Baroda, for example, Residents would try to encroach upon his powers in his absence; their advice was seldom offered for Baroda's benefit, but for the Government of India's.

This was the start of his troubles with the Government of India that were to last over twenty years. Already sensitive about the interventions of his Residents in domestic affairs, Sayajirao increasingly felt they were there not to advise him and support his rule, but hoping to catch him out so they could report his mistakes back to Calcutta. With no reliable dewan and Elliot, much missed, back in England, it was all too easy for Sayajirao to fall below the British government's impossible standards. More importantly, his belief that good government was not simply a matter of good administration, but should embrace visions of a new India, was seen as a threat. Though his state was admirably run – in many areas, such as education and breaking down caste barriers, far ahead of British-administered India – complaints were made against the Maharaja when Sayajirao, a teetotaller, drank the Queen-Empress's health in water rather than champagne, or attended official functions in a morning suit, rather than traditional costume. The British preferred their puppet princes in fancy dress: Curzon was horrified when the Raja of Pudukotta asked permission to come to a viceregal garden party in English clothes. Sayajirao's rank and wealth made him difficult to discipline, but his insistence on behaving as an equal rankled.

For the next five years, he and Chimnabai remained in Baroda. Their children were taught by a series of British tutors and governesses, and sent to Baroda College. 'In this transition epoch,' as Sayajirao put it, he and his wife were determined to give them all the advantages of a western education. 'They may discard some of the prejudices and sentiments of their people. Yet underneath the English frockcoat they may still retain their sense of duty to their country and their people.' What was most important to hold on to was the love of their country, 'and if they retain that, they will be really good Hindoos'.

Sayajirao was himself a man of simple but deeply held faith. He saw all religions as essentially the same in varying forms, worshipping one god, and underpinned by respect for human life and happiness. 'Therefore if a man be a Hindu, let him be a Hindu and conform to the religion of his fathers; for it makes no difference. If he be a Christian, by all means let him remain a Christian; if a Musulman, a Musulman.' He was well aware of the rifts that divided India, believing she could not be a united nation with her ancient religions and castes in place.

Perhaps the hardest element of their children's upbringing to manage was the Baroda family's riches. Sayajirao himself was so unworldly that, observed a friend, 'until a few years ago [that is, the early 1900s] he did not trouble to know one coin from another, [and was] utterly indifferent to the value of the treasures which surrounded him, except in so far as they are beautiful, useful, and seemly'; but this disingenuousness was perhaps the best way to deal with his overwhelming wealth, and a response to the dramatic change in his early circumstances. 'Rich children have their own dangers,' observed Sayajirao, disappointed by Fatesinh's mediocre performance on his Oxford entrance exam in 1898. There were too many temptations for them, and not enough to work towards.

Sayajirao cannot have been an easy father, though. As he himself admitted, 'When I married and had children of my own, I did not know *how* to be anything else than Maharaja. My children have said to me, "You are always the Maharaja." I have never ceased to look after them; but there has been no intimacy.' Perhaps because he had had to reject so completely his life before being chosen as Baroda's heir, he could never recapture the carefree ease of his childhood. Also, his desire to govern well amounted to an obsession.

Everything else in his life, including his family, came second to serving the state.

It was a great sadness to him that he couldn't break through these emotional barriers, either with his children or his wife. Though he and Chimnabai loved and respected one another, and complemented each other in many ways, there was no romantic spark between them. Chimnabai attributed this to her having married so young: 'I do not know what it is to be passionate. These people are fools who say that if an Indian woman does not marry she will be a prostitute [a common justification for child-marriage]. That is not true . . . The majority of our women do not know what is meant by the word "passion": they have never felt it.' But her devotion to her husband was still the only restraint on her actions and opinions. Nothing in her bearing or behaviour gave the impression of submissiveness and docility held up as the ideal for a Hindu wife.

In December 1899, Chimnabai was seriously ill. The gynaecological operation she needed was a sophisticated one, and it was not thought safe to have it done in India. The Maharani also refused to be operated upon by a man – she said she did not mind dying, if necessary, but she did not want a male doctor – and there were no female gynaecologists of the requisite standard in India.

The situation was complicated by two factors. India was engulfed by a terrible famine following the failure of the monsoon that summer. Neither Sayajirao nor Chimnabai wanted to leave their people in such distress – especially not when the Viceroy was touring the country offering succour to the starving. By the end of the year 3.5 million people were receiving relief, but it was not enough, for the famine intensified and became the worst of the century. Despite efforts to relieve the country's plight, the British official line was harsh: 'while the duty of the Government is to save life, it is not bound to maintain the labouring population at its normal level of comfort'.

The Viceroy, Lord Curzon, had also declared that maharajas must not leave India except in exceptional circumstances; the tacit threat of deposition, the last recourse of the British administration against princes who failed to obey their dicta, hung behind his words. Aristocratic, arrogant Lord Curzon was a zealous imperialist. He believed British rule in India was Britain's greatest achievement and would not countenance the idea of self-rule, even on some distant future day. In his exacting eyes Indians – and, it must be said, much of the rest of the world's population, including women – were an inferior race unfit to govern themselves.

Sayajirao had been summoned to the office of that most head-masterly of viceroys the previous June in Simla. Curzon opened the interview by expressing his desire to establish more intimate personal relations with the principal 'native chiefs' (he was on guard against calling them princes in case they got ideas above their station); Sayajirao returned his compliments. Then Curzon launched a stinging attack on Sayajirao: his unwillingness to co-operate with the Government of India, his being 'somewhat punctilious' about his rights and 'always expecting some encroachment upon them', and his 'questionable loyalty' to the Empire. On the defensive, Sayajirao was forced to backtrack, repeatedly asserting his fidelity. Curzon was unimpressed, Sayajirao even less so. From then on, his 'uncooperativeness' only grew more marked.

Curzon was hypocritical in his attitude to the princes. On one hand, he praised them for keeping alive Indian customs and traditions, sustaining the line's 'virility' and saving 'from extinction the picturesqueness of ancient and noble races'; by this token they were mere ornaments of Empire, historical remnants that needed preserving like the monuments he campaigned so energetically to save.★ He declared he wanted the princes to be partners in the ruling of India, yet sought to diminish their role in that partnership. He wanted them taught English manners, yet hated the idea of them going abroad. Above all he complained bitterly that Victoria invested them with an aura of royalty they ought not to possess,

★ Curzon was the driving force behind the conservation of many of India's historic buildings, including the Taj Mahal. 'After every other viceroy has been forgotten, Curzon will be remembered because he restored all that was beautiful in India' (Jawaharlal Nehru quoted in Rose, *Curzon*, p. 239).

grumbling 'that almost anyone with a turban and jewels was regarded in Europe as a prince and treated as if he was a descendant of Nebuchadnezzar'. Native chiefs – especially those of what he called the third rank – demonstrating their 'royalty', for example using writing paper stamped with gold crowns (one maharaja later got around the ban on this by deliberately using the paper from the Hotel George V in Paris, 'embossed with a crown fit for a giant'), infuriated Curzon.

There was a deliberate policy in the late nineteenth century to squash maharajas' pretensions to royalty by changing the language used to describe them: they were not to reign but to rule; they ascended the gaddi rather than the throne; their troops, diminished largely to ornaments since the rebellion of 1857, were called forces rather than armies; their governments were just durbars. Most significantly of all, their relationships with the British crown were described as feudal allegiances, rather than alliances of equals. 'The native chiefs are not sovereigns,' Curzon insisted to Edward VII. 'They have been deprived of the essential rights and attributes of sovereignty.'

This was not a view shared by the princes. Though these measures dented their *amour propre* rather than actually limiting their power, the issue, for the princes, was one of respect. Maharaja Nripendra of Cooch Behar wrote directly to Edward VII in 1908 complaining about the 'uncertainty of precedence of Indian Princes at the King's Court'. Edward responded with strong assurances that princes – as theoretically independent sovereigns and allies rather than subject peoples – should take precedence over the British aristocracy. But the lack of historical models and the sensitive nature of the problem meant it was never satisfactorily resolved.

In May 1900, determined to defy Curzon, Sayaji failed to inform the Viceroy of his plans to leave India and took his family to Europe. This was a direct challenge to Curzon's authority and one that ensured his enmity for the remainder of his tenure in Calcutta.

Sayajirao and Chimnabai enrolled Fatesinhrao at Oxford, and Jayasinhrao at Harrow; the boys would remain in England while their parents returned to India. Their English education, still rare among Indians even of the princely class, was 'a very bold experiment', wrote Sayajirao. 'It will depend upon his [Fatesinhrao's] wisdom to make a success' of it. Sadly, this wisdom, or the strength to resist the temptations with which Fatesinh was faced, was lacking.

Chimnabai underwent her operation at the hands of the celebrated female gynaecologist and surgeon Mary Scharlieb. Mrs Scharlieb had links to the new, progressive India championed by Chimnabai and Sayaji: she was the daughter of an English lawyer from Madras and had been the personal physician of the theosophist Mme Blavatsky. Blavatsky's closest friend, the activist Annie Besant, had lived in India since 1893 and made its independence her crusade; she founded the Indian Home Rule League in 1916 and was selected as president of Congress. Dr Scharlieb instructed Chimnabai to take chloroform in an anteroom, before being carried through to be operated upon. Smiling firmly, Chimnabai declined the drug, and walked into the operating theatre to await the procedure wide-awake.

The Maharani had recovered well from the operation, reported Queen Victoria, whom she visited in December 1900 on a 'very dull dreary day'. The Queen reported her 'still very pretty' and speaking 'now quite fluent English'. The five small Gaekwad children accompanied Chimnabai to Buckingham Palace to be presented to the octogenarian Queen in her stiff black gown. All wearing white brocade jackets and pyjama trousers and little gold caps, they looked indistinguishable. Victoria asked which one of them was the girl: 'five pairs of dark brown eyes stared back at her, and then, because they all enjoyed fooling grown-ups, one of the boys stepped forward'. Suspicious, the Queen peered behind the bold little line, and saw Indira's giveaway ponytail snaking down her back.

Before the Barodas arrived home in the spring of 1901, Curzon sent out a formal circular forbidding princes to leave India without Government of India permission. If they wanted to go abroad for their health, for example, they needed to produce a medical certificate from a British government-approved doctor. The document pointedly reminded the princes that their power was guaranteed by the Supreme Government, and requested in return that they devote their energies not to pleasure but to the welfare of their subjects. 'Such a standard of duty is incompatible with frequent absences from the State, even though these may be represented as inspired by the pursuit of knowledge or by a thirst for civilisation.' Curzon did not deny that travelling could be beneficial to ruler and state, but 'the result of European tours, particularly if too frequently repeated, is more often a collection of expensive furniture in the palace and of questionable proclivities in the mind of the returned traveller, than an increase in his capacity for public or political service'.

Sayajirao called it 'cruel and humiliating', a deliberate limitation of the princes' power and therefore their capacity to rule, and declared his intention of travelling to Europe as often as he pleased and spending his summers at Indian hill-stations. He refused, he said, to be treated like a cow-herd, a reference to his family name, Gaekwad, which literally meant cow-herd. The Viceroy, expecting meek compliance, was furious. Other rebel rajas were easier to subdue: though the princes of Pudukotta and Kapurthala – minor in rank but major in size – tried to convince Curzon they needed to consult European specialists about their obesity, their petitions were rejected.

Queen Victoria died in January 1901. Within forty-eight hours of her death, Lord Curzon had written to Edward VII's private secretary asking for permission to hold a magnificent coronation durbar in his honour – with Curzon, as Edward's stand-in, playing the central part. He wrote to all the Indian princes, asking them to ride behind him on their elephants in the main procession. 'I am afraid it would seriously inconvenience me to join it,' replied Sayajirao, through his Resident. In turn Curzon, by now out to humiliate Sayajirao, ordered the Baroda bodyguards to wear blue rather than their usual red livery at the durbar, because his own viceregal servants would be wearing red. The Governor of Bombay wrote to tell Curzon of a 'curious rumour, probably mere "gup," that Baroda would plead illness at the last moment, and not go'.

Eventually Sayajirao decided he would attend the durbar, but he wrote to Curzon saying he was coming 'not of his own accord' but because 'it was forced upon him under the threat of an insult'. All his actions − closely observed by the British − demonstrated his reluctance to be there. His stepmother, Jamnabai, had just died, so he had the excuse of mourning for his absence from the procession. He was present at the actual durbar, or ceremony, which took place on 1 January 1903 in Delhi.

Sayajirao was not alone in his ambivalence about the way Curzon and the British were hijacking Indian customs and using the princes as colourful window-dressing for their imperial fantasies. Curzon, condescendingly, even said he wanted the princes not to be spectators but actors in the extravaganza; their attendance was mandatory. Though he issued a statement saying he wanted to consult the 'chiefs'' wishes and dignity in every way, maintaining if not enhancing their privileges, his actions belied his words. In private he wrote, 'What are they but a set of unruly and ignorant and rather undisciplined schoolboys?' At the durbar, the princes were segregated from India's British rulers: the British camps were at the centre of the site while the Indian princes were scattered around the edges; the princes were ordered to arrive the day before the European guests; while the provincial governors of British India marched in the main viceregal procession, the Indian princes did not.

The princes found the whole thing demeaning. The mighty Maharaja of Udaipur, most independent and most respected of all the Indian rulers, proud that none of his ancestors had paid court to the Moguls in their ascendancy, refused even to go to Delhi because he would not go as a vassal. Worst of all, large swathes of India were still suffering from the effects of the famine when Curzon spent hundreds of thousands of pounds on his *folie de grandeur*; Congress leader Lal Mohun Ghosh called it 'a pompous pageant to a starving population'.

After the public ceremonies of what his critics dubbed the 'Curzonization', Curzon sat in the Mogul Diwan-i-Am, or imperial Hall of Public Audience, at the Red Fort in Delhi (which he had had restored), to receive his princely guests at the Durbar Ball.

When it was Sayajirao's turn to approach the Viceroy's throne, bow and return to his seat, he stopped and delivered a short speech, requesting 'the Viceroy to convey to His Majesty the King-Emperor his hearty and loyal congratulations on his coronation'. There would be no confusion about to whom exactly Sayajirao was paying his respects.

Sayajirao's attitude was reflected in Chimnabai's manner with the European ladies she met at this time. Fiercely patriotic, she resented being made to kow-tow to the British as much as her husband did. On a visit to Bombay, she neglected to call on the Governor's wife. Sayajirao was asked if it was because she thought it beneath her dignity to call on a British woman; he pleaded purdah though Chimnabai was well known to oppose the custom.

No doubt Chimnabai's imposing self-possession was intimidating. The writer M. M. Kaye remembers, far from feeling superior to Indians, being made acutely aware 'that it was *I* who was not the equal of some well-bred and high-caste lady who would not only not socialise with the British, but would not allow her men folk to enter the living-rooms of her house wearing western clothes . . . and who, if she could not avoid taking the hand of a European, would first cover her own in a fold of her sari'. Chimnabai didn't need to use religion and caste as an excuse to avoid contact with the British – indeed, she became fond of those individuals she got to know – but, always proudly wearing a Maratha sari, she never contained her resentment of what she saw as British impositions.

In 1904, quite deliberately, Sayajirao hired the Bengali intellectual Romesh Chandra Dutt as Baroda's Finance Minister. Dutt came from a traditional Hindu family and had been educated at Presidency College in Calcutta, a school intended to train Indian administrators that Nripendra, Maharaja of Cooch Behar, also attended. Dutt did not tell his devout parents before he went to England to sit the ICS exams in 1869, because he knew how distraught they would be at his losing caste by crossing the ocean. His diligence paid off: he was the first Indian to be awarded a first-class degree from Oxford University, came third in the ICS exams, and later became the first Indian to hold executive charge of an administrative district.

In 1897, Dutt retired from the ICS; four years later he challenged Curzon about the famine that had ravaged India in 1900, arguing that the high assessment of land revenue had been a significant contributing factor behind the widespread starvation. Later, he became President of the Indian National Congress. He was also a historian, economist and novelist who translated into English the great epics of Indian literature, the *Mahabharata* and the *Ramayana*. Dutt believed that, by learning about and taking pride in their history and culture, Indians would develop a sense of national pride which would have its own momentum, carrying them into a new era of unity and autonomy. Hiring Dutt was a clear statement to the British government of Sayajirao's determination to be independent.

This was a tremendously exciting time to be involved in Indian nationalist politics, the first stirrings of a coherent opposition to the Government of India, and Bengal, Dutt's native region, was the centre of the movement. On 29 September 1905, Curzon's decision to divide Bengal – ostensibly because it was too large and too populous to function as a single administrative unit but in reality because he feared the growing power of its nationalist intelligentsia – became law. To many Indians as well as Bengalis this was seen as a deliberate attempt to 'divide and rule'. Within a month the first swadeshi movement, the boycott of all foreign goods, had begun as a protest. This grass-roots movement pervaded India and served both as a rallying-call to all Indians – it was something in which everyone could participate regardless of gender, caste, clan or financial situation – and a foundation for later forms of passive opposition to British rule. 'Really Lord Curzon was a blessing in disguise,' said the activist Annie Besant, 'for his oppression forced the nation into resistance.'

In parallel with this defiance of British rule surged a renaissance of Indian culture, language, history and the arts. The circle of Bengali activists in Calcutta included the Nobel Prize-winning poet Rabindranath Tagore, the mystic Aurobindo Ghose and

G. K. Gokhale, Mohandas Gandhi's early mentor and one of the founding fathers of the Congress movement. Most were from a tiny liberal minority of wealthy upper-middle-class (generally brahmin) families, businessmen, lawyers and administrators who had profited from their links with the British government but found themselves frustrated by the British stranglehold on power and influence in the colony.

Many had been educated in England – the exuberant poetess, Sarojini Naidu, was one of the first Indian women to graduate from Cambridge – and still retained close links with Indian intellectuals and activists there. In London in 1905, Naidu's brother Chattopadhyaya was one of the founders of the *Indian Sociologist*, which declared that loyalty to India precluded loyalty to Britain.

Their lives were examples of the new India they hoped to create: Sarojini Naidu, 'the nightingale of India' as she was known, married a man from outside her caste and clan; many, like the Brahmo Tagores, rejected the idolatry of traditional Hinduism. Many also had links to Sayajirao and Chimnabai: Ghose had worked for Baroda; Gokhale was a friend; in 1906, Naidu asked Dutt to send Sayaji her first volume of poetry, *The Golden Threshold*, and became lifelong friends with Chimnabai.

Sayajirao gave the inaugural speech at the Social Conference of the eighteenth Indian National Congress in Bombay at the end of 1904. His speech dealt with the evils caused by caste discrimination, and women, who were handicapped by child-marriage, strict purdah and ignorance. These were not idle words: in Baroda, Sayajirao instituted a Hindu Remarriage Act in 1902, an Infant Marriage Prevention Act in 1904, and legislation making primary education compulsory (in 1907) and a standardized penal code and criminal procedure. He even introduced divorce – something his children used to tease their mother about mercilessly. Sayajirao was becoming an Indian hero, the model of a modern, progressive prince.

At the risk of alienating his orthodox Hindu subjects Sayajirao also took the revolutionary step – long before Mohandas Gandhi's arrival on the political scene – of clothing, feeding and schooling Baroda's untouchables, financing the education of the great outcaste leader Bhimrao Ramji Ambedkar, author of India's constitution, proving his belief that, as he put it, 'this caste business is all rubbish'. When Sayajirao was told about Ambedkar, a brilliant outcaste boy who needed an education, he summoned Ambedkar to see him at his Bombay palace. He waited all day for the boy to appear and finally, that evening, gave up on him and decided to go out. As Sayajirao passed through the palace gates he saw Ambedkar waiting outside. Because of his low status, the guards had not let the boy in, even though Sayajirao had invited him to the palace. Years later, after his Ivy League education, Ambedkar became Sayajirao's secretary; even then, the servants at Laxmi Vilas refused to serve him at table. 'Everything I am, I owe to your grandfather,' Ambedkar told Sayajirao's granddaughter Ayesha, many years later.

An important element of the liberal, nationalist thought to which the Barodas subscribed was the emancipation of women: they did not believe India could be free when half its population was confined behind the purdah. In 1887, Mahadev Govind Ranade, a Marathi judge and one of the founders of the Indian National Congress, set up a parallel organization, the National Social Conference, which had the move towards nationwide female emancipation as one of its chief aims. From this time, the women's movement in India was inextricably linked to the nationalist movement.

Chimnabai's friend, the lawyer Cornelia Sorabji, said women in India were divided into two groups. Ten per cent were 'progressives', literate, comfortably off and largely independent of ancient customs; they had generally been educated – as in the case of both Chimnabai (through her husband) and Sunity Devi (through her father and then through her husband) – because their families were unusually enlightened. The other 90 per cent lived in seclusion, according to the old customs, and had access neither to education nor to modern ideas. The challenge for activists was to reach this 90 per cent.

In 1903, before leaving India, Chimnabai presided over a large ladies' meeting at Bethune College in Calcutta where the poet and nationalist Sarojini Naidu made one of her earliest public speeches.

In Paris, the Maharani befriended the noted Parsi revolutionary Madame Cama, one-time secretary of Dadabhai Naoroji and the first person to raise the Indian tricolour (in green, saffron and red, which became the green, saffron and white of the modern flag) in Europe. On their return to India in December 1906, Chimnabai again took the chair of the Indian Ladies' Conference, a branch of the National Social Conference.

Indeed, 'the whole family is sympathetic to the Nationalists,' noted the Fabians Beatrice and Sidney Webb on their tour round India in 1912, 'and feel themselves born to be leaders of the Indian people'. At Oxford, the Barodas' second son, Shivajirao, hosted a weekly meeting of the Oxford University Indian Club; one motion raised was, 'In the Opinion of this House Western Civilization is the Degradation of the East'. Princess Indira, who spoke French as well as she did English, left a copy of Pierre Loti's lyrical *L'Inde, Sans Les Anglais*, lying open in her bedroom. Loti celebrated an India that would have been unrecognizable in the dispassionate efficiency of the India Office: wild, ancient, throbbing with life; inhabited by a noble, mysterious, spiritual people, and sensually intoxicating with its exotic scents and intense colours.

The Aga Khan recalled a late-night conversation with Sayajirao at about this time, in the Governor of Bombay's summer residence in Poona, in which it is clear he was beginning to think through the ramifications of independence. 'British rule in India will never be ended merely by the struggle of the Indian people. But world conditions are bound to change so fundamentally that nothing will then be able to prevent its total disappearance,' Sayaji said. 'The first thing you'll have to do when the British are gone, is to get rid of all these rubbishy states. I tell you, there'll never be an Indian nation until this so-called Princely Order disappears. Its disappearance will be the best thing that can happen to India – the best possible thing.'

None of this pleased the British while Sayajirao continued to rail against their presence in India and Chimnabai to ignore their wives. The year 1903 was punctuated by Sayajirao's correspondence with his Resident, Colonel M. J. Meade, on the subject of European trips: on the insult inherent in insisting he and his wife file their itineraries with the government, and the issue of whether princes who stayed in India were any better as rulers. 'The home-bred Indian idea of a raja is not that he should work hard and be a slave to duty, but that he should live at ease and enjoy himself, and anyone who did otherwise was popularly considered an idiot,' he pointed out.

Finally, in September 1904, Sayajirao held his nose, screwed up his face and swallowed the medicine. He asked Colonel Meade to 'do what is needed' to procure permissions for himself and his family to travel to Europe. His health was weak, and he needed a change of scene. His children were to attend European schools. But he stated firmly that this was not a retraction of his views on Curzon's policy restricting the princes' movements.

A lengthy exchange of letters ensued, causing Sayajirao 'more trouble and worry than you would probably imagine,' as he told Meade. The Maharaja took it all personally, and found dealing with the British as baffling as it was frustrating and humiliating. The following March, Sayajirao asked his dewan to write to Meade, explaining that he had been away just over four years of his twenty-two-year reign, and that though he did not relish being absent, and missing the Prince and Princess of Wales's visit scheduled for autumn 1905, his ill-health necessitated it. At first, the Government of India tried to use Sayajirao's proposed absence as an opportunity to limit his powers. They explained that if he was not there, Baroda's Resident, rather than its dewan whom Sayaji had appointed, would take control of its government. Sayajirao resisted. Finally, they agreed he could leave without forfeiting his authority.

The Gaekwads arrived in London in May 1905. Sayajirao called on the Secretary of State for India, Mr Brodrick, on 5 May. His call was returned two weeks later. But only the minimum of courtesies was extended to them. The *froideur* was evident. They were not invited to the reception at Court for Curzon's homecoming in December, 'an omission which it is understood they have much resented', though they did attend a garden party at Windsor in June. Sayajirao, in riposte, wore a frock coat instead of the Indian court dress that was specified by the invitation. Chimnabai, as always, wore a sari.

To the annoyance of the India Office (as detailed in their 'Secret and Political' file on the Barodas' journey), Sayajirao communicated their movements only when he needed help – customs facilities organized, or meetings arranged. Otherwise, officials were left having to find out where they were from newspaper reports, which took a keen interest in the rich Maharaja and his beautiful, proud wife.

They wintered on the Continent, between Italy, Switzerland, Austria and Germany. Their party, consisting of the Maharani and Maharaja, a secretary, an English lady companion, and a professor advising Sayajirao on museums, arrived in Berlin in mid-October 1905. The children had been left at school in England, Shivaji at Harrow and Indira at a finishing school in Eastbourne.

The highlight of their tour was the visit to the United States in the summer of 1906. Sayajirao was amused by the public's 'rather naïve disappointment . . . at his not appearing before them as a bediamonded Raja, but in ordinary European dress', while Chimnabai thought the masses vulgar and ignorant: 'Why should they stare at me on the streets as they do at tigers in a circus parade, merely because I wear different and more reasonable garments than their own?' But both of them adored America's informality and individualism, and felt at home there in a way they never did in Britain. They agreed with the Begum of Bhopal, who said that though she liked and admired the English, 'you Americans are more energetic, more progressive, you have a broader vision'. They left Jayasinh, Chimnabai and Sayajirao's eldest son, at Harvard that autumn, before sailing back across the Atlantic to London.

Their sons were an increasing source of concern. They were 'fast', uninterested in study, extravagant and dissolute. For Sayajirao, who never drank because of the 'misery and suffering' it caused, his sons' weakness for alcohol – like their disinclination to work – was a mystery. Sayajirao was inclined to withdraw when he was angry or disappointed, so Chimnabai was forced into the role of mediator, which upset them both. But they were determined not to crush their children's spirits, as Sayajirao wrote to an American friend about disciplining Jayasinh two years later: 'I should be particularly sorry if the control went so far as to interfere with the healthy development of his character.' Sadly, the alcoholic Jayasinhrao died a few months later, aged only twenty-three, leaving behind a widow, Padmavarti, two little daughters and a three-month-old son, Pratapsinh, now Baroda's heir. Caught 'in a gap between two civilisations, Western progress and Indian tradition', Jayasinh had been unable to find a middle ground.

In 1907, the Reverend Edward St Clair Weeden arrived in Baroda for what he later called *A Year with the Gaekwar* (the Anglicized spelling of Gaekwad). A young protégé of Sayajirao's tutor Elliot, Weeden had accompanied Sayajirao to Switzerland in 1893 as his reader; he had been a family friend ever since. His son had toured England with Chimnabai and Sayaji's son Fatesinh before he went to Harvard. Breathless with wonder, Weeden adored every second of his year in Baroda. His record of it reads like a schoolboy's account of an outing.

Armed with a small lancet and a bottle of antidote (he was terrified of snakes), Weeden arrived in Bombay as the steaming heat of the summer months was fading. He was met off the boat in Bombay by the Thomas Cook representative, who took him to the Taj Mahal Hotel for a bath. Then he was taken to the majestic, Victorian Gothic Victoria Terminus and put on the sleeper to Baroda. His bed was made up in a compartment, with fruit, iced drinks 'and a box of excellent Indian cigars at my elbow, and all around me lay India, the day-dream of my life realised at last, with its vast jungles, through which elephants and tigers might be roaming and which were sure to be full of snakes'.

In Baroda, Weeden was captivated by Chimnabai and her beautiful daughter, Indira. 'It is impossible for me to give any adequate impression of Her Highness, [and] . . . the daughter in whom she lives again.' The Maharani, he wrote, 'is of middle height [a polite way of saying small], but carries her head so proudly and yet so gracefully that she appears taller than she really is'. Her eyebrows were carefully shaped, European-style, and she wore the red marriage mark, or bindi, on her forehead. Her dark, glossy hair, dressed close to her head, was hidden by the end of her sari, sometimes of white (an unconventional choice, since white was traditionally a colour only widows wore), and often shot through with gold thread.

Chimnabai always wore Indian clothes, whatever the occasion and wherever she was; it was a mark of her proud patriotism. The sari was drawn over her head like a halo, and 'falls over the perfect outline of her exquisite figure and is gathered between the knees, showing the ankles encircled with pearls and the small bare feet, which are as beautifully kept as her hands'.

Weeden thought she surpassed all other women in two features: 'her magnificent teeth, revealed within the firm mouth by her rare and charming smile, and her arms, which are the most comely in the world'. So dazzled was he by her that it took him a little while to notice 'the collar of emeralds as large as pigeons' eggs around her neck, and the chain of priceless pearls that falls from her shoulders to the waist'.

He found she was as intelligent and strong-minded as she was beautiful.

The Maharani has a fine perception of affairs diplomatic and political; she holds strong opinions of her own on almost every subject and expresses them forcefully and wittily . . . Sometimes when she is excited by an argument she begins to speak in Mahratti [Marathi] very rapidly and with eloquent gestures, making the Maharaja shake with laughter.

She loved racing, cards and 'had a nice sour sense of humour'; she drove her rationalist husband mad by regularly consulting astrologers, soothsayers and pandits.

Chimnabai enjoyed conversation and debate, but there were few women in Baroda with whom she could indulge this passion. The Indian ladies there were gradually learning to read and write, and coming more into society, but it was an uphill process. Their lives were still unimaginably sheltered compared with hers. The few

English women in Baroda – wives of local officials – were hard to get to know, as they were seldom stationed there for more than a couple of years, 'and she dislikes the feeling that people may come to see her merely out of curiosity as a sort of spectacle. "Though indeed," she added with a smile, "I might have got used to that in America, for there they made a regular peep-show of us."' She hired a series of English lady companions who became intimate friends, but her most constant attendant was her daughter, Indira.

Indira Raje, 'the stormy petrel of the family', had returned recently from boarding school in Eastbourne, on England's south coast, where her fellow students were the daughters of viceroys, ministers and other maharajas. Her schoolwork was not the only thing on Indira's mind in 1908. Though at sixteen she was practically on the shelf by old-fashioned Indian standards, her parents did not want her to marry young, declaring, 'She must think for herself.' They took her to Chimnabai's home state of Dewas Senior to introduce her to the eligible Maratha Maharaja there, but he was in love with someone else. 'The Prince of Dewas Junior,★ however, was so smitten with Indira that he joined her in the train back to Baroda, his eyes idiotic with love, having brought no more baggage than a hastily-borrowed handkerchief.'

Even in her teens, she had an electric effect on men; this only intensified as she matured. Indira had inherited all her parents' strength of mind and dignity. 'Possessing all an Indian woman's grace and rhythm of movement,' wrote an English observer of the adult Indira, 'her added intelligence and sparkling wit made her irresistibly attractive to men.' Chimnabai's companion, Miss Tottenham, described Indira in 1911 as of medium height, like her mother (actually both were petite), with a graceful, well-developed figure. 'Her nose, which was not quite as beautiful as her mother's, was pierced as for a nose-ring, but that afternoon her only ornaments were diamond and ruby bangles and long diamond earrings. It was a pleasure,' continued Miss Tottenham, 'to watch the

★ Dewas Senior and Dewas Junior were two Maratha states in central India ruled by related families.

expressive and responsive small, well-cut features' as they con-
versed. 'What a perfect specimen of the flower of Indian womanhood was this Princess of Baroda!' Poor Reverend Weeden
confessed he was constantly hoping she might catch him performing
brave deeds – anything, presumably, but wrestling with snakes.

Soon after Weeden's arrival in Baroda in the autumn of 1907,
the Gaekwad family celebrated Divali, the Hindu festival of lights,
which falls on the darkest night of the year, in November or
December. Divali is the festival of Laxmi, goddess of wealth and
prosperity; the Maharaja performed puja (worship) to his Treasury
and Chimnabai to her jewels. The palace floors were decorated
with intricate rangoli, patterns in fine, brightly coloured sand and
gold and silver dust, and tiny candles burned around all the parapets
and on all the windowsills and balconies. The windows were left
open so that Laxmi, like Father Christmas down western chimneys,
could bring her blessings into the house.

Fifty guests were invited for an Indian banquet in the durbar
hall. Gold-mosaic apsaras, Hindu angels, glittered down on the
party. Each person sat on a tiny inlaid wooden stool behind a large
silver thali, or plate, on which were set smaller silver bowls filled
with fragrant curries. Between the places stood large silver vases of
flowers. Incense and laughter filled the air. Bangers and fireworks
crackled outside and inside, the guests played cards to win Laxmi's
favour for the coming year.

One day the Barodas took Weeden out of Baroda city for a
shikar, rising early to shoot duck over a mist-covered lake. Breakfast
was laid out for them on their arrival at camp. Chimnabai was said
to be the best Indian woman shot: in England she was a member
of the Ham & Petersham Rifle Club, and in Baroda Weeden saw
her take down two heron at breakfast without leaving the table.
That afternoon they rode out on horseback after blackbuck.

Later, he witnessed one of the cheetah-hunts for which Baroda
was famous. A tame cheetah, hooded like a hawk and on a lead,
was carried out in a bullock cart. When blackbuck were sighted,
the leather mask was whipped off and the cheetah was after them.
Her tail stuck straight up in the air the moment before she pounced.

They returned home in a strange caravan: the cheetah and her keeper in the cart were followed by a camel carrying the bag; three men on horseback made up the rear.

As the temperature rose that spring, Sayajirao and Weeden went to Matheran, a hill-station in central India, to escape the heat. They drove through the park surrounding Laxmi Vilas at twilight, with servants holding torches standing every couple of yards to illuminate their path. On the other side of the park railings stood the Maharaja's private train station, with his own saloon-car waiting for him at the carpet-covered platform. The royal carriage, lit by electric lights and cooled by electric fans, consisted of two large living compartments, plus two bathrooms and a kitchen. The woodwork on walls and ceiling was intricately carved, gilded and enamelled; mirrors hung on the walls; teak shutters covered the windows and the door handles were pure silver.

In Matheran, when they went out for a walk, the two men were followed by six servants in long scarlet coats, with the Baroda crest embroidered in gold on their chests, 'bearing a chair slung on two poles called a jhampan in case he got tired, and one of them carried his puggari [pugree or turban] wrapped in a large green silk handkerchief'. Sayajirao's walking attire was a natty 'brown velvet knickerbocker suit, worsted stockings, and a Homburg hat.' At midday, they stopped in a clearing in the woods, where a large table laid for lunch was waiting for them. One smaller table bore books, another games – cards, chess, draughts and dominoes. After lunch, Sayajirao retired for a nap to a tent erected nearby, which had his bed in it.

In November 1909, for the first time since Sayajirao had locked horns with Curzon at the turn of the century, the Gaekwads welcomed the Viceroy to Baroda. Lord Minto, author with Secretary of State Morley of the Minto-Morley reforms which were the first step on the road towards Indian self-rule, was a popular viceroy. Lacking Curzon's intellectual arrogance, or the pomposity and small-mindedness that marked so many British officials in India, he was liked and respected by the men he dealt with day-to-day – no small achievement in those days of mutual inter-racial suspicion. He voiced, for the first time, the principle of 'non-interference in the internal affairs of Native States', on the basis that 'methods sanctioned by tradition in states are usually well-adapted to the needs and relations of the ruler and his people'. This was a far cry from Curzon's lack of confidence in the princes. Minto's personal style was appreciated: his 'grace of manner and unerring tact [and] . . . peculiar gift of putting one at ease . . . drew the best out of men because he looked for the good in them'. 'His Excellency rained gentlemanliness on me,' was how an Afghan warlord described his manner.

In his speech on 15 November 1909 welcoming the Viceroy and his wife and daughter to Baroda, Sayajirao applauded recent political developments in intentionally loaded words: 'Loyalty has always been considered in the east as one of the first virtues in a people. But loyalty, when merely sentimental, is of small value. It should be real, genuine and active. To secure such loyalty there should be a community of interests between the subjects and the ruling powers. The former should have a share in the administration of their country and should feel that the Government is their own. It is for this reason that I hail with pleasure those great measures of Reform which your Excellency initiated and which His Majesty's Government have accepted.'

'His Majesty's Government have accepted' was the correct phrasing: Edward VII was vehemently opposed to changing India's government, for example having an Indian on the Viceroy's executive council, using all sorts of arguments to justify his racism (chief among them, 'You will never be able to get rid of that native again') and only reluctantly agreeing to it. Even so, the reforms were not successful: the first Indian member of the Executive Council, Brahmo Sinha, resigned a few months after his appointment, saying, 'No self-respecting man can remain here now that he sees the Government of India from inside.' There was still a long way to go.

In the India Office collection of the British Library is a small, gold-tooled, red leather book stamped in gold, 'Autumn Tour of

His Excellency the Viceroy and Governor General 1909', with a red leather loop for a gold pencil to fasten the covers shut. Every minute of the viceregal schedule is detailed in it, as well as background notes on every place they visited, down to the number of ponies that died in the Gwalior campaign in Chitral in 1895 (twenty-two). Their train compartment plans were drawn out: Her Excellency's saloon contained a lavatory, a box room, a bedroom, bathroom and sitting room, and two maids to administer to her; the dining car could seat twenty-four; there were ten secretaries and 120 Indian servants in the viceregal entourage.

The notes on Baroda explain that the administration was 'nominally carried on through a minister, but the present Gaekwar, who takes a great interest in State affairs, gives his Ministers little powers and is constantly changing them'. 'Our visit to Baroda was most interesting and puzzling,' wrote Minto to Morley, a few days later. 'The social and political atmosphere entirely different from that of the other Native States we have visited. The Gaekwar extremely clever, full of information, and friendly; his speech at the usual banquet the essence of loyalty.'

Lady Minto also noticed the atmosphere of discontent in Baroda. Chimnabai, she observed, paid only lip service to the custom of purdah. 'She has been very pleasant and hospitable, and is clever, taking a great interest in politics, and playing a prominent part in the affairs of the State.' Her strength of character, speculated the vicereine, may have been the cause of the cool relations between Chimnabai and the Maharaja: 'He finds her terribly difficult to manage.'

The mood may have been one of friendly rapprochement, but there was a more serious subtext to the Mintos' visit. Two days before their arrival in Baroda, they had narrowly escaped two coconut bombs thrown at them in the nearby city of Ahmadabad. On 27 January 1910, the Calcutta correspondent of *The Times* reported that the government's efforts to suppress sedition were going well everywhere except Baroda. Every prince but the Gaekwad had promised to adopt any measure the British proposed to counter its threat; Sayajirao had given only a 'qualified assurance' of his readiness to assist, and disclaimed knowledge of how far such sentiment had spread in the princely states.

Sayajirao himself protested his state's innocence of these claims. 'Sedition and anarchy find no place in my state and my subjects are peaceful, law-abiding and engrossed in their own occupations,' he declared in a speech given at Baroda College in September 1909. 'No one has greater faith in their good sense than I have. I trust that the same good sense will keep them safe in the future from acts which are foolish and criminal, and that it will not be necessary for the State to adopt measures for their repression.'

Years later, Sayajirao ruefully remembered that this attitude, and his zeal for reform, won him more than a few friends among the radical nationalists. In 1904, he chaired a meeting of the Arya Samaj, a nationalist Hindu revival society; in 1909, he presided over a meeting of the Poona Sarvajanik Sabha, a social reform association with nationalist sympathies. He became something of a celebrity in patriotic journals such as *Amrita Bazar Patrika*. 'There may even have been talk,' wrote his first biographer, 'of the possibility, if India ever became a Republic, of his being the first President.'

By the spring of 1910, Sayajirao had been in Baroda nearly four uninterrupted years. Wanderlust rose in him again, and this time further shores beckoned. At the end of March, he, Chimnabai and Indira sailed east, instead of west, from Bombay. Their first stop was Colombo, the capital of Ceylon, after three days' sailing; then Penang and Singapore, Hong Kong and Shanghai. They spent nearly a month touring Japan. Sayajirao admired the Japanese ability to borrow from the West without jeopardizing their own culture and customs. He and Chimnabai also admired the Japanese aesthetic: the museum in Baroda has a large collection of Japanese bronzes and ceramics; no other country's art, except India's, is as well represented there.

There was some official concern over the Barodas' visit to Japan, because on recent visits two Indian princes had offended their fastidious Japanese hosts. In the early 1900s, the Francophile

Maharaja of Kapurthala (a close friend of Nripendra of Cooch Behar) told the British Ambassador to Japan that, while he had seven official wives at home, he had taken the one he was with only because she spoke French. He called her his 'travelling wife'. While he was there, the Ambassador continued, he'd added two or three 'public ladies of Japan [to his harem], which led to unpleasant-ness and an unfortunate scene in one of the theatres of Tokio'.

The other disreputable visitor had been an unnamed son of the Maharaja of Cooch Behar, and his sin was probably overindulging in sake – alcohol was his family's great weakness. 'His failing was one which aroused pity, but which seemed ineradicable, which was the more to be deplored, because in other respects he seemed a well educated and amiable young man.' These incidents, accord-ing to the Foreign Office, 'left much to be desired, and . . . afforded grounds for somewhat unfavourable comments on the part of the Japanese. The latter look upon the native rulers of India as the result of the British system of education, and it is obviously undesirable that they should be represented by unworthy specimens.'

From Yokohama the Barodas sailed for twelve days across the Pacific to San Francisco, and travelled overland across the United States and Canada, collecting Jayasinhrao from Boston before taking ship in New York. They were met in London in July by Shivaji and Dhairyashil and spent a few months there before, finally, returning home to Laxmi Vilas in December 1910.

They were in Baroda for only a few months before returning to England. There were several reasons for going again so soon: George V's coronation was in June; Indira, newly betrothed to the Maharaja of Gwalior, needed to shop for her trousseau; and Chimnabai had a book coming out.

The Position of Women in Indian Life was published in London that summer. The young Labour MP Ramsay MacDonald hailed it as 'an extraordinary revelation of the educated eastern mind of the present day' and recommended it as a guide as much for English as for Indian women. It is dedicated to 'Indian women' with a quote from Ibsen as its epigram: 'Women must solve the problems of humanity.' It is a practical book, its aim the awakening of Indian women 'from their lethargy of ages, to enable them to take their proper place in Indian public life' using the lessons Chimnabai herself had learned and observations she had made in her travels. Cooperative credit societies, borstals, model farms, manufacturing and agricultural schemes were all discussed in detailed, workable terms, always with an emphasis on education – the first and most necessary step for Indian women to take on the path towards emancipation.

It reads like a feminized expression of Sayajirao's policies and reform programmes: this, as much as Baroda's enlightened government, was the result of their traipsing round factories, museums and schools in every corner of the world, and it demonstrates how inextricably interlinked Chimnabai and Sayajirao's views were. As in John Stuart Mill's ideal of a marriage of equals, each could 'enjoy the luxury of looking up to the other, and . . . [had] alternately the pleasure of being led in the path of development'. They shared a single vision of an independent India, and of humanity's potential.

Like Sayajirao, Chimnabai was a passionate nationalist. Her book was written specifically for Indian women, and she warned against too slavishly following western patterns. 'Every country by intelligent observation can learn something from other lands, but at the same time each should strive to preserve its own racial characteristics, just as each sex should endeavour, not to ape the other, but to make the most of its own particular distinctions of character.'

One of the most obvious influences on *The Position of Women in Indian Life* was the Italian revolutionary Giuseppe Mazzini (1805–72), whose autobiography (along with nationalist tracts such as 'Choose! Oh Indian Princes', 'Free Hindustan' and the speeches of Aurobindo Ghose) was banned in Baroda on the British government's order in August 1911, just after Chimnabai's book was published. Mazzini was a hero of the Indian nationalist movement at home and abroad. Vinayak Savarkar's revolutionary underground 'Free India Society' was modelled on Mazzini's 'Young Italy' movement during the Risorgimento, and sanctioned armed resistance to alien rule; its headquarters was the so-called India House, in Highgate in London, where *The Indian Sociologist* was published. Mazzi-

was a favourite author of both Chimnabai and Sayajirao who saw in his passionate, egalitarian writings, emphasizing the rights and duties of the individual, drawing parallels between political independence and gender equality, much from which Indian men and women could learn.

The Position of Women in Indian Life also heralds grass-roots, women-run schemes such as cooperative credit societies that would flourish in India nearly a century after the book was published. Chimnabai's book is not a feminist manifesto, though. She believed progress could be made only through cooperation with men, not through antagonism to them. Each sex needs the other, and their differences should be accepted, not denied. But for the first time in India, women had the opportunity to fulfil their potential, and Chimnabai wanted to encourage them to do so. Education would be their salvation: 'Only by education can a woman fit herself to be the companion and inspiring helpmate of her husband. Only by information can she gain the ability to direct her children's course and follow their careers with loving, intelligent sympathy.'

The paternalistic argument for educating women so that they could be better wives and mothers was a common one. Especially in India, it de-clawed what many saw as a radical, risky innovation: women demanding equality with men. The Women's Indian Association in the 1910s declared their ambition 'to present to women their responsibilities as daughters of India; as wives and mothers they have the task of guiding and forming the character of the future rulers of India'.

But this in no way diminishes Chimnabai's message: 'The highest aim of women's education should be to fit her to work freely and bravely *with man*; or if not with him, then alongside him, for the benefit of the human race.' Like Mill, she believed strong women were necessary elements of any healthy community; femininity was not compromised by strength, and men would benefit as much as women from respecting their mothers, sisters and wives, and from not believing themselves intrinsically superior to half the world.

Though Chimnabai aimed her book at the 90 per cent of India's women Cornelia Sorabji warned were cut off from the developments in social and political thinking that would free them from centuries of submission and ignorance, most of them would not have heard of Chimnabai, still less have been able to read her words. Instead, the publication of *The Position of Women in Indian Life* demonstrated to the emancipated elite, in India and abroad, that the leaders of the Indian women's movement were beginning to demand new rights and new possibilities on their behalf.

When Sunity and Nripendra Cooch Behar visited England for Queen Victoria's Jubilee in 1887, they caused a sensation. Arriving a matter of months before Chimnabai and Sayajirao Gaekwad, Sunity Devi was the first reigning maharani ever to visit Britain and the reception she got there was overwhelming.

She found the journey itself hard. In order to accustom herself to European food before embarkation, 22-year-old Sunity tasted meat for the first time, and disliked it so much she could eat very little for the early days at sea. In contrast to the Barodas, who brought with them Indian cooks and even a cow so they could continue to eat the food they were used to, the Cooch Behars were determined to embrace European life. Initially depressed and daunted, Sunity spent mealtimes crying in her room. But with Nripendra, her three children, two of her brothers, and a large staff comprising an English secretary and adviser and Indian servants to cheer her up, she soon recovered her spirits.

On their arrival in May London was unusually cold, swept by bitter winds, but they were quickly caught up in the capital's busy social season. Sunity Devi took her children for drives through Hyde Park, gave sailor-suited little Rajey a wooden yacht to sail on the Serpentine lake and took Jit to tea with the Princess of Wales at Marlborough House. The extended Jubilee celebrations included dances, receptions, garden parties and dinners. Sunity and Nripendra saw Letty Lind dance and a performance of *The Winter's Tale*, and went to the opera; they dined with the Prince of Wales, and stayed at Windsor Castle where they were thrilled to find, adjoining their luxurious gilt bedroom, a state-of-the-art en-suite bathroom. They visited Edinburgh and Brighton, and Sunity got lost in the maze at Hatfield House and had to push her way out through the hedge to escape. They refused an invitation to Glamis Castle, in Perthshire, because the Maharani was afraid of the ghosts for which it was famous.

The friends Sunity felt closest to in London were Princess May (later Queen Mary), 'a tall graceful girl, with a wild-rose freshness and fairness, and gifted with . . . [a] simple unaffected charm of manner'; the Duchess of Teck, who radiated good-natured kindness and offered to chaperone Sunity through the Jubilee celebrations; and the feminine, delicate Princess of Wales, Alix, whom the Maharani described as being as good as she was beautiful. It was with her that Sunity Devi was, over the years, to feel the closest bond, despite the warmth the entire royal family showed all the Cooch Behars. 'Fate has dealt heavily with us both,' Sunity wrote, many years later. 'We have each lost our idolised first-born. We have each lost the best of husbands. We have equally sorrowed.' The subtext to this, which Sunity was far too loyal (and fastidious) to mention, was that though both Nripendra and Edward VII may have been adored husbands, both were only ever faithful in their fashion.

On their arrival, Queen Victoria asked Sunity Devi to call on her at Buckingham Palace before she was formally received at Court. Nripendra chose and ordered his wife's gown, a pale-grey satin dress; having visited Britain himself some years earlier, he knew what was expected. Though she scarcely ever drank alcohol, Sunity was so nervous that she accepted a glass of port from her maid, which she promptly spilt down her dress. Everyone cried, 'How lucky!' but Sunity could not help a pang of disappointment at ruining her dress. Despite the immense dignity of her presence, Victoria was so gracious that the Maharani quickly relaxed. 'Her conversation was simple and kindly, and every word revealed her queen, woman and mother. I was delighted to find that I had not been disappointed in my ideal, and felt eager to go back to India that I might tell my country-women about our wonderful Empress.'

The following day Sunity was formally presented to the Queen at a royal Drawing-Room, an afternoon reception at Buckingham

Palace. She wore a heavy white and gold brocade gown beneath a crêpe de Chine sari, and carried a pair of kid gloves. Unlike those of the other ladies present, Sunity Devi's neck, chest and arms were well covered; she was shocked at how décolleté were many of the ancient duchesses in attendance on the Queen in the middle of the day, and how cold they looked in consequence. While the British considered 'native' dress dangerously revealing, pious Indians found British society's behaviour scandalous by their standards.

The Queen noted in her diary the beautiful clothes Nripendra and Sunity wore to the Jubilee garden party at Buckingham Palace. 'She [Sunity] gave me a lovely pendant, a carved ruby set [necklace, earrings and bracelets] with fine large diamonds, and he an inlaid ivory writing and work-box in one. I gave her a miniature of myself.' Sunity was thrilled to be the only woman the Queen kissed in greeting that day, and was amused by the remarks of a newspaper commenting afterwards on 'the Indian Princess receiving more attention than any of the others'.

The Maharani impressed everyone she met with her composure: she looked as if she had been used to these strange foreign ways all her life, yet always retained 'the innate dignity of a high-caste native lady'. Queen Victoria clearly made something of a pet of her. But Sunity confessed she sometimes found it hard to decipher how she ought to behave. When she was presented to the Queen after their first meeting, she was told that she need not kiss her when she curtseyed since she had already been privately received; so when Victoria tried to kiss her, Sunity moved away. 'Why would not the Maharani kiss me?' Victoria asked the Princess of Wales. Sunity blushed deeply when the future kaiser, Prince Wilhelm, kissed her hand on being introduced to her, though she admitted to admiring his beautiful manners.

At the State Ball, Nripendra told her that if the Prince of Wales asked her to dance, she must, as it would be such a great honour.

'I can't, I simply can't,' replied Sunity. 'You know I do not dance.'

'Never mind, you cannot refuse your future king.'

Sunity hoped desperately that the Prince would overlook her, but sure enough a message was brought to them soon after they arrived asking her to honour His Highness with her hand. She replied that she must refuse as she never danced. A message came back: 'It was only the Lancers [a quadrille], and H.R.H. would show me the steps.' Again she refused, and by now her stand was attracting attention: the Kings of Greece and Denmark clamoured to teach her to dance, and, agonizingly embarrassed, she heard the Princess of Wales complimenting her tiny feet. She tried to tuck her shoes up out of sight under her blue and silver gown, but her skirts were too short to hide them completely. When supper time came, much to her relief, she went in with the royal family, and Prince Bertie teased her gently about turning him down.

The morning of the Jubilee celebrations dawned brilliantly, the dazzlingly sunny conditions known, in Victoria's heyday, as Queen's weather. Sunity, in an apricot gown and sari combination, needed a parasol for the hot, dusty drive to Westminster Abbey, but the immaculately behaved crowds shouted for her to close it so they could see the face of the only maharani present. 'Don't,' Nripendra whispered, 'you'll get sunstroke.' But she put it down and was heartily cheered in thanks.

Towards the end of the summer, Sunity Devi was, as she put it, 'in delicate health', which prevented her accepting an invitation to Sandringham. The situation was explained to the Queen, who offered to stand as godmother to the expected baby. This was a great honour, and Sunity appreciated it fully. 'It is so very gratifying to me to find that your Majesty takes such kindly interest in my children and me,' she wrote to her. She and the Queen exchanged photographs, affectionate letters and anxious telegrams concerning Sunity Devi's safe departure from England and arrival in India.

The only thing Sunity Devi was unhappy with during their stay in England was the fact that her beloved husband was not given a Jubilee decoration. 'If a boy goes to school . . . and does his best but does not get promotion, what encouragement is there for him to work?' she demanded of the Duke of Manchester at a dinner in

London. 'The Maharajah has done more than any other Ruler to improve the condition of his State, and I think his efforts deserve recognition.' His Grace was amused, and suggested she bring it up with the Prince of Wales. 'I'm sure he would be delighted at your championship.'

Sunity went back to India in November, leaving Nripendra behind in England, hoping to do some hunting during the winter months. A cable was waiting in Bombay to inform her that Nripendra was to be honoured with the GCIE (Grand Commander of the Indian Empire), 'but although greatly honoured and proud, I was sorry that it was not the GCSI [Grand Commander of the Star of India, a higher distinction], which I am sure is what HM meant to give.' Her sisters were waiting to greet her, exclaiming that she had only grown lovelier while she was away. The Sen girls travelled on to Calcutta together, where the Viceroy told Sunity Devi how charmed the Queen had been with her; she had written specially to him to say so.

She spent her pregnancy in Calcutta, and Victor – named for his godmother – was born on 21 May 1888 at Woodlands. The Queen sent him a large silver cup for his naming ceremony that November. But not everyone in Cooch Behar was pleased with their ruling family's new intimacy with the British crown: the Dewan of Cooch Behar, Calica Das Dutt, was said to have asked, 'What have they gained by going to England? Instead of having the Queen as godmother to the little Raj Kumar [prince] it would have been better if the Maharajah had had some guns.'

After her successes in England, Sunity Devi 'began to "live" in a worldly sense', seeking to show by example that an Indian woman could have social interests and British friends and still be a good, traditional wife and mother. She grew so emancipated that she even went out for carriage rides with men other than her husband, though she was always in the nursery to hear her children say their prayers and kiss them goodnight.

Sunity and Nripendra became renowned hosts, famous for their parties in Calcutta and Darjeeling or Simla, where the family usually retreated during the rainy summer months. They gave luncheons, garden parties, 'Indian' dinners eaten cross-legged on the floor, and fancy dress balls – even one *poudré*. At Woodlands, there were polo tournaments and weekly tennis parties attended by up to 200 people. When the band played the National Anthem, little Jit sang 'God Save Our Gracious Queen' from the upstairs veranda, to the delight of the guests.

Perhaps the most celebrated feature of life in Cooch Behar – especially among British grandees, hundreds of whom sought invitations – were the shikars, or shooting parties. The names of the guests over the years read like a roll call of the Victorian and Edwardian aristocracy, including Hamiltons, Sutherlands, Mintos, Lansdownes, Pembrokes, Galloways, Sassoons, Ilchesters, Lonsdales, Jerseys, Keppels and Tichbornes.

Nripendra was a fine sportsman, brilliant at tennis, rackets, football, polo and cricket, and a famously good shot – especially of the big game for which Cooch Behar was famous. For centuries, the elephants of Cooch Behar had been captured and trained for warfare; in Nripendra's time, they were used for hunting. 'No man knew better than he how to outwit tiger, bison, buffalo, and rhinoceros in the tangled plains of high grass and swamp which fringe the Eastern Himalayas. He understood thoroughly all the wiles of the game, and if "Cooch Behar" could not beat a tiger out of the grass up to the rifles, there was no man who could.' Like the huntsman and gentleman he was, Nripendra rarely shot when he was entertaining, but preferred to lead the beaters so his guests had the chance to make a kill.

Lord Frederic Hamilton (brother of the future Secretary of State for India) went up to Cooch Behar to shoot in 1891. He and his party arrived at the palace after dark, and found the vast, domed durbar hall lit up, with the Maharaja and his children roller-skating around the marble floor, inlaid with the Cooch Behar coat of arms, to the strains of a thirty-five-piece band led by a Viennese conductor. They drove up towards Assam along a road created specially for the party. Oakley, an Australian trainer who taught the children to ride, was a reckless driver and his passengers clung to the sides of the coach-and-four as they hurtled through the jungle, past trees hung with wild orchids that glimmered through the dimness, and across rickety temporary bamboo bridges spanning the many rivers in their path. At the end of the road they found a small city of white tents, forming three sides of a square on the banks of a rushing river.

Each guest had his own Indian tent, spacious enough to hold dressing tables, desks, armchairs and chests of drawers as well as beds. One entered through a covered canvas porch; inside the tents were hung with cotton fabric printed in soft reds and blues and carpeted with dhurries. Private bath tents stood beside each bed tent. The central general living and dining area was a large, open-sided tent, or shamiana, beside an open fire kept lit through the night to keep the animals away. Four hundred and seventy-three servants accompanied the party, including mahouts and syces (elephant and horse grooms, respectively), taxidermists, armourers, boatmen, waiters, three gardeners to arrange flowers in the tents and on the tables, and the thirty-five-man string orchestra.

Hamilton and his companions stayed in their temporary town for five weeks. In the morning, they were up with the dawn, woken by a bare-footed bearer with a cup of tea, to walk or ride through the jungle, or fish for the fighting mahseer that filled the sparkling river. At breakfast, as they sat beneath the fluttering shamiana, khaki-clad and stoutly booted, enjoying piping hot bacon and eggs, or fresh mahseer, the shikaris, or gamekeepers, stood beside the table to tell them where the day's tigers were to be found. Then the party was off after them, settled comfortably in howdahs specially made with gun racks at the front and holders at the back for lemonade, biscuits, nougat and novels for the ladies. The guns they used varied according to the game they were after, and ranged from mighty four-bore elephant rifles with a massive recoil, to lighter guns for other game, including leopard, boar, deer, peacock and snipe.

The rulers of both British India and princely India were united by their shared obsessions with hunting and sport, their peace-time substitutes for warfare. Disputes over rank or precedence were forgotten on the tennis court or the polo ground, and most especially in the jungle, hunting big game. The princes were not blind to the way British grandees used them for their shooting – they knew their states were seen by some British visitors as 'playgrounds where they could get a nice free holiday with some good shooting' – but it was in their interest to provide their guests with good sport, and this they endeavoured to do. When they got on well, camp life was the ideal informal meeting ground, where friendships could be formed and disagreements ironed out. It was always vital, though, for the most important guest to bag the biggest tiger. Some tape measures were made with 11-inch feet, to ensure a viceroy got a 10 footer; others measured tigers by pressing the tape measure down every 4 inches 'instead of taking the measurements, as true sportsmen did, from nose to tail'.

The hunters usually returned to camp at sunset, in time for a hot bath before dressing for dinner. In the moonlight that Hamilton specified was golden in India, not silver, the men wore white tie and tails, and the women evening gowns and jewels. Countless fireflies flickered like stars. The European guests were served European food on silver plates while the Cooch Behars ate richly aromatic curries brought to them in large square silver boxes. At night, the campers could hear tigers' roars echoing through the jungle; one evening, by the light of the full moon, they saw a tiger drinking from the opposite bank of the river.

Though Nripendra held firm views on women wearing makeup, drinking and smoking, he was more indulgent with his daughters than he had initially been with his wife. The Cooch Behar children were brought up in a cosmopolitan mix of eastern and western customs. They wore Indian clothes in Cooch Behar, but European everywhere else. In family photos the boys look sweetly serious in miniature sailor-suits and the girls are dwarfed by white leg-of-mutton sleeves, hair tied back from their faces with vast ribbon bows, dark eyes huge and earnest, waiting for the slow click of the shutter that would release them to play.

Sunity and Nripendra faced the same problems as the Barodas: they wanted their children to be Indian but still have all the advantages of a British education – polish, sophistication; social graces. There was the further, perennial problem of trying to bring up royal children in their home states, where everyone deferred to them in everything. 'I want my sons to be brought up as ordinary boys, not as Indian princes,' declared Nripendra. How were they to avoid being spoiled at home? The answer, much to Sunity's regret, was to send them away.

In 1893, Rajey became the first eastern Indian prince to attend Mayo College, traditionally the training ground for Rajput princes. 'Whether the Maharajahs in that part [modern Rajasthan] did not wish it or whether there was any caste prejudice I cannot say,' commented his mother pointedly. Since the Rajputs were notoriously proud, and hated the thought of mingling with non-Rajputs, it is more than likely there was some caste prejudice at play, and Sunity Devi, for all her delicacy, would not have remarked so acidly on it had there not been.

Modelled on the English public school system, with a British headmaster, Mayo was enlivened by some peculiarly Indian touches: in 1875, the Maharaja of Alwar, Mayo's first scholar, arrived there on a caparisoned elephant at the head of a procession of elephants, camels, horses and 500 servants, to the sound of a troupe of trumpeters. In order to instil in them gentlemanly British virtues, the boys played cricket, polo and tennis. Each student was expected to perform a puja daily, though no further religious activity was encouraged.

Rajey left Mayo in 1894 to attend prep school in England. His distraught mother, echoing her husband's mother and grandmothers all those years before, had pleaded for him to stay in India. She argued that when he came back to Cooch Behar, he would find his people backward, and not want to stay there to rule; that his health would suffer; that he would miss home and his family. But Nripendra was confident the discipline would be good for Rajey.

He spent three years at Farnborough, from where, during his holidays, he often stayed with the Duke of Connaught, Queen Victoria's favourite son, and his family. In a heartrendingly brave letter from Bagshot, Rajey informed his mother, whom he would not see for four years, 'I have a room to myself, a table of my own, a penknife, a pen and pencil on the table.' He began at Eton in 1897, and went up to Oxford in 1900.

His brothers followed him to English schools though the Indian government tried to prevent their parents from joining them there too often. In 1894, six years before Curzon forbad all princes from travelling abroad, the Cooch Behar finances (as in all the princely states, the state and privy purses were not separate) were in so 'embarrassing' a condition that the India Office in London recommended Nripendra be 'discouraged' from further expensive trips to Europe. Offering his house in Simla as collateral, Nripendra was trying to get loans in England because he had exhausted his contacts in India. 'He left me under the impression that it was a necessity for him to get the money *somehow*,' reads a note in an India Office file dated 26 October 1894. The government tried to help him budget, advising him to limit his expenditure to an annual sum of Rs 2,50,000* in 1895, but he refused to do so. By 1903 Nripendra's personal expenditure accounted for a third of Cooch Behar's annual revenue.

Maharajas were expected to be munificent. Nripendra's servants praised his extravagance as an attribute of his kingship, describing him spending money 'in such a festive way'. Lavish displays of wealth were intended to be, and were viewed as, displays of majesty. With this cultural inheritance, it would have been very hard for Nripendra to learn to manage his money and, indeed, he never did.

For her part, Sunity Devi believed these 'money difficulties, which I know for certain did not exist', had been created by the Government to prevent her joining Rajey in England. In her 1921 autobiography, written some years after she had seen two of her sons die, she spoke out against the practice of sending Indian children to school abroad. 'I am of the opinion that my people do *not* require a Western education,' she declared defiantly. 'People

---

*This is the Indian notation system, indicating 2.5 lakhs (see Glossary), or 250,000 rupees.

seem to forget that thousands of years ago India produced astronomers, poets, and sages, when most of the European races of today were cave-dwellers.' Her sons returned from England speaking French and Greek, but not Sanskrit, Urdu or Bengali, and no longer fluent in the local dialect of Cooch Behar.

What made it all the more galling was hearing Lord Curzon remark that 'the Cooch Behar boys were too English, and it was hard on them to have been sent away from Cooch Behar when they were so young'. Indignantly, Sunity pointed out that it had been the Lieutenant-Governor of Bengal who advised them to send their children away. She also decried the lack of any practical education for future maharajas. To rule well, they needed a vocational understanding of legal, accounting, engineering and agricultural matters more than a classical education. A maharaja's younger brothers and sons were also in a difficult position, forced to live on an allowance without any opportunity to make themselves independent.

Even the army was closed to them due to the rigid prejudice of the British. In 1898, Nripendra wrote to the ex-Viceroy, Lord Lansdowne – a personal friend who had enjoyed their generous hospitality in Cooch Behar and Calcutta, and of whom Sunity wrote that his fondness for Nripendra 'made the other Maharajahs very jealous' – asking for his help to get Rajey into Sandhurst. There were no Indian officers in the Indian Army, for fear that they should develop independent power bases, but Nripendra had volunteered for the Tiran Expedition on India's North-West Frontier with Afghanistan in 1897–8. He had served as ADC on General Yeatman Briggs's staff and been awarded the honorary rank of colonel and the CB (Companion of the Bath) for his distinguished service. But, remarkable as Nripendra's active loyalty to the Empire was, Lansdowne hesitated to grant his friend's plea. 'Much as I should like to oblige the father, I fear we ought to refuse,' he wrote in an internal memo to Lord George Hamilton, brother of the Frederic Hamilton who had taken such pleasure in his shooting in Cooch Behar only a few years before. 'Candidates are not suitable unless they are of pure European descent.'

Others in the Indian government agreed. Lansdowne's successor as viceroy, Lord Elgin – another friend of Nripendra's – said there was no special reason to indulge Cooch Behar, and doing so would result only in an undesirable flood of native princes wanting to join the army. The principal reason against this was that British soldiers could not be expected to serve under Indian officers, but other reasons were offered: whether being in the army really was the best preparation for ruling; whether Indian subjects might feel alienated from their overly Anglicized Indian soldier-princes; whether divisions would spring up between those families who sent their children to England and those who did not. 'It would not be good for the Army,' Elgin concluded darkly, 'nor, I think, for them.'

Sunity, as ever, had her own views on the situation, underestimating the profundity of British bigotry. 'I wonder why no Viceroy of India has ever given any of our young princes a place on his staff,' she mused. 'It would appeal tremendously to our people and prove that the much-discussed English training meets its reward. Our Princes mix on terms of equality with Englishmen at the public schools and universities. Yet, in their own land, they are denied positions of honour!'

Three years later, Nripendra was still campaigning for an exception to be made for his boys. In June 1901, he wrote to the Lieutenant-Governor of Bengal, Sir John Woodburn, of how 'the possibility of obtaining for my sons a career and profession in life' was 'a constant anxiety to me'. The solution, he believed, was for them to join the British Army or civil service. 'Failing this, there is nothing left for them to do but lead purposeless, indolent lives.' Rajey, his heir, required discipline rather than a career; but his three younger sons needed an opportunity to make their own way in life. He had given them, Nripendra said, the 'habits, training and education of European life' he had himself received – surely, one can almost hear him protesting, this must be enough for you to count them your equals? Not until 1918 did Sandhurst, the British Army's officer training college, begin to accept Indian candidates, though Nripendra was eventually allowed to buy Rajey a commission in the Westminster Dragoons.

Lord Curzon, who had previously regarded Nripendra as the 'spoilt child' of the British royal family, was impressed by his impassioned plea. Despite his antipathy towards the princes, the Viceroy proposed the formation of a '*corps d'élite* of native gentlemen' that would in due course provide Indian officers for the Indian Army. This was to be an Imperial Cadet Corps, attached to the viceroy's court, but not officially part of the army. The cadets, aged between seventeen and twenty, must speak English, and would be drawn from the four princely schools – Mayo College, two Rajkumar Colleges in Rajkot and Raipur, Aitchison in Lahore, and Daly in Indore. Their uniforms were dazzling ivory achkans with facings of sky blue and gold, blue turbans with gold tassels, and heavy sashes of cloth-of-gold. Though her tall, handsome boys looked marvellous in their uniforms, Sunity Devi still was not satisfied with Curzon's compromise. She said he had 'forced' Rajey to join the Corps, and she was horrified at their basic living conditions. 'The Maharajahs' sons lived in some ordinary buildings like a barrack.'

The Maharaja's eldest daughter, Girlie, married in 1899, aged fifteen. A match with another princely family could not be made, because no other maharajas were Brahmos, and most were still polygamous, one of the most important proscriptions of Brahmoism. Her groom was Jyotsnanath Ghosal, grandson of Debendranath Tagore and member of one of Bengal's most distinguished families. He had passed into the Indian Civil Service and an illustrious career in administration was predicted for him. The wedding was held in a large marquee in the garden at Woodlands, according to the simple Brahmo rites to which both families subscribed. Girlie wore the traditional red and gold sari accessorized with an abundance of jewels; Ghosal was in eau-de-nil Benares silk. Eight hundred guests dined there after the ceremonies, at a party so immaculately planned that even the drivers were given dinner in earthenware pots tied up with muslin. In Cooch Behar, the state offices were closed for a week, prisoners were freed from jail, taxes were excused, and alms were given to the poor.

★

In 1901, the Cooch Behar family travelled to Britain en masse for Edward VII's coronation, at which Nripendra was one of his three Indian ADCs (the others were Sir Pratap Singh and Scindia of Gwalior), riding in the procession behind his new king. At the review of the troops at Buckingham Palace, Sunity Devi was awarded the CI (Imperial Order of the Crown of India) – the only woman there to be so honoured.

They rented a house outside Bexhill-on-Sea on England's south coast. The younger girls were enrolled at Ravenscroft school in nearby Eastbourne, where another student was Indira Gaekwad. The family spent some months in another house near Slough called Ditton Park, closer to Jit and Victor's school, Eton College. Jit and Victor used to sneak out on Sundays for curry teas and cricket in the garden. They loved Eton, though Hitty, at preparatory school in Farnborough, wished he could stay at home with his mother. 'When he came home for the week-ends, every time I saw him off in the train big tears would roll down his cheeks and make my heart ache till I saw him again.'

While his younger brothers were still enjoying innocent schoolboy pleasures such as cricket and lemonade, Rajey's tastes had developed. In 1901 he was nineteen, and very much in love. The American actress Edna May also enjoyed an extended visit to Bexhill in the summer of 1901, staying in the Hotel Metropole. Twenty-three-year-old Edna, a friend of Ellen Terry, was a classically beautiful musical artiste who was the most famous performer of her day. She took London by storm in 1898, with a record 697 appearances in *The Belle of New York*.

The only evidence of their love affair is circumstantial: over the following two or three years they both spent substantial periods of time in Bexhill, and Rajey's niece records the family legend that Rajey, refused permission to marry the beautiful but unsuitable actress he loved, resolved to drink himself to death on champagne. His dependence on champagne, and his related ill-health, began at this time.

In the summer of 1902, Rajey had a bad fall playing polo at

Trouville and was unconscious for several days. During this period, the French doctors 'kept him on nothing but champagne'. Although he made what was described as a full recovery, Sunity Devi said that after this time he was never the same. It is not clear whether the change in him was brought about by the accident or derived from excessive champagne imbibed immediately after it.

Sunity often described Rajay and her other grown-up children as being 'ill', and from what is known of their lives and deaths from other sources it is likely these illnesses were alcohol-related, though she would have savagely refuted this. Alcoholism and its attendant vices (in Victorian eyes) – a fondness for low life in all its guises – ran rampant among the Indian princely families. The death in 1923 of Sayajirao's eldest son, Jayasinhrao, was caused by alcohol abuse and his younger half-brothers suffered from the same weakness. Other maharajas and their families were similarly blighted. 'It is extraordinary how many Ruling Chiefs are apt to die from excessive drink,' observed Lord Hardinge, adding his belief that their 'excesses' were the result of polygamy.

Drinking was seen as a 'badge of Western civilisation'. When one prince was rebuked by his Resident for squandering his state's resources on women, cars, aeroplanes, drink and drugs, he replied bitterly, 'You have taught me all I know.' Extended periods spent in Europe did aggravate the problems of identity encountered by Indian princes at this time of transition and uncertainty: returning, they felt alienated from their people, and yet they never truly assimilated into or were accepted by British society.

Another facet of this dependence on alcohol, especially among the immediate male relatives of a maharaja, was that British influence denied them their traditional subsidiary role in government as well as the arena of warfare. Maharajas' uncles, brothers and sons were made redundant by the increasingly professional administration of most states, but were still kept reliant on their coffers. For the heirs, there was the classic predicament: they were useless until their fathers died, an event for which they might wait for a lifetime, always under the intense pressure of other people's expectations of them. Feelings of emasculation, powerlessness and inadequacy drove many non-ruling princes – and some ruling ones, struggling to assert their predominance over the insidious influence of the British – to drink.

The fact that at the turn of the century alcoholism was not seen as a physical addiction but as a disease of the nerves only made it a harder problem to deal with. Fresh air, sport, mineral water and fortifying drinks such as Bovril and Ovaltine were recommended 'cures'. For serious cases, drugs such as strychnine and nux vomica were administered as aversion therapy, but nothing could be relied upon to prevent an alcoholic continuing to drink.

Indian princes were also often separated from their families for long, lonely periods of their childhood, and thrust into frightening new situations in which the only thing that made them special was their status – essential attributes of which were extravagance and self-indulgence. Young Indian princes were seldom refused anything at home – how could they be expected to learn self-discipline there? – and in England they were alone and always different from everyone around them. The strength of character needed to resist the impulse to self-destruction was not always allowed to develop. 'Having learned many languages, having travelled in many places and having been born a hero at birth, are of no avail if one does not have the knowledge [of] what õne's duty is in one's life,' lamented Nripendra's biographer.

William Gerhardi, a novelist and friend of Indira Gaekwad's in the 1930s, described the 'strange mix of inferiority and superiority' that prevailed among the princes of India. On one hand, the maharajas were absolute monarchs, adored by their people and fêted abroad. On the other, they were not allowed to join European clubs, or European armies, on account of their colour. According to Gerhardi, this explained their sometimes farcical obsession with princely status and privileges. 'Listen to one maharaja addressing another as "Your Highness" across the tennis court – "thirty–fifteen to Your Highness". The word flies back and forth with such rapidity, it might be the tennis ball.' It took a very strong man to rise above the paradoxes of his position. Sayajirao, faced with an exclusively white club in the Baroda cantonment, 'made the superbly disdainful gesture of buying it a new pavilion'.

Not everyone was capable of this level of determined nonchalance. Just as she ignored Rajey's addiction to champagne, Sunity Devi was determined to rise above his desire to marry an unsuitable girl. She attributed his waywardness to his British education: 'Boys who are educated in England do not always get the chance of seeing the right and bright side of English society, and perhaps get married to girls who are not of their class.' Rajey was caught between two worlds, and so finding him a bride was an almost impossible task: the parents of Indian girls of the right caste and position were unlikely to look favourably on a Brahmo, even if he were a maharaja, and marriage between Indians and non-Indians was practically unheard of at this time. Some maharajas did marry foreigners – the Maharaja of Kapurthala married a Spanish dancer, Anita Delgrada, in 1910 – but they were never considered principal, or even official, wives. No English or European girl from the appropriate background would have married an Indian, and those from lower classes – such as the beautiful Edna May – would have been rejected out of hand by Sunity Devi.

During the 1900s, despite their financial worries, the Cooch Behars divided their time between England and India. In the winter of 1905–6, the future George V, then Prince of Wales, visited Calcutta and the whole family was involved in welcoming him. Nripendra sat on the reception committee for their Highnesses; the boys paraded in their glamorous Corps uniforms; and Sunity's baby, Sudhira, presented the Prince and Princess with bouquets. That winter, Rajey was the youngest man, and sole Indian, at an Old Etonian dinner held for the new viceroy, the Earl of Minto, in Calcutta.

Lord Minto's wife, Mary, began holding purdah parties for the consorts of her husband's Indian allies. She brought Mary, Princess of Wales, to one of these gatherings on New Year's Day 1906. There were sixty women present; many had never before seen a white woman. Mary Minto regarded her guests with as much curiosity as they did her:

Some were wearing gorgeous jewels, large rings covered with precious stones hung from their noses, and as many as six huge rings from their ears. Others had large diamond solitaires struck through their nostrils: one small child had a pear-shaped diamond fastened to her nose which fell over her mouth. Another child of eleven was conspicuous, dressed in yellow satin sparkling with precious stones; ropes of pearls with large tassels were suspended from her head; necklaces of uncut emeralds and pearls hung thickly round her small neck, while her arms were covered with jewelled bangles.

Sunity Devi, more experienced than her countrywomen, acted as interpreter between the two cultures: 'The Maharani of Cooch Behar told me that many of these ladies had no idea what life was like outside purdah; some of them are so strict [such strict Hindus] they will not drink a drop of water in her house.'

Lady Minto was a willing student. One day, Sunity dressed her in a Bengali bridal sari of rich scarlet and gold and she was driven the long, hot few miles home across the maidan, the large park that runs through the centre of Calcutta, as an Indian woman. When she arrived at Government House, she sent a message to her husband that a maharani was waiting to see him in the hall. She was delighted her disguise was so effective he did not immediately recognize her.

Minto was less successful than his wife in reaching out to Indian womanhood. He was amused in 1909 to receive a telegram from his Secretary of State, John Morley, at India House in London, inquiring about the status of women living in harems. 'I will do my best!' he responded. 'I think I told you that Scindia [Gwalior]'s Maharani sang "Comin' thro' the Rye" to me from behind the purdah [curtain], but as yet I have not looked into the zenana.'

Though no hint of it stains Sunity Devi's relentlessly positive autobiography, the mid-1900s saw a serious rupture emerge between her and Nripendra. Like many men of his class and background – Indian and English – Nripendra was consistently unfaithful to Sunity, though he was the first maharaja of Cooch Behar to be monogamous. In his aristocratic milieu, the presence of a wife and a family never impinged on a man's pleasures. In

March 1907 Minto's private secretary, Sir James Dunlop-Smith, described Nripendra to Morley who, he said, well knew Cooch Behar's 'matrimonial difficulties'. Cooch Behar had 'sown his wild oats and paid for the process to the utmost farthing. He is now, I think, taking life seriously, but any day he and she may have to part.'

The India Office files offer no further comment on the affair except a postscript a year later, again from Dunlop-Smith, after another meeting with Sunity Devi. 'Poor dear lady, she doesn't seem to be any happier than she used to be and poured out all her woes to me. I spoke to the Bengal Government authorities and I hope I may have done something to smooth matters but after all the only person who can help her in this matter is her own husband.'

As with pecuniary embarrassment, it was unlikely that Nripendra would change his attitude. Infidelity – or rather, the liberty to pursue his own whims without regard to his wife's feelings – was so entrenched a part of a maharaja's majesty (and a husband's authority, in the aristocratic British circles in which Nripendra also moved) that it was a rare man who, like Sayajirao, could turn his back on it.

An incident described by Nripendra's servant and biographer, Choudhuri, is revealing: in the early days of his reign, a wily politician brought his beautiful daughter to dine with Nripendra at the palace in Cooch Behar. Sunity Devi was cloistered in the women's quarters. 'The daughter was charmed at Raja's [Nripendra's] wealth, beauty and manner and hospitality,' reported Choudhuri.

She began to look at the Raja attractively avoiding the sight of her father. The Raja noticed . . . he fixed his sight at the wise man. And then controlling his feelings only looking at the daughter in opportune moments began to discuss a subject of serious nature. Then both of them began to discuss the subject so attentively that the daughter of his could not see any opportunity to look at the Raja the way she wanted.

Choudhuri was naïve: he seems not to have realized the politician had brought his daughter as bait for Nripendra, and praised his king for virtuously resisting her charms. But scenes like this would have occurred all the time, in Calcutta and London as well as Cooch Behar, and it is unsurprising that Nripendra sometimes succumbed.

Unhappy, Sunity threw herself into new projects. She was consulting Sir James regularly during this period because she wanted the absent Vicereine's help in a scheme to improve the welfare of her countrywomen, and hoped Dunlop-Smith would communicate her plans to Lady Minto. She hoped to establish a public-funded industrial institute for women, teaching knitting, weaving, embroidery, lace-making and other crafts in three schools in Calcutta, Madras and Bombay. 'The natural resources of a country are a sacred trust to its citizen,' she told him. 'The rich and the poor, the young and the old, the strong and the weak, the skilled and the unskilled have each an allotted function . . . Each is to endeavour to realise their unfulfilled destiny.'

Her institute was intended to allow women to develop their share of this national responsibility. The plan, Dunlop-Smith commented condescendingly, 'reads beautifully – I wonder who wrote it for her', though he feared it was premature, and doubted its chance of success. 'Indian men have not shared with their women the gifts that we have been showering on them for over a century.'

The institute would have two funding centres, in Calcutta and Baroda, which indicates a degree of cooperation from Chimnabai and Sayajirao, though there is no evidence of friendship between the two families at this time. Chimnabai and Sunity, with their shared interest in women's issues, were meeting fairly regularly. Chimnabai opened the Indian Ladies' Conference in Calcutta on 31 December 1906, at which Sunity was present.

Like Chimnabai, Sunity Devi was a keen proponent of education, especially for women, though she preferred to encourage specific institutions rather than act as patron to associations, Chimnabai's role. She founded a school in Darjeeling for children of both sexes and all castes and a ladies' technical school in Calcutta, and took a keen interest in her father's Victoria College for girls in

Calcutta. Her gentler attitude towards the British and her willing-
ness to believe the best of people made the British see Sunity as a
more acceptable face of Indian womanhood than unafraid, uncompromising Chimnabai.

In November 1908, 22-year-old Prince Jitendra hired a 40 horse-
power Daimler and went for a drive in the English countryside. In
the passenger seat beside him was a Miss Morrison; another car held
a second couple. Jit's car was involved in a crash with a local man,
Thomas George, driving a 6 horse-power Rover. Jit offered George
£35 on the spot as reparation; George rejected it. A few months
later Jit paid him £105 for 'alleged injuries' – George said his son
had been laid up for eleven weeks as a result of the accident – and
the repair of the car, which George estimated would cost £50. But
the case – the first surviving record of the adult Jit – dragged on for
several years. In 1911 George demanded more money and received
a further £25.

This case is typical of the way in which Indian princes were
treated in Britain: they were assumed to be vastly rich, and no
one with the slightest claim on them hesitated to press charges.
Complaints of debts were constantly sent through to the India
Office – whether the suits against them were always strictly defens-
ible is debatable but as a rule all princes, even the richest, could be
lax about paying their bills on time – and, though the Government
of India preferred not to interfere in these cases, sometimes they
had no option but to do so.

In June 1911, for example, Jit was in court for owing a certain
Alfred Moore £109. Although he was a debtor, as a member of a
princely family he was entitled to avoid appearing in court by
pleading his sovereign rights. But Jit declared he did not intend
to demand immunity: he wanted to pay Moore back. All the
proceedings were faithfully reported back to the Government of
Bengal.

Another problem was the difference between the way these
things were handled in India and in England. A few years later,
Alan Mander, Baby Cooch Behar's English husband, hit and killed

an Indian woman on a road in a village near Calcutta. Horrified, he rushed to the nearest police station to report his crime and make some kind of reparation payment to the woman's family, and found the police totally unwilling to deal with it. They told him since it was only a 'coolie woman' he did not need to report it – but if he had run over a dog instead he would have had to.

Not even the most virtuous of the princes was exempt. Just before Sayajirao Gaekwad left London in October 1911, two officers tried to serve him with a writ at his hotel. The staff at Claridges refused them access, and Sayaji left London, but the case went ahead in his absence. Sayajirao – perhaps the only Indian prince never known to have kept a mistress, and one whose moral standards were so high that even the dancing girls at his palace were a mother and daughter of spotless reputation – was cited as correspondent in a divorce case. George Statham alleged that Sayajirao had committed adultery with his wife, Beatrix, in Scotland that August.

This apparently spurious divorce case provided ammunition for the Government of India's continuing efforts to undermine Sayajirao. He had not had to appear in court when George Statham cited him in his divorce; princes and their families were exempt from jurisdiction in most cases. The judge presiding in the Statham case, against the express wishes of the British government, upheld the convention, declaring Sayajirao was, for the purposes of English municipal law, an independent ruling sovereign and not a British subject. What 'a disagreeable surprise', commented the Government of India in March 1912. George and Beatrix Statham, on receipt of the large sum of £5,700 from Sayajirao to withdraw the case, 'arranged our differences'.

Victor Cooch Behar, the late Queen's godson, 'a pleasant mannered boy, and the most promising of the brothers' according to the India Office, also failed to fulfil his potential. He began studying at Cornell University in upstate New York in March 1908. The plan was that he would learn about the American tobacco industry in order to grow tobacco in Cooch Behar. A Bengali gentleman, Mr Majumdar, was sent with him to America to settle him down at college before going to the still-segregated south. Majumdar was to tour the tobacco farms in Virginia and the Carolinas 'so if there is any difficulty or unpleasantness owing to racial feeling he will sample it first' – an early twentieth-century version of the slave hired to taste his master's food in case it contains poison. The following January Victor and a friend went from New York to Cuba for two months to study tobacco production there, but then he returned to England for the summer and autumn of 1909. He spent his time there with his father 'to no good purpose', according to the India Office files.

By this time Nripendra and Sunity were largely living apart. In March 1909 Nripendra had written a moving letter to Pretty and Baby informing them of his and Sunity's decision to separate, and reminding them that, though he believed their remaining with their mother would be the best thing for them, his happiest moments had been spent in their company. It was signed 'Nip the Unhappy'.

The Cooch Behar family were reunited in London in the autumn of 1910 following Edward VII's death that spring. In his memory, his widow, Alix, 'looking more *spirituelle* and lovely than ever before' in her deep mourning, gave Sunity a brooch with the initials A and E entwined on it, and Nripendra a gold cigarette case and a ruby scarf pin that had belonged to Edward. Although they missed his funeral, they were allowed to see his body in the vault beneath St George's Chapel at Windsor, and placed a wreath of orchids on his coffin. Both Sunity and Nripendra knelt and wept through their prayers for the man they had loved as a friend as well as a king.

Though Edward's death marked the passing of an era, in Cooch Behar nothing seemed to change. In about 1908, Major Gordon Casserly of the 120th Rajputana Infantry was posted to the tiny outpost of Buxa Duar in the north of Cooch Behar – a place so remote that the narrow-gauge railway could run into and out of it only during the day because the elephant and bison in the Terai jungle through which it passed were so aggressive at night. Casserly was much impressed by his first meeting with the generous, urbane Nripendra, who 'had been everywhere, seen everything, and knew most of the interesting personalities of the day'. What struck him most was Nripendra's loyalty to British rule, founded, according to Casserly, on the heartfelt conviction of its benefit to India. 'If ever, during my lifetime, the British quitted India, my departure would precede theirs,' he recalled Nripendra saying. 'This country would be no place to live in then. Chaos, bloodshed and confusion would be its lot.'

Casserly visited the Cooch Behars several times during his term at Buxa Duar, most memorably observing the annual state durbar which, it seemed to Casserly, resembled nothing so much as a 'magnificent stage scene': it was a spectacle too glittering, too picturesque, to be real.

The durbar took place at night. The palace's façade, a long line of archways, was illuminated by hundreds of white-gowned servants bearing flickering torches, its windows, doorways and roofs outlined with nightlights. The state elephants, painted and bejewelled like courtesans, stood patiently outside along the approach to the great durbar hall, shifting their weight heavily from foot to foot, swinging their trunks and flapping their leathery ears. Above them, on the steps into the hall, crowded guards and retainers. The state band played on the lawn beside the palace. Carriages and palanquins deposited Cooch Behar's officials and aristocracy on the palace steps.

The Maharaja, resplendent in a coat and turban of pale, delicate blue, surmounted by a diamond aigrette, the mark of his majesty, entered the great hall followed by a procession of white and gold clad ADCs. From behind a screen in a gallery high above the hall, Sunity Devi, Pretty and Baby looked down over the ceremony. To the blare of trumpets and the enthusiastic rendering of the Cooch Behar national anthem by the state band, Nripendra walked across the marble floor, inlaid with the Cooch Behar crest, and mounted the steps to his silver throne, standing beneath a cloth-of-gold canopy given to him by Queen Victoria as a reward for his loyalty. One arm of the throne was carved into the shape of a lion, the other a tiger. Behind it, guardsmen stood sentinel, their swords gleaming.

Silence fell as Rajey, in the scarlet coat of the Westminster

Dragoons, Jit and Victor in the white, blue and gold uniform of the Imperial Cadet Corps, and Hitendra in a cloth-of-gold achkan entered the hall. Proud and graceful, they halted in front of the dais, and then each in turn approached his father to pay him homage, holding his sheathed sword horizontally before him, in a salute that means 'I place my life and my sword in your hand.' Nripendra touched the hilt of each sword, meaning 'I accept the gift and give you back your life.' The princes then took their places on the dais flanking their father's throne, two standing on either side of him.

Only then, with much salaaming and retiring backwards, did the dewan, officials and zamindars, or landowners, of Cooch Behar approach their king, offering him their swords or gold coins which he 'touched and remitted'. An official was on hand to record the amount of each gift proffered so it could be returned to the donor later. Ceremony over, a 2-foot-tall gold hookah was brought into the hall and placed next to Nripendra, who smoked as the dewan sat at his feet examining the account books. When he had finished, the Maharaja rose from the throne and, attended by his sons and ADCs, passed through the bowing crowd out of the hall.

Half an hour later, the family gathered in the drawing room before dinner. Nripendra and the four boys had exchanged their uniforms for more casual clothes.

The pretty young princesses seemed more to be masquerading in an attractive fancy dress than wearing their national costume; for they had been brought up by English governesses and educated in England, had danced through the ball-rooms of London and Calcutta in the smartest Parisian toilettes, and were as much at home in the Park or at a gala night at the Opera as in their own country.

The family dined in the white and gold dining room, its walls lined with the silver and gold sporting trophies Nripendra and his sons had won, waited on by scarlet and gold liveried servants, chatting in Eton drawls about polo, parties and the latest plays.

After dinner, the young men went back up to the galleries

above the durbar hall to watch the nautch dancers moving lazily around the marble floor beneath them, but the sweet smell of incense and the insistently repeating music were overpowering, and Rajey suggested they go for a drive in the moonlight. They returned to the palace in the dim light of dawn, refreshed by the cool night air and invigorated by racing, and Casserly climbed into bed in a room 'fitted like the best bedroom in a European *hotel de luxe*'. He was overwhelmed by what he had seen and experienced in Cooch Behar that night: 'It seemed too splendid, too glowing with colour, to be real life.' This, perhaps, was what made it so hard for the Cooch Behar children to find their way outside the boundaries of their beloved home-state. Cooch Behar was a fairyland, already an anachronism in the changing, modern world with which they were utterly ill-equipped to deal.

Maharani Chimnabai's English companion, Frances West, was due to leave the Gaekwads' service at the start of 1912. She introduced Chimnabai to her friend Edith Tottenham at the party the Maharaja of Gwalior gave to celebrate his betrothal to Indira in London in August 1911, and it was arranged that Miss Tottenham should come to Baroda for a trial period before Miss West left the following January.

Like the Reverend Weeden, who had visited the year before, Miss Tottenham was immediately enchanted by Baroda and the Gaekwad family. The Maharaja paid the two ladies a visit in the house he provided for Miss West, which Miss Tottenham later took over. 'In his simple white attire, charming and friendly, he sat in a low chair and appreciated out loud the life of a small house, our lack of responsibilities, of trammels of caste or community; and especially my freedom to travel wherever love of adventure beckoned.' Chimnabai wasted no time in inquiring about Miss Tottenham's politics, which were conservative. 'The Maharani said concisely: "I am sorry. You ought to be Liberal!"'

Miss Tottenham arrived in India in time to attend the great imperial event of the century – the 1911 Durbar, held to celebrate the coronation of King George V and Queen Mary and the first visit to India by a ruling British monarch. It was here the announcement was made that India's capital would move from Calcutta to New Delhi, as yet unbuilt.

Today, outside the clamour and sprawl of greater Delhi, all that remains of Coronation Park is a monumental obelisk standing in neglected wasteland. Beside it lies a scrubby walled park containing an immense and lonely sculpture of George V flanked by vacant sandstone plinths that once bore statues of India's viceroys. Their names have been erased by time; only Lord Minto, one of the two remaining standing, is recognizable by his generous walrus moustache. The marble king surveys his empty realm high above normal human height. To modern eyes the ruins are a sad commentary on British vainglory but in December 1911 Coronation Park was the beating heart of an unprecedentedly massive and apparently unchallengeable colonial body. The Coronation Durbar was the zenith of the Raj and of Britain's imperial dreams.

The festivities began on 7 December, when the King and Queen arrived at Coronation Park, though the preparations had been going on for months and guests had been arriving since the end of November. Sayajirao attended the opening reception on the first day. After the party, George mounted a white horse and processed for five miles through orderly lines of 200,000 onlookers. The obediently cheering crowds looked in vain for their King: they had expected to see him wearing a crown and mounted majestically on an elephant – in Indian eyes the only mode of transportation fit for a king – but George had refused to ride an elephant and was sensibly protected from the sun by a sober grey-banded sola topi. He told Lord Hardinge later that he was disappointed not to have been applauded by his subjects. Hardinge recorded smugly in his diary that at least the crowds had had no trouble recognizing him: 'At the same time as I passed along the people cheered and I could hear them say, "There is the Lord Sahib, but where is the King?"'

Events were arranged for the purdah ladies, too. Chimnabai attended a purdah party given for Queen Mary in the garden of the Red Fort in the centre of old Delhi. Attentive as usual to her clothes and jewellery, Chimnabai thought carefully about what to wear. The Maharani wanted, recorded Miss Tottenham, according to her customarily naïve interpretation of Chimnabai's motives, 'to wear jewellery which in taste and value would do special honour to the West, of which the Queen was the great representative' and so she selected just two strings of the magnificent Baroda pearls. At the party, an Indian woman, 'decked out with bright and showy cheap stones in filigree-gold setting', reproached Chimnabai for her simplicity. 'Is this nothing?' replied Chimnabai proudly, knowing her pearls were worth more than any other decoration in the room.

Later, she was delighted to be told by an Englishwoman who had accompanied the Queen to the reception how impressed Mary was by her taste and discrimination in not covering herself with jewels like her less sophisticated countrywomen.

The issue of clothing, as important for Sayajirao on this occasion as for Chimnabai, reveals the depth of the cultural differences between the British and their Indian subjects. Indians thought wearing shoes indoors polluted a clean house; the British thought bare feet were dirty. British people bared their heads as a mark of respect while Indians covered them. Confusion was compounded by the fact that there were no guidelines for Indians in European dress: if Sayajirao wore white tie without a pugree he was considered rude, though a British man would never have dreamed of wearing a hat with evening dress. Saris reveal a woman's waist, which appalled Victorian ideas of propriety; European evening gowns, exposing the bosom, horrified Indians.

The British were not thought to wash enough; dancing with partners was horrifying; eating with implements, while in a chair, went against every Indian religious and cultural convention. Chimnabai was sophisticated enough to be amused rather than shocked to see on the mantelpiece of the wife of the Governor-General of Bombay brass pots used in Indian lavatories. There was almost no common ground on these basic issues, and customs which seemed completely matter-of-course to one group were inexplicable, and often highly offensive, to the other.

The uproar over Sayajirao's 'inadequate' bow to George V in the main ceremony was aggravated by the fact that the Maharaja was known to sympathize with anti-British activists and had turned a blind eye to their presence in Baroda. K. G. Deshpande, an official in the Baroda Revenue Department, had founded a nationalist school and printing press in Baroda in 1907. The attempted assassins of Lord and Lady Minto in Ahmedabad in 1909 were former students of this school, but Sayajirao had refused to dismiss Deshpande.

Over the first decade of the twentieth century, the mood of Indian resistance to British rule had changed. The reasonable,

[Shivaji] attempt to disguise their violent hostility to British rule in India.'

Miss Tottenham, who watched the durbar ceremony, insisted that Sayajirao's only faults had been absentmindedness and concern that his son, Dhairyashil, to whom he had given his necklace, should shine on such a momentous day. He did not feel the need for ostentation, she said, when the King-Emperor was so magnificent; and, having spent so much time in European society, he knew glittering jewels marked a maharaja as little more than a painted savage. 'Dearly was the Maharajah of Baroda to pay for his "civilisation".' As for the unemphatic bow, it was only a 'bad moment': he was just in a muddle. Sayajirao's official biographer, in 1928, toed the same line. Sayajirao had forgotten to put on the Star of India, that was all, and the 'mental disturbance' caused by the Statham divorce case was getting to him. No disrespect was intended.

The Aga Khan made no effort to sugar-coat his friend's behaviour. He said Sayajirao resented having to bow publicly to George V, and consequently paid his uneasy homage casually and haphazardly, shocking everyone, British and Indian. For his part, King George 'felt sore' about the incident for years, though he accepted Sayajirao's apology.

Sayajirao's great-grandson, and his most recent biographer, says that Sayajirao's long-serving dewan, Sir V. T. Krishnamachary, told him Sayajirao had 'categorically stated that he had intentionally dressed and behaved in the manner he did' and offered his apology to Hardinge knowing 'the intended damage had been done'. This may have been just post factum bravado, but it is corroborated by Sayajirao's sustained bitterness towards the rigid Hardinge. When the Viceroy returned to England in 1915, Sayajirao refused to see him off in Bombay, as was customary, and sent after him a telegram reading, 'BON VOYAGE. MAY INDIA NEVER SEE THE LIKE OF YOU AGAIN.'

It would take years for Sayajirao to repair the damage done on that day in Delhi. Back in Baroda, his Resident, Henry Cobb, took the opportunity to spell out to him in a tense interview the implications of his 'disloyalty'. Sayajirao showed, Cobb reported, 'genuine alarm' and protested that he and Chimnabai had had dinner with Madame Cama in Paris only because they had been promised Indian food. According to Cobb, the Maharaja thanked him heartily for his warning; he had not realized, apparently, just how seriously the British viewed his uncooperative attitude.

His confidence badly shaken, Baroda did take Cobb's advice. Deshpande was sacked. Sayajirao wrote a series of letters to Sir George Clarke, Governor-General of Bombay, early in 1912, expressing loyalty, and appealing for Clarke's help in changing people's false impression of him. There's even a rare letter from Chimnabai, thanking Sir George and Lady Clarke for seeing her at Government House. 'It is always satisfactory to have a personal explanation,' she concluded cryptically; there is no indication of who made the explanation, or what it was about. Chimnabai's writing-paper was putty-coloured, with the address, 'Bombay, Gajendra-Gad' embossed in silver on the top right, and a delicate, apparently hand-painted, red and jewelled gold crown above a curved silver sword with a tiny gold hilt and the initials G, S and R entwined on a silver shield on the left.

Sayajirao also issued, under Government of India pressure, the statement against 'sedition' he had been resisting for the past decade. The words must have stuck in his throat:

The interests of Native States are inseparably bound with those of British India, and all persons who conspire to subvert the Government in the one, offend equally against the other. The maintenance of the cherished relations of true friendship and good understanding which have uniformly existed between the Baroda State and the British Government has unceasingly claimed my anxious attention, and the preservation of peace and order and the advancement of the material, intellectual and moral well-being of my people, which has been the constant aim of my life, are dependant on the maintenance of those cordial relations; and any attempt within the limits of this State to disturb those relations will meet with my entire disapproval and will be impressed with a firm hand.

All their efforts were, for a while, an uphill struggle. British opinion was largely against them. Crowds hissed in London theatres when Sayajirao appeared on screen in the cinematograph of the Durbar. The *Pall Mall Gazette* reported in February 1912 that their son, aged fourteen (their youngest son was in fact nineteen and no longer at school) refused at first to bow to the Queen when she visited his school, 'and when forced to do so by his tutors behaved in a manner worthy of his sire'.

But not everyone's sympathies were with the King and Hardinge. 'I cannot say I thought he was judiciously treated', said Lord Minto, Hardinge's predecessor as viceroy, noting that the well-respected Maharajas of Gwalior and Bikaner had pleaded his case, and that people were 'predisposed to expect a disloyal attitude from him'. Other English friends emphasized that 'discontent is not sedition'. The socialist founder of the Labour party, Keir Hardie, hijacking the debate to support his own argument, hotly defended Sayajirao in the *Pioneer*. Hardie described Baroda as a 'calm, sedate well-built man in the white robe of a bearer, who moved about with native dignity, doing all that was required of him as a gentleman but remembering always that his country is in the dust with the heel of the foreigner on her neck, and refusing to add to her oppression by kissing the foot of the oppressor'. Sayajirao must have been grateful for Hardie's support, whatever he felt about his immaculate court outfit being described as bearer's robes.

The Cooch Behars had travelled to England in May 1911 on the recommendation of Nripendra's doctor and the Maharaja entered a nursing home for a course of Nauheim treatment, with Sunity there too as companion for him; his illness had brought them back together. But the cure was ineffective, and Nripendra developed pneumonia that he could not shake off. His heart and kidneys were no longer strong. As the months wore on he grew thinner and, though his mind was clear, he was too frail to walk or drive in the sea air at Bexhill which it had been hoped would improve his condition. During his last two months the family was gathered together at his bedside, trying not to give in to tears in front of him, urging him to take a mouthful of food or a sip of barley-water. A few days before he died he asked Sunity, sitting at his bedside, what her plans were.

'My plans are your plans,' she replied. 'When you are better we shall return home.'

'I know my plans and I should like you to make your plans,' he told her gently.

The end was very close. He spoke to each of his sons. On the evening of 18 September 1911, Nripendra died peacefully, with a gentle smile on his face, surrounded by his children and holding his wife's hands. The cause of death was given as arteriosclerosis and a dilated heart. Outside on Bexhill pier, the band of the Rifle Brigade struck up a funereal march.

George V ordered a grand military funeral for his loyal servant, with the rites due not to an Indian maharaja but to a British colonel: even in death Nripendra's allegiance was to the Empire first. In Bexhill, the coffin was draped in a Union Jack, with Nripendra's helmet and sword placed on top of the flag, and guarded the night before the funeral by the Royal Sussex Regiment. The next morning Rajey – now Maharaja – clad in the ivory, blue and gold of the Imperial Cadet Corps, led the long procession of mourners from the seafront to the station at Bexhill. His father's coffin was drawn by six horses to the strains of Chopin's *Marche Funèbre*. The shop-windows and houses they passed had their blinds down and the town's flags were all flying at half-mast. Dense banks of local mourners lined the route, attesting to Nripendra's local popularity; Bexhill's Mayor walked in the procession. Three motorcars bearing flowers followed behind.

The coffin travelled to Victoria in a special funeral car and, on its arrival in London, headed a cortège of mourning carriages to Golders Green crematorium. Hindus are always cremated; despite their flirtation with British culture, nothing would have persuaded Nripendra or Sunity to refuse that final rite. The service at Golders Green was a Brahmo one, and the eulogy was delivered by Sunity's brother, praising Nripendra for his principal characteristic, love of his fellow man. Nripendra's favourite saying, said Profulla Sen, was

'God is love' and with him, these were never empty words. A trembling Rajey, struggling to control his grief, said a final prayer over his father's coffin, his hand raised in a salute. 'In the name of God, the Almighty Father, I commit these last remains of my beloved father to your keeping. That in him which is immortal will always live, the mortal dies and perishes in the flame. God keep and bless him in Your holy care.'

In Cooch Behar, a procession of mourners walked barefoot through the town in Nripendra's memory; his favourite elephant accompanied them, tears streaming down its wrinkled cheeks.

Dedicating a fountain in Bexhill to his father's memory two years later, Jit spoke movingly of Nripendra's endearing personality, his efforts 'to bring the East and West together', and his achievement in bringing 'the little known State of Cooch Behar into such prominence'. To his mother he expressed the simple, fatalistic faith that sustained him during his grief. 'We may think Father has gone too soon. He was young and strong and many lives depended on him, but God is merciful and God knows best. If God loves us he would not do anything that would hurt us. It is all for the best, and we must believe it.'

On 13 January 1912 – twelve days before Indira Gaekwad was due to marry the Maharaja of Gwalior in Baroda – Rajey was installed as the new Maharaja of Cooch Behar. In a dramatic and unprecedented move, at his own request, he rode on elephant-back through the capital's streets so that every one of his subjects could see him face to face. He dismissed his unpopular dewan, and insisted on being installed according to Brahmo rites, declaring he did not recognize caste distinctions.

Every honour was paid to Sunity Devi: at Rajey's first annual durbar, he ordered the tributes of paan, attar and flowers to be laid at her feet. At his second durbar, he told her he would not live to see another. 'How thoughtful he was, how loving, how devoted,' said Sunity. 'And yet there was always something sad about him. He seemed more like a prince out of some old legend than a modern young ruler.'

★

Private concerns dating from the Durbar of 1911 had proven as troubling for Sayajirao and Chimnabai Gaekwad as public events. By the spring of 1913, they had been forced to take their daughter, Indira, to Europe to prevent her running away with Prince Jitendra of Cooch Behar; for her part, after two years of passionate clandestine correspondence, the Princess was more determined than ever that she would marry no one but Jit.

In defiance of her parents' continued opposition to the match, Indira was preparing for her new life. As if to underline the dramatic break she intended to make, the new clothes she was buying for her makeshift trousseau were European instead of Indian, much to Chimnabai's displeasure: tight-fitted coats and skirts and small, brightly coloured cloche hats. As the family toured Europe's spas, Indira, abetted by her maid, continued to receive mysterious telegrams and letters.

In St Moritz, the Barodas' family doctor, who had travelled with them from India, nervously said, 'I hear the Cooch Behar family are at some place down the line. More than that, there are two men, known to belong to that State, staying in Room 121 here!' The following week, Miss Tottenham was sitting with Indira in her room when a small box arrived for her, bearing on it the words, 'The Princess of Baroda. From Room 121'. It contained two sets of underclothes. Miss Tottenham was appalled. 'My friends think I might need some more undies on my way to them from this hotel,' said Indira calmly.

This was the deciding incident. It was clear now, eighteen months after Indira had first broken off her engagement to Gwalior, that she would marry no one but Jitendra. The only way to prevent her eloping with him – or worse – was to consent to the match. There would be no dowry, though; and neither Sayajirao nor Chimnabai wished to attend the wedding or give it their blessing. Indeed, until the last minute they hoped Rajey – Jit's elder brother, the Maharaja of Cooch Behar, who was seriously ill in a nursing home – would die in time to stop Indira marrying Jit. She might run away with a younger son, they reasoned, but surely no maharaja would marry another maharaja's daughter without his approval.

Indira was sent to London in the charge of Miss Tottenham after bidding her unresponsive mother an emotional farewell. Bursting into tears, Indira knelt at her mother's feet, stammering muffled words of remorse and regret. Chimnabai managed to control herself until her daughter left the room and then sank, weeping uncontrollably, into a chair.

The two mysterious men from Room 121 were also on the platform of St Moritz station, and when Indira received a note on the train she brightened visibly. 'I can see you from my carriage every now and then,' she read. 'Cheer up, Childie. You will soon be with Jit . . . This train is shaking so. With love and a big kiss . . .'

Indira and Miss Tottenham travelled across Europe in the summer of 1913 apparently unaware of the militarization escalating around them as the brinkmanship leading up to the First World War intensified. London, said Miss Tottenham, 'tingled that August with the thrill of what some of the papers called "Indian Princess's Romance". Reporters thronged the hotel lobbies . . . Britain [was] agog.' 'Indians were rare in England and the saree was still strange enough to attract considerable attention,' remembered Rashid Ali Baig, the son of Indira's host in London. 'Indira Devi, in any case, attracted more than attention, for to describe her beauty as ravishing would by no means be using an overworked cliché. Reporters flocked to our home, endless photographs were taken and we small boys lived in a haze of reflected glory.'

Before the wedding could take place, its legality needed to be secure, and a settlement had to be drawn up to protect 'the premier Princess of India, who was giving up everything' for love. Fearing Indira would rebel against these delays, the Barodas had given Miss Tottenham formal permission physically to restrain her charge from taking matters into her own hands. An unusual agreement was apparently reached 'by which the Princess becomes immediately after marriage possessed of all the Prince's revenue and property and he is dependent on her for everything'. According to their daughter, this is untrue, but Sayaji did obtain for his daughter an allowance of a lakh (1,00,000) of rupees a year. On 23 August *The Times* announced that the arrangements for Jit and Indira's marriage had been concluded, and that the wedding would take place the following week. 'We understand that the circumstances in both families have made it necessary to celebrate the marriage as quietly as possible.'

The night before her wedding Indira wrote movingly to her father, from whom she had received a heavily insured parcel containing a pair of diamond gypsy earrings. 'She assured him of her desire to be worthy as his daughter, and again of her devotion and her appreciation of all he had ever done for her; and she begged him not to be indifferent to her. She also expressed the hope that he would forgive her, and some day receive her and Jit.' Miss Tottenham had to urge her to write to her mother, reminding Indira of how much she loved her and how tender her heart was underneath it all. Indira burst into tears and picked up her pen again.

The morning of 25 August dawned unseasonably dull. When Miss Tottenham came into her room to wake her, Indira was reading the chapters marked for her in the Brahmo manual by Jit's mother, Sunity Devi. 'The religion seems to me a very pure form of our own,' Indira said. 'I think my heart will be quite honest when I have to say in the initiation ceremony that I renounce any other faith. I haven't got any faith, you know, really, and this seems good.'

The first ceremony of the day was Indira's initiation into the Brahmo faith. Sunity Devi had left Rajey in a rest-home in Cromer where he was undergoing a cure for alcoholism. In a white and gold silk sari, she arrived at the hotel just before 10 a.m. In the drawing room there, to the mournful song of conch shells and enveloped in the rich spicy scent of incense, Sunity welcomed Indira into her faith. Afterwards the eager Jit, wearing a dark-grey lounge suit and a straw boater, drew up outside in a motorcar filled with white lilies and chrysanthemums.

At noon, Miss Tottenham accompanied Indira, slight and girlish in a gown and matching toque of rose du Barry moiré silk trimmed with white lace, to Paddington registry office where Jit and Sunity Devi were waiting for them. There the couple were married according to British civil rites. A photograph they sent out later as a 'wedding souvenir' on a white card tied with narrow silver ribbon shows them awkwardly holding hands and looking into the camera, Jit suspiciously, Indira uncharacteristically meek. On their arrival back at the hotel, bride and groom changed into Indian clothes – an old-gold sari for Indira and a slate-blue achkan for Jit – for the Brahmo blessing during which their joined hands were wreathed with white flowers.

The whole party then sat down for a wedding breakfast at a table laden with red and white flowers, and Indira's face glowed with joy as she showed her husband and Miss Tottenham a telegram she had just received from her father, wishing her 'all happiness and a steady good life of usefulness'. Even at his daughter's moment of personal fulfilment, Sayajirao's thoughts were of duty and responsibility. But there was no word from proud Chimnabai.

After everything, Jit did not begrudge for a moment his efforts to win Indira which, he said, called to his mind the title of a popular book, *Across the World for a Wife*. '*Tant mieux*! A drink at the end of a strenuous game is the more acceptable.' That evening, the newlyweds motored down to Maidenhead for their honeymoon, a time, according to Jit, 'of perfect joy, of happiness, and bliss'.

Three days after the wedding Miss Tottenham returned to St Moritz, where Maharani Chimnabai anxiously awaited every detail of the past weeks and her 'lost' daughter. Though she wept on seeing Miss Tottenham, the Maharani was coaxed into a smile by tales of the detectives posted at Cromer to report back on Rajey's health, and was pleased by how discreetly *The Times* had presented the Barodas' attitude to the match. Her resolution not to see Indira again was unchanged.

Three weeks after Jit and Indira were married, Rajey died of pleurisy caused by alcoholism. They rushed from their honeymoon to his bedside in Cromer. At Rajey's funeral, it was a sombrely suited Jit who placed his hand on the coffin and recited the final prayer. Jit became Maharaja of Cooch Behar, with Indira his maharani.

Rajey's last illness had begun when he caught ptomaine poisoning (severe food poisoning) in Calcutta six months earlier. Desperately worried about her son, who continued pale, melancholic and obviously ill, Sunity Devi accompanied him to England that May. In London they separated, Sunity to the Cadogan Hotel where she stayed with Girlie and Baby, and Rajey and his staff to the Curzon Hotel. 'I seldom got news of him,' Sunity remembered. 'I do not know who to blame for this, but it made me miserable at the time.'

From London, Rajey went to the Derby on a freezing, rainy day and caught a cold which turned into a fever. Admitted to a nursing home, he told Sunity his days were numbered. 'I know my time has come. Do you remember, mother dear, how all the fortune tellers have said I shall not live to be thirty-two?' Sunity Devi, remembering the prophecies, was just as unnerved: palmists over the years had only ever seen a short life-line, and no marriage-line, on his hand. Rajey died a few months later in another nursing home in Cromer, where it had been hoped the sea air would be good for him. His only wish was that he could have died in Cooch Behar.

His ashes were sent back to India and placed in the marble mausoleum built in a rose garden on the banks of the Torsa river, beside his father's. The memorials stand near a ruined summer house where the ranis of Cooch Behar used to bathe, and where Nripendra had his early lessons; from there the snowy peaks of the Himalayas can be seen far off in the distance, and sweet-scented roses and lilies bloom.

Indira and Jit postponed their return to India after their wedding and Rajey's funeral. Though the new maharani's parents made no effort to see her while they were in London in the autumn of 1913, her favourite brother, Dhairyashil, braved their disapproval to visit Indira. Miss Tottenham would have liked to see her too, but, because 'the Cooch Behars still felt keenly the "snubs" they said they had received prior to the marriage', did not. Knowing Chimnabai's current frame of mind, she was glad Chimnabai did not unexpectedly encounter Indira in the theatre or out shopping, a favourite pastime of both mother and daughter.

Jit bought Indira a 7-inch brown sealskin motor case with silver-gilt fittings, engraved with 'Babs', one of his nicknames for her, and a silver-gilt hairbrush in a matching case; the set cost £24 8s 3d. He was a man unafraid of romantic gestures: for their four-month anniversary, Jit gave his wife a tiny blue enamel airmail envelope engraved inside 'August 25th – December 25th Love from Jit'. Now in the possession of their granddaughter, it still contains a browned scrap of paper perhaps 2 by 3 inches, reading in Jit's pencilled handwriting, 'To the cutest little thing that breathed on God's earth. May there be many more of these monthy [*sic*] celebrations All my love Jboy.'

The newlyweds sailed for India just before the Barodas in October 1913. The arrival in Cooch Behar the following month of the new maharaja and maharani in an open motorcar, to the haunting sound of conch shells, the traditional Bengali welcome for a bride, ended purdah there – except, as their daughter points out, in the tigerskin-carpeted billiard room.

Purdah was abolished in Baroda when the Maharaja and Maharani returned from Europe in the autumn of 1913, a few months after their daughter Indira's marriage. As the saloon train drew up at the palace's private station in Baroda, Sayajirao turned to Chimnabai, who was waiting beside him for his instructions, and said, 'Oh, you just come with me.' Usually, when the train came to a halt, Chimnabai would have descended from it, heavily veiled and behind a screen, and got into a curtained carriage for the short ride to the palace, while her husband greeted the officials waiting on the red carpet to meet him and then drove home in an open carriage.

This time, for the first time, an unveiled Chimnabai followed her husband into the public gaze of his people. Bowing and smiling, Sayajirao stepped out of the train on to the platform; Chimnabai, also bowing and smiling, was right behind him. They climbed into an open carriage-and-four for the short drive back to Laxmi Vilas. Chimnabai's aunt, who had boarded the train at the station from a purdah carriage to welcome them home and had never before been out in public, was an astonished participant in this historic moment. She told Chimnabai later that 'she was absolutely blind with nervousness, she saw nothing, she looked at nobody, she just watched my heels in front of her!'

Centuries of purdah were over in Baroda. Its demise had been gradual. Sayajirao had waited to remove purdah 'till women are able to understand the change and know how to treat others'. As with other advances that were radical in Indian eyes, he recognized the need for an almost imperceptible initial change in attitude before any public demonstration could be made. Chimnabai's 1911 book, *The Position of Women in Indian Life*, had quoted Sir Francis Bacon on this subject: 'It were good that men in their innovations would follow the example of Time itself, which, indeed, innovateth greatly, but quietly, and by degrees scarce to be perceived . . .'

Although Baroda was one of the first states to break with purdah, opinion across India was moving into line with Sayajirao and Chimnabai's thinking. Before Curzon's durbar in 1903, Nripendra Cooch Behar told Sunity Devi she could only attend the ceremonies out of purdah, even though most of the other Indian women there, such as the ruling Begum of Bhopal, would be veiled and cloistered, and even though she herself lived in purdah in their state of Cooch Behar. 'Unless I was given my rightful position by his side,' she recalled, 'he would not take me.' That year, too, the Raja of Nabha told a British official how important it was that high-born Indian girls be educated and emancipated. 'We educate our sons, teach them English and Western ideas, and then marry them to girls who have had no education. The result will be a breed of mules.'

Middle-class Indian women whose prosperous husbands took them abroad had also learned new freedoms, and hoped to continue to enjoy them on their return home. 'I have been with my husband to England,' recalled one of the women interviewed in *Mother India* in 1929.

While we were there he let me leave off purdah, for women are respected in England. So I went about freely, in streets and shops and galleries and gardens and to the houses of friends, quite comfortable always. No one frightened or disturbed me and I had much interesting talk with gentlemen as well as ladies. Oh, it was wonderful – a paradise! But here – there is nothing. I must stay within the zenana, keeping strict purdah, as becomes our rank, seeing no one but the women and my husband. We see nothing. We know nothing. We have nothing to say to each other. We quarrel. It is *dull*.

Chimnabai's desire to break down purdah played a huge part in persuading Sayajirao to make this change. ' "You talk about the emancipation of women and this and that and yet we are all put in purdah," ' one of her granddaughters recalls her saying to him. ' "Whether you will allow me or not, I am going to give it up." And she did give it up, although she always insisted that unmarried girls were not to be taken into public places and that when men came – particularly Maratha men – we should cover our heads with our saris.' This sensitivity to custom was typical of the Barodas' approach to the changing times. Out of respect for the stricter religious practices of their friend, the Maharaja of Mysore, Chimnabai and Indira seldom rode and never hunted when they visited his state, although both participated openly in these sports in Baroda and England. When more orthodox friends such as the Mysores or the Kashmirs visited Baroda, purdah was observed for their sake.

Three days after they returned to Baroda in 1913, Chimnabai appeared in public at a garden party at the palace. She accompanied her husband to a gymkhana in the British cantonment, and sat beside him at a prize-giving ceremony at the High Court. In 1915, arriving at the annual Nag Panchmi festival, Chimnabai descended from her painted elephant unveiled. When the ceremony was over, 'she drove away in a four-in-hand through the city in a most unpurdah fashion!' commented Miss Tottenham, who thoroughly approved of the new practice and enthusiastically tutored the more adventurous of Baroda's ladies in English.

Encouraged by Sayajirao, Chimnabai even began to play tennis in public. Tennis was one of her passions: she played every morning at 7.30, before her piano lesson (another passion) with Miss Tottenham. Monkeys plagued the brand-new asphalt courts at Laxmi Vilas. Ball boys wore green and gold uniforms, the men wore flannels and Chimnabai wore her sari. Beneath spreading, shady trees beside the courts stood tables laden with cool drinks and cigarettes for weary players. Chimnabai also loved roller-skating, an early twentieth-century craze, and used to zoom along the palace's long, peach-coloured marble corridors between the men's and women's quarters, her sari flying out like a flag behind her.

Despite Chimnabai's example, purdah lingered on in some parts of India until well after Independence. In some cases it declined gradually, simply fading away; in others, a sudden event precipitated it, sometimes surprising even those involved. The behaviour of the princes and their wives was crucial to the changing customs in India's strictly hierarchical society. Without royal examples, the deferential middle and lower classes would not have contemplated such a radical departure from centuries of tradition. The Maharani of Kutch was still in purdah in 1950 when the President of India, Radha Krishnan, visited Kutch. As the Maharani came out of the palace towards her curtained car, the President invited her to join him in his car. It would have been rude to refuse his request, so she climbed into his car and, then and there, ended purdah in her husband's state.

In August 1914, Chimnabai and Miss Tottenham were in the spa town of Carlsbad, dieting (or 'reducing', as they called it) when England declared war on Austria. Archduke Franz Ferdinand, heir to the Austrian throne, had been killed by a Serb nationalist on 28 June 1914. A month later Austria invaded Serbia; Russia responded, provoking Germany, which in turn provoked France and England. All over Europe, 'General Staffs, goaded by their relentless timetables, were pounding on the tables for the signal to move lest their opponents gain an hour's head start.'

Together with other guests at the Savoy Hotel, Chimnabai and her attendants were stranded in Carlsbad while diplomatic negotiations stalled over how to return foreign nationals to their home countries. One night, angry, violent crowds stormed the hotel gates demanding the arrest of the Savoy's French chefs, and baying for the hotel's French and Russian guests. Chimnabai stood unseen in the shadows on her balcony, watching the mob rehearse for war.

The next day the Maharani redoubled her efforts to get from Austria to Sayajirao in Switzerland, but permits and safe-conducts were increasingly hard to come by. When they set out two weeks later, clutching hastily arranged currency and papers from the Austrian Foreign Minister and the Governor of Carlsbad, they had to return to Carlsbad because the German officers on the border with Austria argued that 'India is British Dominion, therefore the

Maharani is British, therefore she is against us . . .' Unbeknown to them, the Maharaja of Baroda, along with the other Indian princes, had just publicly offered all his state's resources to the British war effort; the German soldiers knew exactly what a maharani was. They were lucky they did not get through.

Finally, after they had been stranded for nearly a month, the capable, diplomatic manager of the Savoy took their predicament in hand. He instructed them to leave all the preparations to him and to follow his orders to the letter; he would arrange for two cars and drivers he could vouch for to take the Maharani and her party to Zurich via Linz and Innsbruck.

Miss Tottenham woke early on the morning of 24 August and supervised the packing of the two cars. Into one went Mrs Burrows, the housekeeper, carrying Chimnabai's jewels in an old canvas bag, the clerk Ambergaokar, and Chimnabai's maid, Yumna. They carried their money in a battered tin box. Chimnabai's car, in which she and Miss Tottenham travelled, was piled high with 'tins of benzine [fuel], provisions, bottles of soda water, dressing-cases, cushions, rugs, books and papers'. Their suitcases, strapped to the back of the motors, were carefully wrapped up in brown paper. Herr Aulich, the hotel manager, saw them off with a huge bunch of pink roses, and the distinctly discomfiting words, 'Do not turn back.'

It was a glorious, unwarlike, late-summer day. Rowan trees, heavy with red berries, overhung the roads. At the beginning of August, the Kaiser had promised his young soldiers, departing for the front, that they would be 'home before the leaves have fallen from the trees'. The harvest was being brought in by the very old and the very young. In Pilsen, a regiment of cackling geese ran angrily at the cars across the cobble-stoned streets, wings out-stretched; near Budweis Chimnabai saw wild duck on a lake, and longed for her gun.

They reached Linz at dusk. There they waited what seemed like an age for their papers to be approved, but eventually their imperturbably smiling guide returned to the cars and said they could continue to Gmunden. They drove on another four hours, through village after village guarded by bayonet-bearing soldiers, before they reached Gmunden. The following day they drove until midnight again, through the mountains to Innsbruck, where posters plastered throughout the town proclaimed that the road to Paris was open – Namur had fallen. They rushed on towards the Swiss border.

As they neared the frontier, at yet another passport check, Miss Tottenham asked the courier selected by Herr Aulich if he needed the 'open order' given to her by the Governor of Carlsbad. ' "*Nein, nein!*" ' he replied. ' "I have got you through the police on these," ' and with a somewhat roguish look he put into my hands the individual passports duly visaed [stamped] at each big town where we had been obliged to stop. I glanced over them,' Miss Tottenham continued, 'then nearly choked with hilarious laughter. The whole party, including myself, was written down as WEST INDIANS FROM SOUTH AMERICA.'

When the story was explained to Chimnabai, she sat silent and affronted as the cars climbed the last few miles through the Tyrol to Feldkirch. That explained why the expensively crested luggage had been so carefully covered up, and why they had so easily managed to get as far from Carlsbad as they had. The courier – perhaps on Herr Aulich's instructions, but no one knew – had paid the clerk at Carlsbad five kroner to describe the party thus: 'the police did not know the difference between East and West Indies, and South America was neutral'. Presently Chimnabai began to shake with silent, irrepressible laughter.

By the time they reached Switzerland, Sayajirao had arrived in London, and they faced a new challenge: crossing France, immobilized in preparation for Germany's invasion. They got to Lyons, and were forced to wait there for a night before they could get a seat on a train to Paris. A train full of pitiful, wounded soldiers passed through Lyons while they were there.

War brought a series of uncomfortable firsts for Chimnabai: her maids shared her carriage and, while the bulk of her baggage, much against her better judgement, crossed Europe separately with a clerk, she helped load her own cases on to the train. 'What would your ladies in Baroda say if they could see Your Highness doing this?' asked Miss Tottenham, as she handed a heavy suitcase up to Chimnabai on the train. 'They will cry when I tell them!' she responded, grasping the bag more firmly.

Paris was silent and empty, its shops and restaurants closed, its windows boarded up. Only a few newspapers were still in print and their single-page issues adorned bare kiosks. Allied flags hung in clusters as the city awaited invasion. Chimnabai reached Galeries Lafayette just before it shut its doors and bought a supply of silk stockings.

Amazingly, their luggage from Carlsbad, transported separately, had reached the Ritz in Paris and was dispatched to London. The hotel was putting its furniture into storage and the best it could do for breakfast was thin coffee and coarse bread. In the lobby, British soldiers just flown in from Compiègne discussed their four-day defeat in the Battle of the Frontiers, the first engagement of the war, in sad, angry voices. Guns boomed in the distance, and the Germans were said to be within 30 miles of the capital as the French Army retreated in front of them.

The train they boarded from Paris to Le Havre, according to the porter, also carried documents from the Banque de France, hidden in dress-boxes. At junctions, they passed gaily swagged and gar-landed trains filled with fresh-faced English and French soldiers on their way to the front, unaware of what awaited them. By the time they reached Le Havre at 2.15 a.m. the steamer to England had gone, and there were no tickets to be had for almost a week. Hundreds of motorcars abandoned by fleeing Belgians stood beside the quay. Meanwhile, the Germans marched on towards the coast, Le Havre was being evacuated and there was talk of the town emptying its petrol supplies into the sea. Finally, room was found for them on a hospital ship, as the expected train full of wounded soldiers from the front had not arrived. They waited in South-ampton for the night mail train, arriving in London 'with the milk' to be met at Waterloo by the commissionaire of Claridges.

India responded to the Great War with almost unanimous patriotism. Even the then largely unknown pacifist Mohandas Gandhi raised an ambulance corps in Britain (as he had done in South Africa during the Boer War) at the start of the war and, on his return to India in 1915, refused to support further agitation for Home Rule during the hostilities. He trusted, as many Indian nationalists did, that after the war a grateful and victorious Britain would reward India with self-rule for her immense contribution to the war effort. As he put it, if India shared in the responsibilities of Empire – over 1 million Indians fought and 62,000 died in Britain's war – then it could expect, too, a share in its privileges.

The princes were especially fervent in their support for Britain. Many wanted to demonstrate their gratitude to the British for having created an India in which their states, wealth and influence were secure. Many also saw the war as an opportunity to revive their traditional martial role in the Empire's service. Sir Pratap Singh, aged seventy, was one of the first to arrive at the European front in the autumn of 1914, declaring, 'I wish to die leading my men, sword in hand.' For once, this support was reciprocal: the Maharaja of Bikaner was given a seat in Lloyd George's War Cabinet.

There was dissent as well as support. Fateh Singh, mighty Maharana of Udaipur, refused to support the British cause. 'When there is a fight in India, Europeans don't come here to die, so why should we send our Indians to die when Europeans fight?' Despite this, when peace was made he still received the GCIE (Grand Commander of the Indian Empire). 'It is the sort of thing that pattawallas [attendants] in offices wear,' he said. 'Put it on the horse. It looks better on the horse than the king.'

Sayajirao's loyal contribution to the war effort – more in the spirit of Gandhi than Pratap Singh – pleased the Government of India and helped restore confidence between Britain and Baroda. His Resident reported in 1916 that 'all his sympathies are with the British Empire in this war'. Baroda sent 150 cavalry horses to Europe and gave Rs 12,000 a month to the government; he also donated Jaya Mahal, his Bombay house high up on Malabar Hill, for use as an officers' hospital during the hostilities.

Relations improved still more after the war when the hated Hardinge, sped on his way by Sayajirao's telegram, was replaced as viceroy by Lord Chelmsford. Chelmsford made the first viceregal visit to Baroda since the Mintos ten years earlier. Chimnabai, whose disinclination to kowtow to Hardinge in Simla had caused comment in the Resident's report in October 1917, was delighted to show the Viceroy round Laxmi Vilas.

'After tea we showed him all the palace, and when he saw the long corridors and palm courts and the balconies, he was delighted,' she told Miss Tottenham. 'Twice he said, "I shall make my wife quite jealous!" And he said it a third time when I showed him my library, and my boudoir and my dressing room, and then our bedroom and the gold bedsteads. He was really impressed. Do you know,' she concluded triumphantly, 'I believe he had thought we were jungly people!'

Chelmsford, for his part, paid tribute to Baroda's impressive government, praising Sayajirao not just 'as a theorist or idealist, but as a practical administrator . . . By wise promotion of a system of political and social order, aiming at the combination of all that is best in Eastern and Western civilisation, the ruler of an Indian state may do much to show the path of progress to the peoples of India.'

At the same time, the Resident in Baroda filed a warm report in Sayajirao's favour, describing him as well liked and full of enthusiasm for the administration of his state and his people's welfare. 'The common belief that the Maharani is the dominant partner in the palace is incorrect,' Wilkinson added. 'She and the Gaekwad are often on bad terms and for days at a time live apart, but he is master in his own house.' This new cordiality was marked by Sayajirao's receipt of the GCIE (Grand Commander of the Indian Empire) in January 1919 and, the following spring, by the cessation of the post-durbar six-monthly reports on Sayajirao's attitude towards the British.

The year 1919 marked a turning point in Barodan–British affairs. It was also a critical moment for the British Government in India. Despite a devastating influenza epidemic and rising inflation, after the war many Indians were optimistic about the possibility of being given a greater degree of involvement in their government. These hopes were shattered in the Punjab, the Sikh heartland north of Delhi, in April 1919. In Amritsar, discontent with repressive British rule erupted into demonstrations and then riots, during which three Europeans were killed. The infamous General Dyer imposed martial law on the volatile city and when several thousand protesters gathered in a large enclosed garden in the city centre, he ordered his soldiers to open fire on them. An estimated 379 unarmed Indian civilians were killed and another 1,200 wounded.

Though the provincial Governor refused to condemn Dyer's massacre, Morley, the Secretary of State, insisted the General be sacked. Despite this official disapproval, Dyer returned home to a hero's welcome and a subscription of £26,000 raised by the readers of the *Morning Post*. But Indians were appalled. Nobel Prize-winner Rabindranath Tagore resigned the knighthood he had been granted in 1915, and, from his ashram near Ahmedabad, Mohandas Gandhi (whom Tagore dubbed Mahatma, or Great Soul) renounced his hopes for conciliation or cooperation with the British.

While Indian relations with the paramount power disintegrated, Chimnabai and Sayajirao continued to struggle with their sons; their disagreements over how best to deal with them were a major factor in the arguments the Baroda Resident had reported. In 1917, the youngest, Dhairyashilrao, was reduced to using his sister Indira, still estranged from her parents but now corresponding with them, as a mediator. Dhairyashil was 'selfish, egoistic . . . [with] no idea of his duties', responded Sayajirao, 'but I bear him no ill will'. The Anglicized Dhairyashilrao, for his part, found the idea of working in a Native State – even his own – abhorrent, reinforcing his father's opinion of him as a wastrel. In February 1920, with restrictions on Indian officers in the British and Indian armies just lifted, Sayajirao bought him a commission in the Indian Cavalry.

At least Dhairyashil did not drink. His eldest brother, Jayasinhrao, whose strong American accent was a legacy from his years at

Harvard, was charming and well liked, 'almost European at heart', but with 'little character or ability', according to Wilkinson, who clearly thought that referring to an Indian as 'almost European' was high praise indeed. But alcohol was rapidly destroying his health. In September 1919, on the recommendation of a doctor and 'mental specialist' in Bombay, Jayasinh was taken to England for medical treatment of insanity caused by delirium tremens.

High-spirited Shivaji, Chimnabai's favourite and the most passionately nationalistic of the three boys, was also an alcoholic. He was a born rebel: 'he inveighs against all authority (his father and Indian chiefs as well as British), thinks that whatever is is wrong, and is generally cross-grained and wrong-headed'. His poor relations with Sayajirao dated back many years; he considered beneath him the state work he was given, which disappointed Sayajirao, and left him bored and frustrated. He died of pneumonia in 1919.

Sayajirao believed that discipline and responsibility were the highest ideals to which humanity could aspire, but he could not persuade his sons to share his attitude. For their part, they dismissed him as not having been 'born royal', and scorned him for living for duty before pleasure. Since none of them would inherit the gaddi, what was the point in their serving the state?

This placed immense strain on the Barodas' marriage. Sayajirao, feeling saddened and let down, was unmoved by his sons' pleas for more money or advances on their allowance; Chimnabai, heart-broken by the feuding, felt isolated with her worries about them. During Shivaji's last illness Chimnabai asked Sayajirao's secretary what her husband was reading. A history of world religions, came the reply. Chimnabai asked the secretary what he thought his master's religion was. 'The Maharaja Sahib says he is an agnostic, that his religion is the service of humanity.' 'Humanity?' she responded bitterly. 'The man who has power and money does not know humanity.' And it is perhaps true that Sayajirao found mankind as an abstract concept easier to deal with than individuals – especially his own troublesome, troubled children.

That May, Sayajirao and Chimnabai escaped Baroda's summer

heat – and, perhaps, their worries – in Ootacamund, or Ooty, the southernmost (and, according to Miss Tottenham, the most beautiful) Indian hill-station. Their 'cottage' there, Woodstock, was like an English country house, surrounded by luxuriant gardens of roses, hollyhocks, sweet peas, heliotrope, geraniums, fuchsia, honeysuckle and forget-me-nots. Ooty sits in the Nilgiri, meaning blue hills, from the eucalyptus trees that forest them. The woods are interspersed with neatly clipped tea gardens and plantations of cardamom, cinnamon and chillies, and are home to sparkling trout streams, dramatic waterfalls and ravines and wild arum lilies. There, in the fresh mountain air, smart holidaymakers such as the Barodas played tennis and golf, rode and hunted, in pink coats, with the Ooty hounds, walked, fished and socialized at the Club.

From Ooty the Gaekwads drove south to Kerala, heading a small convoy of motors. Their Rolls led the procession, with another behind it to provide spares in case of a breakdown. Behind that followed their attendants, in a series of less well-sprung vehicles. At each village their cavalcade stopped to visit schools, hospitals and factories; bands welcomed them more enthusiastically than tunefully; they were hung with marigold garlands and watched processions of eager schoolchildren parading in their honour.

They stopped off for a shoot in the Venganad Hills, behind the Malabar coast. Carried up to their camp in manjils (hammocks suspended from long poles), they found a small chalet, with silk hangings on the walls and soft carpets covering the mud floor. Chimnabai shot a 9-foot-high elephant, from the ground rather than from a hide, as was the custom in the scrubby woods of Rajasthan, or aboard another elephant, the method in jungle areas such as Cooch Behar. Shooting from the ground was dangerous and required nerve as well as skill; only experienced shots dared attempt it. Two days later she took down a bull bison. A photograph shows her beside her kill in her sari, proudly holding her gun.

Finally, in Trivandrum, at the southernmost point of India, Mrs Raman Tampi addressed a speech to Chimnabai on behalf of the ladies of the town:

Your Highness's munificent contributions for the furtherance of education, your patient and selfless devotion to the cause of womankind, and the high and noble principles which guide you in your domestic and social life have written your name in our hearts in indelible characters. Sectarian considerations or geographical limitations do not circumscribe the sphere of your unostentatious beneficence.

As newly installed Maharaja of Cooch Behar, Jit faced tough financial decisions. In 1911, his father had left Rajey debts of nearly £37,000, owed to seventy-nine tradesmen, including £1,590 to Asprey's, and outstanding bills owed to Penhaligon the perfumers, the gun shop Holland & Holland and Rolls-Royce. In turn, on his death, Rajey bequeathed his debts to Jit. The entire family was in hock up to its eyeballs. The list of creditors reads like a catalogue of the family's interests: jewellers, bookshops, photographers; a billiard table manufacturer; the sports equipment maker Spalding; and Hilditch & Key, a Jermyn Street gentleman's shirtmaker and outfitter. Though the Calcutta-based nationalist newspaper *Amrita Bazaar Patrika* had called Cooch Behar 'almost as model a state as any in India' in September 1911, it was not large enough to sustain so many members of a royal family, all expecting to live in the grand style to which they were accustomed.

Though Sayajirao had tried to ensure before their wedding that Jit, if he became maharaja, would settle on Indira an allowance of Rs 1,00,000 a month, she was not even given pin-money at first. When she needed cash she had to ask an ADC for it. Eventually, a servant told Jit he must give his wife pocket money. The humiliation of this period of dependence stayed with her: she insisted that all her children have pocket money and learn how to budget it, and when her granddaughters were growing up she always emphasized to them the importance of having money of their own, 'so you don't have to ask your husband for money for sanitary towels'. Years later, Indira set up a trust for her grandchildren that they were not allowed to break until all four of them were over sixty. This, she explained, was to stop them from wasting the money – and their youth – on booze.

Very quickly, there was another person for Jit to provide for. Ila Devi was born in October 1914, her name suggested by Lord Carmichael, the Governor of Bengal, of whom the entire Cooch Behar family was fond. Indira asked him to suggest a name for her first daughter that began with 'I' and he proposed they call her 'it' in Latin, *illa*, thus neatly using her mother's initial and rhyming with her father's name.

For Indira's twenty-third birthday on 28 January 1915, Jit gave his wife a book of his own poetry, dedicated to her. It is a slim volume, bound in midnight-blue satin. On the title page is a black and white photograph of an uncharacteristically demure, sari-clad Indira, gazing pensively at a posy of roses in her lap. 'Wishing her very many happy returns of the day,' reads the handwritten inscription, 'and every happiness imaginable.'

The poems are blithe and witty in tone, full of private jokes and references, and divided between fond accounts of life in Cooch Behar and Darjeeling, a mock ode to the 'Coochy Lancers' and even a musing on the origins of the Great War, 'Quoth the Kaiser'. 'In Memoriam' praises Nripendra's memory; 'To Mother' is a Sunity-inspired account of religious awakening. The majority are addressed to Indira. 'All's Well That Ends Well' tells the story of their courtship, beginning,

> Once on India's coral strand
> > There lived a Princess fair;
> And many a chieftain sought her hand,
> > But ended in despair

'To "I"' describes the rapture Jit feels clasping his elusive bride in his arms ('Lips sweet and passionate, / Pressed close to mine, / Intoxicate me / Much more than wine!') and in 'Your Necklace' Jit expresses his desire to be Indira's necklace, lying on her bosom, and his jealousy at the thought of another 'clasping' her, his 'lawful prize'. 'Love's Uncertainty' is the second poem in the book, and gives some idea of Jit's light-heartedness and the dynamic of their relationship.

I gave my heart to a maiden fair,
With lustrous eyes and wavy hair:
Her love with every thought and care
                    I cherished!
Her happiness was all to me;
I thought she loved me tenderly.
And had she not, you clearly see
                    I perished.
But now I'm not so sure about
Her love, 'cept when her pretty pout
Dispels in toto every doubt
                    About her love for me.
Of course *I* love her as before,
And I would give the world and more,
If she'd give only half just for
                    Her husband T.O.T.

Ila's birth marked the first thaw in the coldness that had existed between Indira and Chimnabai since she eloped. Indira sent a telegram informing Ila's grandparents of her birth, and Chimnabai responded by sending a Maratha cook to Cooch Behar to make Indira the food she loved from her childhood.

It would be still two more years – and another baby's birth – before Chimnabai relented enough actually to respond to the many letters Indira had written her since running away with Jit four years earlier. Chimnabai, writing in 1917 from Baroda at Divali, the most family-oriented of the Hindu holidays, told of her own and Sayajirao's ill-health, the marriage of a granddaughter, Shivaji's wife Kamala's impending confinement, and anxiously asked about Dhairyashil, who was estranged from his parents in response to what he saw as Sayajirao's unreasonable demands on him, but kept in touch with his sister.

Though Sayajirao had seen Jit with Indira at the Princes' Conference in Delhi in 1916, and again in Bombay later that year, Chimnabai was not yet ready to embrace him: 'He has caused me too much pain. Wait!' she cautioned. It was not until six months later, on the neutral ground of the racecourse in Poona (a propitious place to encounter racing-mad Chimnabai, provided her horses were winning) that they were eventually reconciled.

By then, the almost inevitable grip of alcoholism had taken hold of Jit – only thirty-two in 1918, and with every blessing life could give him but temperance. The following February, having sought permission from the India Office to go abroad for the sake of his health, Jit, Indira and their three small children, Ila, Bhaiya and Indrajit (and a piano, a typewriter and a pram), sailed from Calcutta to Marseilles, and thence overland through Paris to London. They were back in England again the following spring, when Jit completed a cure at a Folkestone nursing home and, on 23 May, Indira gave birth to her second daughter, Ayesha.

Ayesha's real name was Gayatri – a good Hindu name containing the letter 'G' that the royal astrologers recommended – but when she was born Indira was deep in Rider Haggard's 1887 bestseller, *She. A History of Adventure*, and always called her Ayesha after the mysterious goddess at the heart of Haggard's novel. Valentine Castlerosse told the novelist William Gerhardi 'that Indira Cooch Behar was "She", straight out of Rider Haggard', and it is not difficult to trace elements of Indira's personal philosophy back to this book. 'Trust not to the future, for who knows what the future may bring!' was the fictional Ayesha's message. 'Therefore, live for the day, and endeavour not to escape the dust which seems to be man's end.' Ayesha was thus, from the first days of her life, cast in her mother's image as successor and, perhaps, rival.

In the early years of the 1910s, as Maharaja of Cooch Behar, unmarried Rajey had continued to accord his mother all the honours and dignities due to a principal maharani. 'Mother, your rooms will never be given to another woman while I live,' he had told her. 'They are always yours, and if I ever marry, I'll build a new palace.' One can almost hear the implicit reproach to Jit in Sunity's recollection of this promise in her 1922 autobiography, but Indira's arrival in Cooch Behar in 1913 meant that Sunity Devi was no longer the first lady there.

From then on, Sunity Devi spent most of her time in Calcutta and London, ethereally white-clad, writing sentimental Indian story books that she hoped would enlighten British readers about their far-off colony and inspire Indian women to lead better lives. She concluded her autobiography with the words: 'It is my great hope that before many years have passed Indian women will stand in their right place and once again India will cry aloud, "I am proud of my daughters."'

One book was a misty biography of the Buddha's wife, Yashodara, which incorporated Sunity's favourite themes of princely virtue, wifely devotion approaching martyrdom, and the parallel quests for true love and religious truth. Another was a collection of Bengali folk stories and vignettes of life in the forests of Cooch Behar. In Sunity's imagination, wives were always tender, children innocent, a tiger's roar thrilling and moonlight softly radiant.

Even her autobiography has a touch of the fairy-tale about it: Sunity Devi was eminently capable of rising above facts she preferred to ignore. Nripendra's infidelities and extravagances are brushed away; Pretty's estranged husband, Lionel Mander, is described as just 'appearing' devoted to her; Rajey's wayward attachment to Edna May is glossed over by the wish he would meet a girl of his own class. She even declared herself to be as fond of Indira 'as of my own daughters'.

The only reference to her children's tragic weakness for alcohol (she describes them simply as being 'ill') is an old legend Sunity relates, apropos of something else entirely. In the story, cholera-stricken villagers were told that putting a large stone statue of their god into the Ganges would lift the plague from them; but they could find no one strong enough to lift it. An old man dreamed that the god appeared to him and said his statue could be moved only by one pure in heart, who truly loved god. All the villagers tried in turn to lift it, but to no avail. Finally the local drunkard stumbled into the temple grounds and declared no one loved god better than he did. He lifted the statue as if it were a feather and carried it to the Ganges, his face pressed to its marigold-garlanded chest. 'The awe-stricken throng were speechless with amazement that a poor drunkard should be chosen to show them how, under a cloak of failings and frailties, there existed a heart which remained pure, and wherein was to be found "the invisible kingdom of God," which is all truth and all love.' My children may have suffered, was the message, but it was weakness rather than evil, and it may even have brought them closer to god.

Nine Ideal Indian Women was dedicated to Sunity's old friend Queen Alexandra. It told the lives of nine virtuous Indian princesses from history and mythology who were united by their self-sacrificing love for their husbands and their fatalistic resignation to adversity. One of her heroines – her namesake, Sunity – was typically innocent, unworldly and beautiful as she was brought out before her prospective husband – much, no doubt, like the real Sunity in 1878. She entered her father's court

with child-like obedience and simplicity . . . [and] like a rare flower glided to the foot of the throne. The golden border of her sari blended artistically with its rich texture, while the clinging folds of the soft silk hid and revealed the beauty of her maiden form. Her head was slightly bent, and the delicate, high-bred face looked somewhat serious and the tremulous lips betrayed that the facing of so many eyes was an ordeal to her . . . Costly rubies and pearls clasped her beautiful neck and wrists, and the tiny gold bells on her anklets made a delightful tinkle as she walked forward.

The prince who had come to marry her was enraptured: 'He thought her voice was the sweetest music he had ever heard, and that her face framed in the silken sari, was like a pure white lotus floating in a lake of limpid green water.'

But the idealized world Sunity Devi created in these books was a far cry from the way life turned out for her and her children. The temptation to judge her refusal to address her husband's infidelity and her children's tragic alcoholism is as irresistible as it is anachronistic, but it is clear from the little evidence we have that Sunity took an ostrich-like approach to problems with which she did not want to deal. Unlike Chimnabai, a clear-eyed pragmatist, Sunity Devi saw the world through relentlessly rose-coloured glasses. Despite the important work she did to better the conditions in which her countrywomen lived, she never truly grasped the predicaments facing them because she persisted in the Panglossian belief that, contrary to her own personal experience, everything would be all right in the end.

This dichotomy between imagination and reality was displayed with cruel irony in the lives of her children. Perhaps the saddest story is that of her eldest daughter, Princess Sukriti, or Girlie, who had married high-flying Jyotsnanath Ghosal at Woodlands with such fanfare in 1899. Twenty years later, Girlie had left Ghosal, her excessive behaviour having apparently ruined his chances of senior office in the ICS. In April she rented a house in Devon for herself and her two children, and left it six months later not only in terrible condition, but owing her landlord £100. 'She has made herself notorious in this neighbourhood during her short stay,' the outraged Brigadier-General Llewellyn informed the India Office in 1920, 'by smashing (or her party did) the windows of the village school, general rowdiness, and leaving a number of local debts.'

The following February, Ghosal placed an advertisement in the *Morning Post* giving formal notice that he was no longer responsible for any debts his estranged wife might incur. By March, Girlie, now aged thirty-seven, was featuring again in the India Office files. She, her teenaged son, Archie, and her 'secretary', a young man called Raymond Charles Combi, contacted the British Consul-General in Paris. They were 'quite destitute' – had only four francs between them – and their hotel had confiscated their luggage because they could not pay the bill. The Secretary of State authorized an advance of 1,000 francs.

Ten days later, the India Office received a telegram pleading for help in paying for their tickets back to India. It read, dramatically, 'Stranded'. Funds were forwarded to Girlie through Mr Sinclair, the Consul-General in Genoa. She and Combi, whom Sinclair wrongly assumed was a relation, arrived in his office on 1 April. Sinclair booked a berth for Girlie on the SS *Pilsna*, sailing to

Bombay from Trieste two days later. He guaranteed their hotel bill in Genoa and gave her some spending money. After he had seen Girlie on to the train to Trieste, he discovered that she and Combi had not only shared a room but entertained in it and run up a large drinks bill. Because of her 'habits', Sinclair told the India Office tactfully, he recommended she travel with a nurse.

Mr Townend, the clerk to the British Consul in Trieste, and his wife met Girlie and the 'gentleman' with whom she was travelling off the Genoa train. They took them sightseeing before boarding the SS *Pilsna*. In the cabin, Girlie was asked for her ticket and passport, but Combi (always referred to in this correspondence as 'the gentleman') refused to hand them over to the officer. He 'said the Princess would not go without him and that he had no money left' and disembarked with her documents. The astonished Townends took Girlie back to the Savoy Hotel, retrieved her passport and ticket from Combi, and took her to the station to catch a night-train for Venice where she could re-board the *Pilsna*. As they waited on the platform, Combi appeared with the police, 'much excited', and tried to have Mr and Mrs Townend arrested for abducting 'his wife'.

At 2.15 that morning, the Townends, released by the police, returned to the Savoy. Accompanied by the hotel's porter and head bookkeeper, they went up to Girlie's room. She was in bed and Combi was wearing his pyjamas and an overcoat. Townend asked 'the gentleman' to leave the room while Girlie dressed. She allowed Mrs Townend to lead her out of the hotel as Combi, still in his pyjamas, shouted after her, 'Don't leave me, Girlie!' Fainting and hysterical, Girlie was in no state to travel on to Venice then, but at 8.15 she and Mr Townend motored to Venice where, having missed the *Pilsna* by five minutes because Girlie suffered a fresh breakdown en route, he left her in the care of the Vice-Consul. Back in Trieste, Combi was arrested briefly and, penniless, returned to Genoa.

Mr Sinclair, exasperation triumphing over diplomatic discretion, wired the India Office that Girlie 'is quite irresponsible, apparently intemperate, and incapable of travelling alone'. She refused to leave for India without Combi, though the India Office flatly refused to pay his passage as well as hers – on moral as much as financial grounds. Combi arrived in Venice on 22 April; he and Girlie checked out of the hotel the following day, and the episode appeared to have drawn to an unsatisfactory close.

The penultimate entry in the file dealing with this incident is a letter to the British Consulate in Venice from the company which owned the SS *Tevere*, on which Girlie eventually set sail for Bombay on 1 July 1921, requesting payment of her hairdressing and drinks bills and Mr Combi's ticket: he had 'embarked clandestinely without having paid his first-class fare'. The last entry, in 1922, notes the India Office's receipt of Jit's repayment of his sister's expenses in Italy.

The Cooch Behar palace archives contain fat files of requests for money from Girlie (and Victor and Baby). In the summer of 1939, aged fifty-five, Girlie was staying at Woodlands – still unable to live on her allowance and still hoping to be looked after and taken care of. The housekeeper said she was being a 'good girl', Girlie reported, at the end of a series of letters complaining about her veranda flooding, her allowance being late and the bearer not being allowed to use the kitchen for her early-morning tea. Her great-nephew, Habi, later remembers encountering Girlie – who ran away to Darjeeling with a British taxi-driver sometime around Independence – at parties, her clinking pockets full of filched bottles. He went to Darjeeling to bury her when she died in 1958.

Indira's old school friends, Pretty and Baby, married a pair of English brothers, Lionel and Alan Mander. Pretty was the only one of Nripendra's children mentioned in his obituaries. She was, said *The Times*, popular in London society and 'specially noted for her charm and beauty'. Sunity Devi described her as 'just like an English girl, although at home she lived as an Indian Princess'; a photograph shows her level, seductive eyes gazing out of an oval, fur-swathed face. Her European tastes and manners worried her mother, who knew how unhappy Girlie was with her Bengali husband, but was apprehensive about inter-racial marriage. Eventually Pretty married an English film star, Lionel Mander, but the marriage failed long before Pretty's death in 1923.

Although Sunity Devi said her youngest child, Baby, was the most wilful of her children – 'she never would do anything unless she wished' – she seems to have had the most contented adult life of the Cooch Behar children. At five years old she had been betrothed to the Yuvraj of Kapurthala, son of one of Nripendra's closest friends, the licentious Francophile prince, but she fell in love with her sister's handsome brother-in-law, Alan, and, against her family's wishes, was determined to marry him. Sunity Devi, struggling to come to terms with Rajey's death, wished she could keep her youngest with her a little longer. Almost at the same time as the Barodas were taking Indira abroad to distract her from her love for Jit, Sunity Devi took Baby on an extended cruise – but the devoted Alan followed them round the world. Eventually, as Baby threatened to enter a convent if she could not marry Alan, Sunity Devi consented to their marrying at Woodlands in February 1914. 'Now my life has come to that stage that I must not be heard,' she wrote in her memoirs, 'my love must pray silently for the happiness of my children.' The Yuvraj was furious: he threatened to kill Mander for this slight to his honour.

Alan went back to Europe to fight that September and, though he survived the war, he was shell-shocked and never really recovered emotionally. He and Baby lived for a while in Kingston, while he spent her dowry on his attempts to be a racing-driver, and then in Chelsea. Sunity Devi was there when Baby's first child was born in July 1920. Their warm house, her second daughter Garbo remembers, was a real Indian home, smelling richly of spices.

Jit was fading fast in the autumn of 1922: he died two months later in a London nursing home on his thirty-sixth birthday. His widow returned to India almost immediately, with seven-year old Bhaiya – the new maharaja – and two of his sisters, Ila and Ayesha, who remembers Indira, 'dressed entirely in white [the Indian colour of mourning], crying a lot and shutting herself in her cabin'. Their father's ashes went with them to be placed in the increasingly crowded memorial garden in Cooch Behar. Jit was the third of the seven Cooch Behar offspring to die young; Princess Pretty, separated from Lionel Mander, would follow the next year.

All through the spring of 1923, in Calcutta, telegrams, letters and visitors expressing sympathy for Jit's death and loyalty to Bhaiya flooded into Woodlands. Indira, a widow at only thirty and single mother of five, was made Regent for her son and president of his Regency Council.

Though Indian women had long been sheltered from male company, there was an equally long tradition of women participating in government from behind the purdah. This was more to do with the capacity of individual women than the systematically repressive society in which they lived. Exceptional women could subvert custom, while custom could accommodate their strength and ambitions. Senior women in an extended family often dominated household affairs and decisions; so too did they sometimes take on increased responsibility in a wider sphere if their fathers, husbands or sons were unable to. When Nripendra's father died the previous century, the ranis of Cooch Behar tried in vain to assert their control over the state's administration; the fact that they did not succeed reveals more about the British determination to impose their will on every corner of princely India than about any kind of sexual discrimination. In Baroda, Maharani Jamnabai, admittedly resourceful and strong-willed but just out of her teens, had been made Regent while a new heir to the gaddi was found.

From behind the purdah, Indian women had always been fiercely proud of their states. Rajput women, in particular, came into their own when their honour was under threat – and their husbands were failing to defend it. In 1561, the Mogul emperor Akbar's general Adamkhan conquered Malwa. Its Hindu king, Baz Bahadur, was betrayed by his men and fled the city. Adamkhan requested an interview with Baz Bahadur's deserted queen, Rupamati, who was as famous for her poetry as for her beauty. She agreed to receive him. He was led into the palace, through the most secret rooms of the zenana into her apartments, and found her lying on a couch, beautifully dressed and made-up – dead.

Just over a century later, Jaswant Singh, Maharaja of Jodhpur, led 30,000 Rajputs into battle against the Mogul emperor Aurangzeb. It was a massacre, and Singh returned to Jodhpur with only half of his men still alive. His wife closed the city gates against them, and ordered Singh to turn back and 'vanquish or die'. It took him a week to persuade her to relent. The Maratha heroine Laxmibai, Rani of Jhansi, dressed as a man to lead her troops against the British during the Sepoy Rebellion, and was shot dead during a skirmish in 1858.

Four successive begums ('begum' is the Islamic title for a married woman of high rank) ruled Bhopal, an important Muslim state in the centre of India, from 1820 to 1926. Under their leadership, Bhopal was, like Baroda, a well-run state filled with new hospitals and orphanages, and marked by improvements in child welfare, public health and education. A sensitive, respectful British Resident there had ensured good relations with the Government of India. The state's founder, Nuzzar Mohammed Khan, had died at twenty-eight leaving his nineteen-year-old wife Regent for his infant daughter, Sikandar Begum, who in 1868 left the throne to her daughter, Shah Jahan. Though it was a Muslim state, only the last of the four begums, Sultan Jahan, lived in strict enough purdah to remain veiled whenever she was in public; despite her own achievements, she was an ardent opponent of the emancipation of women. She attended the Coronation Durbar in 1911 behind a swathe of cloth-of-gold.

Though women like the Begum of Bhopal and Maharani Jamnabai provided historical role models for Indira in her new position as Regent, and her own mother's example had heralded a dramatic shift in how consort maharanis viewed their influence and responsibilities, the fact that Indira would be ruling outside purdah in her own right (albeit in her son's name) was unprecedented. She would have to define her position herself.

Her widowhood, in a country that ritually shunned widows, was a separate problem. Widowhood was the worst fate that could befall an Indian woman. Nineteenth-century pandits and elders in south and west India commonly greeted women with the words, 'Mayst thou have eight sons, and may thy husband survive thee.' The point of pre-marriage horoscopes was not to determine whether a young couple were personally compatible, but whether the prospective wife would die before her husband. If the charts said she would not, the marriage was called off. But a wife who died before her husband was dressed up as a bride in all her marriage finery and celebrated for her virtue; her husband, however, was not expected to prove his love by joining her on the pyre.

Outliving your husband showed that you had not nurtured him properly – it was the manifestation of lifetimes of bad karma – and a widow was expected to live out the rest of her days doing penance for her sin and revering her dead husband. Sunity Devi admiringly described visiting the Dowager Maharani of Burdwan when she and Nripendra were on honeymoon there. 'She worshipped her late husband's slippers, which she placed before his chair, just as though he were alive and sitting there.'

Traditionally, widows broke their wedding bangles when their husbands died, and never again wore ornaments of any kind. They shaved their heads every two weeks, dressed in simple white cotton saris, seldom ate anything but plain rice for their lone daily meal, and slept on thin, coarse matting. Remarriage was unthinkable, though in 1856 the laws had been changed to permit it. They could not attend any kind of family celebration because their presence alone was thought to bring bad luck. It was unlucky just to see a widow's face first thing in the morning.

Widowhood was especially hard for young women. Some were still children when their husbands died, and, desperate and afraid, they were the widows most susceptible to arguments glorifying sati, the custom in which widows throw themselves on their husbands' funeral pyres. The best thing a widow can do, according to ortho-dox Hindu theology, is to join her husband in death. This not only absolves her own sins – she is immediately released from the cycle of birth and rebirth – but also ensures salvation for her husband and the seven generations that follow her. Sati had been outlawed by the British in 1829 but still persisted in the more orthodox Rajput states, increasingly rarely, through the twentieth century.

Often, sati was not seen as a cruel result of social and community pressure but as the highest act of selfless love. Even reformers such as Sarojini Naidu viewed sati through a haze of romanticism: a woman willing to die in flames rather than live on without the man she worships. In Rajput forts generations of women dipped their hands in the red powder that is the mark of a good wife and pressed their handprints on to the stone walls as they passed on their way to their husbands' funeral pyres; these poignant, anonymous imprints of piety and devotion endure to this day. Padmini, a Rajput princess of Chittor, led her saffron-clad ladies to a mass sati, called jauhur, rather than surrender to the Pathan king of Delhi in 1303. In 1587 Chittor fell again, this time to the Mogul emperor Akbar. As 8,000 Rajput warriors charged out to their deaths, nine Rajput queens, five princesses and the wives and daughters of scores of chieftains died in the flames of a second jauhur.

Indira, 'so full of fire and fun', was not the kind of woman to retire from life altogether because her husband, however beloved, had died. The strength she had shown in choosing to marry Jit, against all the pressures of her family and the society in which she had been raised, had not been diminished by marriage. Though their union had been a passionate one – attested by the five children she bore in nine years – Jit's alcoholism had come between them.

Years later, Indira told her granddaughter that while he was out drinking with his cronies, she would be curled up with her nose in a book, absorbed in something with which he had no connection. For all his wit and gaiety, and his adoration of his wife, Jit, like his brothers and sisters, preferred to skim the surface of life. The tension between their parents, the concerns about money and the family's tragic weakness for drink, none of which were acknowledged or discussed, left them incapable of facing life's challenges head on. Indeed, the powerful glamour they possessed as a family may have stemmed from their perpetual efforts to make believe that everything was marvellous, all of the time: they were always performing. Their very charm made it hard for them to be vulnerable when they needed to be, and hard, too, to be strong.

By 1923 Indira had watched two of her brothers as well as her husband die from alcohol abuse, but her response was utterly characteristic of her. She embraced life, seized what had been given her with both hands. When Jit died, she was more convinced than ever that happiness could not be found in one other person. Family was important, friends were important, lovers would be important; the most valuable lesson life had taught Indira was that she must be responsible for herself.

While Indira took up the reins of government in Cooch Behar, Chimnabai continued her campaign to help emancipate India's women. 'If only the right spirit could stir India's women today,' she sighed to Miss Tottenham, echoing Sunity Devi's sentiments, 'what wonderful things could happen.'

The women's movement had come a long way since the early days of activism in Bengal when Sunity Devi and Chimnabai first met. Its leaders were still, by necessity, from privileged backgrounds but its organization and aims were vastly more sophisticated. The Women's Indian Association, linked to the suffragettes in Britain, was founded in 1917 and demanded equal rights for the first time, and the National Council of Women in India, a philanthropic group whose membership was drawn from the privileged elite of Indian women, was set up in 1925. In 1926, Chimnabai accepted its presidency and she was also made president in 1928, and again from 1930 to 1934 and 1936 to 1937.

In 1927 Sarojini Naidu (now an important member of Congress and one of Gandhi's early supporters) persuaded Chimnabai to preside over the first All-India Women's Conference at Poona. 'No one is better fitted than Her Highness to preside over our deliberations on this occasion,' said the conference's opening speaker, introducing Chimnabai and describing her 'wide experience and enlightened judgement' and the years in which she and Sayajirao had worked to promote education for women and better the conditions in which they live. Chimnabai, who paid for the publication of the conference's report, was described by Sarojini as 'the fairy god-mother of that Cinderella of Indian education – the interests of India's girls'.

The conference originally intended to discuss improving education for women, but found it could not address this without addressing all the social problems women in India faced. 'Here, with the rising tide of revival of Indian culture; here, at the beginning of what may be rightly regarded as an Indian renaissance, we are assembled to discuss that which, more than all else, goes to the root of a rebirth of a great people,' said Chimnabai at the beginning of her speech to the conference. 'We are assembled to discuss those things which are essential for the education and general well-being of the future mothers of the race.'

For the nation's good, she continued, women must have healthy souls as well as healthy bodies: they must have all that is implied by the phrase (a favourite of Sayajirao's) *mens sana in corpore sano*. The curse of sati was no longer upon them, but child-marriage was still a problem. 'If we are to have strong and vigorous sons and daughters, we must have strong and mature mothers.' When child-marriage was eradicated, she believed, education for women would follow.

The greatest evil of all, though, was purdah.

The woman behind her purdah is as much a captive as a bird in a cage. Pent up behind the purdah she is steeped in ignorance and allowed to grow and to flourish like a pet animal. No ray of light nor enlightenment can penetrate into the zenana. She is given away in marriage without any will of her own. A popular adage compares a daughter to a cow. Like the unfortunate cow she licks the hand of the butcher raised to sever her throat.

Chimnabai's final point was a plea on behalf of the women of her own class – India's princesses. A Bombay newspaper had recently carried an anonymous letter from a rani entitled 'The Status of an Indian Princess. A Tale of Woe. (By one of them.)' (see Appendix p. 303) in which the unfortunate woman bemoaned the 'strain of life-long neglect and ill-treatment' under which she and other royal women suffered. Inspired by the social changes taking place all around her ('Even we behind the purdah have felt the breath of the new spirit ... Even we dare to dream in terms of self-determination'), she vividly described the restraints and cruelty of the regime in which she lived, and cried out for understanding and help. 'In expressing my sincere regret that this princess, who is as unknown to me as she is to you, should have had to adopt this method of stating her grievances,' said Chimnabai, 'I must nevertheless welcome the sign that the position of this group of women in our land is at last finding an expression.'

While Chimnabai crusaded, her husband turned inwards. Sayajirao was plagued now by crippling gout as well as neurasthenia, and was increasingly depressed. Civic altruism had not translated into private content. Two of his sons were dead; another languished in a German clinic, too ill to see his parents; his beloved daughter's husband, to whom he had never been fully reconciled, had left her a widow. Relations with his wife had been sorely damaged by their differences over how to handle their errant children. 'What have I done that God should punish me so severely that all my sons have indulged in things that I detested,' he lamented, 'and died as a result so early in life?'

In August 1923, tragedy struck again. Chimnabai and Sayajirao were in Paris when Sayajirao opened the newspaper to read his own obituary. But the papers had made a mistake: it was Jayasinhrao, their 28-year-old eldest son, who had died of a stroke en route from Berlin to Flushing. The paper, in its amended report the following day, said that Jayasinh had had 'heart disease' for some time. Sayajirao was 'too overcome by grief, too stunned by shock' to go to his funeral.

The Maharaja's premature obituary makes interesting reading, though. Baroda's pursuit of a match with the already married Maharaja of Gwalior for his only daughter had apparently disappointed social reformers who had venerated him. He was also criticized for the 'coolness' with which he received viceregal instructions to deal with unrest in the 1910s. Events at the 1911 Durbar were made much of.

Spending even more time abroad was some consolation. From the early 1920s he and Chimnabai stayed in Baroda only in the temperate winter months. The sea journey from India could now take as little as two weeks, and some of the European legs could be done by air – in March 1921 Sayaji flew from London to Paris in a

Farman Goliath. Increasingly, he feared he had neglected his family for his state, and longed to make it up to them. He bought Lord Tennyson's old house, Aldsworth, in Surrey, in 1920 and brought the whole family over from Baroda – including grandchildren and great-grandchildren – for an English summer of cricket and tea on the lawn.

In the winter of 1924, Sayajirao bought a house in Paris near the Parc Monceau. When their health permitted, he and Chimnabai continued to tour round Europe. In 1928, when Indira rented a house in England's fox-hunting country, Sayajirao rode to hounds for the first time, aged sixty-five. They met President Roosevelt in Washington in 1934, admired the spirit of nationalism (as it seemed) at the Berlin Olympics in 1936, big-game hunted in East and Central Africa in 1937 and, that same year, cruised up to Iceland.

The Maharaja's interests in art, culture and music flourished. N. H. Spelman, *The Times*'s art critic, bought paintings by Rubens, Titian, Fragonard, Romney, Turner and Poussin for Sayajirao's collection. From 1916 until his death, a festival was held in Baroda every Holi, attracting the best singers, dancers, magicians and mimes in India as well as its premier musicians.

As he got older, Sayajirao's views fell out of step with the development of political thought in India. The man who had been hailed as a potential prime minister of an independent India was now criticized by left-wing nationalist groups for his long absences from Baroda and occasional personal extravagances and pointedly reminded of his obligations to his people. For the first time, increasingly confident middle-class revolutionaries dared question the right of the princes to rule (and live off) vast Indian territories; the fact that Sayajirao had once been considered an exemplary and liberal head of state did not exempt him from this rigorous new scrutiny.

Katherine Mayo described asking a group of pro-Home Rule Bengali Hindus in Delhi in 1927 what they would do with the princes when India was independent. ' "We shall wipe them all out!" exclaimed one and all the others nodded assent.' Incendiary material attacking the princes was published with increasing frequency. 'We all have different ways of beginning the day,' stormed one such book, published in 1930. 'The Englishman begins on bacon and eggs, the German on sausages, the American on grape nuts. His Highness prefers a virgin.'*

Sayajirao and Chimnabai had long been respected by individual members of Congress. Through their friendship with people such as Sarojini Naidu, they were in contact with the new wave of activists. However, their status was an automatic stumbling block: how could a maharaja and a maharani genuinely back reform when they were a part of the old order that needed overturning? Naidu was close to Mohandas Gandhi, himself the son of a dewan of a minor Gujarati state near Baroda, and increasingly the most important figure in the Indian independence movement. Though until 1937 Congress's policy was non-interference in princely states, Gandhi was as outspoken in his opposition to the princes as to the British. He saw the princes as 'puppets, created or tolerated for the upkeep and prestige of the British power'. Their unchecked authority was 'probably the worst blot on the British crown'. 'It is no credit to the Princes that they allow themselves powers which no human being, conscious of dignity, should possess. It is no credit to the people who have mutely suffered the loss of elementary human freedom.'

To nationalist Indians of more temperate views, Sayajirao remained an inspiration. Young men emulated 'his Highness's perfect manners, punctuality, national aspiration, fearlessness, learning and knowledge', recalled a Hyderabadi nawab.

The princes, along with many Indian politicians, had supported Britain's war effort partly in the hopes that India would be accorded dominion status, on a par with Canada and Australia, after peace was made. They hoped to chart a new destiny for themselves in a free India. A dignified Sayajirao presented the address to Viceroy Chelmsford at the first Conference of Ruling Princes in Delhi in 1916. He concluded with the hope that a council of princes with real powers and responsibilities would be formed.

---

* This was a dig at the Maharaja of Patiala whose enormous sexual appetite was notorious.

This did not happen; five years later Baroda was one of the ten important states who refused to join the purely advisory Chamber of Princes set up by the conference. Sayajirao had hoped that a princely chamber would have some say in the form an independent India would take, but he was quickly disillusioned by the domination of the chamber by a group of northern princes led by Patiala and Bikaner and by the limited proposals made. The chamber was a sop to princely aspirations and an attempt by the British to build the princes up as a counterweight to Congress's increasing power, not a first step towards self-rule.

While the sessions of the Chamber of Princes in the 1920s and 1930s turned out to have been ineffectual politically, they were at least a good spectator sport. Even the cars the princes arrived in were astonishingly splendid. The following description has been used so many times by commentators on princely India that it has come to exemplify the eccentricities and extravagances of a lost era, summing up all that we imagine those lives to have been like:

There are cars which were gold-plated and cars which were silver-plated, cars with hoods of polished aluminium and bodies of costly woods, cars in purple, lavender, sky-blue, orange, emerald green, vermilion, cars upholstered in satins, velvets, brocades. One had mounted on its roof a searchlight as large as those used on destroyers; another was fitted with steel shutters, presumably to save its owner from assassination; a third had on its runningboard a small pipe organ on which an attendant played his master's favourite airs.

The gold-plated motor was the sadistic Maharaja of Alwar's smooth-running Lanchester, custom-made to his specifications in 1924. The rear portion of the car was a facsimile of the British coronation coach; two footmen perched there as if it were a real carriage. The steering wheel was made of ivory. When Alwar died in 1937, his corpse was driven to the cremation ground in this car.

In the winter of 1930, the Gaekwad was one of sixteen representatives from the princely states to a Round Table Conference held in London and intended to inaugurate an integrated debate on

1. The King-Emperor's camp, Delhi Durbar, 1911

2. The Royal Pavilion at the Delhi Durbar, 12 December 1911

3. Miss Tottenham, Chimnabai and Indira, *c.* 1911

4. Indira's fiancé,
Maharaja Scindia of
Gwalior, *c.* 1911

5. Jit in 1913

6. Sayajirao in 1875

7. Laxmi Vilas palace, Baroda

8. Chimnabai playing the sitar with her ladies-in-waiting in a courtyard in Laxmi Vilas

9. Cooch Behar palace

10. Sunity Devi as a young woman

11. Indira as a child, *c.* 1895

12. The Viceroy and Lady Curzon riding to the Durbar in Delhi, 1903

13. The Maharani and Maharaja of Baroda outside Laxmi Vilas, 5 July 1905

14. Chimnabai, showing off her skill as a sportswoman with an uncharacteristic smile for the camera, c. 1910

15. Hitty, Nripendra, Pretty, Baby and Jit, c. 1908

16. Bexhill, *c.* 1909:
Pretty, Nripendra, Jit,
Sunity Devi and Baby

17. The dining room at
Cooch Behar

18. The devoted widow: a white-clad
Sunity Devi, soon after Nripendra's
death, with his photograph

19. Jit and Indira on honeymoon in August 1913: a time of 'perfect joy'

20. Indira and Ila, 1915

21. Sayajirao, the elder statesman, in 1919

22. Jit and Indira with their family in Bexhill just before Jit's death; the children, from left, Ila, Menaka, Ayesha, Indrajit and Bhaiya

23. Indira and Khusru Jung hunting in Leicestershire, late February 1928

24. Indira and friends in Le Touquet, June 1928

25. Indira and her brood on their travels, *c.* 1930: from left, Ila, Bhaiya, Indrajit, Indira, Ayesha, unknown and Kajumama

26. Indira and Douglas Fairbanks with friends in Cooch Behar

27. Sayajirao's Golden Jubilee procession setting out from Laxmi Vilas, 1931

28. A reception for Sayajirao and Chimnabai at the Vatican, 1932. Indira is fourth from left, Chimnabai fifth, Sayajirao seventh

29. 'She': Indira at forty

30. Ayesha with her dog in Darjeeling

31. Indira's boudoir in Cooch Behar. She sits in front of her portrait by de Laszlo with Ila's daughter Devika; on the floor lies the Schiaparelli rug made from leopards shot by Ila

32. Indira flanked by her sons at a durbar in Cooch Behar, mid-1930s

33. Ayesha and Jai dancing in London in the early days of their courtship, c. 1938

34. Jai, in the centre of the picture, is met by Bhaiya as he arrives in Cooch Behar to marry Ayesha in May 1940

35. Gandhi and Sarojini Naidu on the Salt March, 1930

36. Ayesha and Indira watching a performance in Cooch Behar, 1940s

37. Ayesha and Jai on shikar in Cooch Behar, 1940s

38. Ayesha and Bhaiya on an elephant, Cooch Behar, 1940s

39. Hunting in Cooch Behar, 1940s; Jai is in the centre looking at the tiger

40. Nehru perched on the Mountbattens' carriage on India's first day of Independence, 1947

41. Ayesha and Jagat, 1949

42. Indira and Habi in St Mark's Square, Venice, 1950s

43. Nehru and Indira Gandhi, 1956

44. Jackie Kennedy
and Ayesha in
Jaipur, 1962

45. & 46. Ayesha
campaigning in
Jaipur, 1962

47. Jagat in London, late 1960s

48. Ila's son, Habi, with his wife Moon Moon and daughters Riya and Raima, *c.* 1985. Moon Moon and her daughters are Bollywood movie stars – Indian royalty of a different kind

49. Ayesha in 2002, still every inch a queen

India's future. At this time, the idea of federation of which Sayaji was one of the originators – independent India as a union of states, the former British Indian provinces ruled democratically and the former princely states ruled constitutionally by their traditional monarchs – was considered by many to be the most viable option for India's future government.

Congress refused to send delegates to the convention because they felt its aims were inadequate, and because their leader, Gandhi, was in prison in the aftermath of his recent march protesting against the British tax on salt. Congress's non-participation denied the first Round Table any authority at all. As V. P. Menon remarked, 'A Round Table Conference to evolve a constitution for India without the participation of the Congress was like enacting *Hamlet* without the Prince of Denmark.'

At the second Round Table Conference in autumn 1931, Mohandas Gandhi represented Congress, accompanied by Sarojini Naidu. Bhimrao Ambedkar, the outcaste boy Sayajirao had had educated, was there speaking for the 'downtrodden' castes. The mighty princely triumvirate of Baroda, Mysore and Hyderabad unsuccessfully demanded influence within the association proportional to their population and importance. The last Round Table the following year attracted only forty-six delegates. Once again, as it became clear that efforts to influence the British government were effectively ignored, disillusion set in.

Sayajirao no longer derived any joy from politics and administration; he had grown disenchanted with the world. Miss Tottenham noticed him underlining the phrase 'long stretch of sad grey years ahead of him' in a book he was reading. But his fascination with comparative religion and objective truth was a solace as time drew on. The Gaekwad was the first president of the World Fellowship of Faiths, a movement inspired by Sir Francis Younghusband. The Maharaja established a chair of comparative religions at Baroda College. In 1933 he addressed the second World Parliament of Religions in Chicago. Sayajirao's shift in focus was one advocated by the ancient Hindu texts. As a youth, a man should study; as a young man, he should marry, support his family and be an active member of his community; in middle age he should engage in further study and spiritual practice; in old age he should renounce the world and become a holy man. According to this system, women had two life-stages: first as daughters, then as wives.

Though the Maharaja's demands for independence from British control never faltered, British opinion was slowly moving into line with his own. By the 1930s Sayajirao found himself a favoured son of the British Empire, an elder statesman whose opinions were keenly sought against a new political background of widespread civil disobedience and fears of violent revolution. This unsought approval came despite Sayajirao's public praise of Gandhi and his refusal to sanction Gandhi's arrest when he walked through Baroda territory on his march to the sea as a protest against the British salt tax in the spring of 1930.

At his Diamond Jubilee in 1935 tributes poured in from British and Indian friends and associates; the outgoing viceroy, Lord Willingdon, attended his celebrations in Baroda in January 1936. 'Some of his differences with the authorities in Delhi were due to misunderstandings and the proof that no bitterness was left behind is to be seen in the tributes which successive Viceroys have paid him,' said the *Times of India*. An American writer described him at sixty as 'a smiling, cherubic old gentleman': a far cry from the scourge of Lord Hardinge in 1911. Most importantly, though, he was seen as having 'exploded the whole myth of the White man's burden', proving that Indians could be every bit as effective as their European counterparts at ruling themselves.

He began to get away with making speeches – even to viceroys – that twenty years earlier would have threatened his throne. When Lord Reading visited Baroda on his viceregal tour in 1926, Sayajirao met him with the words:

In the new era, the Indian States now claim a place in the sun, and, believing in the justice of the British people, they hope that their current rights and dignities will be fully revived. For my own State, it is only natural in me to hope that its original sovereignty will be restored . . . A hundred years of British peace, progress, and order have now ensued. In the interests of efficient government, and, with the utmost solicitude for the good of the Empire, I suggest to the British Government that the ancient privileges be now fully restored to their friends and allies of old.

In 1906 this would have caused, at best, a diplomatic incident; in 1926, Sayajirao and Reading understood each other.

While freedom-fighters made the association between self-rule and political reform increasingly explicit, much still depended on good personal relations between the princes and their British allies. Lord and Lady Willingdon inhabited Lutyens's monumental red sandstone Government House from 1931, the year it was finished, to 1936. They were the most flamboyant – and, according to Jawaharlal Nehru's sister, Krishna, the most unpopular – of the viceregal couples who lived there. The Willingdons were old India hands; he had been Governor of Bombay before being elevated to New Delhi. Once there, pushy Lady Willingdon lost no time in redecorating their new home in shades of her favourite colour, mauve. Lutyens saw her in 1934: 'I told her that if she possessed the Parthenon she would add bay windows to it. She said she did not like the Parthenon.' She gave a fancy-dress ball for their last Christmas in office at which the Viceroy and Vicereine, apparently without a trace of irony, were Louis XVI and Marie Antoinette, attended by their senior staff as lilac-clad courtiers.

When Lady Willingdon visited Baroda, elaborate preparations were made to ensure that everything was as she liked it; or rather, that everything was purple – including the lavatory paper in the state train. It had been impossible to get hold of the mauve Bronco the Vicereine had imported by the crate, so some was dyed for her. Later, she said to Sayajirao, 'Everything is marvellous in your saloon, but there is something wrong with your toilet paper because I am purple all over.' When a mix-up occurred in Calcutta, and little Ayesha gave her the red roses intended for the Governor of Bengal's wife while Menaka handed her mauve sweet peas to the Governor's wife, Lady Willingdon said firmly, 'No, dear, I don't think these can be for me.'

Chimnabai also had to make special preparations for Lady Willingdon's stay in Baroda. The Vicereine (like Queen Mary) was well known for admiring *objets* in the houses she visited and expecting to be presented with them, but the Maharani had no intention of giving her treasures away. She hid her pearls in a velvet box and buried the box in the gardens. The Willingdons did not leave until after the rains had begun; when Chimnabai had the box dug up it was completely waterlogged and the pearls' settings had rotted away.

Even though she no longer used the constraints of purdah to avoid seeing British officers' wives, Chimnabai had lost none of the fierce dignity she had always employed with them. In 1934, she paid a call on Lady Willingdon in Delhi. As they drew up outside Viceregal Lodge, the ADC opened the door of the Rolls-Royce to allow Chimnabai and her daughter-in-law Kamala to step out. The Maharani, sitting proudly erect, did not stir from her seat until Lady Willingdon came out of the house herself to greet her.

Chimnabai's impatient nationalism did not abate as the prospect of Indian independence drew nearer. She liked to quote Tipu Sultan, defeated by the British under the future Duke of Wellington in 1798, who declared it was better to live for a year as a tiger than a thousand as a lamb. In 1938, the American novelist Louis Bromfield published *The Rains Came*, set in a loosely fictionalized Baroda and written, according to his inscription, partly in Cooch Behar in 1933. The majestic Maharani of 'Ranchipur' was an 'arrogant . . . old lady' who loved gambling and loathed British officialdom. 'At sixty-seven she was handsome, for her beauty was of that indestructible sort which lies in the bones of the face,' wrote Bromfield, describing her 'large fierce black eyes', her 'vivid mobile face' and the 'proud arch of her fiercely sculpted nose'.

While Indira's startling beauty and high-voltage glamour thrilled everyone around her, Chimnabai made no concession to the world and her sternness increased with age. When you look closely at her face in photographs, you can see that she has the same exquisite bone structure, generous mouth and mysterious eyes as Indira, but her expression is always set against the photographer. She looks, quite deliberately, austere and formidable. But in private, when her mischievous laugh bubbled uncontrollably out of her – 'that wonderful silent laugh of hers, her face contorted, her body shaking like jelly, and not a sound out of her mouth' – at the ridiculousness of a given situation, her face must have lit up like a house illuminated for Divali, all the more precious for its rarity.

Sayajirao waged a running battle against Chimnabai over her passion for gambling and racing. When they stayed at the Dorchester, recalls a grandchild, Chimnabai would wait for Sayajirao to go to bed before nipping off to a casino; he, in his turn, would take for ever to get ready for bed, knowing that as soon as he said goodnight she would be off. If she gambled away all her pin-money at cards, Sayajirao refused to forward her more; she hoarded money he had given her for jewels to pay her losses. In Bombay, where Chimnabai was a keen racegoer, her purple Rolls-Royce was the only car allowed inside the racetrack itself. She liked to be driven magisterially along the inside of the track at the same pace as the horses running on the other side of the rail.

In the spring of 1923, Indira was taking charge in her new office as Regent of Cooch Behar. She wanted 'some senior man [as British Resident] in whom she can feel absolute confidence during her absences from the state which owing to her ill-health may not be infrequent', explained her friend the Viceroy to Lord Lytton, Governor-General of Bengal. Since Indira's health, until her last years, was not usually bad, it is likely that she was using it as a preemptive excuse to be away from Cooch Behar as and when she liked in the face of a critical Government of India.

Even while she was abroad, Indira resisted British efforts to interfere in Cooch Behar's government. Lord Lytton complained that Indira thought being Regent was the same as being a 'Ruling Chief'. Her letters to him are strongly worded and well argued. She never lacked confidence or dignity in her dealings with the India Office and, among Indians, was seen as a 'very able, energetic and benevolent ruler'. The approval that meant most to her, though, was that of her father, who 'used to say he wished she had been his eldest son because she had such a good head for government'.

In 1927, worried that Bhaiya was becoming spoilt in Cooch Behar — suspicions aroused by the fact that his friends never gave him out in cricket matches — Indira overrode Jit's wish that their children grow up in Cooch Behar and took her family to England. With them went a dashing Hyderabadi noble, Nawab Khusru Jung, an intimate friend of Indira's and Comptroller of the Cooch Behar state, and his baby daughter. Indira adopted the infant, Kamala, nicknamed Baby, who was immediately assimilated into the family and became like a sixth Cooch Behar child. Bhaiya started at St Cyprian's prep school in Eastbourne and Ila attended Indira's old school, Ravenscroft, also in Eastbourne, while the four younger children went to day schools in London.

When the family had been away from Cooch Behar for fifteen months, in July 1928, the Government of India asked Indira to return to India to attend to her official duties. They said she had told them she would be away for only eight months and nearly twice that period had gone by. Indira's secretary responded that she had already decided to leave Europe but that she would be back to spend the Christmas holidays with her children, who would stay at their English schools.

Her intransigence prompted Lord Birkenhead to send her a firmer letter ordering her to return home and to stay there for at least a year. Indira went to the India Office in Aldwych, London to discuss — or argue — this point, and demanded to see a copy of the original 1816 kharita, or agreement, between Lord Moira, Governor-General of India, and the then raja of Cooch Behar, in which the British 'agreed to abstain from all interference, except in the form of advice and representation, in the unlimited management of the affairs of the State'. She had no intention of backing down.

The next letter in the India Office file is from the Governor of Bengal, Sir Francis Jackson, in January 1929, regarding Bhaiya going to Harrow school. It concludes: 'The Viceroy thinks it would be well to be cautious in referring this to His Majesty's intervention in the case. He would however tell the Maharani that the King

[George V] was greatly annoyed to hear the rumours about her conduct emanating from the Melton Mowbray neighbourhood.'

In the late 1920s and early 1930s Melton, the central town of Leicestershire's fox-hunting country, was the British aristocracy's winter playground. By day, everyone rode to hounds; at night, wild parties were held, often in fancy dress, cards were played for high stakes and revellers habitually swung from chandeliers. Melton was frequented, according to the Prince of Wales, by 'wealthy people who had discovered that the stable door was a quick if expensive short-cut into society . . . [and] ladies whose pursuit of the fox was only a phase of an even more intense pursuit of romance'. Indira rented a house there for the seasons of 1927–8 and 1928–9; it was said she 'came all the way from India to woo' Hugh Molyneux, the future Earl of Sefton, a keen huntsman and ladies' man. She may have set her sights higher than Molyneux: either the dissolute Duke of Kent or the raffish Prince of Wales, a great admirer of Indira's, could have been the unidentified royal British lover because of whom, her family say, she was privately asked to leave England at this time, and which would fit in with the India Office's ambiguous message from the King.

In the files there is a breakdown of the Cooch Behars' expenses over the summer of 1929, a response to the India Office's worries about the high level of Indira's expenditure. Internally, that February, they had discussed removing from her hands control over the state's finances and requiring her to stay in India for a year as a condition of retaining the Regency. The Cooch Behars rented a flat in London where Indira, her six children, their governess, an ADC, an Indian tutor and an Indian bearer lived; clothes for the children cost £600 per annum and laundry £200. There was also the hunting-box in Melton Mowbray, Stavely Lodge, plus livery for eight horses and salaries for seven servants and four grooms. A month on the Continent was budgeted at £1,000. School fees, medical bills and a car were accounted for, but there is no mention of Indira's personal expenses – clothes, chemin-de-fer, jewels and entertaining. Though she was extravagant, she was scrupulous about paying back even the smallest debt.

Discussions with the India Office over Indira's allowance and whether the children should live in England or India continued through the autumn of 1929. Indira made it clear that she would oppose any efforts to reduce her allowance or influence in the council, and opposed Indrajit, her second son, remaining at school in England when she returned to India. Bhaiya's first report from Harrow was glowing. He was first overall in his class, and was described as 'promising' and 'excellent'. But the India Office, as usual, managed to find fault: 'The report is extremely satisfactory,' runs the pencilled note. 'The boy should turn out well if only we can save him from London flats and continental casinos during his holidays.'

In April 1930 Indira began corresponding directly with the Viceroy, Lord Irwin, about Cooch Behar's affairs. Writing from 'The Palace, Cooch Behar' – perhaps, as was her habit, sitting cross-legged on the large, cushion-covered marble throne that stood on the breezy veranda outside her apartments – she expressed her worries that Bhaiya and Indrajit were losing their Bengali across the ocean in England, and her hopes that they could return to Cooch Behar for their summer holidays and again between Christmas and Easter the following year, even if it meant missing a term of school. The misgivings that had plagued Nripendra's mother and the other ranis of Cooch Behar, and Sunity Devi about her beloved boys' upbringing, were still at the fore in Indira's time: was it better to take your children from their home in India and risk them feeling like strangers in their own land for the rest of their lives, or to deprive them of the chance to receive the British education and polish that would allow them to be treated as equals in the wider world?

She also addressed the issue of her allowance. During the first years of her widowhood, she said, she had been in deep mourning and had not needed much money. But her expenses now were much higher and she had been forced to borrow £10,000 from her father. She lived, she insisted, simply and cheaply. 'In England unfortunately second class hotels are not comfortable and I have been compelled to live in first class hotels.' She did not take a private saloon in the train. 'I have not even entertained on any scale befitting my position.' She sent Irwin a list of Indian expenses for which she thought the Cooch Behar state, rather than her personal allowance, should be accountable. These included servants' and ADCs' uniforms, medical and travelling expenses, state motorcars, the Cooch Behar library and entertainment at Cooch Behar Palace, Woodlands in Calcutta, and Colington in Darjeeling.

In total, Indira ran a luxurious establishment of perhaps 400 staff, from gardeners and ball boys up through the three cooks – European, Maratha and Bengali – each running their own kitchens. These cooks travelled with her to sample new recipes in Europe; they would serve the same meal over and over again until they had perfected it. The dignified head butler, Jaffar, was renowned for his magnificent cocktails. Her personal entourage consisted of two secretaries, a typist, ladies-in-waiting and several maids, one Swiss.

This contrasted with the increasingly austere regime at Baroda, where the number of household servants at Laxmi Vilas had declined from 200 in 1883 to just forty in 1926. As Sayajirao and Chimnabai matured, they preferred to live in a simpler manner, though old habits did die hard. They still stayed in their usual suite at the Dorchester when they came to London and travelled through India in their private saloon-car; in the 1920s Sayajirao asked Jacques Cartier to reset his entire collection of jewels in platinum, although the official Baroda jewellers in India lobbied successfully against this.

As her extended absences from Cooch Behar demonstrate, Indira's life in the late 1920s and 1930s was filled with far more than just her governmental duties on Bhaiya's behalf and her attention to her children. Though she never became westernized or mannered, as inhabitants of this world were prone to be, Indira – or Ma, as everyone now called her, friends and family alike – was a prominent figure in the social scene that flitted between London, Paris and Hollywood between the wars, and included Noël Coward, the Douglas Fairbanks Seniors, Jimmy Stewart, the American interior designer Elsie de Wolfe (who lived in the Villa Trianon at Versailles) and various louche members of the British royal family and the European aristocracy. Their hedonism was a lifetime away from her parents' disciplined devotion to duty.

Indian princes provided this proto-jet-set with an exoticism celebrated in a popular song of the 1930s:

> There was a rich Maharaja of Mogador
> Who had ten thousand camels and maybe more
> He had rubies and pearls and the loveliest girls
> But he didn't know how to do the rhumba
>
> (Chorus) Rhumba lessons are wanted for the rich
> Maharaja of Mogador

Unlike many Indian princes and their wives, Indira bridged the gulf between India and Europe 'with charming grace. The more orthodox maharajas affect to depreciate her europeanization; but in actual fact consult her in their affairs and invite her to smarten up their wives, mentally and socially, by her example. To the womanhood of India she stands for social progress. She is, in their eyes, a heroine.' Her daughter Ayesha once asked a friend of Indira's who her friends had been. 'Oh, everyone from the Prince of Wales downwards,' he replied.

'She was part of the European set in Europe but it was always on her own terms,' says Ayesha, and this independence was displayed in her iconic sense of style. After a brief flirtation with western clothes in her late teens – mostly, it seems, to annoy her mother – Indira became known as the most chic Indian woman of her generation. Her method of wearing a sari has been adopted across modern India.

Before Indira, there were so many regional variations in costume that you could pinpoint the area from which a woman came to within a few hundred miles simply by looking at her dress. Maratha saris, like the kind Chimnabai always wore, have a pleated train drawn up between the legs; in Gujarat they are tied closely to the body, the better for working in the fields; in the south saris are drawn round the neck and pinned at the shoulder, and never cover the head; in the Punjab women wear shalwar kameez and in Rajasthan they wear full skirts, called ghagras, with fitted bodices and spangled veils. Indira's method is today as standardized as it can get: the fabric is passed several times round the legs forming the skirt, then the loose end comes up around the waist, beneath the right arm, crosses the body diagonally, and hangs down the back over the left shoulder. This long trailing end is sometimes used, Maharashtran style, to cover the head.

Indira also pioneered the use of silk chiffon, hitherto used only to make negligees, for saris. Her image – a flower-coloured chiffon sari accessorized with a rope of pearls – is today the instantly recognizable uniform of sophisticated Indian women worldwide. Monsieur Erigua, in Paris, specially made chiffon up for her in sari-lengths, 45 inches wide by 6 yards long. Chiffon's racy association with lingerie delighted Indira ('wearing underpants as saris – it was unheard of', says her grandson, highly amused); it was just as unusual – and daring – for an Indian widow to wear colours and jewels, though she was always careful not to wear certain colours, like red, which were considered inappropriate for widows.

Just as her way of wearing a sari was an idiosyncratic mixture of the old-fashioned and the original, Indira loved the rich colours of Indian jewels – pigeon's blood-coloured rubies, emeralds like parrot's wings, sapphires the same deep blue as a peacock's neck – but preferred modern European settings to the heavy, enamelled necklaces, bracelets and nose rings that filled royal treasuries. According to traditional Indian teachings, Indian jewellery was often designed to hit pressure points throughout the body: toe rings, for instance, were thought to make a woman more timid – a desirable quality in a wife. Because the ear was seen as a microcosm of the body, earrings were considered particularly effective. In Ayurveda, India's ancient medical system, jewels are used like crystal therapy: emeralds are supposed to have a laxative effect, and rubies reduce flatulence and biliousness. Though she preferred designers such as Cartier and Asprey, Indira was scrupulous about wearing clothes and jewels in specific colours on the day of the week dedicated to each different Hindu deity: on Mondays, for

Shiva, she wore yellow, for example; on Tuesdays, coral for Hanuman, the monkey god. On Saturday, named for the powerful, turbulent planet Saturn, she wore blue for Shani.

Even her shoes were fabulous works of art. She ordered hundreds of pairs of custom-made shoes from Salvatore Ferragamo, artist-cobbler to the stars, sending him bags of precious jewels with which to adorn them. One pair, which he called 'Nymphia', was made of white canvas water-lily leaves impregnated with phosphorus so they shone in the dark; another was made of green velvet with a spiral of pearls running up the back; yet another pair was black velvet with a diamond buckle and two straight rows of diamonds down the heel. Though Indira loved shoes, when she visited Buckingham Palace to pay her respects to the Queen, in an expression of national pride she approached the throne barefoot, as Indian tradition demanded, and, instead of curtseying, bowed her head and folded her hands together in a namaste.

Indira's dramatic sense of style extended to every area of her life. In her boudoir in the palace at Cooch Behar lay a round leopard-skin rug made by the designer Elsa Schiaparelli from fourteen leopards shot by her eldest daughter, Ila. Indira's bed in Calcutta was made of carved elephant tusks. She gave marvellous parties, infused with the panache that characterized everything she did. There are stories of her dancing on tables at *bals masqués* in Paris, naked but for her emeralds – unverifiable now but an indication of the exotic glamour which surrounded her.

Like her mother, Indira was a reckless gambler, though neither of them ever seemed to win. Indira was even said to have lost a Rolls-Royce to a lover. One friend described seeing for the first time 'the most fabulously beautiful young Indian lady, holding the longest cigarette holder I had ever seen' at the casino in Le Touquet. She was

quite poker-faced but had a pile of chips in front of her to testify to her success and to top it all she had a little live turtle [tortoise], whose back was laden with three strips of emeralds, diamonds and rubies and which she was apparently using as a talisman. Every now and then the creature would crawl away across the table but every time she caught it back. The crowd was totally mesmerised by her.

Her love-life is mysterious but legendary. 'She adored going to bed with attractive men,' recalled an Austrian friend. 'In our circle we called her the Maharani of Couche Partout.' But whatever she did, her innate grace and dignity were never compromised: she was protected not only by her wealth, rank and beauty, but also by an aura of confidence that defied anyone to judge her or disapprove. 'She just got away with it,' says her granddaughter.

In about 1929, Indira invited the novelist William Gerhardi, whom she met in Paris at a dinner party thrown by Douglas Fairbanks Senior and his wife, Mary Pickford, to India. They boarded a sea-plane which crashed into the Mediterranean just off Alexandria. No one drowned, but the plane was wrecked and all the luggage was drenched. On the rescue boat, Gerhardi wrote, 'the Maharani, soaking wet, sat beside me, puffing at a cigarette and smiling to herself at the thrills which life provided, unasked'. Even in a crisis, soaked through and lucky to be alive, Indira remained self-possessed, amusedly detached, delighting in the unfolding of events before her. 'With her, nothing was ever dull and one felt at any moment anything might happen.'

Her captivating looks and style made her a muse as well as an icon. She was photographed by Lee Miller, the Lenare studio and Cecil Beaton. Alfred Jonniaux painted her in Paris in 1932, reclining languidly on a velvet sofa in the Cooch Behar pearls, one red shoe slipping off an exquisite foot. In 1935 the celebrated Hungarian portraitist Philip de Laszlo (who had also painted her in 1919 and 1925) made companion head-and-shoulder oil sketches of her and the dashing Maharaja of Jaipur, one of her closest friends during this period. Her fragile, heart-shaped face and dark waved bob are framed by a sea-green sari; her neck is clasped by a heavy diamond and emerald necklace; her enigmatic eyes are heavily shaded, and seem to encompass all the joy and heartbreak in the world. Oswald Birley painted her side-on, a slip of a woman in a red sari holding a pink flower, gazing at you with that sad half-smile, looking as if she breathes enchanted air. But, as her daughter says, none of her portraits 'captured that electric vitality that made her the focus of attention wherever she went'.

Writers, too, sought to describe her spirit. The heroine of the 1953 novel *Maharajah* was a modern princess called Indira, 'with the air of a young conqueror', who signed her letters with her initial, 'I', just as the real Indira did, and was determined to marry for love. Bohemian, restless and elusive, the fictional Indira was romantically linked to a movie actor, a duke and an American millionaire racehorse owner. There was even a whiff of incest – the fictional princess, unlike the real Indira, loved her brother more than she did any lover or husband – that reflects the more salacious gossip surrounding Indira and her family, and the dark glitter that clung to her because of her proud refusal to conform to respectable society's expectations.

The one person who remained impervious to Indira's charm was her mother-in-law, Sunity Devi, who held firm views about how widows – particularly her adored son's widow – ought to behave. In 1922, she wrote, 'If a widow laughs loudly or dresses in a way that could possibly be called gay, cruel remarks are made on all sides, and if a Hindu widow gets at all a bad name she suffers greatly at the hands of both her own people and her late husband's'; it could have been a prophecy of the bad feeling that would arise between her and her son's merry widow.

This bad feeling simmered even while Jit was alive, aggravated by Cooch Behar's precarious finances. In 1921 Sunity's creditors contacted the India Office about non-payment of debts including thousands to various jewellers. Jit was not taking responsibility for them: 'The Maharajah is now in England and they [a jewellery shop] say that his failure to pay is not due to any want of money as they know that he is spending a good deal elsewhere. They believe that his action is due to the influence of his wife, a daughter of the Gaekwar of Baroda.'

On 2 June 1922, six months before Jit died, Sunity Devi drew up her will. Her goods were to be divided equally between Sudhira, her daughter Gita, and Victor's daughters-in-law. Not only were Indira and her children to receive nothing, the will pointedly reclaims a string of pearls given to Sunity by her beloved Rajey, 'now in the custody or possession of my daughter-in-law Maharani Indira Devi'.

After Jit's death, Sunity Devi left Cooch Behar for good, dividing her time between Calcutta and London and devoting herself to her extended family and her religious life. Apart from disputes over money, Indira's notable lack of devotion to Brahmoism was an important element of the antipathy that existed between her and Sunity Devi, to whom Brahmoism – her father's faith – was ultimate and unquestionable truth. Sudhira's daughter says her mother, like Sunity, never forgave Indira for allowing Cooch Behar to revert to Hinduism. But Indira's spiritual views, though deeply held, were not evangelical, and it would have gone against the grain for her to insist that people should believe and practise what she told them to. If they wanted to be Hindus instead of Brahmos, then Hindus they should be.

In May 1928, Sunity Devi made her last visit to London, accompanied by Victor, her only surviving son, who was in the process of separating from his wife. While there, she fell ill and returned to India the following year. Doctors advised her to check herself into a clinic at Ranchi in Bihar, for a rest cure. She died there, at the Bengal Nagpur Railway Hotel, in November 1932, with her brother and brother-in-law by her side. She was cremated in Calcutta and her ashes brought back to Cooch Behar, though there is a marble monument to her in the grounds of Lily Cottage alongside her father, Keshub Chunder Sen's.

Two weeks after her death, a memorial service was held in London at Caxton Hall. 'In her white Indian robe, her hair turned silver, many of us will remember her as a witness to the power of the higher things in life,' said the Reverend Sparham in his eulogy. 'One could not be long in her company without being conscious of an exceptional spiritual power. Her whole attitude to life and things was charged with a temper of gentleness and goodwill.' An Indian friend praised her social work. Though she was 'the most popular Indian lady in London society', she would be better remembered for 'her work in the sphere of social reform and education for women of India [which] will always remain as a great monument to her memory and a great inspiration to the present and future generations of her sex.'

The Marchioness of Dufferin and Ava, vicereine so many years earlier, paid her a moving tribute. Their friendship, she said, went back nearly fifty years, and she had always been impressed by Sunity Devi's charm. 'Her dignity and her graciousness were the natural expression of a warm heart and a steadfast soul . . . To me she is always *the* maharani.'

As Indira battled with the Government of India for control over Cooch Behar in the 1920s, women all over India were becoming increasingly involved in the independence movement. The desire for emancipation had stirred only a privileged minority to action, but the desire for autonomy awakened a new spirit of courage and determination in India's previously timorous women. Mohandas Gandhi's civil disobedience movement, or satyagraha, launched in December 1920 and rising in intensity over the next two decades, was embraced by women. Emphasizing 'silent and dignified suffering', effectively utilizing boycotts, public protests, strikes, fasting and non-resistance to force and arrests, Gandhi's brand of passive non-violent resistance was a technique for which Indian women of all classes were especially suited, and allowed them to protest against British rule while retaining the vestiges of their modesty.

Women, who bought food and clothing for their families, were also the principal agents of swadeshi, boycotting foreign goods as a political protest.* Wearing Indian clothes, especially made of khadi, or hand-loomed cotton, was an expression of solidarity with India's

* Jawaharlal Nehru's father, Motilal, and Motilal's great friend, the nationalist Bengali politician Chittaranjan Das, vowed to give up their favourite drinks, respectively Scotch whisky and French brandy, in the name of swadeshi. Das died almost immediately, and on hearing the news, Motilal broke his oath and called for a whisky, saying, 'I don't want to die young like Das' (interview, Swarupa Das, 6.4.02).

freedom-fighters. In Baroda, one of Chimnabai's granddaughters remembers wearing cotton saris 'because we had to encourage the Indian handloom industry'.

Gandhi, champion of the oppressed, praised female moral power, endurance, self-sacrifice and courage: 'If non-violence is the law of our being, the future is with woman.' He saw women as men's equals, and encouraged women to do so too. 'Woman,' he said, 'has as much right to shape her own destiny as man has to shape his.' An important element of Gandhi's contribution to Indian politics was his inclusivity and breadth of appeal: under his influence, for the first time, activists were not just educated, middle-class men and women from the sophisticated urban centres of the British provinces, such as Calcutta, Poona and Bombay, but were drawn from all over India, from both sexes, from every clan and from outside caste.

Women even broke purdah to take a more active role in the protest movement. While Jawaharlal Nehru was in prison in 1932, his mother – a middle-aged, upper-caste Hindu woman of delicate health who had lived in seclusion most of her life – allowed herself to be attacked by policemen with lathis as she sat, steadfast and immovable, at the head of a demonstration. People trying to protect her were arrested; she was knocked to the ground and hit repeatedly with canes. She fainted and an open wound on her head gushed blood on to the road. Eventually she was picked up and taken home by a policeman. 'She was full of joy and pride at having shared with our volunteer boys and girls the privilege of receiving cane and lathi blows,' recorded Nehru. In this women's crusade, led by the indomitable Sarojini Naidu, over 5,000 women were imprisoned from 1929 to 1933.

Female activism was not always as restrained as Swarup Rani Nehru's. In December 1931, two Indian schoolgirls asked to see a British magistrate in Comilla on the pretext of obtaining his permission to enter a swimming competition; they shot him. Two months later, Bina Das unsuccessfully fired five shots at the Governor of Bengal while she was collecting her degree at Calcutta University. 'My object was to die and if to die, to die nobly fighting against this despotic system of government which has kept my people in perpetual subjection.' That same year, 1932, Pritilata Waddedar led a raiding party of fifteen young men into the Pahartali Railway Officers Club in Chittagong during which one woman died and twelve more people were injured. All the gang escaped except for Pritilata who swallowed potassium cyanide at the scene of the attack.

Despite these extreme cases, female activism was rewarded by Congress in 1933 with a promise of equal rights in a future independent India in the Fundamental Rights Resolution. The Government of India decreed in 1919, the year after British women joined the electorate, that the individual provinces of British India could decide whether to allow Indian women the vote. Over the 1920s, female suffrage extended throughout India, but only to that rare breed of Indian woman who was well educated and owned property. By the 1937 elections, one-sixth of India's adult population, including 6 million women, had won the right to vote for provincial state legislatures to which they elected eighty women, including Jawaharlal Nehru's sister Nan Pandit. Congress won 716 of 1,161 seats in the 1937 elections.

'The call of freedom had always a double meaning for them [women],' said Nehru, 'and the enthusiasm and energy with which they threw themselves into the struggle had no doubt their springs in the vague and hardly conscious, but nevertheless, intense desire to rid themselves of domestic slavery also.' Margaret Cousins, the feminist activist instrumental in the foundation of both the Women's Indian Association and the All-India Women's Conference, went even further than Nehru with the explicit identification of female emancipation in India with the nation's independence from British rule. 'The movement for the progress and freedom of the women of India is one and the same movement as that for the progress and freedom of India itself,' she declared in 1939.

Winston Churchill was one Englishman whose disapproval of women's rights was nearly an intense as his disapproval of India becoming independent. He saw Gandhi as an insult to the concept of Empire that he venerated, describing in 1931 'the nauseating and humiliating spectacle of this one-time Inner Temple lawyer, now seditious fakir, striding half-naked up the steps of the Viceroy's palace to parley on equal terms with the representative of the King-Emperor'. Gandhi's bemusement with the British had a gentler tone: when he was told that Lord Irwin, the viceroy, prayed before making every important decision, he said, smiling, 'What a pity God gives him such bad advice.'

Nationalist politicians were being greeted by the 1920s with the same kind of pomp and popular adulation usually reserved for maharajas. In 1928, Motilal Nehru, elected president of the Indian National Congress, arrived in Calcutta with his family for the annual convention.

They rode to the opening meeting in a procession with Motilal, Jawa-harlal, Kamala and Indira in a carriage drawn by thirty-four white horses, followed by mounted Congress volunteers, marching women in green and red-bordered khadi saris, a medical unit, and finally a fleet of motor-cycles led by the radical Bengali Congress leader Subhas Chandra Bose.

Despite the ease with which they moved in European as well as Indian circles, the Cooch Behar children were proud national-ists. They each had little spinning wheels, symbols of India's self-sufficiency; they shouted Congress slogans as they played; Mohandas Gandhi and Jawaharlal Nehru were their heroes. When Bhaiya went to Harrow he was thrilled that his room had once belonged to Jawaharlal Nehru, whose name was carved into the bedhead. 'I personally have always held it to be the first duty of an Indian prince that he should also be an Indian nationalist,' declared Hamidullah, Nawab of Bhopal, in 1931. Just as Indian women were able to rise above centuries of ingrained humility to fight for their country's independence, so too did the majority of India's princes value their emerging nation's interests above their own.

Though they had travelled extensively with their mother since they were small and attended schools in the subcontinent and Europe, the place the Cooch Behar children loved best was Cooch Behar. The palace and grounds were a magical, rambling playground. Their days there were always full. The children were up early to ride before breakfast. Miss Hobart and Miss Oliphant, English governesses recommended by Queen Mary, taught them English history and literature and French; two Bengali tutors gave them lessons in Indian history, mathematics, Bengali and Sanskrit. They played tennis, went shooting and roamed the palace grounds on their bicycles, visiting the baby elephants in the pilkhana or swinging, four at a time, in the swing that hung from a massive banyan tree. In the palace grounds Jit had built for Ila a miniature, white-washed house with two storeys and a domed roof in which the children learned to cook and held tea-parties. They had adored pets – monkeys, puppies, baby panthers, a wounded deer which Ila nursed back to health; even Ma had a disobedient Dalmatian.

Indira's endless stream of guests was a constant source of amusement, especially when the foreigners dressed up in Indian clothes, or spoke terrible Hindi to their servants. She loved giving fancy-dress balls at which the male palace servants were always asked to dress in drag. Foreigners had to follow strict house rules when they went on shikar: female guests were forbidden from stripping down to sunbathe as they rode elephants through the jungle, and no staff – from sweepers up to ADCs – were to be invited into guests' tents for any reason. American guests sometimes complained that these strictures were invasions of their privacy, not to mention undemocratic, but no exceptions were made.

Ila, with her huge, soulful eyes, had inherited her father's wit and gift for mimicry; sports-mad Bhaiya soon grew out of his early arrogance, though he still liked to be called 'Yuvraj' or crown prince; Indrajit was 'the mischievous one, always getting into the most imaginative kinds of trouble'; Ayesha, the tomboy, adored Bhaiya, who protected her from Ila and Indrajit's teasing; gentle Menaka trailed after her brothers and sisters. When the author William Gerhardi visited Cooch Behar in the late 1920s, he was impressed by the teenaged Bhaiya and Indrajit's 'vivid hospitality, contrasting with their charming, gentle natures, quiet voices and sad eyes'. For all their love of fun, the Cooch Behars were always described as having sad eyes.

As a child, Ayesha was known as the 'pagly rajkumari', or mad princess, because of the interest she took in the lives and welfare of the palace servants. Earnestly, she inquired how much they were paid and what their living conditions were, and planned detailed improvements for them. Elephants were her overwhelming passion, 'the most important and beloved creatures in the world'. She spent hours with the mahouts in the palace pilkhana, listening to their plaintive songs and learning elephant-lore that had been passed down from generation to generation. Like her brothers and sisters, she knew how to ride an elephant perched on its neck, like a mahout, and loved nothing more than lying down between the massive ears, 'feeling the faint breeze as he flapped his ears, listening to the buzz of the bees, saturated with the peculiar smell of the elephant, the sense of the jungle all around'.

Just as in Nripendra's day, shikars were the focal point of life in Cooch Behar. Two or three big hunts took place each winter in the state's jungle reserves at Patlakhawa or Takuamari, though on any day at the palace a report might arrive of a wild animal that had developed a taste for domestic animals, or even human flesh, and needed destroying. These impromptu hunts were longed-for treats: lessons would be cancelled and the shikar elephants readied for the expedition.

The children spent the first few summers after Jit died at the Barodas' cottage in Ooty, with their grandparents and Baroda cousins. When Bhaiya and the family left Cooch Behar, all the courts, offices, schools and colleges were closed for a day; when

Bhaiya returned, the students of Victoria College lined the palace drive from the crested iron gates (surmounted by a painted stone lion on one side and an elephant on the other) to the portico to cheer his arrival home.

The 1,000-mile journey to Ooty took over a week, with a caravan including thirty horses (and their thirty grooms), luggage filling four lorries, and countless attendants:

a maid for each of the girls and a valet for each of the boys, assorted relatives and companions, two ADCs and their families, six butlers, four *jamedars* or footmen, eight guards, an English governess, two Indian tutors, our English chauffeur and his wife and daughter, four Indian drivers, two dressmakers, one medical assistant, one Indian and one English cook, four kitchen staff, a clerk of the kitchen, the comptroller of the household, his clerk, an accountant and his clerk.

A plump, unhappy thirteen-year-old boy invited himself to lunch in Ooty one summer's day in 1925, with a special request that he be given Indian, not English, food. He was the newly installed Maharaja of Jaipur, and he was desperate for some home-cooked food because his British tutors had restricted him to a plain diet of European cooking. This accords with a description of him at the prize-giving at Mayo College two years earlier, sitting in the front row, 'fat, sulky and magnificent'.

Jai (short for Jaipur, but also meaning victory in Hindi), as he became known, was the son of a thakur, or lord, related to the Jaipur royal family. Jaipur was one of the principal Rajput princi-palities with a 17-gun salute. The aging Maharaja Sawai Madho Singh had no legitimate heir (some said he was afraid of a curse which foretold he would die within six months of having a son), and chose Jai to succeed him in a process similar to that in Baroda when Sayajirao came to the throne. The thakur's two sons were summoned to the royal court to meet the Maharaja. According to tradition, the boys held out a gold coin for him as a symbol of their allegiance.

The Jaipur legend is that while Jai's brother stood there properly waiting, Jai, who was only ten, grew impatient at the Maharaja's slowness in accepting the tribute, dropped his hands to his sides, and pocketed the gold coin. This so struck the Maharaja as a sign of independence and character appropriate to a prince that he adopted the younger boy.

It was not until four months later, when Jai was awakened in the middle of the night and taken to the zenana in Jaipur's City Palace, that he was told he had been selected as the heir to the Jaipur gaddi. He was formally adopted in March 1921, and given the name Man Singh. On Madho Singh's death eighteen months later, he ascended the throne, though he was not invested with his full powers until 1931. Rivalry among Jaipur's noble families meant that Jai had to be guarded for his own safety; the ritual and formality of the Jaipur court were further new constraints. Lonely and uncertain, this was the hardest time in his life, when 'he got fatter and fatter and sadder and sadder'.

Before his death, Jai's adopted father had arranged two marriages for him, to an aunt and her niece from nearby Jodhpur, another ancient Rajput state. In 1924 the miserable schoolboy married Marudhar Kanwar, twelve years his senior. From a distance, her five-year-old niece, Kishore Kanwar, watched her aunt marry her own fiancé – whom she herself would not actually meet until her wedding day eight years later. Marudhar went to live in the Jaipur zenana with the other palace women, and her plump teenaged husband was allowed to visit her there every two weeks. She bore him a daughter, Prem Kumari, nicknamed Mickey by her English nanny, in 1929, and a son, Bhawani Singh, in 1931. So much champagne was drunk to celebrate Bhawani's birth that he was nicknamed Bubbles. The following year Jai married twelve-year-old Kishore.

In 1929, the young Maharaja was sent to England to attend the Royal Military Academy at Woolwich. Jai thrived in this new environment. He loved Woolwich and he loved London: the dancing, the parties, the girls. 'Life from now on,' observed Jai's biographer, 'was to be divided into two separate existences –

responsibilities in India; "fun" abroad.' An important element of this exciting new life was the vivacious Maharani of Cooch Behar, Indira, who had given him Indian food in Ooty all those years before.

Jai came to stay with the Cooch Behar family in Calcutta for the first time the year Bubbles was born. The Christmas season in Calcutta was the highlight of Indian high society's year. Jai, celebrated for his polo-playing as much as his ancient title and incredible wealth, brought his team to compete in the India Polo Association Championship. Sixty gleaming polo ponies, each with its own groom wearing a brightly coloured Rajput turban, arrived at Woodlands from Jaipur. Then Jai himself appeared in an open-top green Rolls-Royce, a slim, elegant figure with dazzling good looks. 'Everyone in Calcutta found him charming and relaxed and yet he generated an air of graceful confidence that was most compelling. He laughed and joked with everyone in his low drawling voice and was very flirtatious which made him all the more attractive.'

Polo was India's sporting obsession, its national game, and Jai was perhaps the best player in the country, with a handicap of nine out of a possible ten. His game was fast, elegant and delightful to watch. During the 1930s his team won the India Polo Association Championship six years running, and he took the team to England in 1933 where they were undefeated. The sports-mad Cooch Behar children regarded Jai as a hero, and Ayesha, a princess, secretly dreamed 'that I would somehow, miraculously, be transformed into a groom so that I could hold his horse for him and hand him his stick and he might inadvertently touch my hand'. He became the romantic focus of all her hopes.

For his part, Jai loved the warmth of the Cooch Behar family atmosphere, something he had missed terribly when he was taken to live in Jaipur's City Palace as a ten-year-old boy. He let the children beat him at tennis, challenged them to bicycle races, told them jokes and let them sip his champagne. From the start, he singled Ayesha out. When he won the polo tournament that winter of 1931, Indira told him he could have anything he wanted as a prize; he requested that Ayesha, then twelve and not yet grown-up enough to wear a sari, accompany him to dinner at Firpo's, the most fashionable restaurant in Calcutta. When Ayesha shot her first panther, he sent her a congratulatory telegram, 'almost as thrilling as the kill itself'. He took her riding and offered her advice on her seat which she was too proud to follow. He exclaimed, good-naturedly, to Ma's maids, who all adored him and reported his words back to an eager Ayesha, 'Oh, that princess of yours! How she stomps around the place! Has she no femininity?'

In 1932, the Cooch Behar family spent a few days with Jai in his newly renovated Rambagh Palace in Jaipur. Once it had been a series of pleasure pavilions and gardens just outside the old city, but Jai had made it the last word in modern luxury. Ayesha was staggered by Jaipur's desert beauty: it is, as a nineteenth-century visitor described it, 'a pink city set on the border of a blue lake, and surrounded by the low, red spurs of the Aravali [hills]'. She 'thought it was the most beautiful place I had ever been to in my life'. Soon after this visit, Jai told Indira he wanted to marry Ayesha when she was old enough. Indira laughed at him, and said, 'I never heard such sentimental rubbish.'

The following year, 1934, Ayesha, Ila and Baby (accompanied only by an ADC, his wife and children and a maid) were sent to Santiniketan (the Abode of Peace), the school run by Rabindranath Tagore near Calcutta. Ayesha lived in the girls' dorm, where she and the other students 'slept on mats on the floor, took cold bucket baths, and used an outdoor latrine'.

Another student at Santiniketan in 1934 was the young Indira Gandhi. Indira Nehru was born in 1917, two years before Ayesha, in the month, as her father noted, that the Russian Revolution began. To India's new wave of nationalists, Indira's lineage was every bit as exalted as Ayesha's. Her paternal grandfather, Motilal, was an aristocratic Hindu lawyer, one of the richest and most sophisticated men in Allahabad (it was rumoured, falsely, that he even had his Savile Row suits sent to England to be laundered), and an influential early member of the Indian National Congress. Her father, Jawaharlal, was schooled at Harrow and Cambridge, and qualified as a lawyer. In 1916, the year before Indira was born,

Jawaharlal met Mohandas Gandhi, recently returned from South Africa to India, at Congress's annual meeting. Gandhi radicalized Jawaharlal, and by the 1930s the two men were hardened campaigners, in and out of British prisons, veteran activists and leaders of Gandhi's civil disobedience movement. Indira Nehru, whose earliest memory was of a symbolic bonfire of imported clothes at her grandparents' house in Allahabad, was heir to this revolutionary tradition.

Santiniketan was a bohemian experimental school, where lessons were held outside in the shade of spreading mango and peepul trees on which Tagore pinned his paintings. Teachers and students went barefoot. Tagore was a universalist: all aspects of Indian culture were celebrated, but European works were not excluded. The otherworldly white-bearded, saffron-robed poet was a legendary figure who, though he no longer taught, took an active and affectionate interest in all Santiniketan's students. Ayesha used to bicycle over to see Tagore in the hut in which he lived, wrote and painted. He prodded her about her handwriting (she could not get used to writing the backwards Bengali 's') and told her and Ila to stop performing the Shiv puja Indira insisted they perform to ensure they found good husbands; 'Gurudev [Tagore] did not believe in idol worship.' Indira did not believe in idol worship, either – except in this one, vital matter.

Ila's puja was more immediately effective than Indira had intended. At Santiniketan, she met and fell in love with another student, Romendra Kishore Deb Burman, a cousin of the Maharaja of Tripura, an eastern jungle kingdom even more wild and remote than Cooch Behar. Though their ancestry was ancient (the Maharaja was the 180th of his line), the Tripuran royal family were progressive patrons of the arts. Rabindranath Tagore had been 'discovered' by a maharaja of Tripura.

In the spring of 1936, just after Ila and Baby had set out for Europe under Chimnabai's charge, someone at a party asked Indira whether it was true that Ila was married. Indira laughed it off, but just to be sure, made inquiries. Ila and Romendra had indeed got married in a Calcutta registry office. Ila, when questioned later, said she knew that Ma wouldn't have consented to the wedding because Romendra was still a student; it was far better to present her with a *fait accompli*.

According to Ila and Romendra's youngest son, Habi, another reason Romendra was considered unsuitable was that he was a teetotaller. Romendra began drinking to be 'accepted into the fold' and would die in 1975 from alcohol abuse 'almost as if to fulfil a family wish'.

Indira was furious about the secret marriage. When she arrived at the Barodas' house in Paris, she and Chimnabai took Ila into a room to have it out with her. Soon, a smiling Ila emerged and shut the door behind her; the sound of raised voices could still be heard within. She explained to an amazed cousin waiting outside that she had 'manoeuvred the conversation around to Ma's own marriage and now Ma and . . . [Chimnabai] were angrily reliving the conflict and estrangement, minute by minute, and had forgotten all about Ila'.

After preparing a trousseau for Ila in Paris and London, Indira took her back to India to be married properly, leaving Menaka, Baby, Indrajit and Ayesha in London in the care of Chimnabai, who was staying in her usual suite at the Dorchester. During that summer, Jai took the seventeen-year-old Ayesha for a drive around Hyde Park and, without preamble, his eyes on the road as he weaved through the traffic, told her that he had long ago decided he wanted to marry her. What did she think? He had preparations to make, if she did want to, and he needed a bit of time to make the arrangements. She also needed to be aware that, because he played polo and flew, he might have an accident; if he did, would she still want to be with him? All the unbelieving, rapturous Ayesha could say was yes.

They kept their engagement secret at first, and met only clandestinely. Ayesha had to use the telephone kiosk in Pont Street, Knightsbridge to ring Jai because the girls' guardian listened in to her conversations in their flat. She would say she was going to the cinema with a friend from the Monkey Club, the finishing school she attended, or one of her sisters, and sneak off to meet Jai in the buttery of the Berkeley Hotel. Jai gave her a ring which she wore only when she was alone at night. It was a heady period. 'Looking back on it now I see that those times were much more fun than an ordinary approved courtship would have been. There was the challenge of outwitting our elders, of arranging secret meetings, of working out how to have letters posted without the knowledge of the ADCs, governesses or clerks,' remembers Ayesha. 'And every now and then there was the marvellous, unheard-of liberty of going for a drive in the country with Jai, of a stolen dinner at Bray, or of an outing on the river in a boat.'

Ayesha and Menaka went off on holiday to Dinard that summer as planned, and then Ayesha went to another finishing school, Brillantmont, in Lausanne. Finally, she plucked up the courage to write to her mother about Jai's proposal; he had become concerned about his fiancée's commitment because when he had seen Indira in India she had not mentioned the matter to him. 'I think the Maharaja of Jaipur must have spoken to you,' wrote Ayesha at last. 'I hope you don't mind our arranging this without asking you first. When His Highness asked me directly about marrying him, there was nothing I could do, so I agreed.' She was still so in awe of him that she could barely say his name in front of other people.

Indira replied that they should wait for two years and see how they felt. She was ambivalent about the relationship for several reasons. She adored Jai and was thrilled at the prospect of having him as a son-in-law – he had spent so much time with them since that Christmas in 1931 that he was like a member of the family already – but she did not like the thought of Ayesha being anyone's third wife and going into purdah in an old-fashioned state where her every movement would be restricted. Also she was fond of Jai's second wife, Kishore Kanwar, and did not want to see her hurt. She 'predicted gloomily that I [Ayesha] would become simply "the latest addition to the Jaipur nursery" '. There would be time enough to see if Jai and Ayesha were serious, and hope she might meet someone else – preferably someone unmarried.

Ayesha's brothers and sisters were also reluctant to give the match their complete approval. Indrajit, always teasing, professed disbelief that Jai, his hero, could stoop to marrying the 'Broomstick', as he had always called his tomboy sister. Ila thought Ayesha was too 'spineless' around Jai to deal with his flirtatiousness. Bhaiya's concerns were more fundamental: he told an indignant Ayesha not to imagine that Jai would 'give up all his girls'. 'Jai isn't going to stop liking girls or taking them out just because he's married to you,' he told her bluntly. 'And really, you mustn't mind.'

A friend of Ayesha's, Sher Ali Pataudi, believed that Jai's approach to his third marriage was matter of fact rather than sentimental. 'To him marriage was a necessity and to produce children a duty, to the state and to the House. So to him one more [wife] made no difference, especially when she could ride well and keep him company in his sport and outdoor life.' Ayesha was ideal because she was 'an attractive modern princess with a most attractive family, well connected and with the kind of upbringing he wanted – modern, European, and yet belonging to the same fraternity.'

But Jai's Rajasthani kinsmen objected to the union. Though a Cooch Behar princess had married a Jaipur maharaja 350 years before and the Cooch Behars were originally descended from Rajput kshatriyas, they were seen by the ancestor-obsessed Rajputs as tainted by generations of intermarriage with princesses from tribal hill states. Nor did the Baroda connection impress the Rajputs, who considered the Maratha ruling clans vulgar, violent arrivistes. The family's recent taste for European high life and their susceptibility to scandal set the seal on Rajput disdain.

Another marriage – an unnecessary marriage, since Jai's wives had already produced sons – would also offend the Jodhpur family from which both Jai's existing wives came, and who were related to the ruling Rajput families of Bikaner, Udaipur, Dungarpur and Jamnagar. The Viceroy, Lord Linlithgow, warned Jai that marrying Ayesha could seriously damage his relations with his neighbouring princes. Jai replied that though the Viceroy could depose him, he could not interfere with his private life. 'The Viceroy, seeing his determination, shook his hand and wished him luck.' But the British government still refused to sanction the match. Any 'congratulations or good wishes' were to be offered only in a 'private capacity' and no British officer was to attend the wedding.

Jai had to go to Udaipur to persuade the Maharana there, the most senior of the Rajput princes, to give him his blessing. Amer Singh, Jai's tutor, who had long worried about his friendship with Indira, told Jai that if he married into a 'good Rajput family' he would attend the wedding with pleasure, 'but not when you marry into that family'. But Jai had done his duty by marrying the women his adoptive father had chosen for him; he was resolved, now, to marry for love.

In 1936 Indira asked her parents, Chimnabai and Sayajirao, to visit Cooch Behar for the first time. The Barodas had not been in Calcutta since December 1906, when Chimnabai had opened the Indian Ladies' Conference there, so they planned to combine a few days in the city with a stay in Cooch Behar. A pamphlet published afterwards in Baroda outlines their trip in minute detail.

The Baroda entourage was uncharacteristically large and official. Besides Sayajirao, Chimnabai and their personal servants, the party included Baroda's dewan, a secretary, an accountant, a doctor and two valets. The Baroda state saloon-car was attached to the Frontier Mail at their private station near the palace for the twenty-four-hour journey to New Delhi. There, 'His Highness [and, no doubt, everyone else] motored to Baroda House in New Delhi and took dinner at the Imperial Hotel.' After breaking their journey, they set off again for another twenty-four-hour train ride from Delhi to Calcutta. At Woodlands, 'Mr and Mrs Sandford of polo fame, Mr Holmes, an Anglo-American millionaire and Mr More O'Ferrall, a renowned equine specialist', awaited their arrival. A full programme lay ahead of the house-party.

On 23 December, Sayajirao received the title of Bhupati-Chakravarty from the principal of the Sanskrit College in recognition of Sayajirao's lifetime of service to Baroda and to India. He was in exalted company: only three other men – Rabindranath

Tagore, Sir M. N. Mookerjee and Sir Francis Younghusband – had been similarly honoured.

Calcutta's glittering Christmas season was in full swing by the time the Barodas arrived. Bhaiya hosted a dinner for them at Firpo's. They went racing – a favourite pastime of both families – and attended balls at Belvedere, the Governor of Bengal's white palace across the road from Woodlands, and at Viceregal House. The Maharaja of Tripura held a cocktail party in their honour and the Maharaja of Kapurthala invited them to dinner to see in the New Year, 1937. Jai's celebrated team beat the state of Bhopal's at polo.

The town of Cooch Behar was decked in flowers and bunting for Chimnabai and Sayajirao's arrival and when their train pulled into the station a 21-gun salute was fired. Cheering crowds filled the streets. 'Naturally she [Indira] was overjoyed to welcome her Father and Mother for the first time to Cooch Behar and in their turn they were happy to be with her in her home and to see Cooch Behar modern and progressive,' reads the account of their visit. 'Altogether a red letter day for everyone.' 'Such a big palace for such a little state,' Sayajirao is said to have commented.

Indira, now forty-five, was still a figure of allure and sophistication. She was a legendary hostess and all her talents were utilized to demonstrate to her adored parents, who had stayed away from her new home for so long, that she had made a home – and run a state – they could be proud of. Inside the palace, as she always did when guests came to stay, she had lain on every bed to ensure the bedside lights were set at the right angle and had a bulb bright enough for reading. She had checked the rooms were filled with flowers chosen to coordinate with their decoration, that the water flasks and biscuit tins on the bedside tables were full, that the beds had both firm and soft pillows, that the inkwells on the desks were filled with red ink as well as blue and that the blotting paper was fresh and unmarked – she always worried that indiscreet imprints of love letters might linger to betray.

That evening, at dinner, Sayajirao returned Bhaiya's speech of welcome in tones that dismissed all the hostility of past years as if it had never existed. Perhaps, having seen his own family grow ever more divided over the years, he was determined to build bridges.

I have known the state of Cooch Behar since the time of your grandfather and grandmother. The latter was a very accomplished lady of amiable disposition and charming manners. Your grandfather was a tall, handsome man of excellent physique, liberal-minded and progressive [Sayajirao's highest praise] and above all a great sportsman. I knew your father and his brothers from their childhood, so that my connection with Cooch Behar, so far from being new, is deeply rooted in the past.

As ever with Sayajirao, the visit was not all fun and games. On 5 January, he laid the foundation stone of His Highness the Maharaja Gaekwad of Baroda's X-ray ward in the Cooch Behar hospital and donated Rs 10,000. X-ray machines were one of Sayajirao's passions: he had enraged Chimnabai on one of their European trips by using money he had given her to buy jewellery in Paris to purchase an X-ray machine for Baroda's hospital.

Bhaiya finished Cambridge later that year and returned to be officially installed as Maharaja of Cooch Behar in an elaborate durbar using an order of precedence dating back to the nineteenth century. The durbar was the focal point of two days of festivities. The military parade (of the 'Coochie Lancers') began at 8.15 a.m. in front of the palace and was followed by a Scouts rally. At 9.30 a birthday gun salute rang out, and then the ritual prayers and devotions took place in Cooch Behar's temples, mosques and masjids. The durbar began in the palace's great hall at 11.30. Guests had been requested to wear any colour but black. On Bhaiya's right stood his sixty-two officers of state and on his left his family, headed by Indrajit. At 2 p.m., alms were distributed to the poor. That evening, the town and palace were illuminated by hundreds of tiny, twinkling lights, and the sky was lit up by a blaze of fireworks. The following day, Bhaiya hosted a garden party at the Cooch Behar club after a sports display in the palace grounds. Indira declared that from now on she would not be known as Maharani Indira Devi or the Dowager Maharani Sahiba, but would adopt the grander title of Her Highness the Maharani Sahiba.

In November 1937, less than a year after their trip to Cooch Behar, Sayajirao grew more ill than usual, though it was an unspecified ailment, more drowsiness than anything else. He was desperate to get home, so Chimnabai and Indira chartered a plane and flew him back to Baroda from Europe and the family gathered at Laxmi Vilas. He died on 6 February 1938. Cooch Behar went into official mourning: a 75-gun salute was fired; offices, courts and schools were closed; the Cooch Behar *Gazette* was published with a black border and even the cinema was cancelled for a night. The principal of Cooch Behar's Victoria College praised Sayajirao for his 'long beneficent rule, high culture, broad outlook, and large-hearted sympathy for all . . . [He] occupied a unique position among the Indian princes and left a rich tradition as an ideal Indian ruler.'

Sayajirao's body was taken to the banks of the river next to the Kirti Mandir, or memorial house, that he had built near Laxmi Vilas to mark his fiftieth anniversary as maharaja. The corpse was laid on the pyre with his feet pointing towards Benares. More wood was piled on the body, and ghee was poured over the pyre. When it was set alight it burst suddenly into flames with an effect 'so striking and unforeseen that I felt my heart beat as though some supernatural apparition had suddenly risen before my eyes'. The mourners watched the blaze burn out. Some of Sayajirao's ashes were cast into the river, others were put into an urn that would be placed in the Kirti Mandir.

Although it would have been inconceivable that she would ever have had a job, as part of her catholic education Ayesha studied at a secretarial college in London in 1938. She learned shorthand as 'Miss Devi' during the day and went to cocktail parties and nightclubs in the evenings with her English friends and various members of her Indian family who were also in London, including Indrajit – nicknamed Diggers – and her uncles Victor and Dhairyashil. For the first time in her life, she was independent, free of the constant presence of ADCs and servants. She went to the cinema, rode on the underground, felt herself one of the jostling crowd at rush hour. When she and Menaka returned home in the spring of 1938, after Sayajirao's death, they submitted again to the old restrictions: though they were not and had never been in purdah, in India princesses could not go out unaccompanied, even to buy a hand-kerchief.

What made up for any petty limitations on her behaviour was being with Jai again. Though they had been in constant contact since their secret engagement eighteen months earlier, they had seen each other only rarely. In January 1938, when Ayesha was in Cooch Behar, the strain was beginning to tell. 'I am feeling miser-able and very unhappy as no news from you,' Jai wrote. 'So drop me a line . . . if you can as you know just one word from you makes all the difference to me. I need not tell you how I feel about you hardly a moment pass [*sic*] when you are not in my thoughts and I just long to see you again.'

But in 1937 Jai had managed to visit Ayesha at her finishing school in Switzerland, pretending to be her cousin, and later that year he spent a few days with the Cooch Behars at Cannes. He joined Ayesha, her mother and her brothers in Budapest in June 1938. For Ayesha, everything was bathed in rosy light when she was with Jai; even the threat of war seemed unimportant. The fact that Jai was in India – taking Indira and Ayesha out for cocktails on the lawn of the Willingdon Club in Bombay, staying with the Cooch Behars at Woodlands for Christmas, shooting with them in Cooch Behar – made everything all right.

Indira rented Moon House in Srinagar in the summer of 1939, when the almond blossom was in flower. Ila brought her infant son, Bhim, and daughter, Devika, to stay in a houseboat; her husband was abroad, serving his cousin, the Maharaja of Tripura, as military secretary. Bhaiya and Indrajit (who turned twenty-one while they were there) came for the polo. Chimnabai and seven Baroda grand-children rented a house nearby. Jai managed to snatch a few days in Kashmir as well. They went on picnics, bear hunts, boat rides across Shalimar Lake; rode, played tennis, cricket and hockey. 'I remember it all as the last idyll of my girlhood,' wrote Ayesha.

Sher Ali Pataudi (uncle of the cricketer Tiger Pataudi), a friend of Bhaiya's and later his commander in the war, spent several carefree weeks with the family in Kashmir. Ayesha enchanted him: he thought her a lost soul, aloof, unfathomable, with an air of 'enduring life without enjoying it' as she waited to marry Jai, whom, he said, she idealized and adored. Still, this did not stop her flirting with Pataudi. Like Jai he wooed her with riding tips while she grumbled to Baby, 'Just my luck, he had to be married.' He read her palm with surprising prescience: 'You will get what you want, but there is no limit to want. Eventually you will get your wealth, but at the expense of real wealth. You will live long – [a] very long life, still trying to find what's real life.' As they walked together, he quoted an Urdu poem to her in his own translation:

I will never forget that yawning stretch of yours,
Like beauty itself taking off to its source.
And then you stopped short – having raised your hands.
When you saw me looking, smiled and dropped your hands.

War broke out in Europe while they were in Kashmir, though no one had any idea what that would mean. Hitler invaded Poland on 2 September 1939 and the following day France and Britain declared war on Germany. On the same day, without consulting Congress – now, after the gradual introduction of more representative government to British India in the mid-1930s, the principal political power in the country – the viceroy, Lord Linlithgow, declared war on Germany on India's behalf. Though Congress opposed Fascism and Nazism, and made their sympathy for Britain's cause clear, nationalists rejected the principle that gave the Viceroy the automatic right to engage India in a 'foreign' war.

For Ayesha, more sobering than the prospect of war was Jai's recent accident. His plane had crashed, killing the pilot and leaving Jai to be dragged, unconscious and with both ankles broken, from the wreckage. Because they were not officially engaged, Ayesha could not rush to his hospital bed. As thanksgiving when he recovered, Jai had heavy silver doors installed in the seventeenth-century

Shila Devi temple at Amber, and his second wife, Kishore, gave the goddess a pair of solid silver legs to celebrate Jai's legs being preserved.

The Cooch Behar annual review of 1939 noted each of Jit and Indira's children's activities. Bhaiya had received his pilot's licence; attended the Chamber of Princes, of which he was an active, respected standing committee member, at its three sessions in Bombay, Simla and New Delhi; raised his polo handicap by one goal and continued his patronage of several sporting clubs. In later years, he captained the Bengal cricket team. Indrajit passed out of the Indian Military Academy at Dehra Dun, and obtained a commission in Bhaiya's regiment, the 7th Light Cavalry, at Bolarum. Ila was living in Agartala with her children. Menaka had recovered from an illness. Finally, that year, Ayesha's engagement was announced.

By that winter, Jai was well enough to come to Calcutta for the season. He told Indira the two years she had prescribed were up. The war had changed everything, and he wanted to be married as quickly as possible. Indira said the wedding could take place within the year, but this was not soon enough for Jai. When he saw her soon afterwards in Delhi, he insisted again. This time, she gave them her blessing. Jai and Ayesha were formally betrothed in Cooch Behar in March 1940 (Jai flew there in his own plane), and the date of their wedding was set by the pandits for 17 April.

Although Ayesha fell ill with diphtheria in the weeks before the wedding and the doctors advised delaying the ceremony so she could convalesce, Jai refused to wait any longer. The only thing left to arrange was her trousseau. Indira had had the foresight to buy heavy bed linen and towels for Ayesha in Czechoslovakia, shoes and bags in Florence and filmy nightdresses in Paris, but she could not remember where she had had the trousseau sent. Finally, it was found at the Ritz in Paris, as the *drôle de guerre*, or phony war, drew to an end and the beleaguered city prepared for another German invasion. Miraculously the trousseau arrived in India before the wedding.

Ayesha was more interested in sports clothes than saris but she duly went off to Glamour, a sari shop in Calcutta, to buy the many saris she would need in her new role as Maharani of Jaipur. With every one she chose the proprietor's face fell, and when she left the shop he rushed to telephone Indira and beg her to come and look at Ayesha's brightly coloured selection. 'Rubbish, rubbish!' she exclaimed when she saw them, and picked out over 200 superb saris for her tomboy daughter, 'in plain and patterned chiffon, with and without borders, some hand-embroidered, others appliquéd, some embroidered in gold, and others of simple, heavy silks'.

'Ayesha, I am afraid, doesn't wear her sari half as well as her mother,' said a family friend, speculating that Ayesha always stood in her adored mother's shadow, defining herself against Indira at the same time as fearing she could not live up to her example. She 'instinctively and yet quite unknowingly tried to copy her mother all her life'. Though she may have lacked Indira's overwhelming panache, Ayesha had a breezy grace of her own, wearing a dark-red Jacques Fath coat with a fur collar over a sari or crisp and relaxed in her sportswear and slacks, taking what she wanted from both Indian and European styles. She always looks fresh in photos and old home movies, as though she has just come in from outside.

The wedding presents were much more exciting than her trousseau: the Nawab of Bhopal gave Ayesha a black Bentley and Chimnabai gave Jai and her a house in Mussorie, in the Himalayan foothills; Jai was given a pair of elephants. Ayesha was unmoved by the exquisite jewels with which an Indian bride is traditionally presented. Her lack of interest in jewellery was in stark contrast to Indira and Chimnabai; when her engagement was announced, the Gem Palace, Jaipur's most celebrated jewellers, knowing her mother and grandmother's tastes and spending habits, rubbed their hands together in glee, but they were soon disappointed in their new maharani. Some years later, Jai gave Ayesha some exquisite, and rather large, diamond drop earrings. She wore them to a small drinks party, horrifying her mother who was also present. 'Don't you know how to dress?' Indira demanded of her daughter. 'Those earrings are too much for a cocktail party. Now, if you were going to Buckingham Palace, they would be perfect . . . If I were a journalist,' she continued, 'I'd describe you as, "The overdressed Maharani of Jaipur".'

The wedding preparations – costing Rs 3,50,000, and requiring a committee of fifty-nine – were complete and the family were getting ready to leave Calcutta for Cooch Behar when Indira's brother Dhairyashil, the only one of her three brothers left, fell down the stairs and died later that night. The family was devastated and the wedding was postponed. The priests said the next auspicious date was 9 May, the day before the German Army would break through the Western Front towards Paris.

For twenty-four hours before the wedding, Ayesha fasted. Just as Chimnabai had done over half a century earlier, she bathed in scented oils, rubbed her skin with turmeric paste and performed the traditional pujas and prayers of a bride. Menaka and Baby stayed with Ayesha that night, just as Sunity Devi's sisters had done with her sixty-five years earlier. When Ayesha woke up, she heard the 19-gun salute fired for Jai's arrival. 'Only then did I believe with total conviction that after all the years of waiting I would actually marry my beloved.'

That day seemed interminable, as she was dressed and beautified, according to ritual, by a gaggle of chattering, excited married ladies dressed in brightly coloured saris given to them for the occasion. Her feet were stained with intricate designs in henna, and Rajput ivory bangles were slipped over her hands. Her forehead was anointed with red sandalwood paste, called sindur, which indicated the straight and virtuous path she was expected to tread as a wife. She was wrapped in the traditional crimson sari and weighed down with ornate gold marriage jewellery. In her lap was placed a banana leaf wrapped round several symbolic items which, according to Cooch Behar custom, would bless the marriage, grant Jai longevity and Ayesha many children: a silver-bound conch shell, red powder mixed with rice, and a little silver mirror with areca and betel nut tied to its handle.

As the cannons were fired and the music struck up, Jai arrived behind a procession of marching bands, scouts, dancing girls and forty richly caparisoned elephants, leading forty of his nobles and their attendants. A Bengali bride's feet must not touch the ground on her wedding day so Ayesha was carried out to meet Jai in the mandap, or marriage pavilion, in a silver palanquin borne by her male relations. Bhaiya gave her away. The religious rites went on for so long that eventually the impatient bridegroom – who had, after all, already sat through two similar ceremonies – called out to the priests to hurry up.

There was another week of celebrations after the wedding, but Ayesha and Jai stayed for only two days before setting off on their honeymoon. They were a stunning pair. 'I personally cannot think of any more striking and attractive couple than Jai and Ayesha when they married,' recalled Lord Mountbatten many years later.

When they reached Calcutta station, Ayesha realized for the first time what going into purdah would mean. Before the wedding, she had been so in love that she refused to see what her friends and family were so concerned about. Now, their railway carriage was completely surrounded by screens while Ayesha was led into the waiting car, the windows of which were curtained; there was a curtain separating the passenger seats from the driver's view. 'This depressed me a lot because I hadn't expected it,' she said later. Indrajit, who was travelling with them on his way to join his regiment, kept nudging her and saying, 'Hey, I hope you're not going to live like this all the time.' Though they stayed the night at Woodlands, all the male servants there were shooed away from the new maharani – whom many had known all her life.

The house they stayed at in Ooty was owned by the Jodhpur royal family, to which Jai's first two wives belonged. In the informal, holiday atmosphere of the hill-station, purdah was barely an issue; as they had always done, Ayesha and Jai played tennis, rode, followed the hunt, went out for picnics. But when Jai went to formal receptions at Government House, he did not take his bride because he did not want her to be embarrassed by being the only maharani there. He promised that she would not live in seclusion for ever: 'When people gradually get used to the idea, you can drop purdah altogether.'

At the end of the honeymoon, Jai left Ayesha in Ooty while he went to Bangalore to play polo. He stayed with Kishore and his four children, and told Ayesha to wait for him to contact her about whether she should join him or wait for him to return to collect her. After a few days, Jai wrote saying he missed her and telling her to come to Bangalore.

Alone and very nervous, Ayesha motored down to Bangalore. Jai was playing polo when she arrived, and an ADC took her to the rooms she would share with him. The ADC returned after a short while with a summons from Second Her Highness, who was in the drawing room and would be pleased if Ayesha would have tea with her. They had met before, but this was an entirely new situation. Kishore was as poised and gracious as ever, but it was not until Jai came back that his relaxed cheerfulness made everything feel natural. That night, Ayesha, Jai, Jo Didi (Jo, short for Jodhpur, was what Jai called Kishore, and Didi means elder sister, so after this she was always Jo Didi to Ayesha) and Bhaiya dined together *en famille*. It was the beginning of a close friendship that neither of them could have anticipated.

In Bangalore, as in Ooty, Ayesha did not have to observe strict purdah. Entertaining was informal and intimate: if they went out to dinner, Ayesha accompanied Jai and if people came to have dinner with them, Ayesha was hostess. 'Although I felt that Jo Didi must resent my presence, she never showed it and perhaps there wasn't so much to resent after all.' Kishore carried on living, as she had always done, behind the purdah, in her own apartments, with her sons – Joey was seven and Pat was five – where Jai visited her as he had always done. Ayesha did not replace her in Jai's life, because she had never really lived with Jai, and her kindness to Ayesha eased the new bride's adjustment to life in Jaipur.

One welcome visitor in Bangalore was Chimnabai, who came to give Ayesha some advice about how to be a queen. 'This entailed, among other things, never going to cocktail parties, never allowing anyone to call me by my first name in the undignified manner my mother did, and never, as I had done, wearing emeralds with a green sari, as they looked much better with pink.' Her grandmother's advice did not help the terrified and uncertain bride when

Ayesha and Jai's train drew into Jaipur station a few weeks later. The blinds were pulled down 'and very gently Jai told me to cover my face'.

Ayesha's first few weeks in Jaipur passed in a haze of introductions, ceremonies and receptions. She settled into her suite adjoining Jai's in the Rambagh Palace, which he had had redecorated for her in pale pink, and acquainted herself with her quarters in the zenana in the City Palace, where she stayed on Jaipur's numerous official ceremonial occasions. Like the other maharanis', her rooms there centred round a small courtyard and had a private durbar hall hung with blue glass lamps.

About 400 women lived in the Jaipur zenana in 1940 – widows, wives, daughters, sisters, aunts and nieces of the Jaipur princes, each with her own retinue. The most senior woman in the zenana was the Dowager Maharani, Maji Sahiba, Jai's adoptive father's widow, who was treated by everyone with the utmost deference. Only during the ladies' durbar at Jai's birthday were his wives permitted to uncover their faces in front of her. The zenana ladies followed everything Jai did with passionate, affectionate interest. 'When Jai's team won the All India Polo Championship, for instance, skirts and shawls were embroidered with polo sticks; when he gained his flying licence, the ladies, who never had – and were never likely to – set foot in a plane themselves, loyally decorated their clothes with aeroplane motifs.'

At Rambagh, Ayesha lived in half-purdah. In the mornings, she was woken by squawking peacocks in the palace grounds. She and Jai went riding together before breakfasting by the pool. She had the run of Rambagh and its extensive grounds, but outside its walls she had to be accompanied, and either veiled or behind the smoked-glass windows of a purdah car. Because she did not speak Hindi she felt like, and seemed, a foreigner. The formality of the Jaipur court meant that Ayesha was always deferred to; she longed for someone to disagree with her, to call her by her name, to be close to. But the smiling zenana ladies just shook their heads gently at her. So grand did this new treatment make her over time that when Indrajit came to stay a year after her marriage he exclaimed with brotherly directness, 'Who the hell do you think you are, Queen Mary?'

In this strange isolation, Ayesha and Jo Didi developed a special friendship. First Her Highness spent most of her time in Jodhpur with her family. Second Her Highness, Jo Didi, was only three years older than Ayesha. She taught the new maharani about the elaborate, confusing rituals minutely observed by the Jaipur court, and initiated her into the pleasures of purdah living – one of which was being able to go to the cinema, where they sat behind a special screen, in pyjamas and dressing gown.

For Ayesha, life with Jai was dominated by polo. At Jaipur, in the evening – at 'cow-dust' hour, so called because the sinking sun sets ablaze the dust particles lifted by the homeward-bound cattle – Ayesha drove out to watch Jai play. She adored the game as much as he did, seeing it more as an art than a sport, but could never relax while watching because of her constant fear he would be injured. They went to Calcutta for the tournaments in December and January, and to England in the summer. During the Jaipur polo season in March, the grounds of Rambagh became a vast tented camp inhabited by the overflow of visiting teams and their attendants. Their friends were Jai's polo-playing pals and their wives, with whom they could be more relaxed than among the stiff nobles of Jaipur who would not let their wives meet the Maharaja's modern young bride.

Religion and ritual were important parts of Jai's public role as maharaja, and although he lacked superstition, Jai performed these rites with devotion and punctiliousness, as he expected his wives to. Govind Devji, an incarnation of Krishna, was Jaipur's deity; Jai began every speech to the people of Jaipur with the words, 'Subjects of Govind Devji . . .' His foreign guests were sometimes surprised to see him get into his Bentley, drive to the fortress of Amber, and sacrifice a goat with his own hand before the temple of Shila Devi. Even when he was abroad, Jai performed his daily puja; during the war and before polo matches, he prayed to the goddess Durga, bringer of victory. Despite her mishmash of religious instruction –

from Sunity Devi's passionately held Brahmoism to Indira's personal faith, by way of Chimnabai's old-fashioned regard for pandits and Sayajirao's inclusiveness – Ayesha grew up to be a devout Hindu. She would not let her mother touch the sacred thread she wore round her wrist because the touch of Indira – a widow – would desanctify it; she avoided travel, decisions or new beginnings on days decreed inauspicious by the pandits.

The overwhelming passion in Jai's life was Jaipur itself. The glamour that clung to him because of his sporting prowess, wealth, good looks and easy charm belied how seriously he took his responsibilities as maharaja. In the words of his penultimate dewan, he was 'an enlightened ruler'. Perhaps, like his fellow-adoptee Sayajirao, he understood better than many princes the swings of fortune, and this lent him compassion; perhaps his childhood loneliness had taught him the importance of extending a hand to others; perhaps the old maharaja had simply chosen his heir well. 'All that we have and all that we are is because of Jaipur,' he told Ayesha, 'and we must give back as much as we can.' Ayesha saw that the people of Jaipur felt a special kinship with her husband. They knew they could stop his car or Jeep any time, for any reason, and he would listen to their complaint or ask after their families. 'Jai embodied for them the qualities of affection, protectiveness and benevolent justice that they associated with the ideal father,' said Ayesha, years later, lamenting the loss of this type of mutually concerned, respectful intimacy between ruler and ruled in modern India.

When the Second World War broke out in September 1939, the Viceroy said he wanted India's princes to remain in their states to organize the war effort there, raising money and troops to send to Europe. For the Rajput maharajas in particular, with their long and honourable military traditions, this was tantamount to being imprisoned. The Maharaja of Bikaner spoke at his sixtieth birthday durbar on 22 October 1939 of 'the dearest wish of my heart as a Rathore Rajput to take my place in the fighting line . . . I long ago also offered to place my own sword and that of the Maharaj Kumar [crown prince] at the disposal of his Imperial Majesty . . . I admit that I am neither as young nor in such good health as when I went off to fight in France, Flanders and Egypt a quarter of a century ago. But no Rajput is ever too old to fight.'

Though he cabled Linlithgow on the day that war was declared begging to be sent to a fighting front, Jai was initially attached to the 13th Lancers, stationed for training at Risalpur, and Ayesha was allowed to go with him to live as an ordinary officer's wife. After the oppressive decorum of life in Jaipur, she adored being a house-wife, with only six servants, as opposed to the several hundred at Rambagh, and entertaining informally, on equal terms with the other officers' wives. 'Best of all', though, 'there was the utter freedom of being one's self.'

Just before Christmas 1941, Jai's regiment was called up to active service on the North-West Frontier. The Axis nations had been trying to develop a power base in Afghanistan since the late 1930s, hoping to replace the pro-British amir with the deposed Ammanullah, in exile in Rome. For their part, the British suspected the Germans and Italians of seeking to distract their attention from the Egyptian and Sudanese fronts by provoking unrest in

Afghanistan, but they could not afford to allow the Axis to establish a foothold there.

Ayesha returned to Jaipur alone for Christmas. Because of the children's English governesses and nurses, the holiday was celebrated with the traditional trappings: a decorated tree, presents and, the *pièce de résistance*, a bearded, rosy Father Christmas lumbering across the manicured lawns of Rambagh aboard a massive state elephant. Though Ayesha missed Jai terribly, his children helped make up for his absence. All four of them were there, and she began to get to know them, taking them for drives in her car, going riding or shooting with them, bicycling or playing table tennis just as she had done all through her childhood in Cooch Behar.

But she still missed her family, and Jai encouraged her to go to Calcutta for New Year with a tacit admission of how hard her new life was to adjust to. 'It must be pretty awful for you at home shut up and surrounded by evil thoughts all the time. Please darling go and enjoy yourself and remember I just live for you and you alone . . .' She arrived in Calcutta on New Year's Day 1942, in time to celebrate Indrajit's engagement at Ma's last party at Woodlands before the house was turned into a military hospital.

When the Japanese took Singapore that February, the war suddenly became immediate to India and Indians. Over the following months the Japanese Army marched into Burma and Malaya, where they were welcomed by the people as liberators, and headed towards India with their slogan 'Asia for the Asiatics' ringing ominously in British ears. Indian soldiers began deserting in their thousands to join a Japanese-controlled Indian National Army. For the first time since the British consolidated their power and created a framework for nationhood in the mid nineteenth century, India's security, both internal and external, was dangerously uncertain.

It was an uncomfortable, lonely time for Ayesha, newly wed and separated from her husband. Away from Jai, she was unsure of how to behave. Her marriage had attracted a lot of attention; she felt as though she was being constantly watched by people hoping both to see her make a mistake and to see evidence that their happiness was a sham. She was also lonely. As a married woman, she was no longer included in the fun, informal parties and expeditions Menaka and Baby organized.

Jai returned from the Afghan border that spring, but, still longing to see action in the Middle East, finally persuaded George VI to let him join the British Life Guards, to which he had been attached in London in the 1930s. He was the first Indian ever to receive a commission in the Household Cavalry, and was prouder of being the only Indian prince to be a captain in the Life Guards than he would have been of being an honorary Lieutenant-General or Major-General in the Indian Army. He sent the King an ecstatic, grateful telegram assuring him 'of the unflinching loyalty and ever-lasting devotion of myself and my house to your Imperial Majesty's person and throne'.

Jai and Ayesha went to Mahabaleshwar, a hill-station near Bombay, so he could say goodbye to Chimnabai. Every morning the old Maharani and Mohandas Gandhi met as they took their constitutionals. Gandhi, while disapproving of war in general and angry that the British had not consulted India before declaring war on her behalf, had initially sanctioned the war against the Axis powers. He was content to put India's movement towards independence on hold while the war was fought. When that ardent imperialist Winston Churchill became prime minister in May 1940 he rejected the recent British line on India – the relatively conciliatory idea that dominion status would be granted as soon as possible after the war – and Indian hopes were dashed once again.

Although he and Jai had never met, in 1937 the British had told Jai to arrest Gandhi as he travelled through Jaipur, which he had not succeeded in doing. 'Ah, so you're the naughty boy who tried to arrest me? I've met you at last,' said Gandhi with typical disingenuousness to Jai when Chimnabai introduced them.

Chimnabai vehemently disapproved of Jai going away. She 'gave me a long lecture [about] how stupid I was going to the war serving in the British army. I should remain at home where there was a lot of work to be done'; the inference was, work to prepare for the day when India would be free.

Ayesha and her mother saw Jai off from Bombay on their first wedding anniversary that May. 'A sight I shall never forget was her standing on the pier,' he recalled, years later. He was sent to Gaza and then Cairo where he was made liaison officer for the Indian State Forces.

In August 1942 Gandhi asked all Congress members to join the Quit India movement. 'We shall either free India or die in the attempt,' he declared. 'We shall not live to see the perpetuation of our slavery.' The British response was immediate. The entire Congress leadership was arrested, though because twelve key Congress politicians – including Jawaharlal Nehru, Asaf Ali, Vallabhbhai 'Sardar' Patel and the current Congress president Abul Kalam Azad – were imprisoned in the same place they used their time there to formulate future policy. Gandhi was held separately in the Aga Khan's palace, where goats were tethered in the garden to provide milk for him. Prominent female Congress members, including Sarojini Naidu and Kamaladevi Chattopadhyaya, were also confined. Across British India, strikes and agitation provoked increasingly violent clashes with the police, and hundreds of protesters were killed as the British grimly maintained their control. This harsh repression 'severely undermined the moral basis of British rule and of the war effort itself'. By the end of 1942, 60,000 people had been arrested.

Because activists concentrated their campaign against the British in the provinces of British India, the princely states largely escaped this new wave of domestic turbulence and continued supporting the Allied cause. In Jaipur, Ayesha worked for the war effort. She went to Red Cross work parties at the Ladies' Club, and began meeting the women of Jaipur she had not encountered in the zenana – women from all walks of life. Her presence encouraged more women to patronize the club, which soon became a hub of Jaipur social and charitable life. Even the purdah ladies, encouraged by Jo Didi and Ayesha, knitted socks for the Jaipur forces abroad. Ayesha organized raffles, tournaments and collections for Indian soldiers in Europe and British casualties in India, and raised Rs 10,000 for the war effort with a silver trinket fund.

These activities, under the cover of patriotism and devotion to their menfolk, encouraged the breakdown of purdah in Jaipur. 'There are old ladies in Jaipur today who say that Ayesha was their liberator, that she opened up for them a world which they might otherwise never have seen,' recorded Jai's biographer in 1985. 'While some were grateful, others were horrified.' But her grandparents on both sides had bequeathed her a sense of paternalistic responsibility, a desire to give back to the community which exalted her, and she always strove to live up to their legacy.

Ayesha also turned her energies to reforming the domestic administration of Rambagh Palace. She discovered, to her shock, that comestibles were ordered 'not just by the crate, but by the dozens of crates'. Unchecked extravagance had led to terrible waste and petty corruption. Jo Didi, for instance, had Evian mineral water specially ordered from France for her own use; Ayesha now found out that even the governess's dogs drank it. If the cook made a crème brulée for four people, he ordered two pounds of cream; when questioned, 'he replied grandly that for the Maharaja no amount of cream was too much'.

Her new regime was unpopular in some quarters, and subtle ways were found of making this unpopularity known. The Home Minister arrived for a meeting with Jai and asked for an iced coffee; he was told trenchantly, 'Third Her Highness has forbidden visitors to be offered drinks with milk.' 'The new Maharani was doing unimaginable things,' wrote Mrs Bhartiya, the Inspectress of Schools in Jaipur.

She had started going to the kitchen and supervising it, she was on the fields playing badminton and tennis, she had bobbed her hair, wore slacks, drove the car, watched polo, and could be seen riding, not only in the Rambagh palace grounds but also on the roads, alongside the Maharaja. It was reported that officers and employees of the Household were on tenter-hooks because of the watchful, though discerning, eyes of this impossible 'She'.

The success of the Ladies Club had been a first step towards encouraging the women of Jaipur out of purdah; the next step was a girls' school. Because the high-born women were the most cloistered, Ayesha decided it should be a school for girls of noble backgrounds, who until then had spent their childhood in one zenana and their adulthood in another. The Maharani Gayatri Devi (MGD) School opened in 1943, with twenty-three students.

If Ayesha was changing life for Jaipur's women, the brilliant Sir Mirza Ismael, appointed dewan by Jai in 1942, was changing life for its whole population. Under his guidance, and with Jai's complete support, the once-autocratic state was moving towards a constitutional monarchy. The prime minister began to preside over cabinet meetings; two elected bodies, a Legislative Council and a Representative Assembly, were established in 1944. 'Without violating tradition or endangering efficiency', without alienating the people from their maharaja or him from them, the slow march to democracy in Jaipur had begun. Sir Mirza was also a passionate conservationist, described by Cecil Beaton, who visited Jaipur during his tenure, as 'the arch-enemy of corrugated iron sheets'. The four years (1942–6) during which he worked alongside Ismael transformed Jai's attitude to government, and gave him 'a definite sense of the way in which he wanted things to go – a sense, also, of which way they were going to have to go in the post-war world'.

As the worldwide war effort intensified in 1942–3 and India's strategic importance was recognized the demands and hardships of wartime increasingly dominated life. In New Delhi, Jaipur House was given over to the WRENS. Tents sprang up throughout the spacious city to accommodate the personnel of the headquarters of the South-East Asia Command, the US Tactical Support, the Joint Intelligence, the Indian Command and the Delhi District. Men who had viewed war as a dangerous but exciting playground now experienced its terrifying reality. The officers of one regiment about to leave for the Far East told Jai they were taking their polo kit; within two months he and Ayesha heard that they were prisoners of war of the Japanese.

There were private sadnesses as well. In 1944, First Her Highness died from liver failure. Bubbles, then only thirteen, had the awful responsibility of lighting her funeral pyre. When he and Joey came to Ayesha's rooms afterwards, he was silent. 'My heart went out to him in his shock and sadness, and I promised myself that in the future I would always look after him.' Bubbles, only twelve years younger than his stepmother, became Ayesha's devoted shadow, affectionately calling her 'mother'.

The following year there was another tragedy. Ila, so bright and vibrant, died (according to varying reports) of ptomaine poisoning or pneumonia. Her three children, who had not been told of her death, were brought to Indira in Darjeeling. 'No one had had the heart to tell them what had happened, and neither did we.' Ayesha took the two elder children, Bhim and Devika, to Jaipur with her, 'and gradually, still without any direct information from me, they seemed to understand that their mother was gone forever'.

In Cooch Behar, ever closer to the action in Asia, Bhaiya served in the South-East Asia Command, from 1943 led by Lord Mount-batten. Within two weeks of hearing that he would be given this 'staggering job', Mountbatten had written affectionately to his old polo chum Jai, asking him to join his staff. 'I shall always remember the thrill and pleasure of playing polo with you and I feel that together we shall knock up a heavy score against the Japanese.' Almost immediately Mountbatten received a coded telegram from the Viceroy, Lord Wavell, advising him not to appoint any ruling prince, including Jaipur, to his staff.

The war effort along the Burmese border was critical, where the British had to contend with the Indian National Army as well as their Axis enemies. Subhas Chandra Bose, a Bengali nationalist activist who refused to accept Gandhi's call for non-violence, saw the British involvement in the war as an opportunity to attack India's oppressors when they were weak. Women joined the fight: influenced by Bose, in Singapore in October 1943 a band of Indian female freedom-fighters, the Rani of Jhansi Regiment, was formed, named for the Maratha queen who had died resisting the British in 1857. 'We had no hatred,' said Aruna Asaf Ali, wife of a Muslim Congress leader in prison with Nehru, and an underground resistance fighter. 'In fact, it was the other way around – it was their [British] values which made us revolt.'

Every fortnight local news of the war was published, heavily loaded with British propaganda. It was a frightening time. 'The enemy are very near us now and I do not know what the future holds for our country,' wrote Indira from Cooch Behar to Queen Mary, the Queen Mother, in May 1942, as Singapore, Malaya and Burma fell in succession. 'India is very open and vast and so unprepared in many ways for an invasion, that there can be nothing ahead for us but merciless slaughter. However at the moment the Japs seem out to finish China. We can breathe in peace for a few more months.'

The road to the front in Burma passed through Cooch Behar. An American Army base was opened in the town, which became known as 'The GI's Shangri-La'. Bhaiya, dividing his time between Cooch Behar and Calcutta, made friends with an American pilot, Peter Goutiere. Goutiere describes seeing Bhaiya for the first time at the bar of the 300 Club in Calcutta:

He was tall and handsome, and looked very much like Stewart Granger. His uniform was black, with high caftan collar buttoned up, and there were silver shoulder epaulets with fringes and dark blue trousers with a dark red stripe down the sides. The boots looked like patent leather, with spurs. He was a fascinating looking individual, and appeared to be enjoying his company with laughter [sic].

Even his trousers had a dashing cut, part military, part cowboy.

The palace under Bhaiya's stewardship had a more sporty, masculine flavour, concentrated on the shikars he, like his grandfather Nripendra, adored arranging for his friends, fast-living soldiers, jockeys and pilots as well as fellow-playboy princes such as Jai and Aly Khan. Bhaiya had a special communion with his elephants, and was an unfailingly generous host, never taking a shot himself unless an animal was wounded or dangerous.

Like Jai, Bhaiya had requested permission to see active service during the war, but it was not until May 1945 that he was allowed to leave his duties in Cooch Behar 'to experience thrills' (as he put it) on the Burmese front. He served conscientiously, impressing his commanding officer so much that he wrote to Field Marshal Sir Claude Auchinleck 'about his devotion to duty and how everyone with whom he came into contact had respect and regard for him'. This recommendation brought Bhaiya a KCSI (Knight Commander of the Star of India) a few weeks later.

From 1943 to 1944, eastern India had to contend with a famine as well as the war effort and the bitter struggle towards independence. Wartime inflation and military supply requirements, devastating tidal waves and a cyclone and the loss of 1.5 million tonnes of rice usually imported annually from Burma (now in Japanese hands) caused widespread starvation in Bengal. Though the Viceroy, Archibald Wavell, fought hard to procure extra grain for India from the reluctant Churchill, his efforts could not alleviate the atmosphere of distrust and desperation and prevent a further descent into administrative chaos.

Bhaiya sought to save Cooch Behar from the famine's ravages by issuing a proclamation forbidding farmers from selling their excess rice outside the state. Hundreds of thousands of lives were lost, but Cooch Behar escaped the worst of the catastrophe. There was a lack of clothing as well as food: 'every now and then we read of women committing suicide for want of being able to cover themselves,' Indira reported to Queen Mary from Cooch Behar in May 1945.

Indira took twenty girls and five boys, all orphaned by the famine, to live with her at the palace in Cooch Behar. The girls were taught to cook and sew, and she arranged marriages for them; the boys were taught trades, and one became her cook. This was typical of the way Indira liked to help people. She always said she was happier giving one person Rs 5,000, which would really make a difference to them, than Rs 100 to fifty people which would just be frittered away.

'But with Peace in Europe,' continued Indira's letter, written two weeks after VE Day and at about the time the Japanese-backed Indian National Army surrendered in Rangoon, 'everyone has more courage to face trials in the East, hoping for Peace here too soon.' Victory in Japan was just three months away, but it would be a long time before India could claim to be at peace.

After so many years of waiting, independence came to India suddenly and savagely. The outbreak of war and Churchill's highly conservative premiership combined to stall both democratic reform in the provinces of British India and talks on the form a future government might take throughout the subcontinent. In the early 1940s the concept of Empire, supported by a loyal phalanx of princes, was once again ascendant in official British eyes, only to be countered by an uncompromising Gandhi and his Quit India movement.

With peace in 1945 and a Labour government ruling a country sucked dry by war came a dramatic shift in the British government's attitude to India. Congress's leaders were released from prison and went to Simla to meet with the Viceroy, Lord Wavell. In February 1947, the prime minister, Clement Attlee, sent Admiral Lord Mountbatten, Queen Victoria's great-grandson, out to India on the understanding that he would be the last viceroy to rule India in the name of the King-Emperor.

The ambitious Mountbatten had toured India in 1921 as ADC to his cousin the Prince of Wales, and had headed the South-East Asia Command from Delhi during the war, so he knew India well. Despite his lofty social connections – a crucial viceregal accessory, especially where the Indian princes were concerned – his politics were liberal enough to appeal to the Labour politicians who just wanted Britain out of India and his manner informal and inclusive enough to charm Congress politicians such as Nehru. His critics called him a vain, 'publicity-crazy' intriguer who lacked the vital qualities of sensitivity and thoughtfulness that characterized his predecessor, Lord Wavell. But Mountbatten also had a magnetic personality with huge persuasive powers; this, combined with his determination to hand India over quickly, made him powerfully effective in the difficult situation with which he was presented.

In February 1947, Attlee declared that the British government

would relinquish power in India in August 1948. In June, Mountbatten announced that an agreement had been reached between
the leaders of Congress, the Muslim League and the Sikhs that the
independent subcontinent would be made up of not one but two
dominion states, a predominantly Hindu nation of India and a
Muslim nation of Pakistan. At the same time, almost to his own
surprise, the Viceroy brought the date of independence forward a
year to 15 August 1947.

The most pressing item on Mountbatten's agenda was Partition,
the division of the former British provinces and princely states
into India and Pakistan. In 1947, the inhabitants of the Indian
subcontinent accounted for about a fifth of the world's population.
Of these, 275 million people were Hindus (a quarter of whom
were outcaste Hindus), 50 million were Muslims, 7 million were
Christian, 6 million were Sikhs (living mostly in the Punjab north-
west of Delhi), 100,000 were Parsis and 24,000 were Jews. Under
the British and in the princely states, these different groups had
coexisted in relative peace, united by their subjection to foreign
rule or their loyalty to the traditional ruler. As independence
approached, resentment and hostility between Hindus, Muslims
and Sikhs developed with worrying speed and throughout the early
1940s parts of India were stained with blood spilt in communal
rampages the embattled British were increasingly powerless to
prevent.

Communal distrust had been an ominous feature of nationalist
thought since the late nineteenth century. The British were well
aware of potential problems between India's religious groups, and
from time to time (especially in the 1920s and early 1940s) tried to
exploit them to establish some control over the independence
movement, playing the Muslim League off against Congress just as
they had tried to bolster the princes to counteract Congress's
influence.

The Muslim League had been founded in 1906 by a group of
Muslim noblemen led by the Nawab of Dhaka (modern capital of
Muslim Bangladesh) loyal to the British crown who hoped to use
their association with the British to protect their own interests in

the newly divided Bengal. Grateful for their support, the Viceroy, Lord Minto, endorsed their idea of separate electorates for minorities including Muslims; these were instituted in 1909 and set a precedent for communal division which some modern Hindus see as the foundation of Muslim demands for a separate state.

Mohammed Ali Jinnah, fastidious architect of Pakistan, was born in Gujarat – near Baroda, and near Gandhi's birthplace – in about 1876. After training as a barrister in England he joined the Indian National Congress in 1904 as secretary to Dadabhai Naoroji, the first Indian member of Britain's Parliament to whose election fund Sayajirao had contributed in 1892. Motilal Nehru, in whose legal office the young Jinnah had worked, hailed him as one of the independence movement's rising stars. He was one of the first Indians to sit on Lord Minto's Central Legislative Council in 1909–10, where he did not shrink from speaking out against British policy of which he disapproved. In 1913 Jinnah joined the Muslim League, though his loyalty to Congress and the concept of a united India was still unquestioned. Until 1928, he insisted that Muslims and Hindus should fight for independence side by side.

In that year, he petitioned Congress – at the time writing their own constitution for an independent India in response to the Simon Commission proposals they had rejected – to guarantee minority, specifically Muslim, rights in a free India. Some Congress leaders supported him but hard-line Hindu nationalists refuted his claims outright, and his proposal was turned down. Jinnah retreated from nationalist politics and returned to his extremely successful legal practice in Bombay and from 1930 in London.

Meanwhile, the idea of a separate Muslim state was crystallizing in the minds of Indian Muslims who resented the Hindu holy man Gandhi assuming the right to speak for all Indians and feared becoming second-class citizens of a Hindu-dominated India. In 1933 Choudhry Rahmat Ali devised the name Pakistan, meaning 'land of the pure', and an acronym of the north-western provinces he imagined would form the new nation: Punjab, Afghan (the North-West Frontier province), Kashmir, Sind and Baluchistan. Muslims were also a majority in Bengal – though Rahmat Ali had not included it in his plans – and in 1947 Pakistan was created with two 'wings', East and West Pakistan, both administered from West Pakistan.

In 1935 the mood had shifted so dramatically that Jinnah decided to return to India and the independence movement. He was no longer interested in conciliation. Under his leadership from 1937 to his death in 1948, the Muslim League, while theoretically in alliance with Congress against British rule (though he did not endorse the Quit India movement) developed a powerful argument for division, declaring that Muslims would never be granted equal status to Hindus in a united India. Jinnah refused to countenance compromise. By the time Mountbatten arrived in India, the force of Jinnah's commitment to his cause had overridden Congress's determination to create a united India and the idea of independence had become indistinguishable from Partition. The rule of law was breaking down across India and communal violence was flaring up uncontrollably.

On 2 June 1947, Mountbatten presided over a meeting of eight men. Three were Congress leaders – Jawaharlal Nehru, Vallabhbhai Patel and Acharya Kripalani; three represented the Muslim League – Jinnah, Liaquat Ali Khan and Rab Nishtar; and one man spoke on behalf of India's Sikhs, Baldar Singh. Mountbatten formally asked Jinnah for the last time if he would accept a united independent India; equally formally, Jinnah refused. Then the Viceroy obtained the consent of each of the groups to Partition, with the border between Indian and Pakistan to be drawn by an English official. Ten and a half million people would be left on the 'wrong' side of the border, dispossessed and uprooted.

The following day the eight men met again. Dramatically, Mountbatten laid down in front of them a massive document entitled 'The Administrative Consequences of Partition'. Everything in British India (with three months to go the future of the princely states was still not decided; they were the next item on the Viceroy's 'To Do' list) had to be divided equally between the two new nations, from the army and the gold in the Bank of India (and Britain's vast wartime debt to its colony) down to the individual books in libraries: alternate volumes of the *Encyclopaedia Britannica* went to India and Pakistan. A provisional currency for Pakistan was made by bank clerks rubber-stamping a huge pile of rupee notes with the word 'Pakistan'.

Anyone could have anticipated the administrative strain of creating two countries out of a collection of colonial provinces in the space of a few months, but although some foresaw the enormity of the bloodshed that would taint the birth of the two nations no serious efforts were made to prevent its escalation. According to the historian Andrew Roberts, Mountbatten's conviction 'that massive loss of life was inevitable' was a terrible dereliction of his responsibilities to the Indian people.

Joy and pride erupted throughout the subcontinent on the night of 15 August 1947, only to be tempered by the knowledge that it came at the terrible cost of hundreds of thousands of lives. For six weeks, as Hindu refugees from Pakistan struggled to reach India and Muslim refugees from India struggled to reach Pakistan, arson, rape, mutilation and slaughter devastated the Punjab and threatened to ignite Bengal too. Parents killed their children and then themselves to avoid a worse fate of capture, torture and murder. The gutters of Lahore ran with blood. On both sides of the frontier, silent trains arrived at stations with carriages full of corpses and blood seeping out beneath the doors.

Cooch Behar, where 40 per cent of the population was Muslim, had shown, like most of the mixed-faith states, that it was possible for the two religions to live side by side. After Partition and the creation of East Pakistan (now Bangladesh), on the southern border of Cooch Behar, millions of refugees left their homes amid tragic scenes of panic and desolation. Bhaiya personally guaranteed the safety of the Muslims in his state if they chose to stay, and prevented communal fighting there, but the devastation caused in the region was overwhelming.

Jaipur fared better. One third of the population of Jaipur city (as well as its recent dewan, Sir Mirza Ismael) was Muslim, but Jai patrolled the streets at night in an open Jeep to show his commitment to protecting Muslims in Jaipur and punishing any Hindus who harmed them. Demonstrating his point, he sat beside the Muslim colonel of one of his regiments. When one of his officers asked Jai if he should kill some Muslim protesters, Jai replied, 'Certainly not. They are my subjects. Protect them.' His efforts were successful: most of Jaipur's Muslims (about 20,000, or 10 per cent of the population throughout the state) stayed in Jaipur and communal violence was avoided.

Less than six months after Independence, on 30 January 1948, on his way to a prayer meeting which would include, as always, Christian, Muslim and Buddhist as well as Hindu prayers, 78-year-old Mohandas Gandhi was murdered by a Hindu extremist who opposed his religious tolerance. Partition had not quelled the fanaticism that defiled India's new dawn.

After deciding to separate India and Pakistan, Mountbatten turned his attention to the problem of the princes. No one agreed on how integrating the princely states into the new dominions could best be achieved.

Congress was determinedly democratic, with a socialist bent, and disapproved of monarchies in practice as well as in principle. For the past few decades it had dismissed the princes as 'imperial allies'. It was also violently opposed, as was the British government, to the idea of an India fragmented into dozens of small princely states alongside the united former British provinces. Though some princes, following Sayajirao, had initially admired Gandhi and supported Congress against the British, from 1937 to 1939 Congress extended its campaign of civil disobedience to include the princely states as well as British India, and left the maharajas under no illusions about the treatment they could expect from an unchecked Congress.

Throughout the 1920s and 1930s, the princes had tried to use institutions such as the Chamber of Princes to coerce the British into defining what shape a new India would take and what role they would play in it, but their internal rivalries prevented them from ever forming an effectively united pressure group. The British government was an unreliable champion for the princes who had (with some notable exceptions) supported its rule for so long. Talk of federation in the 1930s had come to nothing. The princes resented the apparent lack of British interest in their future, while the British felt let down by the princes, who refused to submit to being built up into a political counterweight to Congress. Towards the end of the war, when the Chamber of Princes came to Simla to meet Lord Wavell in 1944, they harboured 'grave misgivings and apprehensions about the future'. All too aware that the 'states were probably incompatible with a smooth devolution of power', Wavell could not calm their fears.

In 1945, with independence looming, most princes realized they could not expect to continue ruling absolute, personal monarchies. Over the next two years, the most important states – such as Jaipur – moved towards more representative government. But this was by no means a uniform trend. As late as March 1947 only a third of the states were even debating instituting constitutional limits on their maharaja's privy purse, traditionally inseparable from the state's treasury.

The princes were assured by the British government in May 1946 that all the powers they had surrendered in their original nineteenth-century treaties would be returned to them, paramountcy would not be transferred automatically from the British to the new Indian government, and each state would be able individually to negotiate its terms with that new government.

But Mountbatten was convinced by the arguments of Jawaharlal Nehru and Vallabhbhai Patel that the princes must join India. 'As soon as I turned my attention to the problem of the states [in July 1947], it became evident to me that their independence . . . would not be worth a moment's purchase unless they had the support of one or other of the Dominions [India or Pakistan],' he said afterwards. To persuade the princes Mountbatten employed a combination of duplicity, charismatic oratory, a decided flair for high drama, and the judicious use of both carrot (hints dropped about how grateful his cousin the King would be to hear of such-and-such a prince's sacrifice for India's greater good) and stick (dire warnings of the 'communist menace'). All but three* of the men he privately called 'a bunch of nitwits' for resisting settling with Congress before Independence on 15 August 1947 submitted to his arguments.

Ostensibly, the deal was a generous one. Only defence, foreign policy and communications would remain in central hands, as they

---

* The three who held out were Junagadh, a tiny state on the west coast, Hyderabad and Kashmir, which were all invaded and annexed by India in 1947–8.

had been under the British; all domestic administration would still be carried out, as in former years, by the maharaja's government. Democratization was necessary, but could be gradual. Territorial boundaries would be respected and none of the eighteen most senior states, including Jaipur and Baroda, would be asked to merge. Theoretically, as under the British, the states would still be internally autonomous. But the Congress leadership had no plans to keep their promises.

Despite the terms of the agreement, many princes agonized over signing away their independence to an openly hostile Congress, fearing perfidy and concerned for the welfare of their people, but they were not united enough to oppose it and individual resistance was impossible. With what Naveen Patnaik calls 'that last grand gesture of royal magnanimity,' the princes gave up everything they believed in to save their people from civil war and grant them independence from foreign hegemony. Sayajirao's grandson and successor, admittedly not a paragon of a ruler, broke down in tears in V. P. Menon's arms after he signed. Eight Punjabi maharajas signed together in a funereal ceremony. One central Indian prince had a heart attack and died seconds after signing. When the Maharaja of Jodhpur signed, he flourished a tiny revolver (cunningly hidden in a pen) at Patel, saying that he would 'shoot him down like a dog if he betrayed the starving people of Jodhpur'.

Several senior British administrators thought their government had wrongfully abandoned the princes. Dowager Maharani Chimnabai pointedly told a British civil servant in the early 1940s that 'she was surprised to learn that we were now proposing to hand over power in India to the people whom her husband had been blamed for associating with.' Minimal provisions had been made by the British to ease the princes' transition into the new India – small thanks for nearly a century of financial and political support. They did make one gesture of loyalty to the princes: Conrad Corfield, who resigned as liaison between the princes and the India Office's Political Department in June 1947 and left India rather than watch the princes lose rights he felt the British government should have protected, received permission to burn four tons of

Government of India documents relating to the princes' personal lives, thus preventing the new government from using as blackmail information collected by the British.

'Although I accepted the idea that we would in some way be part of independent India, it never really occurred to me that our lives would change so radically once our states lost their special identities,' said Ayesha. 'Somehow I imagined that we would always maintain our particular relationship to the people of our states and would continue to have a public role to play.' Instead, to her great regret, their way of life would be gradually eroded and their strong personal identification with Jaipur and its people weakened. But commendable social aims could not erase centuries-old bonds overnight. In Dhrangadhara, the Maharaja called the elders of his small state together to tell them he had decided to merge with India. 'That is all very well Sir, I know what you have done,' said one elderly village head, 'but who will now wipe our tears?'

Perhaps the last fanfare of princely India was the wedding of Jai's only daughter Prem Kumari, known as Mickey, to the Maharaj Kumar of Baria in 1948, which the *Guinness Book of World Records* called 'the most expensive wedding in the world'. Eight hundred royal guests poured into Jaipur by private planes and trains or fleets of motorcars for the celebrations which lasted two weeks. Every visiting family was allocated a car and an ADC. Even the servants' menus were meticulously planned and their places for viewing the wedding processions assigned. An instruction-book 2 inches thick detailed every ceremony, entertainment and reception being held, as well as the individual programmes for each group of visitors. Henri Cartier-Bresson, travelling through India at the time, captured the wedding on film.

The wedding over, Ayesha and Jai went to the United States, their first trip abroad as a married couple. Neither had been there before, and, post-war, they were 'enormously impressed by the richness of everything – the food, the shops, the cars, the clothes people wore'. The Americans were no less impressed by them, and were fascinated by their domestic arrangements. The first time Jai was asked how many wives he had, the couple laughed; the question quickly became tiresome, however. But Ayesha was charmed by the Americans, by their friendliness, their enthusiasm, their politeness. She loved the salesgirls calling her 'honey', and was amused by the taxi-driver who, on finding out she was from India, insisted on telling her in great detail everything she could do in New York for free. 'I wondered,' she commented, 'whether I looked like a refugee.'

After their return Jai continued working to ensure the integration of Jaipur into the new India was a smooth one. British India and the princely states faced different challenges with the onset of independent rule. For the former princedoms, the changes were fundamental and transformatory, requiring not just an ideological and constitutional change from monarchy to democracy, but also the transition from being semi-independent nations to being regions of a much larger country. 'If you had asked a resident of British India before 1947 who ruled him, the answer would probably have been, simply, "The British"', observed Ayesha. 'If you had asked someone from a princely state the same question, the answer would almost certainly have been "The Maharaja".' This was compounded by the fact that the vast majority of India's population was illiterate and unpoliticized.

Almost as soon as the princes had signed the original Instruments of Accession, in May 1948, Patel and Menon began pressing for them to sign new ones ceding to Delhi their right to pass laws. The princes had no choice, now, but to give up most of their inherited wealth and possessions along with their states' autonomy and their own authority. Jawaharlal Nehru openly said, 'I will encourage rebellion in all states that go against us.' Most states were to be merged together or amalgamated into larger administrative units: Jaipur, along with its Rajput kin-states including Jodhpur, Bikaner and Udaipur, would form Rajasthan; Baroda would become a part of Gujarat. Tiny Cooch Behar was one of six states that retained their original boundaries but was administered from Bengal. Democratization would be imposed and subordination to Delhi would be complete.

In return, the most important princes would be allowed to retain their titles and some privileges – including a public holiday in their former states on their birthday, red licence plates on their cars, gun salutes, exemption from taxes and customs, the right to own arms, fly flags on their houses and cars, hunt in their old game reserves and be afforded military honours at their funeral – and given a privy purse allowance determined by the size of their state. Article 363 of the constitution guaranteed that any future government would honour this settlement.

Out of over 600 states 284 received a privy purse; of these, eleven received over Rs 10 lakhs and ninety-one between 1 and 10 lakhs. The smallest privy purse was just Rs 192 per annum for Katodia in Saurashtra; the largest, for Baroda, was Rs 26.5 lakhs. When Jaipur merged with India, the value of the cash, property and goods Jai gave up was estimated at £15 million; he received a privy purse of Rs 18 lakhs a year (about £200,000), of which he set aside Rs 1,50,000 in a Benevolent Fund for his former retainers.

Both Ayesha and Jai accepted union as an inevitability. Long afterwards, Mountbatten told the authors of *Freedom at Midnight* that Ayesha 'and her very sensible and clued-up husband were under no illusion whatsoever that this [princely India] could continue'. But knowing this intellectually could not rid Jai of the feeling that giving up his throne would be betraying a sacred trust. In 1948, he wrote a formal letter justifying his decision to Bubbles, his heir, who would be effectively disinherited by his signature of Menon's accession papers. 'The sacrifice which seems so great today may prove in the end to be no sacrifice at all,' he argued.

I personally feel that every sacrifice is worth making if you can serve your country better and for a greater cause, when I say SERVE I mean it in the real sense of the word and I do not mean just being a mere figurehead. If I cannot guide the destiny of my people as their Ruler at least I will be in the new set up serving them and looking after their interests, which in itself is more service than giving up completely.

Though Jai 'hated giving up Jaipur and relinquishing his deeply felt responsibility for his people', he knew that he must put his own feelings aside for the greater good of India. Ayesha was less ambivalent: she could not stand the idea of him no longer ruling Jaipur and resented any infringement on his powers or privileges. No maharaja found giving up his state easy. 'It was not merely a matter of losing their possessions or their hereditary right to rule,' wrote the Maharani of Gwalior, 'they were gnawed by an acute sense of guilt that they had let slip a trust passed on to them by their forebears and even more . . . that they had failed their people.'

In December 1948, Congress – now the dominant political party in the new India – held its annual meeting in Jaipur. Jai was recovering from another serious plane crash but that did not stop him and Ayesha inviting Jawaharlal Nehru and Sarojini Naidu to stay with them at Rambagh. The irrepressible Naidu teased Nehru mercilessly and told irreverent stories about the old guard of Congress leaders. Nehru, passionate and incisive, roused everyone to enthusiasm for what he called the 'great experiment': building a new nation, free, just and mighty. He had often been asked, he told them, what was the most exciting period of his life; 'he felt that *this* was the most exciting time, *this* moment when we were all to take part in the most important and thrilling task that justified all those years in jail, the meetings, the marches, the agitation, the speeches.'

One of the ways in which Menon and Patel had persuaded the most senior maharajas, such as Jai, to cede to the Republic was by offering them positions as governors of the newly formed state provinces. The office of Rajpramukh was that of a state governor, with overall supervisory powers over the province, though the duties were primarily the ceremonial ones formerly conducted by maharajas. Initially, Rajpramukhships were to be held in perpetuity by the ruling family to whom they had been given, but before they were instituted this was retracted so they were just held for life. At first, too, the Rajpramukhs were to be commanders-in-chief of the provincial forces; this privilege was also withdrawn.

In March 1949, Jai was initiated as Rajpramukh of the Greater

Rajasthan Union, the administrative area of which Jaipur city was now the capital, and Jaipur was absorbed into India. An old legend held that Jaipur state would endure as long as an image of Narsingh remained in a temple in the hills outside Jaipur city. The idol vanished a few days after Jai signed Menon's new Instrument of Accession.

By 1950, the new Government of India had effectively accomplished a silent, bloodless revolution. India's princely states, in all their extravagant, eccentric, contradictory glory, were now a thing of the past.

In the summer of 1949, Ayesha was expecting a baby, and because she had had two miscarriages her doctor had warned her to be careful. She stayed in Jaipur with Jai as he adjusted to his new duties as Rajpramukh. In October, Ayesha went to Bombay to stay with Indira to await the baby's arrival. He came two weeks early, tiny but healthy, as the lights and fireworks of Divali crackled through the city. The little boy was called Jagat. An old custom held that the person who told the maharaja of the birth of a son was richly rewarded so, in Bombay, Baby and one of Ayesha's ladies-in-waiting raced to the telephone – but it was out of order. The ADC who eventually informed Jai of Jagat's birth was given a new car; the lady-in-waiting who told Indira was given a pair of ruby and diamond earrings.

Over the next few years, life at Rambagh, now the official residence of the Rajpramukh, almost slipped back into the pre-war routine. Grand visitors such as the Mountbattens, Nikita Khrushchev, Jackie Kennedy and Queen Elizabeth came to stay, many lured to India as much by the prospect of staying with Ayesha and Jai as by diplomatic obligations or the wish to see the sights. Eleanor Roosevelt arrived in Jaipur during the riotous spring festival of Holi. To stop her being pelted, as tradition demanded, with painful wax pellets and squirted with brightly coloured water, Jai decided that she must have her cheeks smeared with dye as soon as she reached Jaipur so that anyone seeing her 'would assume that she had already had her share of Holi exuberance . . . Mrs Roosevelt arrived at Rambagh, scarlet-cheeked and puzzled, but otherwise unharmed.'

Jai still made time for polo. In 1950, the Argentine team came to India and played in tournaments in Bombay, Delhi and Jaipur. In England, with Prince Philip a keen player, interest in polo was revitalized. Every year Jai and Ayesha gave a cocktail party after the Queen's Cup at Windsor which the Queen and Prince Philip always attended. When Bubbles, Joey, Pat and later Jagat were at Harrow, Ayesha and Jai spent many happy summers in England with the boys, usually waiting to leave India until after the violet jacaranda flowers came into bloom at the beginning of May.

In England they divided their time between their country houses, first in East Sussex (the Georgian Saint Hill) and then in Berkshire (King's Beeches, near Ascot), and their flat in Grosvenor Square. A guest at a dinner given for them in England in the 1960s remembers the glamour surrounding Jai and Ayesha.

I felt the atmosphere in the room change as they entered. People stopped talking; there was a sense of expectancy, of excitement. Of course, they were both stunningly good-looking: tall, slender, he in a formal Indian bandh-gala [black, high-collared] jacket, she in a silver sari. They moved together through the drawing-room, paying attention to everyone without losing a fraction of their aura of privacy, mystery.

When Jai was asked why he sent his children to English schools, he replied with typical pragmatism, 'What more can an Indian ruler do for his children today than give them a cosmopolitan education? It is unlikely that they will be rich when they grow up. At least they can become good diplomats.' Perhaps because he had missed his own family so much in his formative years, or because maharajas simply did not have much to do with their children when they were small, Jai's relations with his sons, especially the three elder boys, were always distant. Jai was never critical of them; he simply seems not to have known how to be close to them. They, in their turn, idolized him. When they were grown up, he was more relaxed with them, but still reluctant to find fault. An English friend remonstrated with one of Jai's sons for drinking too much. The young man said, 'If my father told me to stop drinking, I would.' But Jai never did. He was equally inhibited with Mickey, who had an unhappy marriage and later turned to drink. 'Jai knew her problems, sympathised with them, but again felt unable to help,' wrote Quentin Crewe, Jai's biographer. 'It was as if he thought that her life was her affair and that she must deal with it herself.'

Jai was softer on Jagat than he had been on the older boys; his relationship with him was still distant, but less formal. All the children were stuck in a strange time warp, no matter how 'modern' Jai and Ayesha were: the way of life into which they had been born – and this applied almost as much to Jagat as to the others – had disappeared, and they had to adjust to living in a new world in which the old values and the old ways of doing things counted for little. The transition was not easy for any of them.

This was true, too, of Ayesha and Jai's relationship. Their marriage was a romantic one in that they had fallen in love and expected their love to sustain their married life together. Though Jai wanted the modern ideal of marriage, and had fallen in love with Ayesha because he wanted a wife who was his partner and equal, he still lived by the same code as Nripendra Narayan, who expected to be able to have 'girlfriends' (as Ayesha described them) as well as a wife. Even if Jai had not been radiantly good-looking and charming, many women would still have found his wealth and status hard to turn down: the combination was a potent, irresistible mixture. How could anyone be expected to refuse him? With his upbringing and cultural inheritance, how could he possibly be expected to be faithful? And, though she subscribed to the same aristocratic code of discretion, how could Ayesha ever learn not to care?

Bhaiya had warned his sister before her wedding that she could not expect Jai to be faithful, and must learn not to mind about it. 'Just because he marries you, you can't expect him to give up all his girls,' he told her seriously. Ayesha was appalled: when Jai married her, she protested, of course he would change. 'Even then, behind my protests, somewhere I knew Bhaiya was right.' Ayesha herself had questioned Jai during their engagement, prompting a 'miserable' letter from him in January 1939 protesting that he had never hidden anything from her, but promising to write and tell her everything, as long as she trusted him and believed in him. By March, peace had been restored between them; Jai signed off a letter with 'all my love beautiful and I think of you every second of my life'.

The issue would remain a thorny one for the rest of their married life. Jai simply did not believe fidelity was important. Writing to the wife of a close friend, he urged her not to let him go 'the wrong way': 'I am only afraid of him taking to drink as you know that weakness is in all our family and we all at some time or other fall to it. Other things don't matter so much . . .'

In December 1946, Indira and Chimnabai – only slightly debilitated by arthritis – were staying at Jaipur House in New Delhi. Indira sent Queen Mary a letter and a Mogul jade attar case via the diarist Chips Channon, who was returning to England from India. 'India is in a sad state nowadays,' she wrote, 'and it is very difficult for our class to adjust ourselves to the new times.' As much as she had longed for her country's freedom, Indira was never reconciled to the new India. In 1962, she bemoaned Darjeeling as 'ghastly'. 'What deterioration since Independence, it is hard to believe,' she wrote to her granddaughter Devika. Half-joking, she called Indian Independence Day 'Doomsday for the Princely States'.

Independence, no matter how eagerly anticipated, had brought with it the destruction of the princely culture in which Indira had grown up and thrived. Its loss left her sick with nostalgia and spiritually homeless. The new order was even harder to swallow as she watched her beloved eldest son struggle to come to terms with a world in which he no longer had a role. It made her want to turn to religion, she said. 'Take my poor Bhaiya's case,' Indira wrote to Jai in 1951, 'he will be 36 this December and yet no wisdom, it breaks one's heart to see this deterioration. These two years of sitting idle since the merger [of Cooch Behar with India] have done their damage . . . I could not be more disheartened and without hope!'

Her concern for Bhaiya was not always constructively expressed, according to her grandson. At a formal dinner in Cooch Behar at about this time,

the head butler served the temple offering of sweets and fruit first to His Highness as the head of the family which Bhaiya turned down saying that he did not believe in such rituals. Ma seated next to him snapped in front of all the guests suggesting that he should then abdicate relinquishing his title and privileges if he did not follow state custom and tradition – he could not have and eat his cake as he wished. Bhaiya left the table quietly but Granny continued regaling [the guests with] how her son was weak – mixed with only whores and jockeys and never with foreign women of his own status like Doris Duke and Barbara Hutton who admired him.

Indira despaired of Bhaiya's lack of interest in eligible women. In the late 1940s, she refused to meet his girlfriend, an American starlet called Nancy Valentine, and deliberately told a friend of Nancy's that if they married Bhaiya would lose his title and she would never be maharani. 'Of course he can be a taxi driver,' she said to the friend, knowing it would be repeated back to Nancy. 'But God help the passengers.' 'Luckily the Government of India disapproved of any such misalliances and refused to recognise the lady in question,' Indira wrote to Queen Mary in December 1951, 'which sorted the situation. I hope in course of time he will find a suitable Indian girl to marry and settle down with.'

Gentle, shy Bhaiya was in an awkward situation. He had been brought up in an informal, unrestricted atmosphere, but for all its glamour there simply were not many suitable Indian girls from similar backgrounds. He wanted to have fun, and properly brought up Indian women – except for his sisters – did not play sports or drink; they would not have joined in with his parties and practical jokes or felt comfortable with his friends. It is hard to imagine an Indian princess of the 1940s wearing knickers, as Nancy Valentine did, that had 'For Bhaiya only' embroidered on the front.

Just as Partition had left millions stranded on the wrong side of the Indo-Pakistan border, the birth of the Republic of India had created princely refugees who could not learn to fit into the new order. As with Indira's brothers and Jai's sons, Bhaiya was a remnant of another age, brought up to be modern in some ways and unable to be free of the past in others; it left him stranded between two worlds.

Indrajit was another casualty. He died in 1951. A spell at a clinic in Bihar, where he tried to run away with his doctor's wife, had not cured him and he had returned to Cooch Behar. There, everyone was strictly forbidden from giving him alcohol. One tragic night, desperate for a drink, he had gone out in the car, knocked his driver out, and driven himself eight hours to Darjeeling. Later on, a cigarette he was smoking in bed set the blankets alight. The servants heard him shouting, but did not go to his rescue because he could be violent when he was drunk. He was burned to death. 'I had lived in dread of some such accident for years and when the catastrophe happened I found myself considerably prepared,' Indira wrote afterwards.

An air of loneliness now surrounded Indira. Like her parents, she loved travelling and continued to tour Europe well into old age. She was still a part of that glamorous circle of socialites she had known before the war, its ranks now swollen by Prince Rainier of Monaco and Grace Kelly, Aly Khan and Rita Hayworth, and Ayesha and Jai. Indira always made a point of visiting the Queen Mother, Mary of Teck, when she was in England. She wrote to May (as she was known) fairly regularly in the 1940s and 1950s until the Queen's death in 1953, and entertained a respect for Mary's 'great graciousness', she said, that she had never felt for 'anyone else of your high position'.

An echo of old restrictions on the princes' movements, formal permission had to be sought to leave the new India. Swarupa Das, a family friend, helped Indira fill out her application for her first trip abroad from the Republic. The form asked the reason for her journey. Indira dictated, 'I've always been to Czechoslovakia to buy my towels, to Ferragamo for my shoes . . .' 'Auntie, you can't write that!' protested Miss Das. 'I've never had to give an explanation for anything,' said Indira indignantly. 'I married the man I wanted to, I've always lived as I pleased . . .'

She took her teenaged grandson Habi to Paris and Rome with her, making him sit in restaurants with her chefs, whom she took to Europe so they could taste the food she wanted them to cook for her, while she sat alone at another table. 'I don't want people to think they're my boyfriends,' she'd say, aged seventy. Habi remembers travelling with Indira with rueful affection. When asked for her name at airport immigration, she would announce, 'Indira of Cooch Behar'. If the official dared press her for her surname, she would reply, 'I have no surname. What do you call the Queen of England? I am Her Highness Indira of Cooch Behar.' Once on an aeroplane a pretty stewardess offered Indira and Habi beef for their meal. 'Granny in one of her infamous stubborn moods (like Chimnabai) was furious and reprimanded the stewardess for insulting us Hindus,' recalled Habi. 'The airhostess apologised and promptly replaced the trays with a cheese and biscuit platter assortment. This infuriated Granny further who snapped that while we may be Hindus we certainly weren't rats.'

In Florence, Indira took Habi and his sister Devika, Ila's children, to the coming-out party of an Italian princess. Paralysed by shyness in a room full of people who did not speak much English, Habi got howlingly drunk for the first time in his life. Eventually he passed out and had to be carried home. When he told Indira what had happened, she wept bitterly, and told him that thirty years before, seventeen-year-old Indrajit had fallen in love at a party and got drunk because he was so shy. Like Habi, he had been carried home unconscious. It was the start of the drinking that had killed him.

Indira hated being alone as she got older, and could be endearingly persistent in her demands on those close to her. 'I'm an orphan,' she would say to Habi when he attempted to go out for an evening without her ('A seventy year old orphan!'). 'You can't leave me here alone.' At her own parties she could be 'very edgy insisting that one of us [grandchildren] stick close by since some of her cronies who had been unsuccessful for years may attempt to molest her'. She spent months at a time in her flat in Queen's Gate in London, but she was glad to be returning home to Bombay in the autumn of 1964, she told Devika. 'I am happy to come back and be amongst you all. It is sad to give up this lovely flat, but such is life! Look at my flat in Calcutta compared to Woodlands [torn down after the war]! Such are the penalties for having weak-minded offsprings!'

When Devika was expecting her first child, Indira gave her some advice about staying detached from one's children which reads almost as a reproach to her own family. 'Remember they are fun when they are babies, then growing up, but once grown up they are no more yours!' she wrote.

All the love, care, anxieties parents have undergone are forgotten and they are out for themselves. In some cases it is different, like Chotomashima [Menaka], your mother [Ila] even Chotomama [Indrajit], but Baramama [Bhaiya] and Baramashima [Ayesha] are for self first! If I had [my] life to live [over], I would depend on no one, marry no one, certainly not produce children; but shower my affections on those whose temperaments suit me and there must be so many in this large world, who need affection, help and understanding.

Later in life, Indira tended to fat; she said eating was the only pleasure left to her. Her health grew steadily worse as she aged, leaving her by her sixties full of aches and pains, reliant on a host of homeopathic and allopathic medicines, with a mouthful of 'clackers' (false teeth), and reliant on crutches (she called them 'sticks') when she was not in a wheelchair. She 'loved medicine – in my heart of hearts I think she was a bit of a hypochondriac', says her granddaughter. 'She never complained but she loved taking pills, those coloured pills.'

Her physical decline did not lessen her allure. Indira's friend Ann Wright took her six-year-old son to meet Indira in Bombay in the 1960s, when she was old, infirm and stout. 'Mummy,' he said, awed, 'she's so beautiful.' She loved children, never spoke down to them, and made them feel important by listening to their opinions and asking them about their lives. She could talk to anyone about anything. The morning after a party full of grandees, she would be found listening to her maids' problems with the same attention she had given to her smart guests.

In Bombay in the 1950s and 1960s, Indira usually woke late; she was always a night owl. When she was ill she might stay in bed until lunch, writing letters and talking on the telephone, holding court; but she always kept up appearances. 'Even if she had a temperature of 102 degrees she'd have her jewels on.' She began a normal day with a large cup of tisane instead of breakfast; then she had a bath – she loved baths, even taking a bathtub on the train with her – and did her puja. She weighed herself on an old-fashioned weighing machine with tiny brass weights. Dressing might take all morning; she was meticulous about every detail of her appearance. She did not wear much makeup, but she swore by Elizabeth Arden face cream.

Before lunch, she had a gin martini – always Gordon's gin. Sometimes, to her grandchildren's anguish, lunch lasted until tea-time. After lunch, Indira, like her mother, carefully prepared paan; she also loved a Bengali milk sweet called prahara. In the afternoon, she went to the cinema, peering at the screen through her diamond and pearl encrusted gold lorgnettes, or went shopping ('Her shopping used to kill me!' says a granddaughter). She changed for dinner, and had another martini then. She smoked a few cigarettes a day, hand-mentholated 555s, in a long cigarette-holder of gold or ivory.

Indira regularly took her grandchildren to lunch with Chimnabai in Bombay. After Sayaji died, Chimnabai had left Baroda, dividing her time between Poona and Bombay. She got on so badly with her step-grandson, Pratapsinhrao, the new Maharaja of Baroda, that in 1945 Indira had written to the Queen asking for the Government of India's help in curbing his misdeeds. 'She has suffered so much mentally due to the unkind treatment from my nephew the Maharaja, that she succumbs very easily and seriously to any little ailment,' she wrote. 'Discontented as she was at the arrangements made for Baroda State after my father's death, she gradually settled down to her lot. But today the Maharaja is out to give her constant new worries too petty and too many to be mentioned.' The British maintained their somewhat inconsistent policy of non-interference in the private affairs of princes in this case, despite the formidable trio of Chimnabai, Indira and Ayesha confronting the Viceroy, Lord Wavell, to ask for his help. But the real problem was that no one could have lived up to Sayajirao's legacy. As his successor's ADC said, 'He was an extraordinary man. My Maharaja was an ordinary man.'

Chimnabai's house in Bombay was off Pedder Road, across the street from Indira's flat. When Indira was in Bombay they saw each other almost every day. The children always had to be on their best behaviour: Chimnabai's grandchildren and great-grandchildren found her as intimidating as the ladies of the Raj had half a century earlier. Her voice failed as she grew older, which did nothing to make her more approachable, and she was forced to gesture imperiously to express her wishes, her eyes sparkling with frustrated determination. Even Indira, who was afraid of nothing, 'trembled like a little child' before her mother until the end of her life, and used to order her grandchildren to tell Chimnabai they were taking her with them to a matinee at the cinema so she did not have to stay behind after lunch for a maternal scolding. Indira's marriage remained a sore point up to the end: Chimnabai was assiduous about not giving Indira any money, even a tiny amount, because she had been cut off when she married Jit.

One day Chimnabai asked Habi, Ila's younger son, what he was studying at school. He replied, 'Shivaji, the Mountain Rat.' There was a shocked silence around the table. Shivaji, the great Maratha hero, had united his people to defy the Moguls under Aurangzeb, proclaiming himself 'Champion of the Hindu Gods' from his mountain fortress at Raigarh. The British had given him this derogatory nickname. Chimnabai, the proud Maratha, turned furiously to Indira: 'Take him away from that school!'

Chimnabai died in Bombay in 1958, aged eighty-seven. It is hard to imagine her facing death, her last challenge, with anything but the dignity and courage that had illuminated her whole life.

In Jaipur in the 1950s, Ayesha accepted the presidency of the Badminton Association of India and the vice-presidency of the Tennis Association of India. These were her first official roles and her first tentative steps into public life. She also opened a school teaching women embroidery and sewing to provide a livelihood for refugees from Pakistan; it is now a polytechnic specializing in secretarial work and domestic science. She held an exhibition of Jaipur arts and crafts (including the traditional blue and white pottery, fresco-painting and tapestry work) in Delhi which was opened by the Prime Minister, Jawaharlal Nehru.

Despite his ideological commitment to socialism, the aristocratic Nehru, a polo fan, became a friend of the Jaipurs during those early years of independence. 'He was a marvellously appreciative guest, with great charm and an almost boyish enthusiasm.' During this period, he also brought his daughter Indira, Ayesha's schoolmate at Santiniketan, to stay at Rambagh. According to the Mountbattens, the young Indira Gandhi was interesting but acid-tongued, scathing about the princes and their way of life.

Ayesha followed Chimnabai's lead and became involved with the All-India Women's Conference (which had absorbed the Women's Indian Association) and its continuing struggle on behalf of India's women. Though equal rights had been enshrined in the new constitution, social biases against female freedoms – the right to education, to owning property, to remarriage and to divorce – were deeply entrenched in Indian culture and much harder to change.

One conference meeting in particular illuminated for Ayesha the strange hybrid she had become in her years at Jaipur, 'partly understanding and sympathising with the zenana way of thinking, but still very much the product of Ma's cosmopolitan upbringing'.

Ayesha had listened approvingly to the delegates' calls for Hindu women to inherit money in their own right, for widows to be allowed to remarry and wives to sue for divorce; these rights were enshrined in the Hindu Code Bill of 1954–5. Beside her sat one of her ladies-in-waiting, deeply upset by the arguments. 'Why should the delegates wish to introduce divorce,' she asked. 'Surely Indian women were much better off as they were. If they divorced their husbands, who would marry them? Who would give them clothes and food and a roof over their head?' Having lived in semi-purdah in conservative Jaipur for over a decade, Ayesha could understand these concerns, too.

Jai encouraged all Ayesha's projects with characteristic generosity of spirit. 'How lucky you are to have a husband who backs you up in everything,' Indira said to her. 'Can you believe that some men are jealous of their wives?' Jai needed support, too. In October 1956, without warning, he was informed that the office of Rajpramukh, to which he had been appointed for life less than a decade earlier, and which had been enshrined in India's constitution, was to come to an end. Instead, he was offered (and turned down) the ambassadorship of Argentina, on the other side of the world. He felt betrayed by the country in which he had placed his trust and to which he had offered his service, but there was nothing he could do except silently submit. He considered running for Parliament, requesting an interview with Nehru to discuss it, but Nehru's response was dampening because he feared Jai would oppose Congress. Also, Jai could not shake off two convictions: first, that as the representative of his people, he should be above politics; and second, that despite his opposition to Congress's policies, Jaipur had always been allied with the ruling power in Delhi.

Like the other former ruling families of India, the Jaipurs struggled to readjust to the changing world in which they found themselves. The Maharani of Gwalior, whose husband had, like Jai in Rajasthan, been made Rajpramukh of Madhya Pradesh, said that in the years following Independence,

We tried to get used to the attitude of mind which seemed expected of us, that our historic heritage in which we took pride was something to be ashamed of; that we had to make amends by good behaviour, which meant unquestioning subservience to our rulers; that Jawaharlal Nehru and his colleagues who had wound up the princedoms were really our benefactors.

One result of his sudden demotion in 1956 was Jai's decision to sell Rambagh Palace to the Oberoi family of hoteliers.* He was the first of numerous maharajas to turn his palace into a hotel, and many disapproved of his action. But Jai was adamant that it was unnecessary to live in such luxury without an official role to fulfil. The sale was part of a general retrenchment over the next few years – he also sold their Dakota aeroplane and relinquished Jaipur House in New Delhi – as well as the result of a feeling that Rambagh deserved to be properly kept up and given a public role it would no longer have if it was kept as a private home. Ayesha found the changes difficult at first: she had liked their plane – it was useful for flying to Delhi to have her hair done – and in the early years used to post a maid outside the poolhouse at Rambagh to keep the hotel guests out while she had her morning swim.

In order to clear space at the City Palace to store the treasures they did not have room for in their smaller new house, Rajmahal, the palace's storerooms were emptied and their contents, from cooking pots to antique Rajput costumes, auctioned off. What they kept – from heavy ceremonial elephant jewellery and brocaded caparisons to exquisite Mogul and Rajput miniature paintings – formed the core of the new City Palace Museum. Jai's durbar hall became an art gallery, another hall was converted into a library containing manuscripts dating back to the twelfth century, and yet another houses the exquisite clothes and textiles that adorned the persons and apartments of generations of Jaipur maharajas and their

*Jai actually pulled out of the sale before it went through, and the Rambagh was made into a hotel by the Taj Group, with which the Jaipur family have since been closely associated. Thus the Rambagh Hotel is still in Jaipur family hands.

ranis. These fabrics – filmy muslins from Dhaka, priceless shatush shawls from Kashmir, nineteenth-century velvet polo clothes with heavy gold frogging, fur-lined coats and sashes decorated with delicate Mogul flower embroidery – had been stored in the palace for centuries, kept fresh by being regularly aired and refolded using different herbs and leaves at different times of the year. Jasmine was used in spring; attar of roses and khus, a sweet-scented grass, in summer; mitti, which gives off a fragrance like that released by scorched earth when the first drops of rain fall on it, during the monsoon; and rich henna in winter.

Jo Didi, even more than Ayesha, could not imagine life outside Rambagh, and her death in the summer of 1958 before they left the palace meant she did not have to make the wrenching move. She collapsed with a diseased gall-bladder and forbad her maids to call a doctor. The maids, 'too obedient to her wishes to summon a doctor on their own initiative', just watched her die.

With Jo Didi's death, after the Dowager Maharani Maji Sahiba's and Marudhar's, the zenana had lost its last important inhabitant, and its function; from then on it just faded away. Years later, Ayesha gave a transistor radio to one of the remaining zenana ladies. After a few months, she delivered some more batteries – and found the woman had no idea what the radio was, let alone how to use it. Still, she had been lighting incense and offering flowers to it daily because the maharani had given it to her. When it was eventually switched on, she ran away screaming.

Jai's removal from office, Jo Didi's death, the sale of Rambagh and their move to nearby Rajmahal, all in a matter of two years, underlined the changes that had taken place in Jaipur since Independence. Physically, too, Jaipur was changing for the worse. The arcaded walkways of the old city were being enclosed as extensions of the shops behind them, balconies and terraces were crumbling off buildings' façades, rubbish lay in drifts in the city's gutters, advertising hoardings were springing up everywhere, parks and commons were being built over. The final straw for Ayesha was seeing the castellated city walls and gates that had enclosed Jaipur for hundreds of years, lovingly kept pink by Jai and his predecessors, being demolished with the knowledge and permission of the state government. She wrote directly to Nehru, who wrote to the Chief Minister of Rajasthan, Mohanlal Sukhadia, and had the work stopped. For the moment, Jaipur's beauty had been preserved, but it was like blocking a hole in a crumbling dam.

It was issues like this that politicized Ayesha. In 1957, Sukhadia – the same man who, a year later, would approve the tearing down of Jaipur's walls – asked Ayesha if she would consider standing for Parliament as a Congress party candidate. Astonished but interested, she began to think about politics in a new way. Her upbringing on both sides – the combined legacies of her grandparents, especially of Chimnabai – gave her the 'moral courage and sincerity of purpose' that made her feel she must 'serve the people in their plight'. Ayesha 'could not just watch and do nothing'.

Her first decision was that she wanted nothing to do with the Congress party. Congress's monopoly on political power in the decade since Independence allowed its virtually unchallenged members to grow fat on the influence and privilege they commanded. Though Congress actively sought the support of ex-maharajas, well aware of the popular followings they commanded in their former states, as soon as princes went into opposition they were accused of gross misgovernment before Independence. In Jaipur, where the people still cheered Jai rapturously whenever he appeared in public, ministers were distrustful and jealous of him, even though he was careful to remain scrupulously neutral.

There was no coherent opposition to the Congress's power until the dignified intellectual Chakravarty Rajagopalachari, who had succeeded Mountbatten as the first Indian Governor-General of independent India, formed the Swatantra, or Independent, party. A long-standing friend of Gandhi's and a senior member of Congress since before Independence, he had broken away from Congress in 1959 over the issue of cooperative ownership of land. Nehru, the radical idealist who had declared as early as 1952 that the princes and their privy purses were anachronisms, wanted to use his position as Indian Prime Minister (which he held from 1947 until his death in 1964) to steer India towards true socialism. He imposed five-year economic plans modelled on the Soviet system and pursued communist China and the Soviet Union as allies.

Rajagopalachari was a liberal conservative, a capitalist who believed the greatest security of individual Indians lay in their ownership of property and their freedom to prosper economically, and wanted India released from the grip of socialist interventionist government. He formed the Swatantra party in the belief that if democracy were to survive in India there must be a flourishing opposition to the monolith of Congress, and disaffected Indians rushed to join it.

In January 1961, the Queen and Prince Philip were due to visit Jaipur. Just before they arrived, on the day of the betrothal ceremony of Jai's son Pat and Ila's daughter Devika, Ayesha asked Jai if she could join the Swatantra party. He said yes, so Ayesha requested the party's secretary to come to Rajmahal that morning. She asked him how one joined a political party; he told her you just filled out a form and paid a subscription. She and Pat joined on the spot and then went off to the reception hall in the City Palace for the betrothal. A home-movie of the ceremony shows the hall, diffuse with rose-coloured light, crowded with men wearing white achkans and turbans in every shade of auspicious saffron, sunflower yellow, tangerine, coral, fuchsia and crimson. No women were present, not even Devika, Pat's bride-to-be; all the women's ceremonies took place in the zenana.

During the reception, Ayesha told a family friend, Swarupa, or Buchie, Das, that she had just joined the Swatantra party. Buchie was aghast, and told her that with the Queen specially breaking off her official visit to come to Jaipur, it would look like a deliberate affront to the Congress-dominated government. Ayesha was worried, and when she got home she asked the ADC whether there had been any calls. He said journalists had been ringing all morning to find out whether the rumours of her joining the Swatantra party were true. Not knowing the truth, he had denied them, and they managed to keep it under wraps until after the Queen's visit.

Jaipur was *en fête* for the arrival of the Queen and Prince Philip. Ayesha received Elizabeth in the open-sided peach-coloured audience pavilion in the great pink courtyard of the City Palace, which was lined with richly caparisoned elephants, horses, camels and bullock-carts. They gave a small dinner at Rambagh before leaving for the shooting lodge. 'We didn't use the gold plates for dinner with the Queen,' says Ayesha. 'We only used them for big parties.'

Four years later Prince Philip, a polo friend of Jai's, would come to Jaipur again on his own during the riotous spring festival of Holi. Unlike Eleanor Roosevelt, he was given no quarter. 'I have never experienced anything like last week in my life,' he wrote afterwards in thanks. 'Every moment was sheer joy and it's only the bruises from polo and the pink stain on my fingers which remain to convince me that the whole thing wasn't some marvellous dream.' The following year he sent them a telegram with 'multi-coloured' Holi wishes, saying he was 'green with envy [at not being there] and pink with nostalgia'. Many years later, in the foreword to a biography of Jai, he wrote, 'To experience the festival of Holi in Jaipur in the company of Jai and Ayesha was to gain a glimpse of the universality of mankind.'

After the Queen and Prince Philip had left Jaipur, Ayesha wrote to Rajagopalachari to tell him that she had joined his party. He thanked her, adding that she was a brave lady. Ayesha was puzzled – what was wrong with a private person joining a political party in a democratic country? – but she understood when the news was made public. Rajasthan's Chief Minister, who had asked her to join the Congress party four years before, told the State Assembly that princes who became involved in politics would have their privy purses revoked. He was silenced by an independent member asking if that would apply to princes who were members of the Congress party, too.

At first, Ayesha had no intention of running for office. Just making her first speech, introducing Rajagopalachari at a public meeting held for Rajasthan's Swatantra party, left her almost paralysed with nerves. Though she no longer lived in purdah, she had rarely appeared in public since her marriage twenty years earlier. But Jai told her that since she had joined the party, she had an obligation to work for it, and gave his blessing to her appearing at the meeting. It passed off smoothly and, as Rajagopalachari spoke, she was transfixed by his inspiring words.

In the autumn of 1961, the Swatantra party formally invited Ayesha to stand for election the following year, and gave her the added responsibility of securing the entire former state of Jaipur. This meant that, apart from contesting one parliamentary seat for herself, she was in charge of seeing that four other parliamentary seats and forty seats in the Rajasthan State Assembly were won. Jai, impartial on principle, refused to join the party and contest a seat, but Joey and Pat both stood alongside their stepmother.

Ma sent Ayesha a card before the election which read, 'I'm getting hysterical, you're getting historical.' She believed former princes entering politics would be the end of them, maintaining that 'if the princes had been content to keep their privileges and a low profile, the government wouldn't have turned against them and taken everything they had left.' She had always sought to stand above politics, even as Regent of Cooch Behar. But she still sent a cheque to support the Swatantra party.

For the two months leading up to the election, Ayesha drove across hundreds of miles of bumpy, unsurfaced roads to campaign throughout the dusty Rajasthani countryside, making speech after speech in her halting, painfully translated Hindi in tiny villages to people who had sometimes walked for 50 miles to see her. Deliberately, she left off showy jewellery, wearing just a rope of pearls and glass bangles, but the village women were disappointed, horrified that their maharani did not wear the anklets that the poorest of them would own. Everywhere, Ayesha was touched by the dignity and self-respect of the villagers she met, despite the hardships of their lives, and the 'deep security [they took] in an inclusive philosophy of life . . . [made her] feel both admiration and, in a way, almost envy'.

It was, she says, a 'campaign of love'. She was met with decorated arches, songs of welcome, celebrations and affection. Hospitality is a point of honour and tradition with Rajputs, however poor they are, and in every village not only would there be singing and dancing to greet her but also cups of tea or glasses of precious water and baskets of fresh fruit or vegetables pressed on her by villagers in their most festive clothes. But this was more than just custom; this was a spontaneous outpouring of love for the Jaipur royal family. Ayesha was deeply moved by the warmth of this reception for Jai's sake, but also terrified that she would not be able to fulfil the hopes these people were placing in her. By voting for Ayesha and her candidates, they were saying, '*You* are responsible for us. *You* are our mother and our father [Ma-Baap, a traditional form of address for a maharaja]. *You* will see that we are properly taken care of.' They were expecting miracles which she could only try to perform.

Equally, she was convinced that they knew how much she wanted to help them. Just before the election, she spoke to a group of village leaders about her worries, saying that she could withdraw her candidature if they thought someone else could represent them better. They told her they wanted her to stand. 'Is it because I'm your Maharaja's wife?' she asked. 'They said it was partly that, yes. And then they said, "The other thing is that you're doing it for us, you can't be doing it for yourself otherwise you wouldn't be in the Opposition. You'd be like the other princes who have joined the Congress party."'

On the evening before the election, in a speech that demonstrated his love and support for Ayesha, Jai suspended his political impartiality and spoke to 200,000 people at a Swatantra party rally in Jaipur, addressing the vast crowd with the familiar form of the word 'you'.

For generations my family have ruled you, and we have built up many generations of affection. The new government has taken my state from me, but for all I care they can take the shirt off my back as long as I can keep that bond of trust and affection. They accuse me of putting up my wife and two of my sons for election. They say that if I had 176 sons [the number of seats in the Rajasthan Assembly] that I would put them all up too. But they don't know, do they, that I have far more than only 176 sons?

As the people roared their approval and pelted them with flowers, Ayesha knew she would win her seat.

The next day, Ayesha drove through the fairground atmosphere of an Indian election day, past sweet-sellers, astrologers and snake-charmers eager to take advantage of the crowds gathered by the polling stands in their best clothes. There was a holiday mood, with whole families going to the polls together to put their crosses next to the picture representing their party: two bullocks yoked together, symbolizing cooperation, for the Congress party; a spreading banyan tree for the Socialists; a sickle crossed with three stems of wheat for the Communists. The Swatantra symbol was a star; it was worn by all the camel drivers in Amber, Jaipur's ancient fortress.

Their victory was on a scale they could not have imagined. In the whole of Jaipur only one Congress candidate was elected; the opposition had swept the board. Joey and Pat won their seats, and Ayesha won by a majority of 175,000 votes – according to the *Guinness Book of World Records*, proportionally the largest majority ever achieved in a democratic election. The streets of Jaipur over-flowed with crowds celebrating their victory, waving from windows and rooftops at the cavalcade of Jeeps and trucks driving through the city, horns blaring. As the procession passed the balconies of the City Palace on which Jai was standing, throwing gold pieces to the people, Ayesha, at the head of it, 'knew that this was really Jai's victory'.

When Ayesha went to Delhi later in 1962 to take her seat in the Lok Sabha, or Lower House, she was accompanied not just by Pat, also taking his seat for the first time (Joey's seat was in the Rajasthan Assembly in Jaipur), but also by Jai, who had been elected by Parliament to the Upper House, or Rajya Sabha.★ Bubbles was there too, in his capacity as Adjutant of the President's Bodyguard. After the upheavals of Independence, they all revelled in this moment of family triumph.

★ India has a two-house system with a larger elected Lower House (Lok Sabha) of representatives from each region and an elected Upper House (Rajya Sabha).

Even though the 1962 elections were the first the Swatantra party had contested, they became the second largest party in Parliament and the main opposition to the Congress party. Though Ayesha protested that Congress had far more members from princely families than Swatantra, Nehru's christening of it as the 'Party of the Princes' stuck. Some of the Congress-affiliated princes, who had in many cases been asked to run by the Congress party, keen to exploit their popular appeal, said to Ayesha, 'If we [meaning we princes] had been in Opposition we'd have had some majority.' 'Why weren't you, then?' she responded.

Former princely families embraced politics in the new India, either hoping to profit from Congress's domination of privilege and patronage or opposing its monopoly of power. Over a third of the 284 families guaranteed privy purses in 1948 have since fielded candidates for the Lok Sabha and still more sat in the Rajya Sabha. From 1957 to 1960, forty-three members of princely families contested elections at state and national level; in the next five years the number went up to fifty-one; between 1967 and 1970 it was seventy-five. About half were at some time members of the Congress party. Politicians from princely families were (and remain) valuable political assets: they have an 85 per cent election rate at the polls and generally lead other successful candidates by an average of twenty percentage points. The unprecedentedly high turn-out in the areas in which they stand has contributed indirectly but significantly to the politicization of unsophisticated areas of rural India.

Unsurprisingly, the family which has produced the most political candidates is the Gaekwads with their 'progressive, participant' attitude to public life: five of Sayajirao's grandchildren and great-grandchildren, three of whom were educated by him in Baroda, entered politics. Ayesha is the only one to have opposed Congress.

In March 1962, Jackie Kennedy and her sister, Lee Radziwill, were due to visit India. Though Mrs Kennedy was America's First Lady, it was only a semi-official visit. When Lee told Jai they were planning to come to India, he invited them to Jaipur. The American

Ambassador in India, John Kenneth Galbraith, was told by the Indian government that Jai and Ayesha were trying to make 'political capital' out of what they insisted was an informal visit by a friend and her sister, who just happened to be the most recognizable woman in the world. The government was 'determined to thwart' this perceived manoeuvre. Hoping to avoid a potentially difficult situation, Galbraith wrote to President Kennedy advising him to persuade Jackie not to include Jaipur on their itinerary. Kennedy refused to interfere with his wife's private plans, and Jackie and Lee went to Jaipur as planned.

'As far as Jai and I were concerned,' wrote Ayesha, 'the visit was certainly meant to be a private, friendly, informal one . . . We had planned to entertain our guests with nothing more than some sightseeing, a polo match, relaxation around the swimming pool, and some riding.' When Ayesha told Jackie that a party was planned for them at the City Palace, she said, in that breathy, child-like voice, 'But Ayesha, I've been told that I'm not allowed to go there.' Galbraith had warned the First Lady that allowing Jai to show her round the City Palace, his ancestral home and still in his possession, would be interpreted as an attempt to present himself still as the ruler of Jaipur.

Eventually, after long telephone calls to Delhi, Jackie was given permission to visit the museum and palace on condition that it was done as quietly as possible – 'an absurd situation,' commented Ayesha, 'since anything Jackie did was news'. So, after a party at Rajmahal during which Jackie had turned on the gramophone and taught the other guests the Twist, Jai drove her and Galbraith at midnight through the quiet town to the City Palace, where they were met by Ayesha. Jai and Ayesha spent several hours showing her the moonlit palace.

Galbraith found Ayesha 'vivacious and extremely good looking' and, rather condescendingly, detected 'a certain determination to inform herself'. He sounded her out on politics: 'she is in favour of free enterprise and also more and better government services; for protection of all existing feudal privileges but also more democracy.' 'Jackie and Lee were in their element [in Jaipur], the intellectual

Galbraith less so,' writes Jackie's biographer, Sarah Bradford, quoting Galbraith: 'The conversation was on horses, mutual friends, social events and polo, scarcely my particular speciality.' Jackie's visit to Jaipur cemented her friendship with the Jaipurs and they were delighted to accept her invitation to stay with her and Jack in Washington later that year.

While their social and sporting lives still occupied much of the Jaipurs' time, Ayesha threw herself into her political duties, dealing with the thousands of requests she received for help in matters ranging from complaints about tyrannical mothers-in-law to requests for money for hospitals, roads, schools and electricity. The charitable trust fund that Jai had set up for the subjects of the old Jaipur state, donating Rs 1,50,000 a year from his privy purse, allowed her to deal with many demands directly. In one case, to provide affordable wheat for Jaipur's poor, she opened a grain shop selling it at cost price. She also campaigned on behalf of other Swatantra candidates outside Rajasthan, and even for one-time Congress Secretary Acharya Kripalani, who had represented Congress alongside Nehru and Patel in negotiations in 1947 and was now standing as an independent. These victories made her proud because she knew they were won on merit, rather than appealing to ancient loyalty to the Jaipur family.

Jai and Ayesha arrived in Washington in October 1962 as the Cuban Missile Crisis reached its peak. The Kennedys cancelled the dance they had planned in their honour, and instead held a dinner party for them attended by (among others) Lee Radziwill, the British Ambassador David Ormsby-Gore and his wife, and Benno and Nicole Graziani. Benno was a journalist with *Paris-Match* who had accompanied Lee and Jackie to India earlier that year. President Kennedy greeted Ayesha with the words, 'Ah, I hear you are the Barry Goldwater [the maverick, independent-minded Republican who would campaign for President of the USA in 1964] of India.' Despite the gravity of the situation he was facing, Ayesha found his boyish, infectious charm so appealing that it was hard to remember he was the President. 'Around midnight, Nicole Graziani made scrambled eggs for the party. "He [Jack] took her hand," Graziani recalled, "and he said, 'You know, maybe tomorrow we will be at war . . .'"'

But both Jackie and Kennedy were determined not to allow their worries to have an impact on their lives. The next day, when Jackie was showing Ayesha and Jai the White House gardens, Kennedy knocked on the window of the Oval Office and called Ayesha in, introducing her to the group of senators there as 'the woman with the most staggering majority that anyone has ever earned in an election'. Little Caroline Kennedy thought Ayesha was marvellous, too: 'Mummy,' she said, 'she's more beautiful than you.'

They left one crisis in the United States to return to another in India. On 20 October 1962, war was declared between China and India. Since the mid-1950s, Nehru's 'high-minded naiveté' had blinded him to the threat the Chinese posed to India's northern border. Pursuing a close alliance between two socialist powers, he had always insisted that the Chinese and the Indians were brothers. But at the same time, the Chinese were secretly building a road for their troops through the remote Himalayan region of Ladakh, and in 1959 they annexed Tibet, forcing the Dalai Lama to seek asylum in India. When China's quietly amassed forces began entering India in September 1962, through Assam and Ladakh, Nehru was apparently unconcerned. On 20 October the Chinese launched a full-scale invasion into Indian territory, sweeping southwards past badly equipped and unsuspecting Indian troops.

Nehru appeared in Parliament 'with head bowed, quite unlike his usual confident, casual self, helpless to explain our unpreparedness'. The Indian Army had been humiliated by their failure to repel the Chinese, and India's self-confidence and prestige had been dealt a devastating blow. On 21 November, the Chinese suddenly declared a ceasefire and withdrew, retaining large areas of Indian territory. The war was over, but India had suffered a bitter humiliation and it was a blow from which Nehru never recovered.

Ayesha was outspoken in her criticism of Nehru, condemning the government's cover-up of China's repeated incursions into India over the previous eight years, and the use of the Defence of

266 *Lucy Moore*

India Act to silence internal opposition. When she spoke out against Nehru she wore a saffron sari – the colour of courage, sacrifice and renunciation traditionally worn by Rajput women committing jauhur when their men had been defeated in battle. When asked about this, with typical disingenuousness, Ayesha said she did not remember what colour sari she had worn: certainly it had not been deliberate.

Despite her political disagreements with Jawaharlal Nehru over the years, when he died two years later Ayesha, like the rest of the nation, mourned the passing of one of India's founding fathers. She was chosen by the Swatantra party to speak about his death on behalf of her party, and talked of his love for India and India's love for him; what she really felt, she later wrote, was 'that the most extraordinary thing about Pandit Nehru was his ability to be at home anywhere: in a palace, at a teenagers' party with the rock-'n'-roll music blaring, or in a village hut'.

Even before Nehru died, some of the shine had rubbed off the dynasty. 'The tragedy of the Nehrus has been on an almost classical pattern: they proclaimed and believed in the principles of social democracy and sustained and promoted their party through the nastiest aspects of unbridled and dishonest capitalism . . . [Nehru himself] in his final weariness was well aware of the sycophancy and corruption that surrounded him, and remained silent while it flourished because he was too vain to acknowledge it and too weak to fight it.'

Nehru was replaced as prime minister by Lal Bahadur Shastri, a gentle, moderate man who lacked Nehru's flair but none of his passion for improving the lives of Indians. Shastri had come to Nehru's daughter, Indira Gandhi (no relation to Mohandas), three days after the Prime Minister's death and urged her to succeed him as Congress leader, but Indira refused. Later, though, she accepted a post in his cabinet as Minister of Foreign Affairs and a group formed around her in the mid-1960s positing her as Shastri's replacement.

Shastri persuaded Jai to take up the ambassadorship of Spain. This put Ayesha in an impossible situation: she did not want to be

separated from Jai, but she desperately wanted to fulfil her obligations to her constituents. Eventually, she went to talk to the Prime
Minister about her dilemma and her worries that Jai was being
sent abroad by Congress party members who feared his political
influence at home. Shastri reassured her and, as she left, asked,
'Must you really be in the Opposition?' For her part, she wished
more Congress party politicians could be like him.

Ayesha and Jai had just begun their new life in Madrid in 1966
when they heard that Shastri had died of a heart attack and Indira
Gandhi had been chosen to replace him as leader of Congress and
Prime Minister of India. The ladies in the Indian Embassy in Madrid
were proud that a woman was to lead their country. Indian history
had always been dominated by its ruling dynasties; the modern
Republic, so strongly associated with the Nehrus, was proving no
different. India was meant to be a democracy, but the new prime
minister, despite her close involvement in her father's fifteen-year
regime, had not yet contested a political seat.

The Jaipurs were happy in Madrid. Spain's dry, hilly landscape,
dotted with crenellated forts and castles, reminded Ayesha of
Rajasthan, as did the gypsy culture and music, and the scent of
jasmine on warm summer nights. But all too often they were apart
when Ayesha returned to India to fulfil her political obligations. As
ever, though, Jai's letters to her from this period were loving and
supportive. 'Just remember I will always stand by you and never
never let you down,' he wrote to her from Spain, calling her 'my
life long companion'.

Even in 1965, on their twenty-fifth anniversary, they only just
managed to be together on the day, at a party in Cannes. As they
flew home afterwards, Ayesha reflected on how much she had
changed since 1940, and how much she owed Jai and his strength
over the years. 'I was no longer the shy little bride, terribly in love
and terribly in awe of her husband and his life, frightened that his
family and the people of Jaipur didn't want her and wouldn't like
her. What I had now become – a fairly independent, relatively active,
and politically conscious woman – was, in great part, Jai's doing.'

Their anniversary party in England that summer was featured in the society pages of US *Vogue*, which named Ayesha one of the ten most beautiful women in the world. 'The Jaipurs' party was charming . . . very small – only intimate friends like the Queen!' gushed the text.

The Maharani, a dream in sari and jewels, with her hair up . . . His Highness the Maharajah, crack polo man, big game hunter, scholar, and world traveller . . . the party, the silver anniversary of the Jaipurs at King's Beeches, Sunninghill . . . English-pretty, it began with dinner for twenty-four in the dining room . . . moved to floodlit, sloping swards where, in an Indian *shamiyana* tent, flamed the barbecue . . . turbaned footmen in pale jackets . . . supper delicious, under cosy canvas white with flowers, chandeliered in silver . . . two hundred guests of international cast . . . just about the most beautifully dressed collection of women at any party in the English season . . . in the drawing room, dancing, opened by H.M. Queen Elizabeth in gold and white lace with the Maharajah; H.R.H. Prince Philip with the Maharani . . . then everybody, from everywhere, danced, danced, danced.

The guests featured in the accompanying pictures were Gianni and Marella Agnelli, the Stavros Niarchoses, Lee Radziwill and assorted European royals.

Looking back on her life, Ayesha saw 1965 'as the last year of untrammelled happiness and success that I've known'. Despite the tragedies of the deaths of Ila and Indrajit, she had always been able to pick herself up after a crisis, dust herself down and go on. She did not question the rectitude or importance of her involvement in politics, and with Jai's support, was able 'to go on, though I continued to be deeply disturbed by the feeling that I was failing to do justice to either my public or my personal life by trying to be in two places at once'.

As the 1960s wore on, however, Ayesha's passion for politics was slowly eroded. Part of the reason she had initially been attracted to the Swatantra party was its secularism, but in 1966 it formed an alliance with the right-wing religious Hindu Jana Sangh (forerunner of the Bharatiya Janata Party or BJP) in order to present a more viable threat to Congress in the person of Indira Gandhi, who was increasingly dominating government and policy. Worried and overworked, far away from Jai in Madrid, Ayesha became seriously ill and missed two critical weeks of campaigning before the 1967 elections.

This was the first election in which Indira Gandhi contested a parliamentary seat herself, though she had campaigned for her father and husband in the past. She travelled tirelessly all over the country on behalf of Congress, including to Jaipur where a Swatantra group protested at her rally. Indira rounded on the troublemakers:

I am not going to be cowed down. I know who is behind these demonstrations and I know how to make myself heard . . . Go and ask the Maharajas how many wells they dug for the people in their States when they ruled them, how many roads they constructed, what they did to fight the British. If you look at the account of their achievements before Independence, it is a big zero there.

In Orissa, Swatantra hecklers threw stones at her as she addressed a crowd. One hit her full on the face, breaking her nose. She continued to campaign with her nose swathed in a white bandage, mark of her brave determination to prevail.

If Indira had enemies, she also won millions of supporters, presenting herself definingly as 'Mother Indira', guardian and protector of her country. As her most recent biographer explains, this was a dangerous political path to tread, based as it was on personality rather than policy:

Her relationship to 'the people' was intimate, parental – both maternal and paternal – and unconnected to political institutions. Children do not choose their parents; parents, both good and bad, possess a natural authority over their children. To what extent was Indira conscious of her strategy and its implications? Undoubtedly she saw it as a means of political survival, but it is unlikely that at this point she fully grasped its subversive and undemocratic overtones.

Nationwide, the results were agonizingly close. Congress lost 95 seats, leaving them with a slim majority of only 44 in the 520-seat Lok Sabha. It also lost its majority in six states, not counting Rajasthan. There, the Congress party won 89 seats and the combined opposition parties 95. The Governor, whose responsibility it was to invite the majority party to form the state government, delayed performing his duty in the allotted time. Ayesha and her associates believed he was being pressured by Congress in Delhi to postpone making a decision to give them time to win over wavering members of the opposition so Congress would retain control in Rajasthan. Having lost six states, winning Rajasthan would be a crucial victory.

The opposition members – their numbers already reduced by one – retreated to a country fort just outside Jaipur, away from the bribes they expected Congress to offer them to defect. While there they learned the government had imposed an anti-riot regulation forbidding gatherings of more than five persons in the area of Jaipur in which the Governor and ministers lived. The next day the Governor of Rajasthan asked the Congress leader to form the next government.

Ayesha and the other opposition leaders met in the centre of the city from where they planned to go to the Governor's house to ask him to reverse his decision. A mob had already gathered, protesting that democracy was being murdered. Ayesha spoke, to ask them not to follow the opposition leaders as they made their protest, defying the new ban, but the swelling throng insisted on accompanying them through the city. The police were waiting for them in the restricted area; the crowds were beaten back and a twenty-four-hour curfew was imposed on Jaipur city. Every opposition leader except Ayesha was arrested.

She and Jai flew to Delhi to plead Jaipur's case with the President and Home Minister. The Home Minister promised to lift the curfew and the President assured Ayesha that she and her allies would have a chance to prove their majority when the State Assembly met. But when the curfew was lifted, the police – not the usual Jaipur police but forces called in from neighbouring states

– opened fire on people as they began returning to the streets, claiming they had not been informed of the lifting of the curfew. Nine people were killed and forty-nine more wounded; the first victim was a boy of fourteen.

As Ayesha and her associates gathered to work out what their next move should be, President's rule was declared in Rajasthan, temporarily giving control of the state to the central government. They were told that the recent bloodshed had so outraged the people of Jaipur that the Congress leader could not form a government. Instead of asking the opposition leader to do so in his stead, the Governor had called for President's rule, which effectively meant handing power to Indira Gandhi and her Congress supporters in Delhi – stalling events until the fragile opposition majority could be seduced away with offers of public office and money. Ayesha, disheartened and cynical, accepted defeat and went to join Jai in Spain, where she heard that enough opposition members had defected to give Congress the majority in Rajasthan and allowed them to form the government despite their initial loss at the polls.

'Nepotism and corruption have reached the limit . . . and the victims as always are the innocent poor. And this from a party that claims to be socialistic!' wrote Ayesha in her diary on 9 January 1967. 'It is ironical, sad and heartbreaking to see what is happening to the wonderful people who are Indians. Proud good people sacrificed for the greed and lust of a few. Justice does not exist. Truth is a thing to laugh at. Honesty is a fool. But hunger and want are real. If I ever give up politics it will be because it hurts too much to see all this.'

A severe drought in Rajasthan was another cause for impotent despair. The government's famine relief work consisted of making the villagers dig water-tanks that would never be filled and clear roads that would soon be covered with sand again, rather than developing electrification and irrigation programmes that would help relieve drought long term.

Disillusioned as she was by politics, Ayesha was unsurprised to discover that the more radical members of Congress, intimidated by the fact that twenty-four former princes or members of their families had been elected to the Lok Sabha in the 1967 elections, were agitating for privy purses to be abolished. It was over this issue that Jai decided to return to India. He wanted to be involved when the inevitable changes were imposed, and became an active, if moderate, member of the Consultation of Rulers of Indian States in Concord for India, which represented the former rulers' interests before the government.

'It is demeaning to have your name taken away from you,' observed Jai's biographer of this period. He and the other princes felt betrayed, diminished and unvalued by the country for which they had given everything taking away their last privileges, the last things that had set them apart. 'Such acts were perhaps necessary in the context of the new world order,' said Mrs Gandhi's aunt Nan Pandit, 'but the change could have been made with more grace and less speed. The Princes were sensitive, especially to small pinpricks like having to give up using titles they had borne with pride for centuries and the retention of which could have harmed no one.' Perhaps the worst of it was that what they had given up willingly could never be recovered.

The princes felt that Indira Gandhi was acting out of spiteful personal antipathy more than political necessity. The Maharani of Gwalior described the lengths to which Mrs Gandhi went to deprive her of the chancellorship of Sagar University: she had to remove the university's right to elect a chancellor altogether simply to get rid of a single chancellor with whom she disagreed. Ayesha, Indira's old schoolmate, was a particular focus of her hatred: the Prime Minister referred to her as the glass doll and even called her a bitch in Parliament.

In September 1970 Indira Gandhi put forward an amendment to the constitution that would abolish privy purses. It was passed in the Lok Sabha by 339 to 154 but defeated in the Rajya Sabha by one vote. Undaunted, Mrs Gandhi used a clause originally inserted by Mountbatten in the accession provisions (allowing the President to derecognize an individual prince who committed a serious crime or misdemeanour) to further humiliate the princes. She made the President officially write to each one of them individually, derecognizing them and stripping them not only of their privy purses but also of their titles. Eight princes sued: when the Supreme Court declared her derecognition of the princes was unconstitutional, Indira dissolved Parliament a year early and called an election that would give her a mandate to push this legislation through.

In 1966, during the celebrations for Bubbles's wedding to Padmini, a princess of Sirmur, Bhaiya had a serious accident playing polo. His horse fell and rolled on him. Bhaiya survived weeks in intensive care, but he never fully recovered, remaining an invalid, restricted to a wheelchair and totally dependent on other people until his death four years later. 'Uncle is improving daily,' Indira told Devika in May, 'but aunty Gina wants to have her own way over everything which is causing Chota Mashima [Menaka] a lot of trouble. She and her husband have been left in charge to check any wrongdoing by aunty Gina. I feel a leopard can never change its spots, however nice and kind one is to the animal.'

In London a few months later, Bhaiya was looking better, 'but mentally still far from well'. His wife, who thought she had married a glamorous playboy prince, found herself tied down to an invalid, and it did not improve her relations with her husband's family. Bhaiya had married Gina Egan, an English model, in the 1950s, much against the wishes of his family. Indira was horrified by the match. When she took a dislike to someone – something she did in an instant – her mind was set, and she would make no effort to get on with the object of her animosity. 'She behaved so badly over Gina,' said a friend, describing how newspaper reports of the marriage made Indira so ill the newly-wed Bhaiya could not leave her side to be with his bride.

Gina and Bhaiya asked Indira to leave the palace at Cooch Behar and she had to comply. Gina also got rid of Bhaiya's devoted ADC and partner-in-crime, Kajumama. Bhaiya saw Ayesha and Jai less and less, and each blamed the other for the break. 'Being the gentleman that he was he defended the actions of marrying the person that he did, stubbornly. He got upset when his wife was slighted in any way.' Bitter about his family's attitude to Gina, depressed by being an invalid, gentle, sensitive Bhaiya drank more and more to drown his sorrows.

Ayesha returned to India in the autumn of 1968 to see Indira whose health had been failing for the past couple of years. Indira's letters through the 1960s bemoaned her aches and pains, the many treatments she was trying out and her resignation to her fate. In 1967, she told her granddaughter she took medicine for gout, and had massage, homoeopathy and biochemical treatment, as well as 'spiritual healing treatment, and if with all this I do not get better, I am definitely not meant to get better, it is obvious'. She was wheelchair-bound and badly affected by cardiac asthma. Still she surrounded herself with young people and retained her passionate curiosity and gift for living.

Ayesha arrived in India a few days before Jai on 6 September, and rang Ma from Delhi. Indira told her to come to Bombay in five days' time, and said she had asked her other daughter, Menaka, to be there too. Ayesha delayed her departure by one day. The morning she was due to fly out, Menaka rang to tell her that Indira's condition had suddenly worsened. As she waited to leave, she watched the hands move slowly round the clock, willing them to speed up. Just before she left for the airport word reached her that Ma had died.

She and Menaka received the visitors who came to offer their condolences, trying not to imagine 'the room with Ma in it, the centre of an endless stream of guests, filling the palace with her easy warmth and fun. Even when she was ill, her involvement with life had been so intense it was impossible to grasp the fact that she was dead.' They settled her affairs and sorted through her things, the little gold paan box still standing on the French table beside her favourite chair, the flowers she had arranged now wilting in their vases, and her portrait by de Laszlo gazing dreamily down over them. 'That was Ma at the moment when the whole world seem[ed] to be her domain and when all the men were in love with her and when she would – any minute now – smile her famous smile and make one of her unexpected remarks, outrageous or infinitely kind. She couldn't be dead.'

Indira had already given away most of her possessions; part of her philosophy was 'Don't hoard': enjoy something for a while, she told Devika, and then let someone else enjoy it. But when her grandson Habi asked to be left some of her portraits, she refused him breezily. 'Darling, the girls [Ayesha and Menaka] have palaces, they'll be properly displayed there,' she explained. 'You'll live in a hovel, you won't have space for them, and anyway who'd see them?' Her true bequest, another grandson told me, was 'an amazing gift of not giving a damn'; it was also the gift of making everyone with whom she came into contact feel special, bringing joy to those she loved, and sharing with them the passionate curiosity and excitement she took in life.

In 1969, Ayesha herself went into hospital for an operation. While she was recovering in the spring of 1970, she received news from Calcutta that Bhaiya's condition was deteriorating. She was too ill to go to Calcutta to see him, but they agreed to meet in England the following month. But Bhaiya did not rally. He cried before he died because he had not passed his knowledge of elephants on to anyone.

Bhaiya and Gina had no children (though even if they had had a son, commented Ayesha, he would not have been recognized as maharaja by the people of Cooch Behar. 'Old customs die hard in India, especially in the princely states') so Indrajit's son Viraj was appointed the next maharaja by the palace priest – just before all the old titles were abolished for good.

The worst blow was still to come. In the summer of 1970, as usual, Jai and Ayesha were in England. Though he had had a fall some months earlier and had not played much polo, on a rainy day at the end of June Jai decided to play in a match at Cirencester. At half-time, Ayesha was sitting in her car chatting to Bubbles, watching the horses, players and grooms milling around on the other side of the field. Suddenly she saw a circle of people surrounding a figure lying on the ground; it was Jai. She rushed out of the car and over to him. 'I remember noticing in some part of my mind that someone had kicked his helmet out of the way and this irrationally angered me very much.'

When they lifted Jai into the ambulance, he was still unconscious, but by the time they reached the hospital he was dead. Ayesha could not believe her loss; for the next few weeks everything seemed unreal, dreamlike. 'Only when we reached Jaipur, the city that contained so much of our life together, did I truly realise that Jai had gone forever.' In her rooms at Rajmahal, Ayesha heard the boom of muffled drums and the shots fired in the traditional 19-gun salute as Jai's funeral procession left the City Palace. The night before, his four sons, white-clad, had kept a night-long vigil by his body while the people of Jaipur came to pay him their last respects. 'The entire city turned out to pay homage to him throughout the night, in an unending stream of sorrowful men, women and children.'

The procession to the cenotaph in Gaitor was a mile long. Jai's body, his head raised so everyone could see his face as he passed, was carried through Jaipur on a gun-carriage, and accompanied by men carrying lighted torches, 600 officers, a dozen former princes, the Chief Minister of Rajasthan and his cabinet members, police bands (their instruments swathed in black) and richly decorated camels, horses and elephants. The chief mahout led the procession, carrying the gold rod given to the Jaipur family by the Mogul emperors. Jai's four sons walked behind him, followed by Jaipur's nobles and the ministers of Rajasthan. 'But this day had nothing really to do with Rajasthan' and everything to do with the old Jaipur. Half a million mourners filled the streets, many clinging to telegraph poles or perched in trees to catch one last glimpse of their beloved former maharaja's body. At the cremation ground, Bubbles lit the funeral pyre, as he had done for his mother twenty-six years before. In London a month later, after Rimsky-Korsakov's *Song of India* had been played, Lord Mountbatten read an emotional tribute to Jai at his memorial service in the Guards Chapel. He concluded with the triumphant cry, 'Maharaja Man Singh ki Jai' (victory to Man Singh the great king) that had resounded through Jaipur for over fifty years.

Though the funeral and memorial were public and ceremonial, Ayesha's grief was private. She had lost the man she had adored since she was twelve, and who, despite his infidelities, 'in the end proved he loved her as much, if not more', according to her old friend Sher Ali Pataudi. 'She must have had something in her to have kindled that deep affection in him, which was so foreign to that class of people.'

Jai's death had ended their 'wonderful partnership', in Mountbatten's words, and Ayesha did not know how she would survive without him. 'There are no words with which I can thank you adequately for the moving and wonderful tribute you paid Jai,' she wrote to Mountbatten. 'Now at least I feel I can carry on and know what I should do even though the reason and centre of my life has gone. Thanks to all you have told me I shall now try to be worthy of Jai's memory . . . Please take great care of yourself,' she concluded. 'You have now a new responsibility – Jai's widow and family. May you live long to help and guide us.'

Tributes to Jai flooded in. Prince Philip spoke of the immeasurable boon Jai's friendship had been to him,

in the things we did together, like playing polo or shooting or just sitting and chatting under the moon in Jaipur . . . Jai had a serene quality, a sort of cheerful calm, which . . . was a most endearing and enjoyable characteristic. He combined with that a very rare quality in men, he was supremely civilised. Kind and modest, with an unerring instinct for the highest standards of human ambition and behaviour.

The man who had looked after the maharaja's dogs for forty years described the happiness he felt watching Jai walk in the garden. 'I was very sad when he went to England. We were all very happy with the news of his coming back. I kept on looking for the aeroplane . . . I would have been the happiest man if Maharaja Sahib had returned. He always liked me. I will always remember him.' After an enthusiastic account of his polo-playing prowess which had attracted 'countless numbers' of cheering fans, a Muslim gardener praised Jai's treatment of Jaipur's Muslims:

He also loved his people very much. He considered it his duty to help people in trouble. He never differentiated between Hindus and Muslims.

When some Muslims wanted to leave Jaipur during the communal disturbances [in 1947], he stopped them and told them, 'No Muslim should leave Jaipur and go. They are all like the hair of my chest.' The Muslims of Jaipur will never forget this.

The Chief Minister of Rajasthan was perhaps alone in breathing a sigh of relief: 'the tiger is gone.'

Devastated by her loss and with the news of more family deaths – Jai's daughter Mickey, Ayesha's cousin Gautam, Jai's elder brother Bahadur Singh – only adding to her feelings of despair and isolation, Ayesha retreated to Rajmahal. She was considering retiring from political and public life altogether when she received two letters, one from the grandmother of the Maharaja of Jodhpur and one from the Rajmata of Bikaner, urging her to put aside her grief and stand for Parliament once again. The 1971 election, called early by Mrs Gandhi to consolidate her power, was 'a referendum on Indira Gandhi herself'. The combined opposition parties campaigned behind the slogan 'Remove Indira'. Ayesha was seen as someone who could effectively counter her looming influence.

Still in mourning, Ayesha campaigned throughout Rajasthan in January and February 1971. For once, the activity did not help her to forget her troubles. She wrote to Pat begging him to come back to Jaipur and help her campaign. 'As for me my life is very sad and I feel very very alone except when the boys are here then I feel someone of his is with me.'

Ayesha was astonished on election day to find that thousands of her supporters' names had been removed from electoral registers. A Returning Officer showed her one register on which the names of individual voters had simply been crossed out; he suggested 'that it must have been a slip of the pen', but no efforts were made to rectify the situation. Every Rajput name had been struck off the list; not a single member of staff at Rajmahal, Rambagh or the City Palace had been allowed to vote.

Tactics like these, alongside Indira's powerful crusading and her slogan, 'Remove Poverty', carried the day for Indira. A hundred and fifty million people voted and Indira swept back to power with a two-thirds majority in the Lok Sabha. It was a triumphant moment for Indira Gandhi, for she, 'the woman – rather than Congress the party – was the victor'. Ayesha won her seat, but the Swatantra party lost 27 of its previous 34 seats.

In this unassailable position, Mrs Gandhi could legislate as she pleased. Having already nationalized the banks in 1969, she now nationalized the insurance and coal industries. She deliberately weakened the judiciary which had dared to challenge her over derecognizing the princes the year before, and instituted the Maintenance of Internal Security Act which allowed the government to arrest and imprison people without trial for up to a year. Some of these reforms were blatantly unconstitutional, undemocratic and illiberal, but in the name of 'the people's interest', Indira could do anything.

The bill derecognizing the princes and ending their constitutional rights was also passed. 'We may be depriving the Princes of luxury,' said Indira Gandhi, who did not deny herself luxuries, 'but we are giving them the opportunity to be men.' What the princes saw as their patriotic contribution to the creation of the independent Indian nation was finally disregarded. Now they were nothing more than ordinary citizens of a nation for which they felt they had sacrificed everything and received in return ingratitude and betrayal. 'Twenty years ago in this same place we were called the co-founders of independent India,' said Fatesinhrao, Maharaja of Baroda, Sayajirao's great-grandson. 'Today, we are branded as an anachronism and later, we will be known as reactionary obstacles to the founding of an egalitarian society.'

In the spring of 1971, tensions between East and West Pakistan had reached crisis point. Although East Pakistan had a larger population and a stronger economy than West Pakistan, since Independence West Pakistan had dominated government and used revenues from the east to build hospitals, roads and schools in the west. West Pakistan declared that Urdu would be Pakistan's national language, though it was barely spoken in the Bengali east. When a civil disobedience movement was launched in East Pakistan in the winter of 1971, the Pakistani Army was sent in to crush the rising, brutally murdering, looting and raping millions of Bengalis. East Pakistan renamed itself Bangladesh and declared itself independent, mustering impassioned support from Indira Gandhi in the Indian Parliament. By the end of the year, 10 million desperate refugees had poured over the border into India.

In December, the Pakistani Army bombed nine Indian air bases in the north and west of the country. India, which had held back from intervening in Bangladeshi–Pakistani affairs for over six months, was now committed to war. Indira officially declared war and announced India's recognition of the state of Bangladesh. The exhausted, ill-equipped Pakistani Army held out for only fourteen days before surrendering.

This was the pinnacle of Indira Gandhi's power. Her 'intoxicating victory' over Pakistan and her radical populism won over even her critics. 'She was the undisputed leader of the country; the cynicism of the intellectuals had given way to admiration; the masses were even more worshipful,' wrote the journalist Kuldip Nayar. 'She was hailed as the greatest leader India had ever had.' In a Gallup poll conducted in 1971 Indira Gandhi was voted the most admired person in the world.

But India was soon disillusioned with her regime. The costs of war and refugee support were compounded by famine in 1972 when the monsoon failed. Over the next years, oil and food prices soared, strikes paralysed the country and unrest simmered. Corruption was inescapable; it had become virtually institutionalized. Indira, interpreting her unpopularity as a 'Get Indira' campaign by the united opposition parties, responded with increasingly repressive measures and mounted a retaliatory campaign of her own.

On 11 February 1975, Ayesha did her morning yoga on the terrace of Moti Doongri, the small, exquisite fort high above Jaipur city in which she had lived since Jai's death, and sat down to breakfast in the freshness of the morning. Five years after Jai's death, she was beginning to feel herself again, and once again to have hope in the future. As she ate, her maid announced some visitors.

'We are income tax officers,' they announced. 'We have come to search the premises.' When she said they could, but she had to leave shortly for her appointments, they told her no one was allowed to leave the house. As they searched the house, Pat telephoned and told Ayesha that Rajmahal, now Bubbles's home, the Rambagh Palace Hotel, the City Palace and museum, Pat and Joey's houses in Jaipur and Ayesha's parliamentary grace-and-favour house in Delhi had all been raided. The inspections, here and in Gwalior, another former princely state whose Rajmata, like Ayesha, opposed Congress, went on for months. Matched Carrara marble floors were taken up, slab by slab, and discarded in untidy piles. Fabulous jewels and gold coins – each piece accounted for – were marvelled over by the incredulous inspectors. It took them nine years to decide none of the gold they found in Gwalior was 'smuggled'.

Perched above the old palace of Amber, Jaigarh Fort, where Jaipur's treasury had been guarded by warlike Meena tribesmen for generations, was also targeted. From the earliest years of the Jaipur dynasty, each maharaja had been allowed to enter Jaigarh only once in his lifetime, just after his accession. He was led blindfolded through the maze of tunnels and passages by the guards, and allowed to choose one thing to take out with him. This custom underlined the ages-old belief that the maharaja was only the custodian of his state's treasures. Many years before, Jai's predecessor had taken from Jaigarh a solid gold parrot about a foot high with a diamond encrusted breast, rubies for its eyes and an emerald hanging from its beak that stood on the mantelpiece of the drawing room at Rambagh. When the tax inspectors arrived at Jaigarh in 1975, the guards told them they could enter the fort only over their dead bodies, though they were eventually persuaded to allow them in.

Another focus of the searches, the heir to the Maharaja of Alwar, refused to allow the inspectors access to his house, his grandfather's former shooting-lodge, where he and his wife lived surrounded by an adored menagerie that included elephants, tigers and leopards as well as dogs and horses. When the inspectors arrived, he set the animals free and barred the doors. His gas and water were cut off, and the inspectors settled down to wait for his surrender. The prince held on for a week and then, made desperate by the howling of his beloved animals, went into the family shrine with his ADC, a close friend. Reports were heard. When the servants ran into the shrine, they found both men lying dead, each with a bullet hole in his skull. Surrender had never been an option; the Yuvraj's was a typically romantic, Rajput solution to the impossible predicament in which he found himself.

On 12 June 1975, Indira Gandhi's election to Parliament in 1971 was annulled by the Allahabad High Court on the grounds of electoral malpractice. Her election as MP for Rae Bareilly in Uttar Pradesh was invalidated and she was debarred from holding electoral office for six years. Indira appealed and her lawyer requested an unconditional stay against the verdict in Allahabad, but all she was granted was the right to remain in office without a parliamentary vote.

Her enemies were determined to force her to resign, but their threats of action gave Indira the justification she needed for suspending normal government. On 25 June, she declared a state of Emergency, assuming absolute control of the government. Power cuts in newspaper offices quelled press criticism, and opposition leaders were seized and arrested without charge in midnight raids. Mrs Gandhi later admitted that people were arrested 'for no reason at all, I mean just personal enmity'. 'No crisis but that of Mrs Gandhi's own political survival necessitated the Emergency,' wrote one of her early biographers. Mrs Gandhi's aunt, Nan Pandit, made no secret of her opposition to Indira's new regime, saying, 'The essence of democracy is the right to dissent.'

At the end of July, Ayesha travelled to Delhi to attend the Monsoon Session of Parliament. The opposition benches were almost empty; Congress members, on the other side of the hall, seemed surprised to see her. That afternoon, back at home, Ayesha was arrested. Her offence – she was never actually charged – was that she had been found in possession of foreign currency when Moti Doongri was searched: £19 sterling, 10 Swiss francs and some other foreign coins had been found on her dressing table during the months of searches. This was in excess of the permitted limit, and the only breach of the law the inspectors were able to find, though her non-cooperation with them (she had refused to allow them to eat their tiffin in her garden) had also been unofficially infuriating. She was allowed to pack a small bag, but not to telephone her lawyer. When Bubbles, who was with her, came out to protest to the policemen, he was arrested too.

Because the jails were full 'chock-a-block full like a holiday resort', Ayesha and Bubbles were taken to the notorious Tihar Jail, on the outskirts of Delhi. 'As we were taken through the gates of the prison I was surprised to find a large garden filled with trees. I said to the Superintendent, "This is not too bad," to which he replied, "But there are walls that surround it."'

Ayesha's room was in a building used by visiting doctors to examine sick prisoners. Alongside one wall ran an open sewer. For the first few days, she shared with another political prisoner, Srilata Swaminathan, but after that she was alone. There was some movement inside the prison, though. Ayesha requested and received permission to walk every evening with Bubbles in the courtyard. Two little boys called Ismael and Islam brought Ayesha roses and their mother, another prisoner, Laila Begum, offered to clean her room. Her cell had no running water or basin, so Bubbles sent her hot water to wash in from his cell. Newspapers were delivered, but they were censored; there was a decent library. Though she and Bubbles saw their lawyers after about a week behind bars, there was very little that could be done for them because of the Emergency. Ayesha's plight attracted much sympathy, in India and around the world. Friends in high places, such as Mountbatten, who had been such a support to her since Jai's death, tried to intervene. Pat had to ask people in Jaipur not to demonstrate in public in case it made her and Bubbles's situation worse.

The days passed. From England, Jagat sent Ayesha a canvas for needlepoint. She received letters from friends and supporters from all over the world. She sent for textbooks and slates to start a school for the many children in prison with their mothers, and also taught them cricket and football. 'It was wonderful to see the amount of cheer she brought to their lives and to hear their laughter; there was nothing that those children would not have done for her.' She played badminton with the younger prisoners, who were mostly pickpockets or prostitutes. Some had more violent histories, though: one inmate – the 'Queen' of Tihar – had twenty-four cases pending against her, four of which were for murder. At night, the women sang songs of protest and defiance. Twice a week Joey visited, bringing news from outside and of the campaign for their release. She was very unhappy in prison, says her niece Devika, but very brave, always joking with her visitors and making light of how bad conditions were.

A month or so after Ayesha's arrival at Tihar, another Rajmata appeared there, the former Maharani of Gwalior and daughter-in-law of the man Indira had rejected in favour of Jit Cooch Behar. She, like Ayesha, was a prominent opponent of the government, later a founder-member of the right-wing and ardently Hindu-nationalist BJP, or Bharatiya Janata Party. At first the inspectors asked Ayesha if she would share her cell with Vijayaraje, but she protested that their interests would clash: the Rajmata meditated for over two hours a day, while Ayesha was up early to do her yoga and liked to listen to her tape player and read late into the night. Instead, Ayesha helped them fit up another room for her. 'We bowed to each other and folded our hands as we would have at a social occasion,' recalled Vijaya, 'but the greeting she came out with was one of agonised concern: "Whatever made you come here? This is a horrible place!"'

The room Vijaya was assigned was heavy with humidity, as it was the monsoon season, and so she ended up sleeping on Ayesha's veranda. Every night, Ayesha listened quietly to the BBC news on the small radio Joey had smuggled into Tihar for her. 'As I switched off the radio, the Rajmata would ask if there was anything about India. There never was.' Because she and the Rajmata were still, theoretically, Members of Parliament, they received invitations to a reception being held for a British delegation to India, and, amused, wondered if they would be allowed out for the evening to attend it.

Bubbles was released from prison after two and a half months, but just as Ayesha's case was about to come to court, habeas corpus was revoked. 'The doors of justice were closed,' and Ayesha began to lose hope. In September, she found a lump in her breast. She became convinced she would die there. 'Only my body will be taken out,' she used to say, and Vijaya would make a pretence of second sight and tell her a date by which she would certainly be freed. 'But when that day passed, she would never fail to point out that my prophecy had not come true. Sheepishly I would confess to a miscalculation and give her another date.'

As the months wore on, the autumn festival of Dussera was celebrated in Tihar, and outside the lamps were lit for Divali when winter began. In November Ayesha's lawyers filed a petition at the High Court in Delhi, contending that her detention was political, and pointing out that she needed medical attention; the government's counter-affidavit declared that Ayesha's violations of the regulations were so dangerous that they could not be made public. She spent Christmas eating a jar of caviar sent to her by an English friend, listening to Cole Porter on her portable tape player.

Before New Year, she was admitted to hospital; as well as the fear of breast cancer, she needed surgery to remove gall-stones. She refused to have the operation while she was still a prisoner, and on 11 January Joey and Menaka took her home. She had stayed in Tihar for 156 nights, the longest time she had spent consecutively in one place in her life. Despite the hardship she endured, she looks back on that time with equanimity and humour. 'I would have been most insulted if she hadn't thought me important enough to put in jail.' The only thing she saved from that time was the caviar-pot she had been sent, which now stands in her bathroom.

At home in Delhi, Joey took Ayesha into the garden to warn her that the house and telephone lines were bugged. When they arrived in Jaipur, she was forbidden from using public transport in case people demonstrated when they saw her. None the less, 600 people were waiting for her outside her house to cheer her return. Though she had been released from prison, she was still on parole and had to inform the authorities of her every move. This restriction was almost unbearably frustrating, she told Mountbatten two years later. 'It's such a waste just existing and not doing anything for Jaipur and India.' Even worse, she had not seen Jagat for two and a half years.

Her memoir, *A Princess Remembers*, came out in 1976. 'Dearest Ayesha we think of you so much and I do admire your courage and fortitude and excellent example of really good behaviour,' Mountbatten wrote to her. 'I only wish your book wasn't being published. I was never very keen on a biography and it can't help much at this time and indeed there is so much more to say in a real biography in a few years' time which would include all which really happened to you during the last two years.' 'We could not prevent the book being published,' Ayesha replied. 'It's full of mistakes!'

Because she was on parole, Ayesha was unable to campaign against Mrs Gandhi in the elections of 1976. The night of the election, the telephone rang in Ayesha's house. She was told that someone wanted to speak to her who would not give her name. When she picked up the receiver, a woman's voice said, ' "Congratulations. Mrs Gandhi has lost her seat." It was the telephone operator. I threw the receiver into the air, picked it up again, and said, "Are you sure?" ' Knowing that the news would not be announced officially until the last moment, the operator had rung to give Ayesha the good news. She rushed to the Jaipur collectorate where the votes were being counted, and a jubilant crowd shouted, 'We have taken revenge for what she did to you.'

Soon afterwards, Ayesha was leaving a party at the British High Commission in Delhi when Mrs Gandhi's car drew up. Indira rolled down the window and both women bowed silently to each other in a namaste, the traditional Indian greeting.

Though she did not run herself, Ayesha campaigned for the opposition candidates to the Legislative Assembly in Rajasthan in 1977. That year she was appointed chairman of the Rajasthan Tourism Development Corporation. She campaigned again in the

1984 elections following Indira Gandhi's assassination but since then she has retired from active political life.

When Sanjay Gandhi died in 1980, Ayesha telephoned Indira Gandhi to offer her condolences; Mrs Gandhi would not take the call. The two women, born two years apart, both heirs to great Indian political families, both worshipped by thousands but loathing each other, were fated to similar sadnesses. Educated alike, they moved in similar cosmopolitan circles but sought meaning and validation in political life. Proud, passionate and demanding, both won admirers and made enemies. Both fought their private battles in public. Both would watch their adored, difficult sons die. But at the end of it all, Ayesha could extend the hand of forgiveness, and Indira Gandhi could not accept it.

Conclusion

Before her arrest, Ayesha had been in the process of moving house from Moti Doongri to the Lily Pool, in the grounds of Rambagh Palace. In the late 1930s, Jai had had a modern pavilion built in a shady green garden near Rambagh's tennis courts, which was used for informal entertaining. Called the Lily Pool after a house Jai had seen in a magazine article, it was a favourite place for alfresco dinners in the summer and tennis parties or barbecues in the winter. In 1968, Jai decided to convert the Lily Pool into a house for Ayesha. Simple, spacious and elegant, it is full of silver-framed family photographs and paintings and the exquisite jade and rose quartz *objets* Jai had placed in the suite of rooms she had as a bride at Rambagh, just a few hundred yards away. 'I like it because it is so open – bright and airy – like living outdoors,' says Ayesha. 'I hate shut doors and do not mind that swallows dirty my lamp shades and chipmunks nibble the fringes of my curtains.'

When the flag is up outside the Lily Pool,

people know I am in Jaipur and they come to ask me for help. If it is a school, a well, a dispensary or anything deserving, I try to write to the authorities concerned. When the poor ask for monetary aid for marriages, medical aid and even housing we provide help from the Sawai Jai Singh Benevolent Fund. Sometimes I am asked for land, money for election expenses, to publish a book, or a train ticket and all sorts of other things. I ask my secretary to direct them to the Governor or the Chief Minister of Rajasthan.

There are always children around the house, playing tennis or cricket. Ayesha continues the royal tradition of keeping open house; she is never too busy for the people of Jaipur or Cooch

Behar. She has managed to translate the traditional concepts of regal responsibility in which she was raised into the modern era, creating a role for herself as a model of progressive royalty. She is a passionate charity worker, a glamorous tourist attraction, utterly dedicated to the causes and people she supports.

Ayesha maintains an interest in the institutions she set up, such as the MGD School, over whose board she still presides. In 2003 the school celebrated its Diamond Jubilee; her stepson Joey's wife, Vidya (the daughter of Indira and Bhaiya's beloved ADC, Kajumama) carries on Ayesha's work there. Ayesha also founded a village school just outside Jaipur called Lalitya Bal Niketan, named for her granddaughter. These schools are much needed institutions: in a 1991 census, the literacy rates in India were 63.86 per cent for men, and 39.42 per cent for women, with the percentages much lower in rural areas. They are the work of which she is proudest, and in which she has the most hope. 'Education is not only necessary for earning a livelihood . . . These students have also been taught to live in a world where dignity, understanding and sensitivity for others matters. This kind of training, I hope, will hold the key for a brighter future.'

Ayesha is still intensely committed to the welfare of children, just as she was when she was a child, the 'pagli rajkumari' of Cooch Behar, trying to improve the living conditions of the palace servants and mahouts. In April 2003, appalled at the devastation caused by the American bombing of Iraq, she pledged payment for the treatment of Ali, a twelve-year-old boy who lost both his arms and was severely burned in an air raid.

Her other childhood passion, animals, remains with her too. The girl who shot her first panther at twelve grew up to be an ardent conservationist, campaigning to protect her beloved elephants and the diminishing natural habitat Indian wildlife urgently needs to survive. She despairs of the deterioration of her beloved Jaipur, and frequently visits Cooch Behar, mourning its decline and poverty since Independence. She hates seeing the once immaculate town sprawling and shabby, the palace that once rang with her family's laughter empty. 'Sometimes I still hum the tune of a song which described the prosperity and gentle beauty of Cooch Behar as the abode of gods in the foothills of the Himalayas.'

On a personal level, she continues the stud farm she and Jai started, breeding polo ponies and, now, race horses; she visits the farm daily when she's in Jaipur. Ayesha takes great pleasure in presenting the Cooch Behar Cup at Cowdray Polo Club in Sussex. She usually spends five or six months a year in England, watching the polo and tennis, seeing old friends there and in Europe. At first, she found life abroad easier than in Jaipur – freer of the heartbreaking memories of Jai and of the politics of Indian life. 'Life here is pleasant and uncomplicated. No back-biting like in India!' she wrote from London in 1982. But two years later she was, she said, 'longing to go home to India despite all the intrigues and bad feelings'.

Ayesha's family life has been the source of tension and grief in recent years. Jaipur's former royal family is deeply divided. In 2003, Bubbles declared his only daughter's son his heir, while Joey and Pat believe he should have chosen one of their sons so that the male line continued. Jai's will has been challenged and a complex, upsetting legal battle drags on. Ayesha is closely allied to Joey and Pat and barely speaks to Bubbles – who as a young man had adored the woman he called his 'mother'. There are also disputes over her own grandchildren's inheritances. Nothing is simple in this family; for all their charm they are as capable of intransigence and vengefulness as anyone. Like her mother and grandmothers, Ayesha possesses formidable strength of character and her sense of entitlement can make her difficult to deal with.

In May 1978, Jagat married Priya, the daughter of Prince Piya and Princess Vibhavati of Thailand. The Queen attended the reception in London. Their marriage soon broke down, and 'the problem of the children' weighed down on Jagat through the 1990s. He died in 1997, weakened by years of alcoholism. In his eulogy, his friend the writer Mark Shand described Jagat as an irreverent, optimistic *bon viveur*, 'the dazzling Prince with flowing locks and flashing eyes, attired in jewels and jeans, turban and tshirt', to whom nothing was too much trouble for a friend and whose infectious chuckle had charmed so many.

Jagat's death sent Ayesha into a deep depression.

It was a terrible loss when my beloved, darling son Jagat passed away. It is something that I cannot get over. And I often wonder had I taken more care of him he might still have been with us today. He was such a good-looking, charming, intelligent person and very popular with everybody, he was generous to a fault shall never forget seeing him lying on his bed in the hospital, not breathing and I knew Jagat was no more. I cannot describe the pain of this moment and every now and again it comes back and I blame myself and I wonder about life and death.

Jagat's death was the worst blow to fall on Ayesha after Jai's death and left her deeply saddened. However, although she has lost her beloved husband and her only son, her younger stepsons, Joey and Pat, and their families, have brought her joy and consolation in old age. In the princely tradition of the Indian extended family, the family she acquired through her marriage has grown to mean as much to her as her own.

For all her trials, Ayesha, in her eighties, lives a full, active life. She is still considered one of the world's most attractive women and a recent poll in the *Eastern Voice* voted her the fourth most beautiful woman of the last century. A journalist from America's *Woman's Wear Daily* telephoned the Lily Pool a few years ago while Mark Shand was staying. 'We'd like to ask the Rajmata how she has kept her looks all these years,' she said. Mark called the question up to Ayesha, who thought for a minute at the top of the stairs. 'Tell her I use boot-black on my hair,' she said mischievously, 'and drink a bottle of whisky a day.'

A life spent in the public eye has made Ayesha a national celebrity in India; her face is more familiar to most Indians than their president's. While I was in India in 2002 on one of my research trips, a special edition of the *Rajasthan Plus* newspaper celebrating great Rajasthani personalities came out. The Rajmata was front and centre, with a photograph ten times the size of anyone else's, and a laudatory paragraph concluding, 'Without mentioning her this would have been an incomplete offering.'

Her diverse interests, extended family and many friends fill her days; her energy is unfailing. She is enormous fun to be with, curious, captivating, sparkling with life. Though she is breezy and relaxed, she never loses the regal dignity and grace that come to her as naturally as breathing. A lively irreverence bubbles up behind her eyes when something amuses her. She is quick to laughter; quick, as Chimnabai was, to anger or annoyance, but equally so to apologize.

She gave a speech at a school just outside Jaipur recently. Her Hindi is still not fluent, so she was reading out what she had first written in English and then translated into Hindi. Halfway through she stopped and looked out at the children sitting band-box neat in their school uniforms in front of her, fidgeting. 'I hate making speeches,' she said. 'What do all of you like to do?' As soon as she spoke directly to them, the children's attention was gripped, and she glowed to see she had touched them.

I arrived at the Lily Pool one day to find Ayesha coming off the tennis court beside her house. She had been practising her strokes – though she had not played tennis, she said, for twenty years – because she had been asked to open a municipal tennis court for the children of Jaipur and was determined to hit the inaugural ball over the net. 'I'm going to have to ask them to make the ceremony a bit later,' she said, laughing, 'I'm too creaky before eleven o'clock to manage it.'

Driving through Jaipur with her – past the very walls she saved, past the Ladies' Club she founded, past MGD School, now one of the most highly regarded girls' schools in India, past tourist shops selling the handicrafts she encouraged Partition refugees to manufacture, past hotels full of visitors attracted to Jaipur as much by the glamour with which she and Jai invested it as by its scenery or shopping – you see her stamp on everything. Her legacy is everywhere.

She often looks back with nostalgia on her youth, that lost, magical world she once inhabited.

One of the most haunting memories of my childhood in Cooch Behar is of coming home on an elephant just before dusk, tired after the excitement of the day's shooting. The air was full of the smell of mustard flowers, and from a distance came the lovely sound of flutes. Far to the north, still visible through the twilight after a very clear day, stands the white half-circle of the Himalayas. This remembered moment immediately takes me back to the happiness and security of my childhood, to a time when my life was untouched by change and the loss of the people dearest to me. Sometimes, as I fall asleep at night during the moist heat of the monsoon rains, it seems that we are all back there still, Ma and Bhaiya, Ila and Indrajit, my husband Jai, and I, and that Menaka and I are not the only ones left alive.

Today all that remains of this vanished world is memories. The marble palaces in which Ayesha and her family once lived are either crumbling into disrepair or populated by rich tourists; the jewels which once adorned maharajas seen by their people as living gods now glitter blindly in bank vaults. For just over a century, India's princely families lived in an extraordinary cocoon of privilege and magnificence, protected from the mass democratization that ushered in the modern era by their complex association with the British Empire. Although most longed, alongside their country-men, for India to break free of its colonial bonds, for the princes independence was an ambiguous prize and adjusting to it meant rejecting the very things that had once defined them. Even Sayajirao and Chimnabai, Nripendra and Sunity, Indira, Ayesha and Jai, progressive and enlightened sovereigns and in many ways models of modern monarchy, were haunted by the dichotomy between their traditional roles as maharajas and maharanis and the demands imposed on them by the new world they suddenly found themselves inhabiting.

Tales of curses cling to India's princely families. Sunity Devi's granddaughter Garbo told me that one of Narendra Narayan's wives, devastated by her infant son's murder at the hands of a rival rani, threw her treasured pearls into the ghat in the centre of Cooch Behar town and cursed the family's male line. Another legend relates how, many centuries ago, a prince of Cooch Behar conquered parts of neighbouring Assam, including a temple at Guwahati, its capital, where the goddess Kali's yoni, or vagina, was said to have been dropped. The temple was thus one of the most mysterious and powerful in India, but the maharaja of the day violated its sacred precincts, either by molesting a priestess or simply looking at one when he should not have. The priests of the temple cursed his family: any member of the Cooch Behar line who came back to the temple would be doomed.

Habi, Indira's grandson and Ayesha's nephew, told me this story, and listed with it a catalogue of related disasters. No member of the family could even look in the direction of the temple without encountering catastrophe, he said. Bhaiya's polo accident occurred two months after he visited Guwahati in 1966. Viraj, the last maharaja, who had business in Guwahati, died within six months of going there; his pancreas, admittedly already fragile, just gave up. Habi himself broke his leg the day after going to Guwahati and was bedridden for six months.

Jagat's loss was the latest in a long line of tragedies. So many of the deaths in these three families – Baroda, Cooch Behar and Jaipur – were untimely and alcoholism was, if not the sole cause, a significant contributing factor in many. They fell down stairs, they caught food poisoning or pneumonia, their hearts were weak: directly or indirectly, alcohol put their lives in peril and yet aware of this weakness they appeared powerless to resist it. They seemed to live under a cloud of nameless melancholy or sense of foreboding that only drinking could assuage. For all their gaiety, humour and love of fun, the Cooch Behars were always described as having sad eyes; and the ones I have met bear this out. Mukul Narayan, a member of the family whom I met in Cooch Behar in 2002, said mournfully, 'None of us is happy.' Perhaps the saddest thing of all for the family now is that, just as the rani's curse foretold, there is no male heir to carry on the line.

I don't know whether I believe in curses – or fairy-tales either, for that matter – but these extraordinary women, so blessed with intelligence, charisma, beauty, wealth and position, seem somehow damned, too, as if the gods really are jealous of those upon whom they have showered blessings. Maybe the Indian concept of karma is more helpful, that they were granted great suffering along with their great boons in accordance with some mysterious, preordained system. Perhaps it's just a truism that no amount of wealth and privilege can protect anyone from heartbreak.

And yet, though Chimnabai, Sunity, Indira and Ayesha were not always able to hold on to the happiness they sought for themselves, they could and did bring so much of it to other people's lives. Despite their individual faults and weaknesses, these four women lived up to their rank, believed passionately in the concept of duty that drove them, and tried to the best of their abilities to share their privileges of education and emancipation with others, even in the midst of private hardship. In their different ways, they were icons, modernizers and revolutionaries, rising above the cultural limitations that bound their countrywomen and inspiring a redefinition of the role of women in modern India. They truly were maharanis, 'great queens'.

Glossary

Hindi, Bengali, Marathi and British-Indian words used in this book

Achkan – knee-length man's jacket
Apsara – a dancing girl at the court of the god Indra or,
  figuratively, a beautiful woman
Arati – evening prayers
Ashram – hermitage
Attar – flower essence, traditionally of rose, used (among other
  purposes) in durbar ceremonies
Ayurveda – traditional Indian medical system

Bagh – garden
Bahadur – hero
Barra – big, elder
Begum – Muslim lady of high rank
Bhai – brother
Bhrust – unsanctified in Hindu eyes
Bindi – mark worn on her forehead by a married (or
  marriageable) woman
Brahmin – the Hindu priestly caste
Brahmo Samaj – a modern, monotheistic form of Hinduism

Cantonment – the British area, usually military, of an Indian
  town
Caste – traditional Hindu social divisions
Chamar – fly-whisk made of a yak's tail
Chaprassi – messenger
Charkha – spinning wheel
Chatri – large parasol
Chik – thin bamboo, generally used for screens
Choli – small bodice worn under a sari, until the late nineteenth
  century usually backless

Choto – small, younger
Crore – 10 million

Dada – grandfather; elder brother
Dalit – someone outside the Hindu caste system; Gandhi called
them harijans, children of god
Deodhi – a zenana's entrance porch
Devi – Bengali feminine honorific suffix, used for women from
noble or royal families; also means goddess
Dewan – minister at a prince's court
Dharma – religious observance
Dhurri – flat-woven rug
Didi – grandmother
Divali – the Hindu winter festival of lights celebrating the goddess
Laxmi
Durbar – royal court or reception; can also be used to mean the
king himself
Dussera – the Hindu autumn festival in honour of the goddess
Durga

Gaddi (or gadi) – throne
Ghagra – Rajasthani full skirt, usually worn with a bodice
Ghat – large water tank
Ghee – clarified butter, often used in lamps lit as religious
offerings

Haveli – merchant's house, traditionally divided into men's and
women's sides
Holi – the Hindu spring festival
Howdah – elephant saddle, generally canopied

Jai – victory
Jamedar – footman
Jati – caste subdivision
Jauhur – mass sati
Ji – suffix denoting affection and respect

Jungly – provincial, backwards, almost wild

Kalgi – turban jewel, worn only by those of royal blood; also,
   sarpech
Kavad – door
Khadi – handloomed cotton, often worn as a statement of India's
   self-sufficiency
Kharita – agreement
Kshatriya – the warrior caste
Kumar/kumari – prince/princess

Lakh – 1,00,000
Lathi – stick bound with iron, traditionally carried by Indian
   policeman
Lingam – phallus, and the symbolic representation of this used as
   an object of worship

Mahal – palace
Maharaja – great king
Maharani – great queen
Maharishi – great mystic
Mahout – elephant groom, driver
Mahseer – Indian fresh water fish
Maidan – large park
Mama – uncle, specifically mother's brother
Mandap – temporary marriage pavilion
Manjil – hammock
Maratha – Indian race originally from central India
Mashima – aunt, specifically mother's sister
Masjid – mosque
Mitti – kind of herb
Mujira – traditional greeting for Indian royalty, bowing low and
   touching their feet

Namaskar, namaste – Hindu greeting, with hands together in
   prayer in front of the heart

Nautch girls – dancing girls
Nawab – Muslim nobleman

Paan – betel nut, eaten as a digestive
Pagli – mad
Palki, palanquin – sedan chair
Panchayat – village council
Pandal – marquee
Pandit – priest, astrologer
Pie, paise – $\frac{1}{100}$ of a rupee
Pilkhana – elephant stables
Prahara – Bengali milk sweet
Pugree – traditional Marathi headgear for men. It closely
    resembles a turban, except that it is kept and worn permanently
    folded into shape, while a turban is folded freshly on to the
    head at each wearing
Puja – prayer, worship
Purdah – literally, curtain; social system by which women,
    especially of the upper classes, are segregated from men

Raj – rule; especially used to describe the period of British rule in
    India
Raja – king
Raje – Maratha feminine honorific suffix; princess
Rajkumar/Rajkumari – prince/princess
Rajmata – queen mother
Rajput – noble race from north-western Indian
Rangoli – patterns in coloured sand and gold and silver dust
Rani – queen
Rao – Maratha masculine honorific suffix
Raoraja – a maharaja's illegitimate, but acknowledged, son
Rupee – Indian currency (approximately Rs 13 to the pound in
    1930s–40s)

Sardar – nobleman, lord
Sari – traditional Indian woman's dress

Sati – Rajput practice of self-immolation in which a widow
    voluntarily joins her husband on his funeral pyre; or the
    woman herself
Satyagraha – non-violent resistance, non-cooperation (literally,
    'the force of truth'); began as a political movement in 1920–21
Shalwar kameez – long tunic worn over loose trousers gathered at
    the ankle; traditional woman's dress of the Punjab area
Shamiana – an open-sided marquee; also, pandal
Shatush – lightweight soft goat wool
Shikar – a hunt
Shudra – the Hindu farming class
Sindur – vermilion powder used for bindis and in a married
    woman's hair parting
Sitar – stringed musical intrument, plucked like a guitar
Sri, srimati – honorific; equivalent to Mr or Mrs
Swadeshi – boycott of foreign goods; began as a political
    movement in 1905
Swaraj – self-rule
Swatantra – freedom
Syce – groom

Tabla – hand drum
Thakur – nobleman
Thali – circular dish with separate compartments for rice, curries
    and pickles
Tiffin – a meal, lunch or tea, often carried in a tiffin-tin
Tikka – priest's sandalwood (or blood) thumbprint on the
    forehead of worshippers; the 'mark of the god'
Tilgul – sweet made from cinnamon and molasses
Tonga – one-horse cart
Tulsi – basil used in Hindu ceremonies

Vaisya – the Hindu merchant caste
Varan – the mother-in-law's traditional welcome to a bride
Veena – stringed musical instrument, played by plucking
Vilas – home

Yoni – vagina, and the symbolic representation of this used as an
   object of worship
Yuvraj – crown prince

Zamindar – landowner
Zenana – women's quarters of a house or palace

Appendix

The Status of an Indian Princess. A Tale of Woe.
(By one of them.)*

It will seem strange that a person of my class should seek the help of the public – and that through the agency of a daily paper; but there are limits to human patience and suffering. It is impossible to bear the strain of life-long neglect and ill-treatment. It is said that even the worm will turn, and we women of the ruling Princes of Hindustan are surely more sentient than the proverbial worm. For generations we have quietly suffered untold and unbelievable wrongs; but this is a new age. Even we behind the Purdah have felt the breath of the new spirit. Our grandmothers put up mildly with insults and humiliations without a word of protest. They accepted their fate ungrudgingly. They allowed themselves to be treated like pet dogs. Our mothers showed a slightly different spirit. They cried and killed themselves when the agony was unbearable, but the new generation has started to protest. Why should we not protest? We are also human. We have received little education, but we had English governesses to instil new ideas into our heads. Even we dare to dream in terms of self-determination.

Persons of my class are married off when they are quite young. My father's house is of middling importance. I was brought up and educated with my brothers. My parents prided themselves on being modern. At the time of my marriage a decent amount of money was paid to my lord presumably for my maintenance, but not a pie has ever been available to me. I did not understand what marriage

* (*c.* 1926; reprinted from Chudgar, *Indian Princes Under British Protection*, pp. 22–6. 'It is generally surmised,' reads the endnote, 'that the writer was once the wife of a Prince of the highest class, once considered very enlightened and progressive, but who had latterly passed much of his time on the Continent.')

was except that I had to leave a happy home and in future I had to stay with strangers. But I was old enough to understand that the Prince who married me belonged to a big house, and I did dream dreams of splendour. When I went to my new home I wanted my governess to accompany me, but that was not allowed. I was well looked after, well-dressed, and kindly treated. One day the news came to me with a shock that the Prince had two other wives and that there were other women also with whom the Prince spent weeks. I was overwhelmed with shame, and I dared not look up into the faces of my servant-women. When the Prince came to me I talked to him about it very cautiously, but he was absolutely brutal about it. He told me things that I refused to believe. I never thought that any man could possibly be so inhuman.

I found out a pretext for returning to my parents. There I created a scene, but my aunt told me horrible stories, and eventually I returned to my master. All pride of family greatness, of purity of married life, was knocked out of me. Purity does not exist for such princely masters. They are above such human considerations of virtue. Throughout my life I have been made to feel that my status in the world depended upon the favour of the Prince. If I am a great personage to-day I may become almost a beggar tomorrow. The State Jhaverkhana (Treasury) is at my disposal, but not one little thing belongs to me. The same thing applies to dresses, motors, horses, and servants. A fairly large sum of money is placed at my disposal in the family budget, but I may not spend, well, practically anything, without the previous sanction of my husband. This total dependence is deliberately enforced. I have been made to pocket insults, and they say that self-respect is a commodity unknown in the Palace. I submitted to all sorts of humiliations, though not without protest. I have been kept caged up. I may not see men except some near relatives. I had no one to whom I could complain or consult.

But I could not bear my children being treated with unfairness and injustice. For their sake I quarrelled with my husband and now we are drifting apart.

God alone knows what has happened to our Indian Princes. Why are there so many of them running after baby faces? Why

have they become so recklessly careless of their name and reputation? When the whole country is being influenced by high
ideals and striving to improve itself, so many Princes are taking a
downward course. Why are some of them imbued with animal
passion to a disgusting extent? It is obvious that some of them go
to Europe just with a view to enjoy personal liberty so that they
may indulge in licence without any check. They are neglecting
their State affairs. The people are angry with them, but what do they
care? The Government is pursuing a policy of non-interference;
perhaps they are giving them the long rope so that they may
eventually hang themselves.

The subjects of the Princes have become vocal and they are
raising their voices in complaint. Perhaps the Viceroy will listen to
them, but how are our grievances to be redressed? I have consulted
political officers, they give me no hope. We are to be treated like
chattels. There is not much difference in the treatment that a
married Princess and a Court courtesan may receive. We have no
rights. We cannot combine as you men may. I consulted a prominent politician who is also a lawyer. He could give me no hopes.
Intrigues with political officers and with the Political Department
are unsuitable to my nature. I want my rights. I want my status to
be regularly defined. I want to fight for the many voiceless women
who are being ill-treated. I say that they are reduced to the condition
which is worse than that of beggars in the street. We are taught to
be slaves. Our duty is merely to satisfy the whims of our master.
We are deprived of our self-respect. If we assert our right of being
human our lord may neglect and punish us. We are threatened
with this every moment of our lives. The Prince has no duty
towards us, we have no rights excepting such as a kindly political
officer might get for us.

Our existence is a mere cipher. We are not taught to take interest
in anything. We are the toys of our master. He may dress us or tear
our clothes away. We are worse situated than the Russian serfs
of yesterday.

You politically minded men rejoice when the Nepal Government frees thousands of slaves, and yet you do not know that side

by side with you live your own sisters, whose existence is worse than nightmare. You will say that there is morbid exaggeration in my account. So said people in regard to Russia, Congo, and elsewhere. You are grieving and praying over the fate of the Indians in South Africa, but will you not listen to the tragic appeal of your sisters?

Bibliography

Unpublished sources
(with endnote abbreviations in brackets)

Files from the Oriental and India Office Collection, British Library,
individually noted in the footnotes (OIOC)
Files from the British Library's manuscript collection (BL)
The Royal Collection, Windsor Castle, by kind permission of Her
Majesty the Queen (RA)
The Cooch Behar Palace archives, by kind permission of the
Government of West Bengal (CB)
The Mountbatten Archives, Hartley Library, University of
Southampton (MB)
An account of Nripendra Narayan by his servant D. D. Choudhuri in
1915; a copy held at the Bexhill Museum, Bexhill-on-Sea (NN)

Published sources
(with endnote abbreviations in brackets)

(published in London except where stated)

By or directly about members of the Baroda and Cooch Behar families

All India Women's Conference on Educational Reform, Poona, 5–8 January
1927
Clarke, A. B., *In Kerala. A Record of a Tour in the South of India with Their
Highnesses the Maharaja and Maharani Gaekwar, June–July 1915*,
Bombay, 1916
Devi, G., *A Princess Remembers. The Memoirs of the Maharani of Jaipur*,
New York, 1976 (GD)

Devi, S., *The Life of Princess Yashodara, Wife & Disciple of the Lord Buddha*, 1929

—, *Indian Fairy Tales*, 1923

—, *The Autobiography of an Indian Princess*, 1921 (SD)

—, *The Beautiful Mogul Princesses*, 1918

—, *Bengal Dacoits and Tigers*, Calcutta, 1916

—, *Nine Ideal Indian Women*, Calcutta, undated

Gaekwad, C. and Mitra, S. M., *The Position of Women in Indian Life*, 1911

Gaekwad, F. P. G., *Sayajirao of Baroda. The Prince and the Man*, Bombay, 1989 (FPG)

Gaekwad, S., *Speeches and Addresses of His Highness Sayaji Rao III Maharaja of Baroda 1877–1927*, 1928

—, 'My Ways and Days in Europe and in India', *Nineteenth Century & After*, vol. xlix, January–June 1901

Narayan, N., *Shooting in Cooch Behar. 37 Years of Big Game Shooting*, Bombay, 1908

Report of His Highness the Maharaja Saheb's Trip to Calcutta, Baroda, 1938

Rice, S., *Sayaji Rao of Baroda*, Oxford, 1931

Sergeant, P., *The Ruler of Baroda*, 1928

Tottenham, E. L., *Highnesses of Hindostan*, 1934

Weeden, E., *A Year with the Gaekwar of Baroda*, 1912

Widgery, A. G., *Goods and Bads. Outlines of a Philosophy of Life, Being the Substance of a Series of Talks and Discussions with His Highness the Maharajah Gaekwar of Baroda*, Baroda, 1920

Memoirs, letters, personal and primary accounts

(published in London except where stated)

Anon., *More Uncensored Recollections*, 1924

Baig, M. R. A., *In Different Saddles*, 1967

Barton, W., *The Princes of India*, 1934

Besant, A., *India: A Nation*, 1915

Bhopal, J., *An Account of My Life*, 1912

Blackwood, H. G. (the Marchioness of Dufferin and Ava), *Our Viceregal Life in India*, 1889

Butler, I., *The Viceroy's Wife. Letters of Alice, Countess of Reading, from India 1921–25*, 1969

Cartier-Bresson, H., *Henri Cartier-Bresson in India*, 1987

Casserly, G., *Life in an Indian Outpost*, undated

Chudgar, P. L., *The Indian Princes under British Protection*, 1929

Collet, S. D. (ed.), *Keshub Chunder Sen's English Visit*, 1871

Coward, N., *Autobiography*, 1986

Cromer, R., *Letters and Second Indian Journal*, York, 1995

Dekobra, M., *The Perfumed Tigers. Adventures in the Land of the Maharajahs*, 1930

De Wolfe, E., *After All*, 1935

Diver, M., *Royal India*, 1942

Elwin, E. F., *India and the Indians*, 1913

Fairbanks, Jr, D., *The Salad Days*, 1988

Ferragamo, S., *Shoemaker of Dreams*, 1985

Fitzroy, Y., *Courts and Camps in India*, 1926

Forbes, R., *India of the Princes*, 1939

Forster, E. M., *The Hill of Devi*, 1921

Fortescue, J. W., *Narrative of the Visit of Their Majesties King George V and Queen Mary to India*, 1912

Galbraith, J. K., *An Ambassador's Journal*, 1969

Gauba, K., *His Highness, or the Pathology of Princes*, Lahore, 1930

Gay, J. D., *From Pall Mall to the Punjab; Or, with the Prince in India*, 1876

Gerhardi, W., *Memoirs of a Polyglot*, 1931

Goutiere, P., *Himalayan Rogue*, Paduca, KY, 1998

Hamilton, F., *Here, There & Everywhere*, 1921

Hardinge, Lord, *My Indian Years 1910–1916*, 1948

Hutheesing, K. N., *We Nehrus*, 1967

Ismael, M. M., *My Public Life. Recollections and Reflections*, 1954

James, R. R. (ed.), *Chips. The Diaries of Sir Henry Channon*, 1967

Kaye, M. M., *The Sun in the Morning*, 1990

Kipling, R., *Letters of Marque*, Allahabad, 1891

Kissinger, H., *White House Years*, 1979

Lawrence, W., *The India We Served*, 1928

Lothian, A., *Kingdoms of Yesteryear*, 1951

Loti, P., *India*, 1928 (originally published as *L'Inde, Sans les Anglais* in 1903)

Mayo, K., *Mother India*, 1927

Mazzini, G., *The Duties of Man*, 1955

Menon, V. P., *The Integration of the Indian States*, 1956

Minto, M., *India, Minto and Morley 1905–1910*, 1934

Montagu, E. S., *An Indian Diary*, 1930

Murray Smith, U., *Magic of the Quorn*, 1980

Nehru, J., *An Autobiography*, Delhi, 1991

—, *The Discovery of India*, New York, 1959

O'Dwyer, M., *India as I Knew It 1885–1925*, 1925

Pandit, V. L., *The Scope of Happiness: A Personal Memoir*, 1979

Parks, F., *Wanderings of a Pilgrim in Search of the Picturesque*, 1850

Pataudi, S. A., *The Elite Minority Princes of India*, Lahore, 1989

Powell, E. A., *Last Home of Mystery*, 1929

Programme of the Ceremonies to be Observed on the Occasion of the Coronation Durbar, 12 December 1912

Ramabai, P., *The High-Caste Hindu Woman*, 1888

Raymond, J. (ed.), *Queen Victoria's Early Letters*, 1963

Reed, S., *The King and Queen in India*, Bombay, 1912

Russell, W. H., *The Prince of Wales's Tour: A Diary in India*, 1877

Sassoon, P., *The Third Route*, 1929

Scindia, V., *Princess*, 1985

Shah, M., *The Memoirs of Aga Khan*, 1954

Shand, M., *River Dog: A Journey Down the Brahmaputra*, 2002

—, *Queen of the Elephants*, 1995

Sorabji, C., *India Calling. The Memories of Cornelia Sorabji*, 1934

Webb, S. and B., *Indian Diary*, Delhi, 1988 (original edition 1912)

Secondary sources

(published in London except where stated)

Ali, A. A., *The Resurgence of Indian Women*, Delhi, 1991

Allen, C., *Plain Tales from the Raj*, 1975

Allen, C. and Dwivedi, S., *Lives of the Indian Princes*, 1984

Allen, C., Dehejia, V. and Falconer, J. (eds.), *India Through the Lens*, Washington, 2000

Bala Krishnan, U. R. and Kumar, M. S., *Indian Jewellery. The Dance of the Peacock*, Bombay, 1999

Ballhatchet, K., *Race, Sex and Class Under the Raj*, 1980

Bence-Jones, M., *The Viceroys of India*, 1982

Blow, S., *Fields Elysian. A Portrait of Hunting Society*, 1983

Brown, J. M., *Gandhi. Prisoner of Hope*, Yale, CT, 1989

Bumiller, E., *May You Be the Mother of a Hundred Sons*, 1990

Cannadine, D., *Ornamentalism. How the British Saw Their Empire*, 2001

Chattopadhyayya, K., *The Awakening of the Indian Women*, 1939

Chaudhuri, N. and Strobel, M. (eds.), *Western Women and Imperialism, Complicity and Resistance*, Bloomington, IN, 1992

Chavda, V. K., *Gaekwads and the British. A Study of Their Problems 1875–1920*, Delhi, undated

Clayton, M., *Foxhunting in Paradise*, 1993

Collins, L., and Lapierre, D., *Freedom at Midnight*, New York, 1975

Copland, I., *India 1885–1947: The Unmaking of an Empire*, 2002

—, *The Princes of India in the Endgame of Empire 1917–1947*, Cambridge, 1997

—, *The British Raj and the Indian Princes. Paramountcy in Western India 1857–1930*, Delhi, 1982

Cormack, M., *The Hindu Woman*, New York, 1953

Crewe, Q., *The Last Maharajah*, 1985 (QC)

Dalrymple, W., *The Age of Kali*, 1998

Dass, D. J., *Maharajah*, Bombay, 1972

De Courcy, A., *The Viceroy's Daughters*, 2000

Donaldson, F., *Edward VIII. The Road to Abdication*, 1974

Drew, J., *India and the Romantic Imagination*, Oxford, 1997

Fitze, K., *Twilight of the Maharajas*, 1956

Forbes, G., *Women in Modern India*, Cambridge, 1996

Frank, K., *Indira. The Life of Indira Nehru Gandhi*, 2001

French, P., *Liberty or Death* 1998

—, *Younghusband*, 1994

Gaekwad, F. P. G., *The Palaces of India*, 1981

Gedge, E. C. and Choski, M. (eds.), *Women in Modern India*, Bombay, 1929

Gilmour, D., *Curzon*, 1994

Grewal, R., *In Rajasthan*, Delhi, 1998

Griffith, M., *India's Princes. Short Life Sketches of the Native Rajas of India*, 1894

Handa, R. L., *History of Freedom Struggle in Princely States*, Delhi, 1968

Harlan, L. and Courtright, P. B. (eds.), *From the Margins of Hindu Marriage. Essays on Gender, Religion and Culture*, New York, 1995

Ivory, J., *Autobiography of a Princess*, 1975

James, L., *Raj. The Making and Unmaking of British India*, 1997

Jeffrey, R. (ed.), *People, Princes and Paramount Power: Society and Politics in Indian Princely States*, Oxford, 1978

Karlekar, M., *Voices from Within. Early Personal Narratives of Bengali Women*, Delhi, 1991

Kelkar, G., *Violence against Women. Perspectives and Strategies in India*, Delhi, 1992

Kopf, D., *The Brahmo Samaj and the Shaping of the Modern Indian Mind*, Princeton, NJ, 1979

Lal, M., *The Law of the Threshold. Women Writers in Indian English*, Simla, 1995

Lee, S., *King Edward VII*, 1925

Liddle, J. and Joshi, R., *Daughters of Independence. Gender, Caste and Class in India*, 1986

Lord, J., *The Maharajahs*, 1972

Lottman, H. R., *The Fall of Paris. June 1940*, 1992

Mankekar, D. R., *Accession to Extinction. The Story of the Indian Princes*, Delhi, 1974

Masani, Z., *Indian Tales of the Raj*, Berkeley, CA, 1987

Michell, G., *The Royal Palaces of India*, 1994

Mitter, S. S., *Dharma's Daughters. Contemporary Indian Women and Hindu Culture*, New Brunswick, NJ, 1991

Mookerji, R., *Asoka*, 1928

Morris, J., *Farewell the Trumpets*, 1978

—, *Heaven's Command*, 1973

—, *Pax Britannica*, 1968

Nadelhoffer, H., *Cartier. Jewellers Extraordinary*, 1984

Nanda, B. R. (ed.), *Indian Women. From Purdah to Modernity*, Delhi, 1990

Parashar, A., *Women and Family Law in India*, Delhi, 1992

Patnaik, N., *A Second Paradise: Indian Courtly Life 1590–1947*, 1984

Peissel, M., *Tiger for Breakfast. The Story of Boris of Kathmandu*, New York, 1966

Popplewell, R. J., *Intelligence and Imperial Defence. British Intelligence and the Defence of the Indian Empire 1904–1924*, 1995

Ramusack, B. N., *The Princes of India in the Twilight of Empire*, Cincinnati, OH, 1978

Roberts, A., *Eminent Churchillians*, 1994

Robinson, A., *Maharaja. The Spectacular Heritage of Princely India*, 1988

Rose, K., *Curzon: A Most Superior Person*, 1969

Roy, A., *Sri Aurobindo and the New Age*, 1940

Saghal, N., *Indira Gandhi's Emergence and Style*, Delhi, 1978

Said, E., *Orientalism*, 1978

Schwab, R., *The Oriental Renaissance*, New York, 1984 (originally published in Paris in 1950)

Sengupta, P., *Sarojini Naidu. A Biography*, 1966

Silvers, R. B. and Epstein, B., *India: A Mosaic*, New York, 2000

Tarlo, E., *Clothing Matters. Dress and Identity in India*, 1996

Thakur, J., *All the Prime Minister's Men*, Delhi, 1977

Tharu, S. and Lalita, K. (eds.), *Women Writing in India*, 1991

Tinker, H., *Viceroy. Curzon to Mountbatten*, Oxford, 1997

Tuchman, B., *August 1914*, 1962

Uberoi, P., *Family, Kinship and Marriage in India*, Delhi, 1993

Vadgama, K., *India in Britain*, 1984

Vasudev, U., *The Two Faces of Indira Gandhi*, Delhi, 1977

Visram, R., *Women in India and Pakistan. The Struggle for Independence from British Rule*, Cambridge, 1992

Younger, C., *Wicked Women of the Raj*, Delhi, 2003

Warner, L., *The Native States of India*, 1910

Warwick, C., *George and Marina, Duke and Duchess of Kent*, 1988

Weintraub, S., *The Importance of Being Edward*, 2000

Zeigler, P., *Edward VIII*, 1990

—, *Mountbatten*, 1985

Fiction

(all published in London)

Bromfield, L., *The Rains Came*, 1938
Cargoe, R., *Maharajah*, 1953
Dekobra, M., *Princess Brinda*, 1934
Haggard, R., *Ayesha. A History of Adventure*, 1905
—, *She*, 1887
Mehta, G., *Raj*, 1989
Mehta, R., *Inside the Haveli*, 1977
Tagore, R., *The Home and the World*, 1919

Notes

(Some notes are not quotations, just text references – these are given out of quotation marks.)

Chapter 1

p. 2   'waving corn': Hardinge, p. 42

p. 4   'This transcended': Reed, p. 68

p. 4   Fifty thousand . . .: I am greatly indebted to Charles Allen for the valuable information he forwarded to me about the three British durbars in Delhi. See his article in Allen, ed., *India Through the Lens*.

p. 5   'If you were': Allen, *Indian Princes*, p. 171

p. 6   'some alteration': FPG, p. 236

p. 9   'had the gifts': Lord, p. 62

p. 10   'like some kind': GD, p. 42

p. 10   'astonishing grace': Interview, Garbo Garnham, 14.08.2001

p. 10   'should be over': Interview, Habi Deb Burman, 1.11.2001

p. 10   'inadequate obeisance': Hardinge, p. 51

p. 11   Their bloodline . . .: The origins of these clans are complicated and vary greatly from source to source. Greatly helped by Charles Allen, in this chapter and the next I have tried to present the most generally accepted account of the early Gaekwads and the Maratha clan to which they belonged.

p. 12   'in private life': Forster, p. 130

p. 12   'Our poached eggs': Fitzroy, pp. 86–7

p. 12   'able, ambitious': OIOC, MSS EUR F166/31

p. 12   'their arrogance': Scindia, p. 108

p. 13   'No one ever': Ibid., p. 81

p. 13   'never set foot': Ibid.

p. 13   'There seems to': Montagu, p. 168

p. 15   During the negotiations . . .: Interview, Habi Deb Burman, 1.11.2001

p. 16   'refuses to keep': Webb, p. 89

p. 17   'enclosed in a': Weeden, p. 165

p. 17   'entirely for personal': Tottenham, p. 47

p. 17   'must have constructed': 'A Knut, a Knight, a Kwery', quoted in Tottenham, p. 128

p. 17   'that she would': Tottenham, p. 74

p. 17   'in stern and': GD, p. 24

p. 18   'Had such a': Tottenham, p. 75

p. 18   'Outwardly the Maharaja':
        Aga Khan, p. 84

p. 19   'most devoted': Tottenham,
        p. 123

p. 19   'the most spoiled': SD, p. 142

p. 19   'full of descriptions': GD, 28–
        9

p. 20   'How money': Tottenham,
        p. 104

p. 20   'that young villain': Ibid.,
        p. 116

p. 20   'The Gaekwad has': OIOC,
        L/PS/10/264

p. 21   'I wish you': Tottenham,
        p. 124

p. 21   'Should I have': Ibid.

p. 22   'Great preparations':
        Tottenham, p. 126

p. 22   'It's Father's own': Ibid.,
        p. 127

Chapter 2

p. 24   'There is no': Quoted in Ali,
        p. 17

p. 24   'Let his defects': Ibid.

p. 25   'We husbands': Mayo, p. 82

p. 25   'I could not': Lawrence, p. 141

p. 27   'biscuit-tin on wheels':
        Weeden, p. 19

p. 28   'that no man': Parks I, p. 59

p. 28   'They were very': Ibid.

p. 28   'A common complaint': Parks
        I, pp. 230–31

p. 29   'all these things': Kipling, p. 24

p. 29   'Zenana life': GD, p. 209

p. 29   'to beg or': Tottenham, p. 313

p. 29   'possessed a sturdy': Aga Khan,
        p. 301

p. 31   Like Khanderao . . .: FPG,
        pp. 29–30 says Khanderao
        commissioned both pairs of
        cannon and the pearl carpet,
        but I have followed Sergeant,
        p. 52

p. 32   'breakwaters in the': Both
        quotes Canning, cited in
        Copland, *The British Raj*, p. 16

p. 33   'If we support': Chudgar,
        p. 107

p. 33   'If it is': Quoted in Said, p. 33

p. 33   'We happen to': Quoted in
        Morris, *Pax Britannica*, p. 124

p. 34   'We started feeling': Allen,
        Indian Princes, p. 67

p. 34   This almost unwitting: See
        Copland, *India*, p. 5

p. 35   'To see the': FPG, p. x,
        Sergeant, p. 24 n

p. 35   'a powerful sovereignty':
        FPG, p. 47

p. 35   'sudden flick': Chavda, p. 153

p. 35   'a beautiful boy': Weintraub,
        p. 221

p. 35   'He is a small': Russell, p. 137

p. 36   'I have never': Sergeant, p. 77

p. 36   'sad, subdued': Russell, p. 193

p. 36   'This boy, aged': Griffiths,
        p. 148

p. 37   'The Little Gaekwar': Lee I,
        p. 384

p. 37   'crystallised rainbow': Russell,
        p. 137

p. 37   'He was weighted': Ibid.

p. 38   'hung with lamps': Russell,
        p. 190

p. 38   'The people seemed': Ibid.

p. 38   'I rather suspect': Gay, p. 90

p. 39   'highly delighted': Quoted in
        Weintraub, p. 223

p. 39 'had the most': Lee I, p. 384
p. 40 'dignified . . . but': Quoted in
       FPG, p. 86
p. 40 'social and public': Gaekwad,
       'My Ways', p. 218
p. 40 'May you always': Patnaik,
       p. 35
p. 40 'the uneducated losing':
       Weeden, p. 22
p. 40 'bridge the gulf': Ibid.
p. 41 'the mild, charitable':
       Sayajirao, quoted in FPG,
       p. 105
p. 42 'an educated lady': 'My Ways'
       p. 223
p. 43 'socks, shoes': FPG, p. 118
p. 43 'indefatigable promenader':
       Sergeant, p. 63
p. 44 'The Maharani bent':
       Vadgama, p. 31
p. 45 'If I do not': Tottenham,
       p. 275
p. 45 'The atmosphere': *Indian
       Princes*, p. 132
p. 45 'I can hardly': 'My Ways',
       p. 224
p. 46 'the tried and': Quoted in
       FPG, p. 147
p. 46 'grasping Reynolds': FPG,
       p. 156
p. 46 'The effects of': 'My Ways',
       p. 220
p. 48 'had an almost': Diver, p.
       114
p. 49 'unite the usefulness': Quoted
       in Gaekwad, *Palaces of India*,
       p. 130
p. 49 'He lost control': *Palaces of
       India*, p. 130
p. 50 'white buskins': Tottenham,
       p. 319

p. 51 'she confessed': Weeden,
       p. 100
p. 51 'Here there is nothing':
       Weeden, p. 7

Chapter 3

p. 52 'according to popular': SD,
       p. 43
p. 52 He seems to . . .: Interview,
       Garbo Garnham, 14.08.2001
p. 53 'He had, before': Chaudhuri,
       p. 418
p. 53 'frank, open-hearted': Ibid.,
       p. 421
p. 53 'he would be': NN, p. 3
p. 53 'When I am': Ibid., p. 33
p. 54 'not a suitable': SD, p. 47
p. 55 'One God': Interview, Garbo
       Garnham, 14.08.2001
p. 55 'nothing sacred': Besant, p. 21
p. 55 'aimed at purifying': Masani,
       p. 77
p. 55 'the Eternal': Besant, p. 21
p. 55 'living proof': James, p. 280
p. 56 'the natives of': James, p. 347
p. 56 'Mr Keshub is': SD, p. 8
p. 56 'If one believes': Ibid., p. 3
p. 56 'I want you': Ibid., p. 4
p. 57 'When India lay': Collet, p. 27
p. 57 'much pleased': Ibid., p. 481
p. 57 'If you desire': Ibid., p. 199
p. 57 'the growth of': Ibid., p. 471
p. 57 'There are some': Ibid., p. 219
p. 58 'good wives': Quoted in
       Beveridge, p. 83
p. 58 'In those things': Collet, p. 473
p. 58 'likely . . . to be': SD, p. 21
p. 59 'an enchanted': SD, p. 16
p. 59 'men spend': Ramabai, p. 26

p. 59   'exacted and received': SD,
         p. 17
p. 60   The very language . . .:
         Harlan, p. 8
p. 60   'the best type': SD, p. 1
p. 60   'We led our': Ibid., p. 24
p. 60   'and if we all': Ibid., p. 48
p. 61   'I thought your': Ibid., p. 49
p. 61   'charmed at the': NN, p. 38
p. 63   'I don't know': Karlekar,
         p. 141
p. 63   'Now give good': SD, p. 65
p. 64   'He was like': Ibid., p. 67
p. 64   'I am, for good': Quoting
         obituary of Nripendra Narayan
         in the *Pioneer*, NN, p. 94
p. 64   'that of a boy's': NN, p. 60
p. 64   'Although he was': SD, p. 116
p. 64   'like an Englishman': Ibid.,
         p. 82
p. 64   'he was entirely': Ibid., p. 78
p. 64   'It was left': Ibid., p. 69
p. 65   'threaten and scold': Ibid.,
         p. 67
p. 65   'In quiet ways': Ibid., p. 78
p. 65   'He who has': Ibid., p. 79
p. 65   'a bevy': Ibid.
p. 66   'I prefer *my*': SD, p. 81
p. 66   'I have often': Ibid., p. 97
p. 67   'advanced Western': Ibid.,
         p. 98
p. 67   'where none of': GD, p. 33
p. 68   'a microcosmic model':
         Gaekwad, *Palaces of India*,
         p. 213
p. 68   'Maharaja, it has': NN, p. 55
p. 69   'Well, your Highness': SD,
         p. 93
p. 69   'very delicate': Hamilton, p. 17
p. 70   'as if a fairy': SD, p. 89
p. 70   'She is very': Blackwood, p. 42

p. 70   'two grandmothers': Ibid.,
         p. 267
p. 70   'which gave': Ibid.
p. 70   'native dress': Blackwood,
         p. 62
p. 71   'never seems': Ibid.
p. 71   'promote female': I am
         indebted to Charles Allen for
         revising this section.
p. 71   'To begin with': SD, p. 217
p. 71   'never made any': Ibid., p. 218

Chapter 4

p. 72   'four of my': Allen, *Indian
         Princes*, p. 23
p. 72   'Fondled, indulged': Chudgar,
         p. 7
p. 73   'Put your foot': *Indian Princes*,
         p. 32
p. 73   'yuvraj would': Ibid.
p. 73   'that "nothing" ': Ramabai,
         p. 14
p. 73   'A bride's of': From Tharu,
         p. 270
p. 74   'a skilful pressure': Ramabai,
         p. 14
p. 74   In 1870 . . .: Ibid.
p. 74   The population census . . .:
         Ibid.
p. 74   'severe scarcity and distress':
         O'Dwyer, p. 102
p. 74   'no one in India': Gaekwad,
         'My Ways', p. 223
p. 75   'What puzzled me': Sorabji,
         p. 58
p. 75   'The boat was': Ibid., p. 57
p. 75   'so that we': Weeden, p. 17
p. 75   'the middle ages': Lawrence,
         p. 73

p. 76   'agitation and intrigue':
Sergeant, p. 94

p. 76   the first articulate . . .:
Copland, *Raj*, p. 189

p. 76   More importantly . . .: James,
p. 339

p. 76   'In this transition': 'My Ways',
p. 218

p. 77   'Therefore if a man': Rice I,
p. 44

p. 77   'until a few': Weeden, p. 31

p. 77   'Rich children': Sergeant,
p. 102

p. 77   'When I married': Ibid., p. 77

p. 78   'I do not know': Tottenham,
p. 266

p. 78   'while the duty': Quoted in
Morris, p. 143

p. 79   'somewhat punctilious':
OIOC, MS EUR FIII/256

p. 79   'from extinction': Quoted in
Robinson, p. 7

p. 80   'that almost anyone': Gilmour,
p. 184

p. 80   'embossed with': Lord, p. 64 n

p. 80   Most . . . of all . . .: Mankekar,
p. 10 and Gilmour, p. 188

p. 80   'The native chiefs': Quoted in
Gilmour, p. 184

p. 80   'uncertainty of precedence':
Lee II, pp. 389–90

p. 81   'It will depend': Sergeant,
p. 107

p. 81   'very dull dreary': RA/VIC/
QVJ: 3.12.1900

p. 81   'five pairs of': GD, p. 18

p. 82   'Such a standard': OIOC, MS
EUR FIII/256

p. 82   'cruel and humiliating':
Sergeant, p. 282

p. 82   'I am afraid': FPG, p. 195

p. 82   'curious rumour': OIOC,
EUR MS FIII/206

p. 83   'not of his': FPG, p. 196

p. 83   'What are they': Thanks to
Charles Allen for this
quotation. Dilks, *Curzon in
India*, Vol. I, p. 75

p. 83   'a pompous pageant': Tinker,
p. 26

p. 84   'the Viceroy to': FPG, p. 197

p. 84   'that it was': Kaye, p. 50

p. 85   'Really Lord Curzon': Besant,
p. 74

p. 87   'this caste business': Weeden,
p. 146

p. 87   'Everything I am': Interview,
HH Rajmata of Jaipur,
26.01.2003

p. 88   'the whole family': Webb,
p. 176

p. 88   'In the Opinion': FPG, p. 226

p. 88   'British rule in': Aga Khan,
p. 301

p. 89   'The home-bred': Sergeant,
p. 113

p. 89   'do what is': OIOC, L/PS/
10/375

p. 89   'more trouble and': Ibid.

p. 89   'an omission which': L/PS/
10/375

p. 90   'rather naïve disappointment':
Sergeant, p. 118

p. 90   'Why should they': Lafayette
Gallery book of postcard
portraits of Indian princes,
2002

p. 90   'you Americans are': Powell,
p. 277

p. 90   'misery and suffering': Barton,
p. 179

p. 91   'I should be': Rice I, p. 136

p. 91   'in a gap': Sergeant, p. 196
p. 91   'and a box': Weeden, p. 9
p. 91   'It is impossible': Ibid., p. 2
p. 91   'is of middle': Ibid., pp. 15–16
p. 92   'had a nice': GD, p. 10
p. 93   'Though indeed': Weeden,
         p. 17
p. 93   'the stormy petrel': FPG,
         p. 231
p. 93   'She must think': Tottenham,
         p. 45
p. 93   'The Prince of': Lord, p. 147
p. 93   'Possessing all': Diver, p. 115
p. 93   'Her nose, which':
         Tottenham, pp. 26–7
p. 95   'bearing a chair': Weeden,
         p. 130
p. 95   'brown velvet knickerbocker':
         Ibid., p. 129
p. 96   'non-interference in': Speech
         given in Udaipur, 1909,
         quoted in Jeffrey, p. 374
p. 96   'grace of manner': OIOC,
         MSS EUR F122/36
p. 96   'His Excellency rained': Ibid.,
         MSS EUR F122/36
p. 96   'Loyalty has always': Gaekwad,
         Speeches, p. 248
p. 96   'You will never': Lee II,
         p. 386
p. 96   'No self-respecting': Tinker,
         p. 50
p. 97   'nominally carried on':
         OIOC, MSS EUR D1227/
         43, p. 101
p. 97   'Our visit to': Minto, p. 359
p. 97   'She has been': Weeden,
         p. 59
p. 97   'He finds her': Lady Minto's
         unpublished journals,
         November 1909

p. 98   'qualified assurance': Sergeant,
         p. 127
p. 98   'Sedition and anarchy':
         Speeches, p. 242
p. 98   'There may even': Sergeant,
         p. 128
p. 99   'public ladies of': OIOC, L/
         PS/10/375
p. 99   'His failing was': Ibid.
p. 99   'left much to': Ibid.
p. 99   'an extraordinary revelation':
         Lord, p. 144
p. 100   'from their lethargy':
         Gaekwad, *The Position*, p. viii
p. 100   'enjoy the luxury': Mill, p. 177
p. 100   'Every country by': *The
         Position*, p. xiii
p. 101   'Only by education': Ibid.,
         p. 15
p. 101   'to present to': Margaret
         Cousins quoted in
         Chattopadhyaya, p. 53
p. 101   'The highest aim': *The
         Position*, p. 28

Chapter 5

p. 104   'a tall graceful': SD, p. 107
p. 104   'Fate has dealt': Ibid., p. 107
p. 104   'Her conversation': Ibid.,
         p. 108
p. 105   'She gave me': Vadgama, p. 35
p. 105   'the Indian Princess': SD,
         p. 118
p. 105   'the innate dignity': Hamilton,
         p. 17
p. 105   'Why would not': SD, p. 109
p. 105   'I can't': Ibid., p. 110
p. 106   'It was only': Ibid.
p. 106   'Don't, you'll get': SD, p. 111

p. 106 'in delicate': Ibid., p. 134

p. 106 'It is so very': RA/VIC/N44/
101, letter to Victoria from
SD, 19.11.1887

p. 106 'If a boy': SD, p. 125

p. 107 'but although': Ibid.

p. 107 'What have they': SD, p. 137

p. 107 'began to "live"': Ibid., p. 138

p. 108 'No man knew': NN, p. 95,
from an obituary in the *Pioneer*

p. 110 'playgrounds': Allen, *Indian
Princes*, p. 204

p. 110 'instead of taking': *Plain Tales*,
p. 139

p. 111 'I want my': SD, p. 161

p. 111 'Whether the Maharajahs':
Ibid., p. 158

p. 112 'I have a': Ibid., p. 162

p. 112 'He left me': OIOC, L/PS/
10/136, File 760/1908/3

p. 112 'in such a': NN, p. 46

p. 112 'money difficulties': SD, p. 162

p. 112 'I am of': Ibid., p. 161

p. 113 'the Cooch Behar': Ibid.,
p. 160

p. 113 'made the other': Ibid., p. 217

p. 113 'Much as I': OIOC, MS
EUR F111/252, 20.02.1998

p. 114 'It would not': Ibid.

p. 114 'I wonder': SD, pp. 168–9

p. 114 'the possibility': OIOC, MS
EUR F111/204, 30.06.1901

p. 114 'habits, training': Ibid.

p. 115 '*corps d'élite*: OIOC, MS
EUR F111/252

p. 115 'The Maharajahs': SD, p. 167

p. 116 'At the': Sunity Devi says she
was awarded this distinction in
1901 but another source dates
it to 1887.

p. 116 'When he came': Ibid., p. 171

p. 116 'In 1901 he was': Younger,
Wicked Women, p. 98 says that
Rajey fell in love with and
wanted to marry an Australian
actress, Elsie Thomas, in
Calcutta in 1904–5. Younger's
facts are somewhat hazy and
she offers no source references.

p. 117 'kept him on': Ibid., p. 175

p. 117 'It is extraordinary': Hardinge,
p. 41

p. 117 'badge of Western': Kopf,
p. 17

p. 117 'You have taught': Gauba, p.
xiii

p. 118 'Having learned': NN, p. 42

p. 118 'strange mix': Gerhardi, p. 370

p. 119 'made the superbly': Lord,
p. 147

p. 119 'Boys who are': SD, p. 161

p. 120 'Some were wearing': Minto,
pp. 23–4

p. 120 'The Maharani': Minto, p. 24

p. 120 'I will do': Ibid., p. 275

p. 121 'sown his wild': OIOC, MS
EUR F166/31, 15.03.1907

p. 121 'Poor dear lady': Ibid., MS
EUR F166/32, 24.03.1908

p. 121 'The daughter was': NN,
pp. 48–9

p. 122 'The natural resources':
OIOC, MS EUR F166/31,
12.04.1907

p. 123 'alleged injuries': Ibid., L/PS/
10/136 File 760/1908

p. 123 In June 1911 . . .: Ibid.

p. 124 'coolie woman': Interview,
Garbo Garnham, 14.08.01

p. 124 Sayajirao – perhaps: According
to Younger, *Wicked Women*,
p. 32, Sayajirao not only had a

European mistress in the 1890s
but also a child by her.
Unfortunately Younger has
not cited her source for this
information so I could not
check it. Younger states that a
major reason for friction
between Sayajirao and
Chimnabai was his
womanizing but no one I
spoke to in India corroborated
this and I found no other
information to back up her
theory. This does not, of
course, mean it was not true.

p. 124 'a disagreeable surprise':
OIOC, L/PS/10/258 File
1076/1912

p. 124 'arranged our': FPG, p. 235

p. 124 'a pleasant': OIOC, L/PS/10/
136, File 760/1908, p. 1

p. 125 'so if there': Ibid.

p. 125 'to no good': Ibid.

p. 125 'Nip the Unhappy': Letter in
the collection of Garbo
Garnham

p. 125 'looking more': SD, p. 188

p. 125 'had been everywhere':
Casserly, p. 220

p. 126 'If ever, during': Ibid., p. 223

p. 126 'magnificent stage': Ibid.,
p. 216

p. 127 'I place my': Ibid.

p. 127 'touched and': Casserly, p. 217

p. 127 'The pretty young': Ibid.,
p. 218

p. 128 'fitted like': Ibid., p. 219

p. 128 'It seemed': Ibid., p. 216

Chapter 6

p. 129 'In his simple': Tottenham,
p. 50

p. 129 'The Maharani': Ibid., p. 53

p. 130 'At the same': Hardinge, p. 46

p. 130 'to wear jewellery':
Tottenham, p. 53

p. 132 'Neither she nor': OIOC L/
PS/10/264, 29.09.1911

p. 133 'Dearly was': Tottenham, p. 36

p. 133 'mental disturbance': Sergeant,
p. 131

p. 133 'felt sore': Aga Khan, p. 81

p. 133 'categorically stated': FPG, p. x

p. 133 'BON VOYAGE': Ibid.

p. 134 'genuine alarm': OIOC, L/
PS/10/264

p. 134 'It is always': BL, ADD MSS
50839f72

p. 134 'The interests of': OIOC, L/
PS/10/264, 28.02.1912

p. 135 'and when forced': Ibid.

p. 135 'I cannot say': OIOC,MSS
EUR F122/36

p. 135 'discontent is not': Tottenham,
p. 91

p. 135 'calm, sedate': OIOC,L/PS/
10/264

p. 136 'My plans are': SD, p. 194

p. 137 'In the name': All details of the
funeral from 'Bexhill's
Maharaja' quoting the *Bexhill
Observer*, 23.09.11

p. 137 In Cooch Behar . . .: SD,
p. 195

p. 137 'to bring the': 'Bexhill's
Maharaja 18', *Bexhill Chronicle*,
13.09.1913

p. 137 'We may think': SD, p. 229

p. 137 'How thoughtful': Ibid., p. 202

p. 138 'I hear the': Tottenham, pp. 130–31

p. 139 'I can see': Ibid., p. 132

p. 139 'tingled that': Ibid.

p. 139 'Indira Devi, in': Baig, p. 8

p. 139 'the premier Princess': Tottenham, p. 135

p. 139 'by which the': Ibid.

p. 140 'We understand': quoted in Tottenham, p. 137

p. 140 'She assured': Tottenham, p. 137

p. 140 'The religion': Ibid., p. 138

p. 141 'all happiness': Ibid., p. 139

p. 141 '*Tant mieux!*': 'A Knut, a Knight, a Kwery', quoted in Tottenham, p. 129

p. 141 'of perfect joy': Jit's poems, private collection, Baroda

p. 142 'I seldom got': SD, p. 206

p. 142 'I know my': Ibid., p. 207

p. 142 'the Cooch Behars': Tottenham, p. 142

p. 143 'To the cutest': Interview, Devika Devi, 28.11.2001

Chapter 7

p. 144 'Oh, you just': Tottenham, p. 144

p. 144 'she was absolutely': Quoted in Tottenham, p. 144

p. 144 'till women are': Rice I, p. 72

p. 144 'It were good': Gaekwad, *The Position*, p. xiv

p. 145 'Unless I was': SD, p. 176

p. 145 'We educate': Lawrence, p. 111

p. 145 'I have been': Mayo, p. 111

p. 145 'You talk about': Allen, *Indian Princes*, p. 169

p. 146 'she drove away': Tottenham, p. 228

p. 147 'General Staffs': Tuchman, p. 78

p. 147 'India is British': Tottenham, p. 183

p. 148 'tins of benzine': Ibid.

p. 148 'home before': Tuchman, p. 123

p. 149 '*Nein, nein!*': Tottenham, p. 187

p. 149 'the police did': Ibid.

p. 149 'What would your': Tottenham, p. 190

p. 150 'with the milk': Ibid., p. 196

p. 151 'I wish to die': Vadgama, p. 94

p. 151 'When there is': *Indian Princes*, p. 77

p. 151 'all his sympathies': OIOC, L/PS/10/264, File 1294/1912

p. 152 'After tea': Tottenham, p. 322

p. 152 'as a theorist': Quoted in Tottenham, p. 318

p. 152 'The common belief': OIOC, L/PS/10/264, 20.09.1919

p. 153 'selfish, egoistic': FPG, p. 298

p. 154 'almost European': OIOC, L/PS/10/264

p. 154 'he inveighs': OIOC, L/PS/10/264 20.09.1919

p. 154 'born royal': Tottenham, p. 214

p. 154 'The Maharaja Sahib': Ibid., p. 264

p. 156 'Your Highness's': *In Kerala*, p. 98

p. 156 'so you don't': Interview, Devika Devi, 28.01.2003

p. 157 'Wishing her' et seq.: Jit's

poems, private collection, Baroda

p. 158 'He has caused': Tottenham, p. 281

p. 159 'that Indira Cooch': Gerhardi, p. 367

p. 159 'Trust not': Haggard, *She*, p. 219

p. 159 'Mother, your': SD, p. 204

p. 160 'It is my': Ibid., p. 242

p. 160 'as of my': Ibid., p. 209

p. 161 'The awe-stricken': Ibid., p. 181

p. 161 'with child-like': Devi, *Nine Ideal Indian Women*, p. 20

p. 162 'She has made' et seq.: OIOC, L/PS/10/896

p. 164 'specially noted': *The Times*, 19.09.1911

p. 164 'just like an': SD, p. 204

p. 165 'she never would': Ibid., p. 147

p. 165 'Now my life': Ibid., p. 230

p. 165 'dressed entirely': GD, p. 43

p. 167 'vanquish or': Robinson, p. 45

p. 167 'Mayst thou': Ramabai, p. 7

p. 168 'She worshipped': SD, p. 80

p. 169 In 1587 . . .: Many thanks to Charles Allen for these details

p. 169 'so full of': Pataudi, p. 207

Chapter 8

p. 171 'If only': Tottenham, p. 229

p. 171 'No one is' et seq.: This quotation and all others from the conference come from Poona pamphlet

p. 172 'The Status': Reproduced in Chudgar, pp. 23–6

p. 173 'What have I': Pataudi, p. 229

p. 173 'heart disease': OIOC, L/PS/10/864

p. 173 'too overcome': FPG, p. 341

p. 173 The Maharaja's . . .: *The Times*, 27.08.1923

p. 174 'We shall wipe': Mayo, p. 284

p. 174 'We all have': Gauba, p. 190

p. 175 'puppets, created': Quoted in Robinson, p. 7

p. 175 'It is no': Quoted in Allen, *Indian Princes*, p. 15

p. 175 'his Highness's': Nawab Mehdi Nawaz Jung, quoted in FPG, p. 353

p. 176 'There are cars': Powell 252; also copied (uncredited) in both Gauba and Ann Morrow, *Maharaja*

p. 177 'A Round Table': Menon, p. 29

p. 177 'long stretch': Tottenham, p. 233

p. 177 As a youth . . .: Harlan, p. 13

p. 178 'Some of his': FPG, p. 376

p. 178 'a smiling, cherubic': Powell, p. 248

p. 178 'exploded the whole': Bromfield, p. 22

p. 178 'In the new': Sergeant, p. 181

p. 179 'I told her': Bence-Jones, p. 265

p. 179 'Everything is marvellous': *Indian Princes*, p. 205

p. 179 'No, dear, I': Ibid. and GD, p. 97

p. 180 She hid her . . .: *Indian Princes*, p. 82. The anecdote says the pearls had rotted away, but since pearls cannot rot, I am assuming that what rotted was

the settings, which in India are
often made of heavy cord
p. 180 In 1934, she . . .: *Indian Princes*,
p. 207
p. 180 She liked to . . .: Tottenham,
p. 67
p. 180 'arrogant . . . old lady':
Bromfield, p. 23
p. 181 'that wonderful silent': GD,
p. 16
p. 181 When they stayed . . .: *Indian
Princes*, p. 82
p. 181 If she gambled . . .: Interview,
Anandrao Gaekwad, 6.11.2001
p. 181 'some senior man': OIOC, L/
PS/11/222, p. 4985
p. 181 'very able': Pataudi, p. 202
p. 182 'used to say': GD, p. 70
p. 182 'agreed to abstain': OIOC, L/
PS/11/222, p. 4985
p. 182 'The Viceroy thinks': Ibid.
p. 183 'wealthy people': Quoted in
Clayton, p. 126
p. 183 'came all the': Blow, p. 122
p. 183 . . . raffish Prince . . .:
Interview, Ann Wright,
23.11.2001
p. 183 . . . unidentified royal British
lover . . .: Interview, Habi
Deb Burman, 1.11.2001. I
have found no confirmatory
proof of this rumour, possibly
just family myth
p. 184 'The report is': OIOC, L/PS/
11/222, p. 4985
p. 184 'In England unfortunately':
Ibid.
p. 186 'There was a': Quoted in
Patnaik, p. 175
p. 186 'with charming grace':
Gerhardi, p. 372

p. 186 'Oh, everyone from': GD,
p. 60
p. 186 'She was part': Interview, HH
Rajmata of Jaipur, 15.09.2001
p. 187 'wearing underpants':
Interview, Habi Deb Burman,
1.11.2001
p. 188 One pair, which . . .:
Ferragamo, pp. 230, 232
p. 188 Though Indira loved . . .:
Kumar, p. 68
p. 188 'the most fabulously': Mrs
Evelyn Walsh, quoted in GD,
p. 87
p. 189 'She adored': Ettie Plesch,
unpublished memoirs
p. 189 'She just got': Interview,
Devika Devi and Sangeeta
Kumari, 28.01.2003
p. 189 'the Maharani, soaking':
Gerhardi, p. 365
p. 189 'With her, nothing': GD,
p. 19
p. 189 She was photographed . . .:
Sadly the photograph is no
longer extant, though Lee
Miller said in an interview that
she had photographed Indira
in Paris in the late 1920s. See
A. Penrose, *The Lives of Lee
Miller*
p. 190 'captured that electric': GD,
p. 19
p. 190 'with the air': Cargoe, p. 76
p. 190 'If a widow': SD, p. 197
p. 190 'The Maharajah is': OIOC,
L/PS/10/280
p. 191 'now in the': CB files
p. 191 'In her white': Indian
appendix to SD's
autobiography, p. 216

p. 191 'One could not': Ibid., p. 215

p. 191 'the most popular': Ibid., p. 217

p. 192 'Her dignity': Ibid., p. 218

p. 192 'silent and dignified': Nanda, p. xii

p. 193 'because we had': Quoted in *Indian Princes*, p. 168

p. 193 'If non-violence': Quoted in Visram, p. 23

p. 193 'Woman has as': Quoted in Nanda, p. 57

p. 193 'She was full': Nehru, p. 154

p. 193 'My object was': Visram, p. 41

p. 194 'The call of': Nehru, p. 157

p. 194 'The movement': Quoted in Chattopadhyaya, p. 52

p. 194 'the nauseating': Quoted in Hutheesing, p. 97

p. 195 'What a pity': Ibid., p. 81

p. 195 'They rode to': Frank, p. 56

p. 195 'I personally': quoted in Copland, p. 76

Chapter 9

p. 197 'the mischievous': GD, p. 53

p. 197 'vivid hospitality': Gerhardi, p. 368

p. 197 'the most important': GD, p. 67

p. 197 'feeling the faint': Ibid., p. 68

p. 198 'a maid for': Ibid., p. 80

p. 198 'fat, sulky': Butler, p. 101

p. 199 'The Jaipur legend': GD, p. 103

p. 199 'he got fatter': Ibid., p. 104

p. 199 'Life from now': QC, p. 62

p. 200 'Everyone in Calcutta': GD, p. 100

p. 200 'that I would': Ibid.

p. 201 'almost as thrilling': GD, p. 109

p. 201 'Oh, that princess': Ibid., p. 115

p. 201 'a pink city': Kipling, p. 15

p. 201 'thought it was': Quoted in Ivory, p. 62

p. 201 'I never heard': GD, p. 115

p. 201 'slept on mats': Frank, p. 89

p. 202 'Gurudev did': GD, p. 117

p. 203 'accepted into the': Undated letter from Habi Deb Burman to the author, December 2003

p. 203 'manoeuvred the conversation': GD, p. 118

p. 204 'Looking back on': Ibid., p. 122

p. 204 'I think the': Ibid., p. 126

p. 204 'predicted gloomily': Ibid., p. 143

p. 205 Indrajit, always . . .: Ibid.

p. 205 'give up all': GD, p. 143

p. 205 'To him marriage': Pataudi, pp. 233–4

p. 205 'The Viceroy': Major Parbat Singh, quoted in QC, p. 139

p. 206 'congratulations or': Viceregal edict, quoted in QC, p. 140

p. 206 'good Rajput family': Quoted in QC, p. 139

p. 206 'His Highness motored': *Barodas' Calcutta Trip*, p. 1

p. 206 'Mr and Mrs Sandford': Ibid.

p. 207 'Naturally she was': *Barodas' Calcutta Trip*, p. 12

p. 207 'Such a big': Interview, Ambikar Rai, 16.01.2003

p. 208 'I have known': *Barodas' Calcutta Trip*, p. 16

p. 208 X-ray machines . . .: Interview, Ajit Sinh, 8.11.2001

p. 209 'long beneficent': CB Files
p. 209 'so striking': Weeden,
pp. 276–9
p. 210 'I am feeling': quoted in QC,
p. 136
p. 210 'I remember it': GD, p. 140
p. 211 'enduring life': Pataudi, p. 214
p. 211 'You will get': Ibid., p. 221
p. 211 'I will never': Ibid., p. 223
p. 212 The Cooch Behar . . .: CB
Files
p. 213 'Rubbish, rubbish': GD, p. 146
p. 213 'Ayesha, I am': Pataudi, p. 231
p. 213 'Don't you know': Interview,
HH Rajmata of Jaipur,
27.01.2003
p. 214 'Only then did': GD, p. 148
p. 215 'I personally cannot': MB,
K154, Mountbatten's eulogy
for Jai
p. 215 'This depressed me': Allen,
Indian Princes, p. 152
p. 215 'When people gradually': GD,
p. 156
p. 216 'Although I felt': Ibid., p. 159
p. 216 'This entailed': Ibid., p. 160
p. 217 'and very gently': Ibid., p. 162
p. 217 'When Jai's team': Ibid., p. 170
p. 218 'Who the hell': Ibid., p. 181
p. 218 'Subjects of': Quoted in QC,
p. 107
p. 219 'an enlightened': Ismael,
quoted in GD, p. 214
p. 219 'All that we': GD, p. 401
p. 219 'Jai embodied': Ibid., p. 185

Chapter 10

p. 220 'the dearest wish': CB Files
p. 220 'Best of all': GD, p. 196

p. 221 'It must be': Quoted in QC,
p. 143
p. 222 'of the unflinching': Ibid.,
p. 147
p. 222 'Ah, so you're': GD, p. 201
p. 222 'gave me a': Quoted in QC,
p. 148
p. 223 'A sight I': Ibid.
p. 223 'We shall either': French,
p. 154
p. 223 'severely undermined': Allen,
Indian Tales, p. 119
p. 224 'There are old': QC, p. 145
p. 224 'not just by': GD, p. 206
p. 224 'he replied grandly': Ibid.
p. 224 'Third Her Highness': GD,
p. 207
p. 224 'The new Maharani': Quoted
in GD, pp. 207–8
p. 225 'Without violating': GD,
p. 214
p. 225 'the arch-enemy': Quoted in
QC, p. 154
p. 225 'a definite sense': QC, p. 160
p. 226 'My heart went': GD, p. 216
p. 226 'No one had': GD, pp. 216–17
p. 226 'I shall always': MB1/C148/2
p. 226 'We had no': Indian Tales,
p. 109
p. 227 'The enemy are': RA/GV/
CC47/1989, 26.05.1942
p. 227 'The GI's Shangri-La': GD,
p. 200
p. 227 'He was tall': Goutiere, p. 87
p. 228 'to experience thrills': RA/
GV/CC47/2224, 21.05.1945
p. 228 'about his devotion': Pataudi,
p. 237
p. 228 'every now and': RA/GV/
CC47/2224, 21.05.1945
p. 228 'But with Peace': Ibid.

p. 229 'publicity-crazy': General Stilwell, quoted in French, p. 180

p. 231 Grateful for . . .: French, p. 44

p. 231 Until 1928 . . .: Ibid., p. 29

p. 233 'that massive loss': Roberts, p. 118

p. 234 'Certainly not': Quoted in QC, p. 173

Chapter 11

p. 235 'imperial allies': Chattopadhyaya, p. 38

p. 235 'grave misgivings' et seq.: Both quoted in Copland, p. 204

p. 236 But this was . . .: Ibid., p. 280

p. 236 'As soon as': Collins, p. 254

p. 236 'a bunch of': Quoted in Raj, p. 626

p. 237 'that last grand': Patnaik, p. 177

p. 237 'shoot him down': Robinson, p. 21

p. 237 'she was surprised': Corfield, p. 168

p. 238 'Although I accepted': GD, p. 224

p. 238 'That is all': Allen, *Indian Princes*, p. 270

p. 238 'the most expensive': Quoted in GD, p. 234

p. 238 'enormously impressed': GD, p. 235

p. 239 'I wondered': Ibid.

p. 239 'If you had': GD, p. 224

p. 239 'I will encourage': Quoted in Zeigler, *Mountbatten*, p. 406

p. 240 'and her very': Quoted in QC, p. 169

p. 240 But knowing . . .: QC, p. 178

p. 240 'The sacrifice': Quoted in QC, p. 182

p. 241 'hated giving up': GD, p. 237

p. 241 'It was not': Scindia, p. 161

p. 241 'he felt that': GD, p. 239

p. 242 'would assume': Ibid., p. 248

p. 243 'I felt the': Shirley Lord in US *Vogue*, September 2002

p. 243 'What more can': Quoted in QC, p. 176

p. 244 'If my father': QC, p. 207

p. 244 'Jai knew her': Ibid.

p. 244 'Just because': GD, p. 144

p. 245 'miserable': quoted in QC, p. 136

p. 245 'all my love': quoted in Ibid., p. 137

p. 245 'I am only': quoted in Ibid., p. 88

p. 245 'India is in': RA/GV/CC47/2302, 8.12.1946

p. 245 'What deterioration': Letter from Indira Devi, undated, May 1962. By kind permission of Devika Devi

p. 245 'Doomsday for': Letter from Habi Deb Burman to the author, 20.12.2003

p. 245 'Take my poor': quoted in QC, pp. 198–9

p. 246 'the head butler': Letter from Habi Deb Burman to the author, 20.12.2003

p. 246 'Of course he': Interview, Swarupa Das, 6.4.2002

p. 246 'Luckily the Government': RA/GV/CC47/2580, 27.12.1951

p. 247 'I had lived': RA/GV/CC47/2580, 27.12.1951

p. 247 'great graciousness': RA/GV/
CC47/2482, 25.07.1950
p. 247 'I've always been': Interview,
Swarupa Das, 6.4.2002
p. 248 'I don't want': Interview, Habi
Deb Burman, 1.11.2001
p. 248 'Granny in one': Letter from
Habi Deb Burman to the
author, 20.12.2003
p. 248 'I'm an orphan': Interviews,
Habi Deb Burman and Bunny
Lakshman Singh, November
2001
p. 248 'very edgy': Letter from Habi
Deb Burman to the author,
20.12.2003
p. 249 'I am happy': Letter, ID,
2.11.1964. By kind permission
of Devika Devi
p. 249 'Remember they': Letter, ID,
18.08.1962. By kind
permission of Devika Devi
p. 249 Later in life . . .: Interview,
Ann Wright, 4.4.2002
p. 249 'loved medicine': Interview,
Devika Devi, 28.11.2001
p. 249 'Mummy, she's': Interview,
Ann Wright 4.4.2002
p. 250 'Even if she': Interview,
Devika Devi, 28.01.2003
p. 250 'Her shopping': Ibid.
p. 250 'She has suffered': RA/GV/
CC47/2224, 21.05.1945
p. 251 'He was an': Interview,
Colonel Shamsher Singh,
8.11.2001
p. 251 'trembled like': Interview,
Habi Deb Burman 1.11.2001
p. 251 'Shivaji, the': Ibid.

Chapter 12

p. 252 'He was a': GD, p. 253
p. 252 'partly understanding': Ibid.,
p. 252
p. 253 'Why should the': Ibid.
p. 253 'How lucky': GD, p. 303
p. 254 'We tried to': Scindia, p. 164
p. 255 Jasmine was . . .: Kumar 68;
these were the herbs used for
the Jodhpur family's clothes
p. 255 'too obedient': GD, p. 266
p. 256 'moral courage': Pataudi,
pp. 208–9
p. 256 'could not just': Ibid., p. 231
p. 258 'We didn't use': Interview,
HH Rajmata of Jaipur,
27.01.2003
p. 258 'I have never': Quoted in QC,
p. 217
p. 258 'multi-coloured': Ibid.,
p. 218
p. 258 'To experience': QC, p. xi
p. 259 'I'm getting': Interview, HH
Rajmata of Jaipur 14.11.01
p. 259 'if the princes': Ibid.
p. 259 But she still . . .: Letter, ID,
13.06.1963 by kind permission
of Devika Devi
p. 259 'deep security': GD, p. 291
p. 260 'You are responsible': Ibid.,
p. 298
p. 260 'Is it because': Quoted in
Allen, *Indian Princes*, p. 273
p. 260 'For generations': GD, p. 299
p. 261 'knew that this': Ibid., p. 303
p. 262 'If we had': Interview, HH
Rajmata of Jaipur, 10.09.2003
p. 262 The unprecedentedly . . .:
Jeffrey, p. 342

p. 262 'progressive, participant':
Ibid., p. 336

p. 263 'determined to thwart':
Galbraith, p. 327

p. 263 'As far as': GD, p. 306

p. 263 'But Ayesha': Ibid., p. 307

p. 263 'an absurd': Ibid.

p. 263 'vivacious and extremely':
Galbraith, p. 329

p. 263 'Jackie and Lee': Bradford,
p. 217

p. 264 'Ah, I hear': GD, p. 314

p. 264 'He took her': Bradford,
p. 240

p. 265 'the woman with': Quoted in
GD, p. 315

p. 265 'Mummy, she's': Interview,
HH Rajmata of Jaipur,
9.09.2002

p. 265 'high-minded naiveté': GD,
p. 316

p. 265 'with head bowed': Ibid.

p. 266 When asked about . . .:
Interview, HH Rajmata of
Jaipur, 14.11.2001

p. 266 'that the most': GD, p. 323

p. 266 'The tragedy of': James
Cameron, quoted in Thakur,
p. 8

p. 267 'Must you really': GD, p. 325

p. 267 'Just remember': Quoted in
Crewe, p. 221

p. 267 'I was no': GD, p. 328

p. 268 'The Jaipurs' party': US
Vogue, 15.09.1965

p. 268 'as the last': GD, p. 328

p. 268 'to go on': Ibid.

p. 269 'I am not': Quoted in Frank,
p. 302

p. 269 'Her relationship': Frank,
p. 303

p. 271 'Nepotism and corruption':
Quoted by Dharmendar
Kanwar in an unpublished MS

p. 272 'It is demeaning': QC, p. 228

p. 272 'Such acts were': Pandit,
p. 233

Chapter 13

p. 274 'Uncle is improving': Letter,
Indira Devi, 10.5.1966. By
kind permission of Devika
Devi

p. 274 'but mentally still': Letter, ID,
26.8.1966. By kind permission
of Devika Devi

p. 274 'She behaved so': Interview,
Ann Wright, 4.4.2002

p. 274 'Being the gentleman':
Pataudi, p. 236

p. 275 'spiritual healing': Letter, ID,
13.04.1967. By kind
permission of Devika Devi

p. 275 'the room with': GD, p. 340

p. 275 'That was Ma': Ibid., p. 341

p. 276 'Darling, the girls': Interview,
Habi Deb Burman, 1.11.2001

p. 276 'an amazing gift': Interview,
Bunny Lakshman Singh,
4.4.2002

p. 276 'Old customs': GD, p. 345

p. 276 'I remember noticing': Ibid.,
p. 349

p. 277 'Only when we': Ibid., p. 351

p. 277 'The entire city': Ibid.

p. 277 'But this day': QC, p. 231

p. 277 'in the end': Pataudi, p. 219

p. 278 'There are no': MB, K154,
Gayatri Devi to Mountbatten,
26.07.1970

p. 278 'in the things': Quoted in GD, p. 354

p. 278 'I was very': Ibid.

p. 278 'He also loved'. Quoted in GD, p. 355

p. 279 'the tiger is': Quoted in QC, p. 232

p. 279 'a referendum': Frank, p. 325

p. 279 'As for me': Letter, GD, 27.01.1971. By kind permission of Devika Devi

p. 279 'that it must': GD, p. 361

p. 280 'the woman – rather': Frank, p. 327

p. 280 'We may be': Quoted in GD, p. 362

p. 280 'Twenty years ago': Ibid., p. 363

p. 281 'intoxicating victory': Scindia, p. 215

p. 281 'She was the': Frank, p. 347

p. 282 'We are income': GD, p. 368

p. 282 'smuggled': Scindia, p. 235

p. 283 When the servants . . .: Ibid., p. 239

p. 283 'for no reason': Quoted in Frank, p. 432

p. 283 'No crisis but': Sangal, p. 199

p. 283 'The essence of': Pandit, p. 14

p. 284 'chock-a-block full': Interview, HH Rajmata of Jaipur, 27.01.2003

p. 284 'As we were': GD, p. 371

p. 285 'It was wonderful': Scindia, p. 245

p. 285 'We bowed to': Ibid., p. 242

p. 285 'As I switched': GD, p. 375

p. 286 'The doors of': Ibid., p. 376

p. 286 'Only my body': Scindia, p. 244

p. 286 'I would have': GD, quoted in Ann Morrow, *Maharaja*, p. 35

p. 287 'It's such a': MB, K154, GD to Mountbatten, 5.03.1977

p. 287 'Dearest Ayesha': MB, K154, Mountbatten to GD, 7.02.1977

p. 287 'We could not': MB, K154, GD to Mountbatten, 5.03.1977

p. 287 'Congratulations. Mrs Gandhi': GD, p. 381

p. 287 'We have taken': Ibid.

p. 288 But at the . . .: QC, p. 240

Conclusion

p. 289 'I like it': GD, p. 388

p. 289 'people know': Ibid., p. 391

p. 290 'Education is not': Ibid., p. 402

p. 290 'Sometimes I still': Ibid.

p. 291 'Life here is': Letter, GD, 6.07.1982. By kind permission of Devika Devi

p. 291 'longing to go': Letter, GD, 15.08.1984. By kind permission of Devika Devi

p. 291 'the problem of': Letter, GD, 3.06.1990. By kind permission of Devika Devi

p. 291 'the dazzling Prince': Unpublished eulogy, by kind permission of Mark Shand

p. 292 'It was a': Quoted by Dharmendar Kanwar in an unpublished MS

p. 292 'We'd like to': Interview, Mark Shand, 24.01.2003

p. 293 'One of the': GD, p. 69

p. 294 many centuries . . .: See also
GD 73: 'There was one Durga
[another form of Kali] temple,
however, in the old ruined
capital called Gosanimare,
where none of us could worship or even enter. Legend has
it that one of my ancestors
mortally offended the goddess
Durga. He had heard that at
night she took on human form
and secretly danced in the
temple. He hid there one night
to spy on her and see this
magical performance, but, of
course, she discovered him and
flew into a rage. As punish-
ment for his temerity, she
cursed him and all his descendants, forbidding them to set
foot in her temple again and
leaving him a silver anklet as a
reminder and a warning.'

p. 295 'None of us': Interview,
Mukul Narayan, 16.01.2003

Acknowledgements

First and most importantly I want to thank the present-day members of the Baroda and Cooch Behar families, especially Gayatri Devi, the Rajmata of Jaipur – to whom I have referred throughout, rather familiarly, as Ayesha – who have been so unfailingly generous with their time, memories and hospitality. Their assistance and enthusiasm made this book possible – and also made the process of writing it an immense pleasure.

Everyone I met in India – friends, descendants, relations and contacts of Chimnabai, Sunity, Indira and Ayesha – bent over backwards to help me, lending me books, photographs and papers, telling me stories and anecdotes and patiently answering all my questions, as well as feeding me delicious Indian food, plying me with whisky, sorting out my complicated travel arrangements and very often, very kindly, having me to stay. Heartfelt thanks to: Habi Deb Burman and Moon Moon Sen; Mota Chudasama; Swarupa Das; Devika Devi; Menaka Devi; Udaya Devi; Urvashi Devi; Anandrao and Sangeeta Gaekwad; Ranjitsinh and Shuphangi Raje Gaekwad; Mrs Sen Gupta; Joey and Vidya Jaipur; Pat Jaipur; Dharmendar Kanwar; Gita Mehta; Mukul Narayan; Ambikar Rai; Devyani Raje; Mr Ranubaba at the Cooch Behar District Library; Reeta Roy; Ajit Sinh; Bunny Lakshman Singh; Madhu Singh; Nangeeta Singh and Chandan Sinha; Pratap Singh; Colonel Shamsher Singh; Vijit and Meenakshi Singh; Roshan, Billy, Anisha and Ruku Sodhi (and Jubri, Matches and Esky); Sunil and Surekha Kejriwal; Deepak Vaidya; and Bob and Ann Wright.

Away from India, too, a great many people went out of their way to offer advice, suggest leads, respond to my queries and generally speed the book on its way. I am enormously grateful to: Arabella at the Lee Miller Archives; Rob Albert and Revel Guest; Charles Allen; Indiajane Birley; Hamish Bowles; Miranda Brankin Frisby; David, Rosanna and Hannah Bulmer; Graydon Carter; Willa Chetwode; Miss Pamela Clark; Sarah Cox; Ursula D'Abo; William Dalrymple; Patrick French; Garbo

Garnham; Michael Goedhuis; Sarah Henderson; Jemima Khan; Sandra de Laszlo; Amabel Lindsay; James Lindsay; Ed Manners and Saskia Nixdorf; John and Julia Moore; Con Normanby; Julian Porter; Stefania Ricci; Charles Schieps; Nick Scott; Mark Shand; Robert Skelton; Andrew Stock; Hugo Vickers; Harry and Vicky Westropp; Victoria Weymouth; and Haydn Williams.

I would like to thank everyone at Penguin (past and present) in London and New York who worked on the book, especially Andrew Kidd, Leo Hollis, Kate Barker and Wendy Wolf; also Juliet Annan, Elisabeth Merriman and her team and Hilary Redmon. Jeevan Deol very kindly proof-read the book, Oula Jones navigated the index, John Gilkes made the maps, Alex Hippsley-Cox did the PR, and once again Bela Cunha did a fantastic job of copy-editing.

Many thanks as well to everyone at Janklow and Nesbit, especially Tif Loehnis and Eric Simonoff.

Finally, I want to thank my family, and dedicate this book to my mother, who taught me the importance of feminism, and my father, who first took me to India.

Index

maharanis, status, 172–3
Maintenance of Internal Security Act,
    280
Majumdar, Mr, 124–5
Malaya, Second World War, 221
Mander, Alan, 123–4, 164, 165
Mander, Garbo, 165, 294
Mander, Lionel, 160, 164, 165, 166
Mant, Major Charles, 49
Marathas, 26–7, 32
marriages, arranged, 11
  as dynastic arrangement, 24
  between royal houses, 25–7
Mary, Queen Consort
  and Chimnabai, 131
  Coronation Durbar (1911), 4,
    129–31
  Indian tour (1905), 6–7, 89, 119
  Indira and, 245, 247
  and Sunity Devi, 104
Matheran hill-station, 95
May, Edna, 116, 119, 160
Mayo, Katherine, 25, 174
Mayo, Richard Bourke, Earl of,
    Viceroy, 33
Mayo College, 111, 115, 198
Mazzini, Giuseppe, 100–101
Meade, Colonel M. J., (British
    Resident), 88–9
Meade, Sir Richard (British
    Resident), 31, 35
Melton Mowbray, Leics, 183
men, fidelity, 16
Menon, V. P., 177, 237, 239, 241
Mill, J. S., 100
Miller, Lee, 189
Minto, Gilbert John Elliot-Murray-
    Kynynmound, 4th Earl,
    Viceroy, 119, 129–30, 231
  assassination attempt (1909), 97,
    131, 132

popularity, 95–6
and Sayajirao, 97, 135
Minto, Lady Mary, 97, 119–20,
    122
assassination attempt (1909), 97,
    131, 132
Mirabai, princess, 42
Moira, Lord, 182
Monkey Club, London, 203–4
monogamy, 120
Mookerjee, Sir M. N., 207
Moon House, Srinagar, 210–11
Moore, Alfred, 123
Morley, John, Secretary of State, 95,
    120, 153
Morning Post, 153, 162
Mother India (Mayo), 25, 145
Moti Doongri fort, 281–2, 284,
    289
Mountbatten, Louis, 1st Earl, Viceroy
  friendship with Jaipurs, 226, 242,
    277, 278, 284
  on Jaipurs, 240
  oversees Independence, 229–30,
    272
  and Partition, 230, 232–3
  and princely states, 235, 236–7
Muslim League, 230–31, 232
Muslims, 230, 278–9
  Congress and, 231, 232
Mysore, Maharaja of, 146

Nag Panchmi festival, 18, 146
Naidu, Chattopadhyaya, 86
Naidu, Sarojini, 87, 169, 177, 193,
    241
  arrest (1942), 223
  friendship with Barodas, 86, 171,
    175
Naoroji, Dadabhai, 47, 88, 231
Narayan, Mukul, 295

FOR THE BEST IN PAPERBACKS, LOOK FOR THE 🐧

In every corner of the world, on every subject under the sun, Penguin represents quality and variety—the very best in publishing today.

For complete information about books available from Penguin—including Penguin Classics, Penguin Compass, and Puffins—and how to order them, write to us at the appropriate address below. Please note that for copyright reasons the selection of books varies from country to country.

In the United States: Please write to *Penguin Group (USA), P.O. Box 12289 Dept. B, Newark, New Jersey 07101-5289* or call 1-800-788-6262.

In the United Kingdom: Please write to *Dept. EP, Penguin Books Ltd, Bath Road, Harmondsworth, West Drayton, Middlesex UB7 0DA.*

In Canada: Please write to *Penguin Books Canada Ltd, 90 Eglinton Avenue East, Suite 700, Toronto, Ontario M4P 2Y3.*

In Australia: Please write to *Penguin Books Australia Ltd, P.O. Box 257, Ringwood, Victoria 3134.*

In New Zealand: Please write to *Penguin Books (NZ) Ltd, Private Bag 102902, North Shore Mail Centre, Auckland 10.*

In India: Please write to *Penguin Books India Pvt Ltd, 11 Panchsheel Shopping Centre, Panchsheel Park, New Delhi 110 017.*

In the Netherlands: Please write to *Penguin Books Netherlands bv, Postbus 3507, NL-1001 AH Amsterdam.*

In Germany: Please write to *Penguin Books Deutschland GmbH, Metzlerstrasse 26, 60594 Frankfurt am Main.*

In Spain: Please write to *Penguin Books S. A., Bravo Murillo 19, 1° B, 28015 Madrid.*

In Italy: Please write to *Penguin Italia s.r.l., Via Benedetto Croce 2, 20094 Corsico, Milano.*

In France: Please write to *Penguin France, Le Carré Wilson, 62 rue Benjamin Baillaud, 31500 Toulouse.*

In Japan: Please write to *Penguin Books Japan Ltd, Kaneko Building, 2-3-25 Koraku, Bunkyo-Ku, Tokyo 112.*

In South Africa: Please write to *Penguin Books South Africa (Pty) Ltd, Private Bag X14, Parkview, 2122 Johannesburg.*